Ordnance Survey Ireland

National Mapping Agency
www.osi.ie

Route Plan	I
M50 Map	II
Outer Orbital Route	III
Inner Orbital Route	IV
Dart, Luas and Suburban Rail Network	V
Dublin Bus Route Network	VI
Dublin City and District Maps	1-68
City Centre Maps	69-76
Town Maps	77-92

Town Maps 77-92

77	Ashbourne	86	Dunshaughlin
79	Balbriggan	87	Kilcock
81	Blessington	88	Lusk
82	Clane	89	Rush
83	Delgany/Greystones	91	Ratoath
85	Donabate	92	Skerries

Tourist Information	93-94
Embassies	95
Index to Hospitals	96
Industrial Estates and Business Parks	97-98
Street Index	99

GW00514856

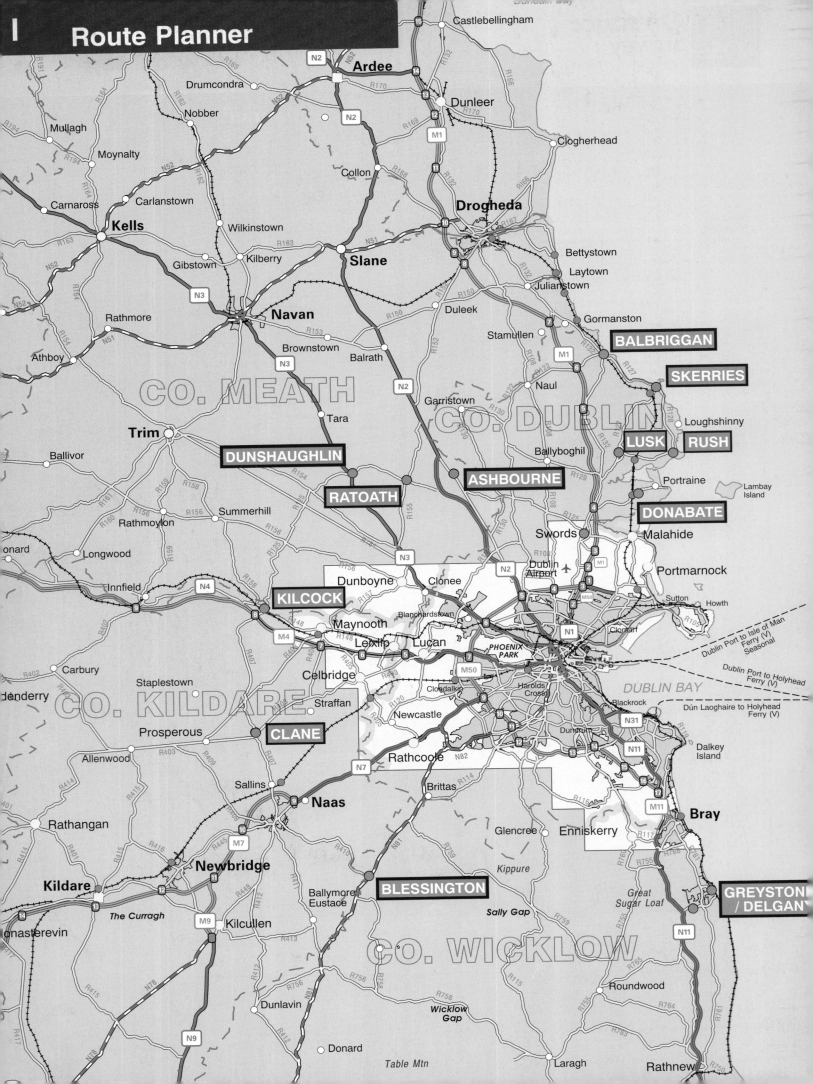

Bray to Ballymount

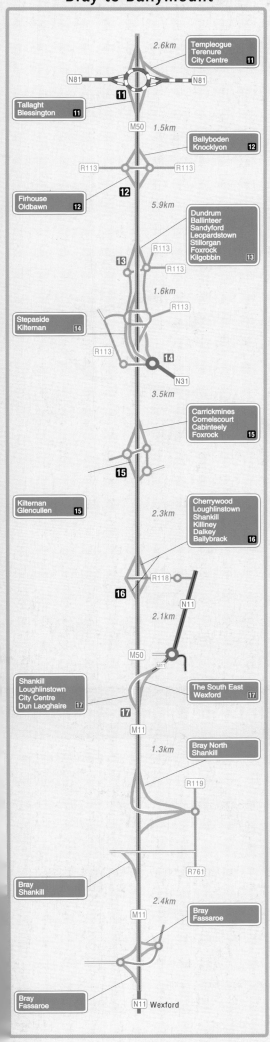

Ballymount to East Wall

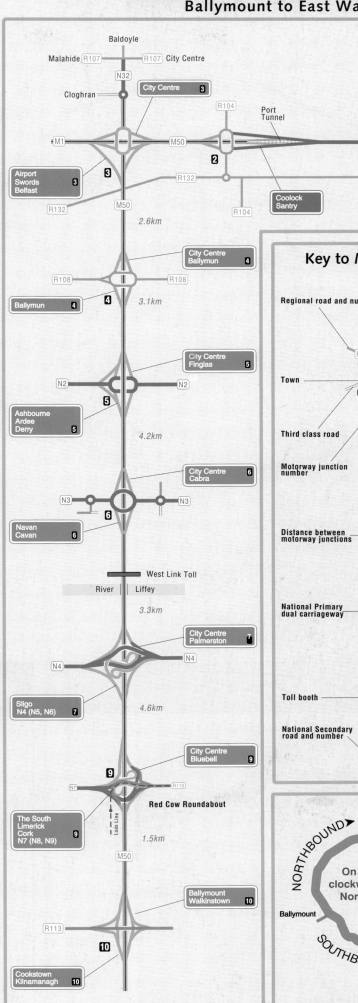

Key to Motorway Schemas

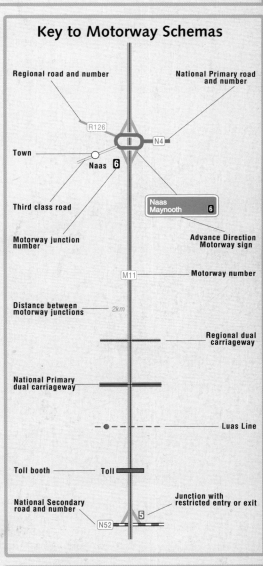

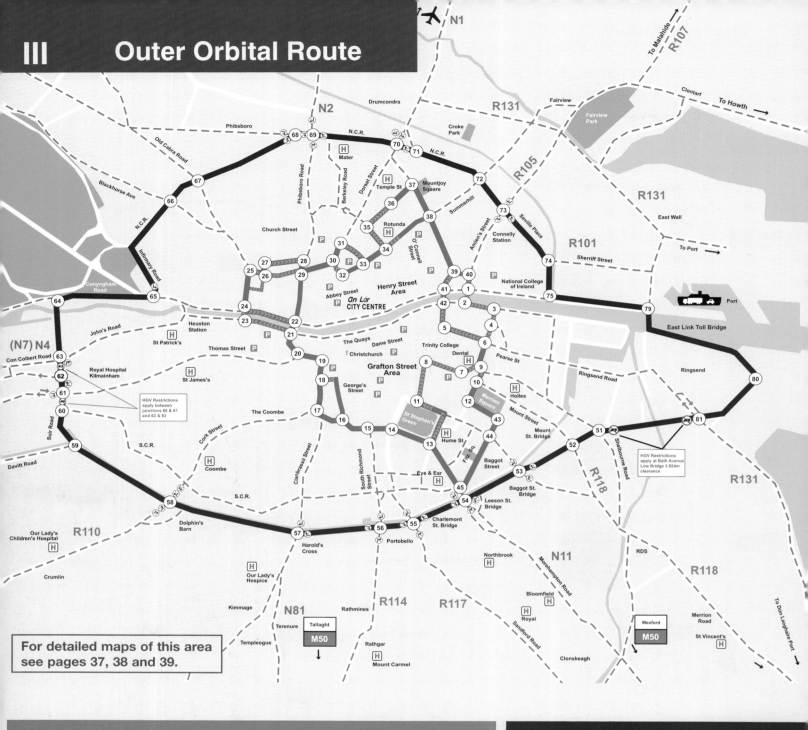

III Outer Orbital Route

For detailed maps of this area see pages 37, 38 and 39.

INNER ORBITAL JUNCTIONS INDEX

J1	Custom House Quay / Talbot Memorial Bridge
J2	Talbot Memorial Bridge / City Quay
J3	City Quay/Lombard St. East
J4	Lombard St. East / Townsend St
J5	Pearse St. / Tara St.
J6	Pearse St. / Westland Row
J7	Clare St./Lincoln Place
J8	Dawson St. / Nassau St.
J9	Lincoln Place / Westland Row
J10	Clare St. / Merrion Square
J11	St. Stephen's Green / Dawson St.
J12	Merrion St. Upr/Merrion Sq. Sth.
J13	St. Stephen's Green / Leeson St. Lwr.
J14	St. Stephen's Green / Harcourt St.
J15	Wexford St. / Kevin St. Lwr.
J16	Kevin St. / Bride St.
J17	Kevin St. / Patrick St.
J18	Bride Rd. / Patrick St.
J19	Christchurch Place/High St.
J20	High St. / Cornmarket
J21	Bridge St./Merchant's Quay
J22	Inns Quay / Church St.
J23	Ushers Island / Blackhall Place Bridge
J24	Ellis Quay / Blackhall Place Bridge
J25	Blackhall Place / King St.
J26	King St. / George's Lane
J27	George's Lane / Brunswick St. Nth
J28	Brunswick St. Nth. / Church St. Upr
J29	King St. / Church St.
J30	Nth. King St. / Bolton St.
J31	Bolton St. / King's Inns St.
J32	Parnell St. / Ryder's Row
J33	Parnell St. / King's Inns St.
J34	Parnell St. / Parnell Square West
J35	Parnell Square West / Granby Row
J36	Parnell Sq. Nth. / Frederick St. Nth.
J37	Gardiner St. Upr. / Mountjoy Square
J38	Summerhill / Gardiner St.
J39	Gardiner St. Lwr. / Beresford Place
J40	Amiens St./Beresford Place
J41	Eden Quay / Butt Bridge
J42	Tara St./Butt Bridge/Burgh Quay
J43	Merrion Sq. Sth. / Fitzwilliam St. Lwr
J44	Fitzwilliam St. Lwr / Baggot St. Lwr
J45	Fitzwilliam Place / Leeson St. Lwr

OUTER ORBITAL JUNCTIONS INDEX

J51	Shelbourne Rd / Haddington Rd
J52	Mount St. Lwr. / Haddington Rd
J53	Baggot St. Br. / Mespil Rd
J54	Leeson St. Br. /Grand Parade
J55	Charlemont St. Br. / Ranelagh Rd.
J56	Portobello / Rathmines Rd
J57	Harold's Cross Br. / Clanbrassil St.
J58	Dolphin's Barn / Crumlin Rd.
J59	Davitt Rd. / Suir Rd.
J60	Suir Rd. / SCR
J61	SCR / Old Kilmainham
J62	SCR / Inchicore Rd.
J63	SCR / St. John's Rd. West
J64	SCR / Conyngham Rd.
J65	Parkgate / Infirmary Rd.
J66	NCR / Blackhorse Ave.
J67	NCR / Prussia St.
J68	NCR / Cabra Rd.
J69	NCR / Phibsboro Rd.
J70	NCR / Dorset St. Lower
J71	NCR / Belvidere Road
J72	NCR / Summerhill
J73	Amiens St. / Seville Pl.
J74	Sheriff St. / Guild St.
J75	Guild St. / North Wall Quay
J79	North Wall Quay / East Link Br.
J80	Sean Moore Rd. / South Bank Rd.
J81	Sean Moore Rd. / Beach Rd.

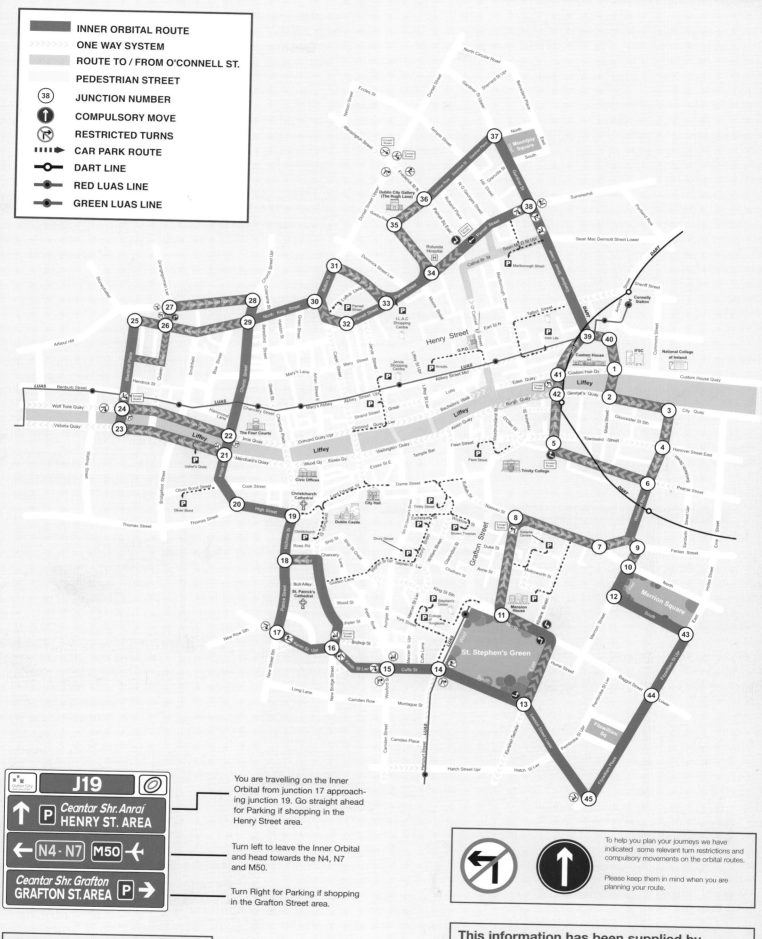

INNER ORBITAL ROUTE
ONE WAY SYSTEM
ROUTE TO / FROM O'CONNELL ST.
PEDESTRIAN STREET
38 **JUNCTION NUMBER**
COMPULSORY MOVE
RESTRICTED TURNS
CAR PARK ROUTE
DART LINE
RED LUAS LINE
GREEN LUAS LINE

J19

↑ P Ceantar Shr. Anrai HENRY ST. AREA

← N4 - N7 M50 ✈ ←

Ceantar Shr. Grafton GRAFTON ST. AREA P →

You are travelling on the Inner Orbital from junction 17 approaching junction 19. Go straight ahead for Parking if shopping in the Henry Street area.

Turn left to leave the Inner Orbital and head towards the N4, N7 and M50.

Turn Right for Parking if shopping in the Grafton Street area.

To help you plan your journeys we have indicated some relevant turn restrictions and compulsory movements on the orbital routes.

Please keep them in mind when you are planning your route.

For detailed maps of this area see pages 69, 70 and 71.

This information has been supplied by Road and Traffic Department, Dublin City Council

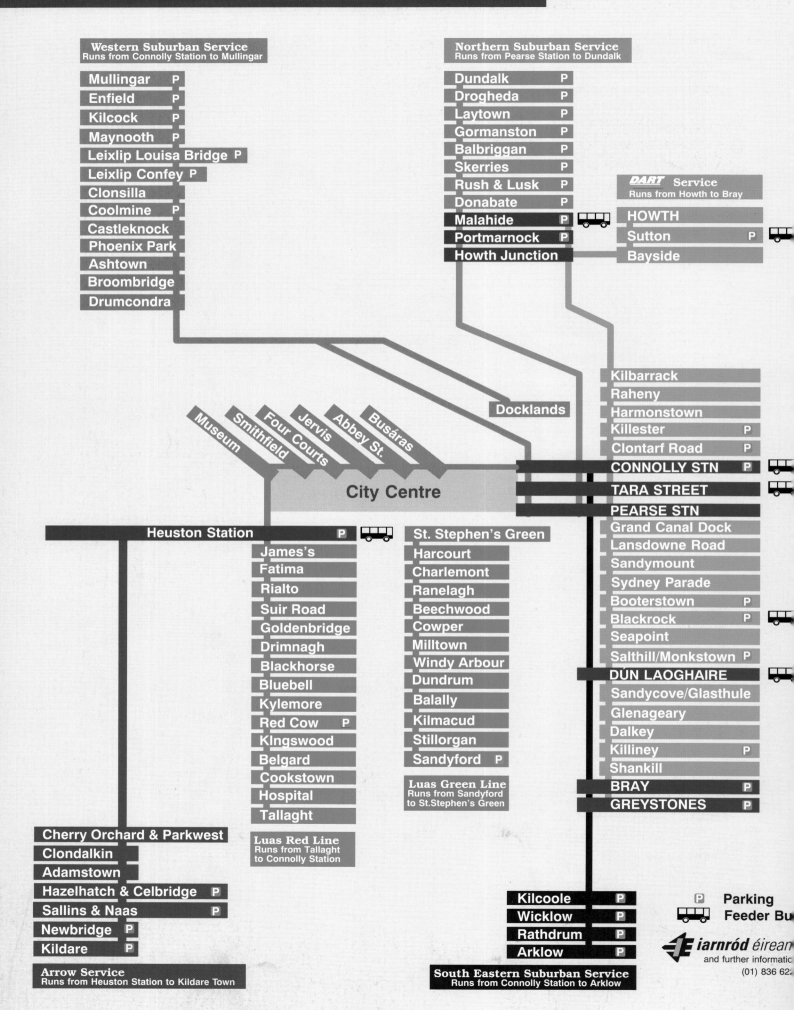

V Dart, Luas and Suburban Rail Network

Western Suburban Service
Runs from Connolly Station to Mullingar

- Mullingar P
- Enfield P
- Kilcock P
- Maynooth P
- Leixlip Louisa Bridge P
- Leixlip Confey P
- Clonsilla
- Coolmine P
- Castleknock
- Phoenix Park
- Ashtown
- Broombridge
- Drumcondra

Northern Suburban Service
Runs from Pearse Station to Dundalk

- Dundalk P
- Drogheda P
- Laytown P
- Gormanston P
- Balbriggan P
- Skerries P
- Rush & Lusk P
- Donabate P
- Malahide P
- Portmarnock P
- Howth Junction

DART Service
Runs from Howth to Bray

- HOWTH
- Sutton P
- Bayside

- Kilbarrack
- Raheny
- Harmonstown
- Killester P
- Clontarf Road P
- CONNOLLY STN P
- TARA STREET
- PEARSE STN
- Grand Canal Dock
- Lansdowne Road
- Sandymount
- Sydney Parade
- Booterstown P
- Blackrock P
- Seapoint
- Salthill/Monkstown P
- DÚN LAOGHAIRE
- Sandycove/Glasthule
- Glenageary
- Dalkey
- Killiney P
- Shankill
- BRAY P
- GREYSTONES P

Docklands

Museum
Smithfield
Four Courts
Jervis
Abbey St.
Busáras

City Centre

Heuston Station P

- James's
- Fatima
- Rialto
- Suir Road
- Goldenbridge
- Drimnagh
- Blackhorse
- Bluebell
- Kylemore
- Red Cow P
- Kingswood
- Belgard
- Cookstown
- Hospital
- Tallaght

Luas Red Line
Runs from Tallaght to Connolly Station

- St. Stephen's Green
- Harcourt
- Charlemont
- Ranelagh
- Beechwood
- Cowper
- Milltown
- Windy Arbour
- Dundrum
- Balally
- Kilmacud
- Stillorgan
- Sandyford P

Luas Green Line
Runs from Sandyford to St.Stephen's Green

- Cherry Orchard & Parkwest
- Clondalkin
- Adamstown
- Hazelhatch & Celbridge P
- Sallins & Naas P
- Newbridge P
- Kildare P

Arrow Service
Runs from Heuston Station to Kildare Town

- Kilcoole P
- Wicklow P
- Rathdrum P
- Arklow P

South Eastern Suburban Service
Runs from Connolly Station to Arklow

P Parking
Feeder Bu

iarnród éirean
and further informatio
(01) 836 62

Dublin Bus operates the bus network in the greater Dublin area. This network extends from Balbriggan in North County Dublin to Kilcoole in County Wicklow and westwards as far as Kilcock, County Kildare.

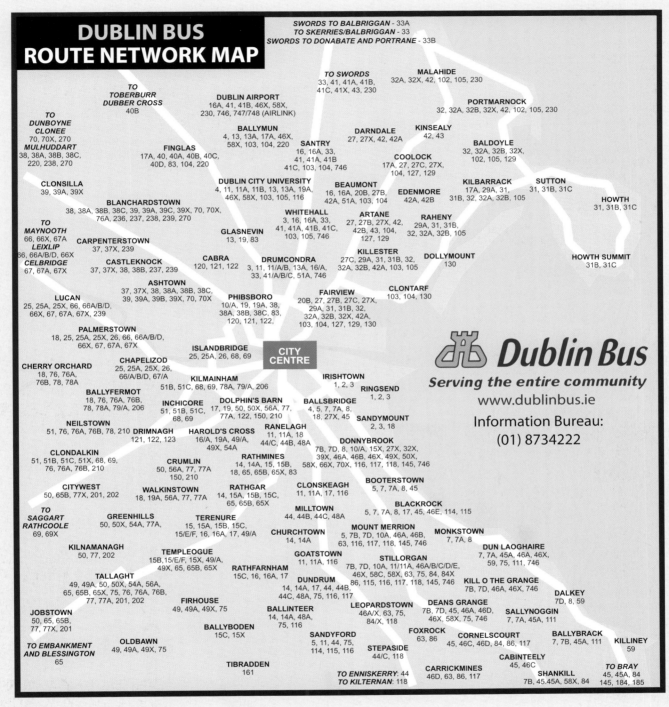

DUBLIN BUS ROUTE NETWORK MAP

SWORDS TO BALBRIGGAN - 33A
TO SKERRIES/BALBRIGGAN - 33
SWORDS TO DONABATE AND PORTRANE - 33B

TO SWORDS 33, 41, 41A, 41B, 41C, 41X, 43, 230

MALAHIDE 32A, 32X, 42, 102, 105, 230

TO TOBERBURR DUBBER CROSS 40B

DUBLIN AIRPORT 16A, 41, 41B, 46X, 58X, 230, 746, 747/748 (AIRLINK)

PORTMARNOCK 32, 32A, 32B, 32X, 42, 102, 105, 230

TO DUNBOYNE CLONEE 70, 70X, 270
MULHUDDART 38, 38A, 38B, 38C, 220, 238, 270

BALLYMUN 4, 13, 13A, 17A, 46X, 58X, 103, 104, 220

DARNDALE 27, 27X, 42, 42A

KINSEALY 42, 43

BALDOYLE 32, 32A, 32B, 32X, 102, 105, 129

FINGLAS 17A, 40, 40A, 40B, 40C, 40D, 83, 104, 220

SANTRY 16, 16A, 33, 41, 41A, 41B 41C, 103, 104, 746

COOLOCK 17A, 27, 27C, 27X, 104, 127, 129

CLONSILLA 39, 39A, 39X

DUBLIN CITY UNIVERSITY 4, 11, 11A, 11B, 13, 13A, 19A, 46X, 58X, 103, 105, 116

BEAUMONT 16, 16A, 20B, 27B, 42A, 51A, 103, 104

EDENMORE 42A, 42B

KILBARRACK 17A, 29A, 31, 31B, 32, 32A, 32B, 105

SUTTON 31, 31B, 31C

BLANCHARDSTOWN 38, 38A, 38B, 38C, 39, 39A, 39C, 39X, 70, 70X, 76A, 236, 237, 238, 239, 270

HOWTH 31, 31B, 31C

TO MAYNOOTH 66, 66X, 67A
LEIXLIP 66, 66A/B/D, 66X
CELBRIDGE 67, 67A, 67X

WHITEHALL 3, 16, 16A, 33, 41, 41A, 41B, 41C, 103, 105, 746

ARTANE 27, 27B, 27X, 42, 42B, 43, 104, 127, 129

RAHENY 29A, 31, 31B, 32, 32A, 32B, 105

GLASNEVIN 13, 19, 83

CARPENTERSTOWN 37, 37X, 239

CASTLEKNOCK 37, 37X, 38, 38B, 237, 239

CABRA 120, 121, 122

KILLESTER 27C, 29A, 31, 31B, 32, 32A, 32B, 42A, 103, 105

DOLLYMOUNT 130

HOWTH SUMMIT 31B, 31C

DRUMCONDRA 3, 11, 11/A/B, 13A, 16/A, 33, 41/A/B/C, 51A, 746

ASHTOWN 37, 37X, 38, 38A, 38B, 38C, 39, 39A, 39B, 39X, 70, 70X

FAIRVIEW 20B, 27, 27B, 27C, 27X, 29A, 31, 31B, 32, 32A, 32B, 32X, 42A, 103, 104, 127, 129, 130

CLONTARF 103, 104, 130

LUCAN 25, 25A, 25X, 66, 66A/B/D, 66X, 67, 67A, 67X, 239

PHIBSBORO 10/A, 19, 19A, 38, 38A, 38B, 38C, 83, 120, 121, 122,

PALMERSTOWN 18, 25, 25A, 25X, 26, 66, 66A/B/D, 66X, 67, 67A, 67X

ISLANDBRIDGE 25, 25A, 26, 68, 69

CITY CENTRE

IRISHTOWN 1, 2, 3

CHAPELIZOD 25, 25A, 25X, 26, 66/A/B/D, 67/A

CHERRY ORCHARD 18, 76, 76A, 76B, 78, 78A

KILMAINHAM 51B, 51C, 68, 69, 78A, 79/A, 206

RINGSEND 1, 2, 3

Dublin Bus
Serving the entire community
www.dublinbus.ie

BALLYFERMOT 18, 76, 76A, 76B, 78, 78A, 79/A, 206

INCHICORE 51, 51B, 51C, 68, 69

DOLPHIN'S BARN 17, 19, 50, 50X, 56A, 77, 77A, 122, 150, 210

BALLSBRIDGE 4, 5, 7, 7A, 8, 18, 27X, 45

SANDYMOUNT 2, 3, 18

Information Bureau: (01) 8734222

NEILSTOWN 51, 76, 76A, 76B, 78, 210

DRIMNAGH 121, 122, 123

HAROLD'S CROSS 16/A, 19A, 49/A, 49X, 54A

RANELAGH 11, 11A, 18, 44/C, 44B, 48A

DONNYBROOK 7B, 7D, 8, 10/A, 15X, 27X, 32X, 39X, 46A, 46B, 46X, 49X, 50X, 58X, 66X, 70X, 116, 117, 118, 145, 746

CLONDALKIN 51, 51B, 51C, 51X, 68, 69, 76, 76A, 76B, 210

CRUMLIN 50, 56A, 77, 77A, 150, 210

RATHMINES 14, 14A, 15, 15B, 18, 65, 65B, 65X, 83

CITYWEST 50, 65B, 77X, 201, 202

WALKINSTOWN 18, 19A, 56A, 77, 77A

RATHGAR 14, 15A, 15B, 15C, 65, 65B, 65X

CLONSKEAGH 11, 11A, 17, 116

BOOTERSTOWN 5, 7, 7A, 8, 45

TO SAGGART RATHCOOLE 69, 69X

GREENHILLS 50, 50X, 54A, 77A,

TERENURE 15, 15A, 15B, 15C, 15/E/F, 16, 16A, 17, 49/A

MILLTOWN 44, 44B, 44C, 48A

BLACKROCK 5, 7, 7A, 8, 17, 45, 46E, 114, 115

CHURCHTOWN 14, 14A

MOUNT MERRION 5, 7B, 7D, 10A, 46A, 46B, 63, 116, 117, 118, 145, 746

MONKSTOWN 7, 7A, 8

KILNAMANAGH 50, 77, 202

TEMPLEOGUE 15B, 15/E/F, 15X, 49/A, 49X, 65, 65B, 65X

GOATSTOWN 11, 11A, 116

STILLORGAN 7B, 7D, 10A, 11/11A, 46A/B/C/D/E, 46X, 58C, 58X, 63, 75, 84, 84X, 86, 115, 116, 117, 118, 145, 746

DUN LAOGHAIRE 7, 7A, 45A, 46A, 46X, 59, 75, 111, 746

RATHFARNHAM 15C, 16, 16A, 17

DUNDRUM 14, 14A, 17, 44, 44B, 44C, 48A, 75, 116, 117

KILL O THE GRANGE 7B, 7D, 46A, 46X, 746

DALKEY 7D, 8, 59

TALLAGHT 49, 49A, 50, 50X, 54A, 56A, 65, 65B, 65X, 75, 76, 76A, 76B, 77, 77A, 201, 202

FIRHOUSE 49, 49A, 49X, 75

LEOPARDSTOWN 46A/X, 63, 75, 84/X, 118

DEANS GRANGE 7B, 7D, 45, 46A, 46D, 46X, 58X, 75, 746

SALLYNOGGIN 7, 7A, 45A, 111

JOBSTOWN 50, 65, 65B, 77, 77X, 201

BALLINTEER 14, 14A, 48A, 75, 116

BALLYBODEN 15C, 15X

SANDYFORD 5, 11, 44, 75, 114, 115, 116

FOXROCK 63, 86

CORNELSCOURT 45, 46C, 46D, 84, 86, 117

BALLYBRACK 7, 7B, 45A, 111

KILLINEY 59

TO EMBANKMENT AND BLESSINGTON 65

OLDBAWN 49, 49A, 49X, 75

STEPASIDE 44/C, 118

CABINTEELY 45, 46C

TO BRAY 45, 45A, 84, 145, 184, 185

TIBRADDEN 161

TO ENNISKERRY: 44
TO KILTERNAN: 118

CARRICKMINES 46D, 63, 86, 117

SHANKILL 7B, 45.45A, 58X, 84

Contact Information

Our Head Office is located at 59 Upper O'Connell Street, Dublin 1 and our opening hours are as follows:

Monday: 0830 – 1730hrs   Tuesday to Friday: 0900 – 1730hrs   Saturday: 0900 – 1300hrs

Please note that the Dublin Bus Head Office is closed Sundays and Bank Holidays.

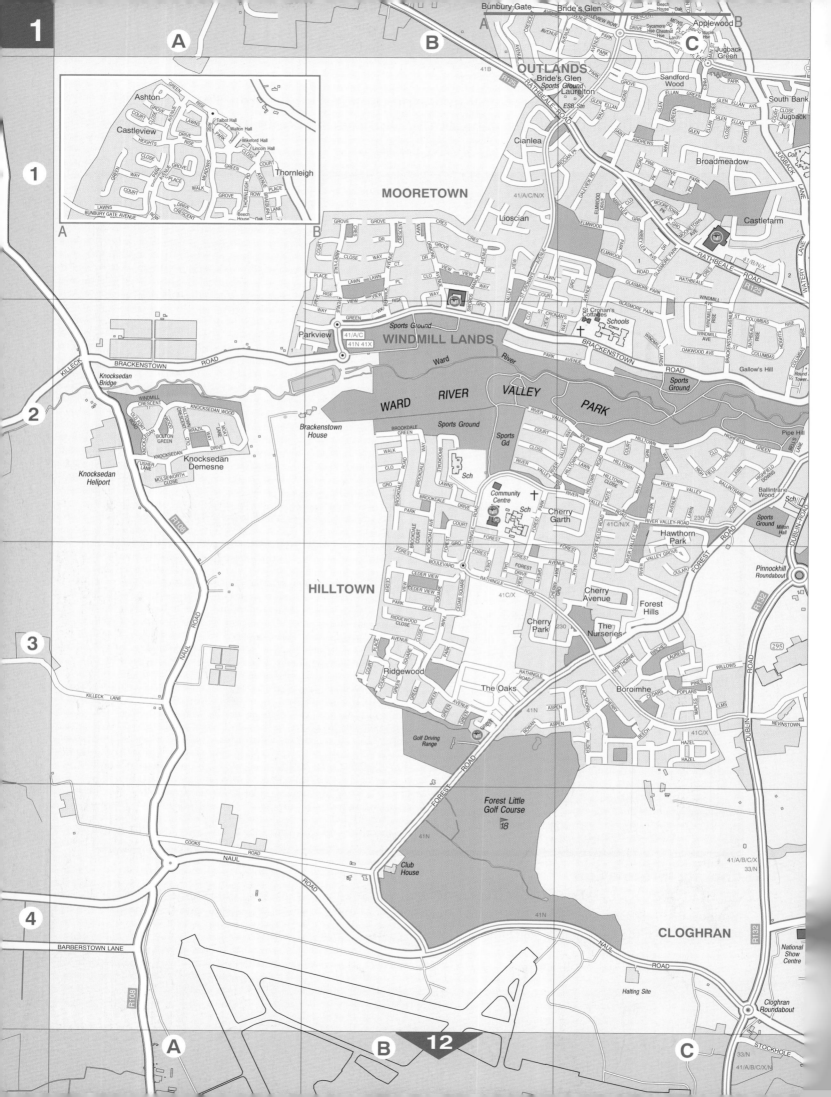

Corballis Golf Links

18

Strand

IRISH SEA

COAST

Biscayne

Castle Robbswall

ROAD

The Lighthouse

Sports Ground

ROBSWALL WALK

PATH

THE CRESCENT

The Anchorage

The Spinnaker

R10g

THE CRESCENT

32A
32X
42N
102

105

230

MONKS MEADON

32

32B

142

LIME TREE

ELMER COURT

AVENUE

RADLETT GRO

WHEATFIELD ROAD

WALK

BRIAR

BRACKEN DRIVE

ASHLEY RISE

KELVIN CLOSE

BLACKTHORN CLOSE

DEWBERRY PARK

HEATHER GARDENS

CONVENT LANE

WALK

Martello Tower

WHEATFIELD GROVE

42N

WENDELL AVENUE

230 102 32X

MARTELLO COURT

1

WENDELL AVE

HEATHER

142

ROAD

CARRICKHILL

32B

105

CARRICKHILL CLOSE

PALM

CARRICKHILL WALK

ROBB

RISE

CRIMMNOCK CRESCENT

STRAND

PARKVIEW

AVE

ROAD

PINE CT

CARRICKHILL HTS

2

BURROW CT

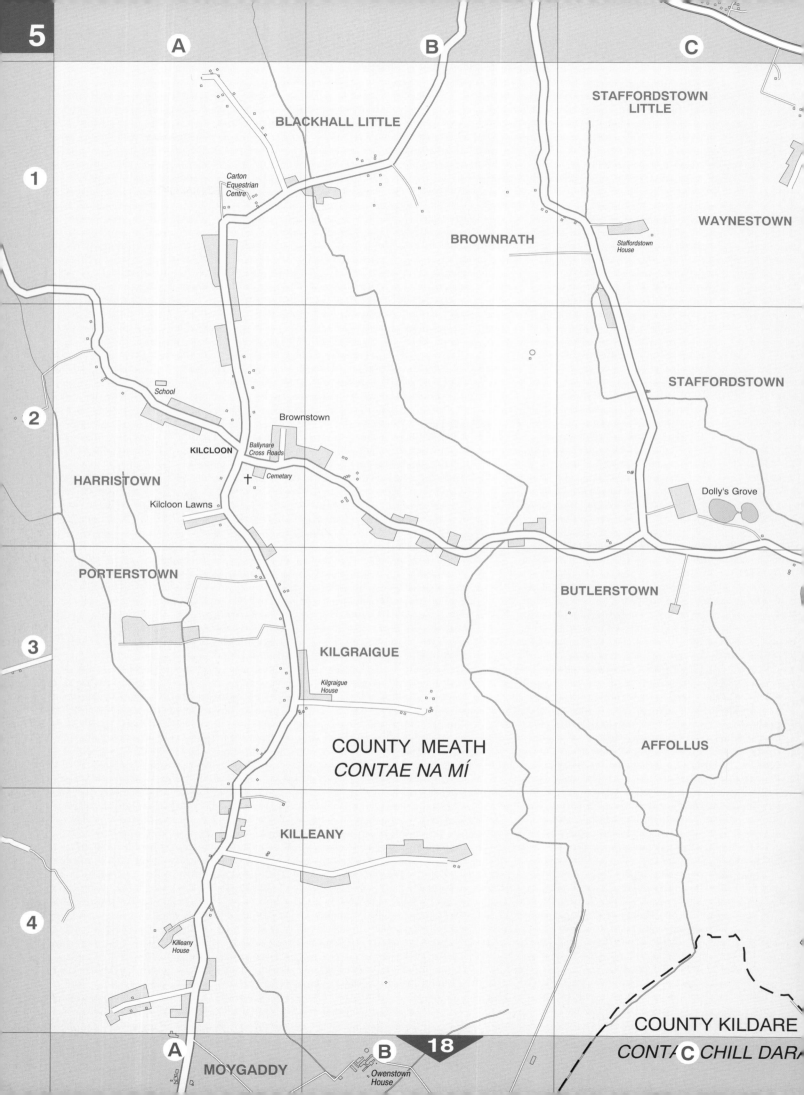

D

E

Warrenstown

F

R156

1

BAYTOWNPARK

CUSHINSTOWN

Brookville
Stud Farm

R156

CORNELSTOWN

Cornelstown
House

307

SARNEY

COLLIERSLAND

2

Ballymacoll
Stud

7

HAMWOOD

BALLYMACOLL

3

R157

Hamwood
House and
Gardens

Killarkin House

Grave Yard

SALESTOWN

4

MILESTOWN

18 Club House

Dungrange
Golf
Course

R157

GRANGE

D

E

F

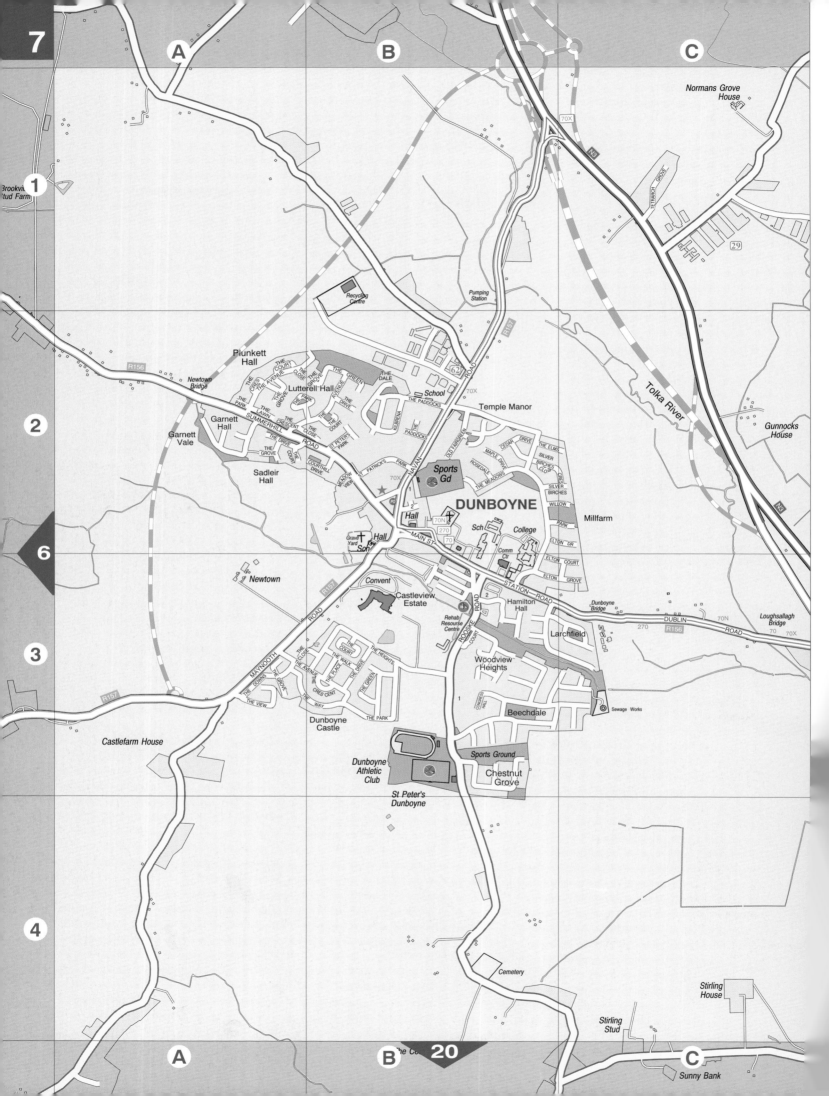

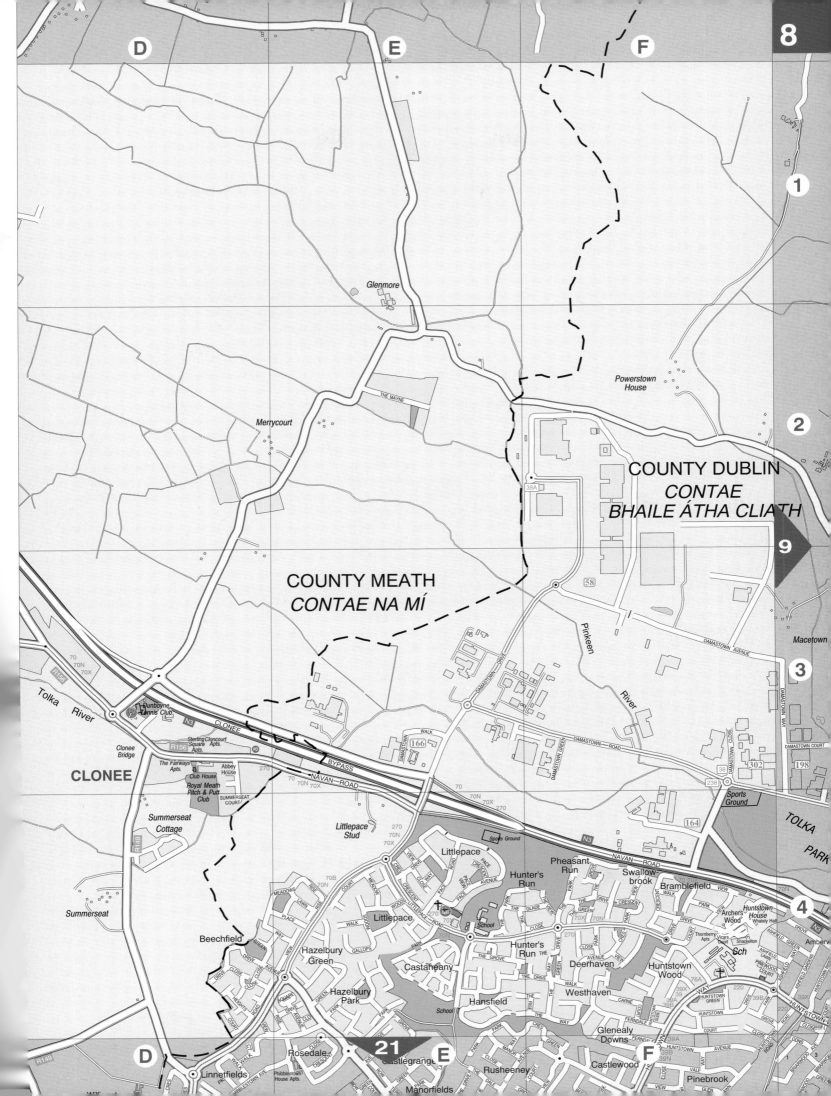

Broghan
New Br.

Broghan House

Pitch
and
Putt

Dúnsoghly
Castle

Newte

KILSHANE

Cement Works

Kilmore House

N2

NORTH ROAD

Woodlands

Kilshane
House

Kilshane Cross

88N

KILSHANE AVENUE

Old Quarry

Sports
Ground

KILSHANE VIEW

KILSHANE PARK

KILSHANE DRIVE

KILSHANE ROAD

Sand &
Gravel Pit

N2

KILSHANE WAY

Burial
Gd

201

Cloghran House

202

236

238

236

13

220

38B

220

Electricity
Station

Kildonan House

ROSEMOUNT PARK ROAD

133

40D

BALLYCOOLIN ROAD

ROSEMOUNT PARK DRIVE

CAPPAGH ROAD

Cappoge
Cottages

203

220

40D

M50

CAPPOGE

Marine

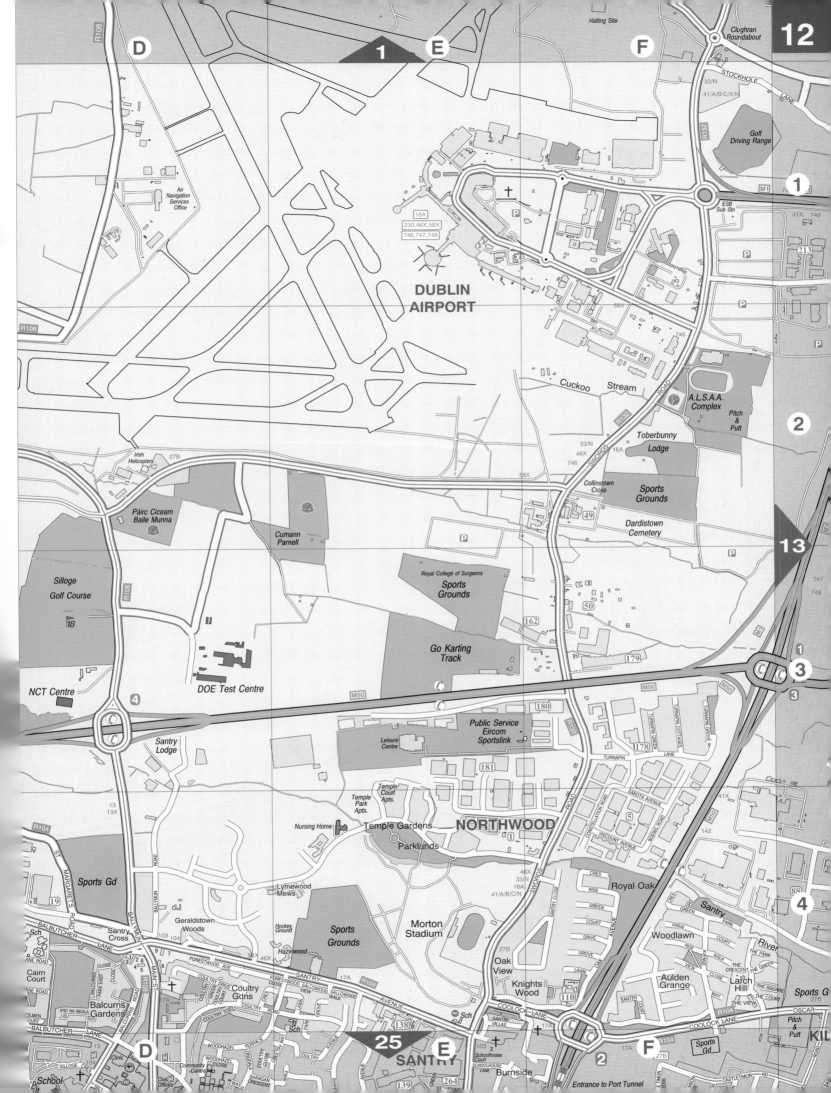

DUBLIN AIRPORT

Air Navigation Services Office

Cloghran Roundabout

Halting Site

STOCKHOLE LANE

33/N
41/A/B/C/X/N

R32

Golf Driving Range

ESB Sub Stn

41X   748

M1

1

213

P

P

2

16A
230,46X,58X
746,747,748

Cuckoo   Stream

A.L.S.A.A. Complex

Pitch & Putt

58X

R132

Toberbunny Lodge

SWORDS   ROAD

33/N
46X
746

16A

58X

Collinstown Cross

Sports Grounds

49

Dardistown Cemetery

Irish Helicopters   27B

Páirc Ciceam Baile Munna

Cumann Parnell

R108

P

Royal College of Surgeons

Sports Grounds

50

162

Silloge Golf Course

18

P

13

747
748

M1

Go Karting Track

179

1

NCT Centre

4

DOE Test Centre

M50

180

R132

M50

M50

3

3

Santry Lodge

Public Service Eircom Sportslink

Leisure Centre

TURNAPIN GREEN

TURNAPIN COTTAGES

TURNAPIN GROVE

178

TURNAPIN   LANE

181

DAKOTA AVENUE

41X

Temple Court Apts.

Temple Park Apts.

13
13A

R104

Nursing Home

Temple Gardens

NORTHWOOD

CONSTELLATION ROAD

BOEING ROAD

VISCOUNT AVENUE

5

Parklands

1

142

Sports Gd

19

Lymewood Mews

46X
33/N
16A
41/A/B/C/N

SWORDS   ROAD

SANTRY CLOSE

CRES

RISE

GREEN

COURT

DRIVE

GROVE

Royal Oak

Santry

THE PARK

88

4

Woodlawn

THE CRESCENT

THE GREEN

River

ST. MARGARET'S   ROAD

BALLYMUN   ROAD

Santry Cross

Geraldstown Woods

Hockey Ground

Sports Grounds

Morton Stadium

27B

Oak View

Knights Wood

110

WALK

THE VIEW

Aulden Grange

Larch Hill

THE SQUARE

THE COURT

Sports G

Hazelwood

Cairn Court

BALCURRIS

Balcurris Gardens

BALBUTCHER   LANE

103 104

9

MAIN ST

FORESTWOOD AVE

FORESTWOOD CLOSE

SALLOWOOD VIEW

SALLOWOOD WALK

SANTRY

46X

17A

R104

AVENUE

COOLOCK   LANE

Santry Villas

17A

R104

COOLOCK LANE

Pitch & Putt

KIL

Sch

ARD NA MEALA

DOLMEN COURT

BALBUTCHER LANE

SILLOGE CRES

13
104

Clinic

School

Coultry Gdns

COULTRY CRES

COULTRY WAY

WOODHAZEL TERRACE

SHANGAN CRESCENT

Community Centre

Civic Offices

138

COULTRY   AVENUE

264

139

SANTRY

25

Sch

Schoolhouse Court

SCHOOLHOUSE LANE

Burnside

103

GRO

Entrance to Port Tunnel

CASTLETIMON RD

OSCAR

ST. TIMON'S

2

D   1   E   F

D   E   25   F   2

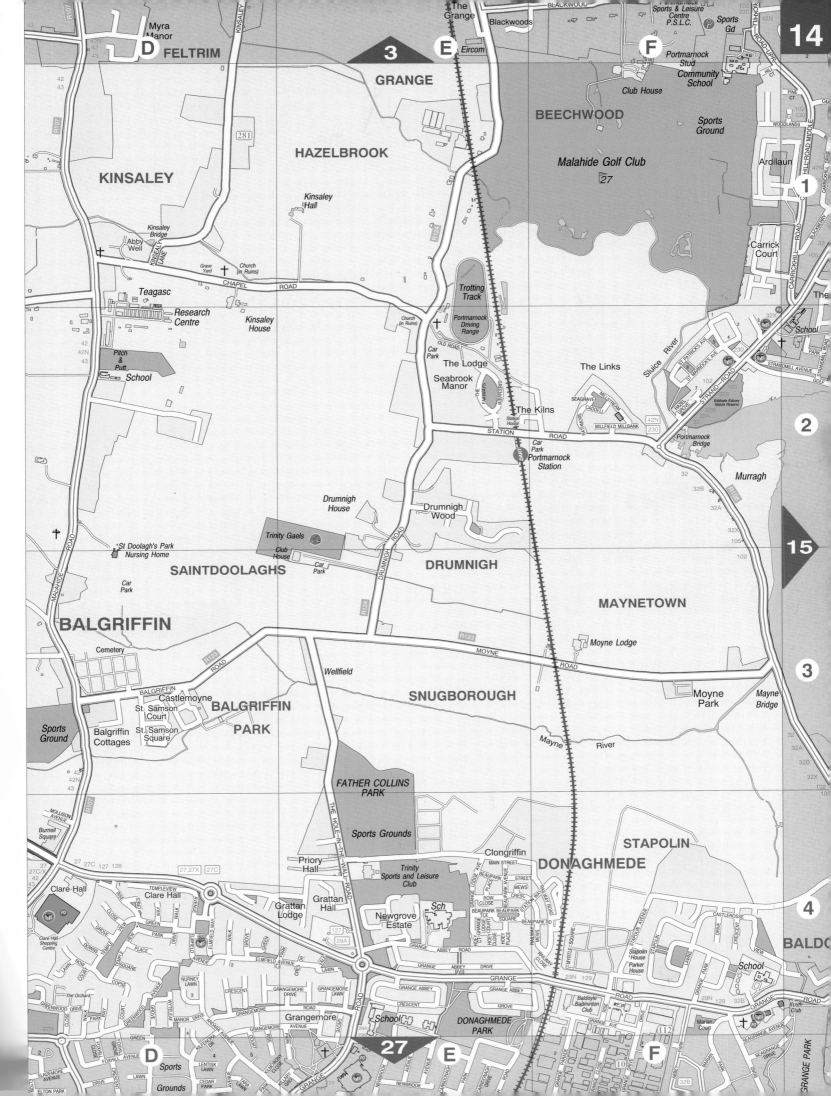

The Steer

Tower

Ireland's Eye

Carrigeen Bay

Rowan Rocks

Thulla Rocks

Thulla

Lighthouse

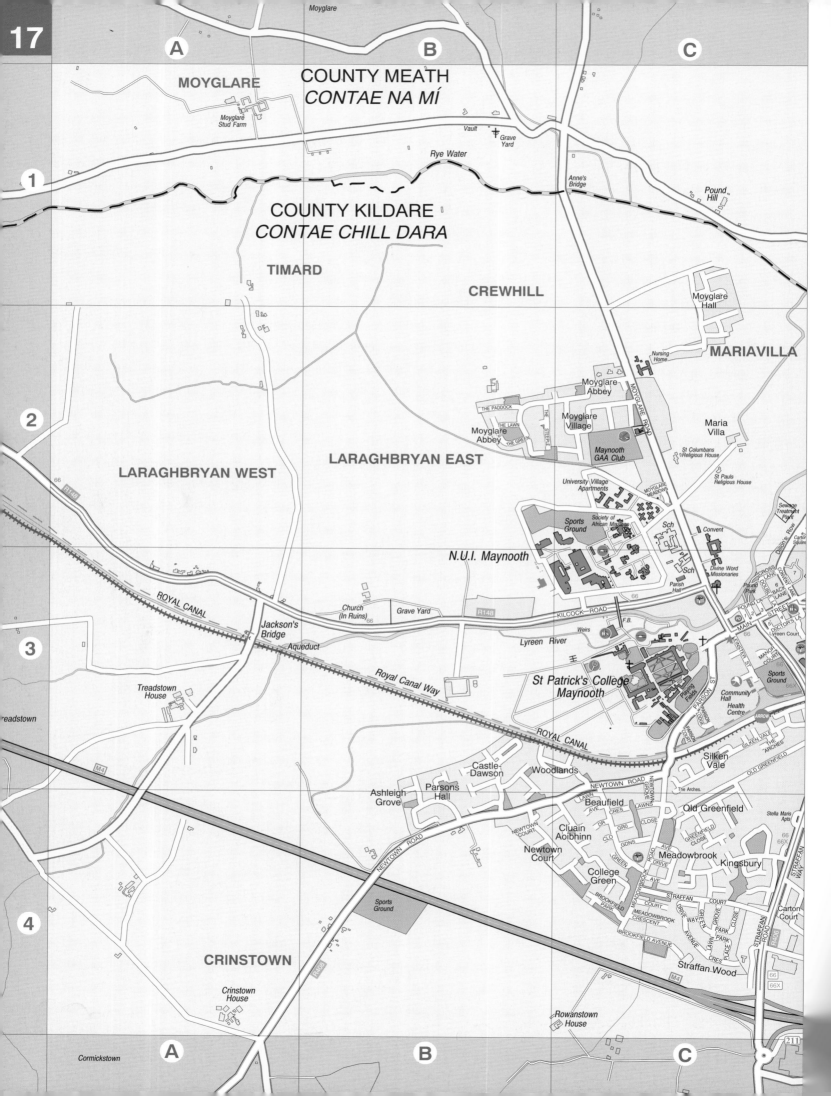

A   B   C

Moyglare

MOYGLARE

COUNTY MEATH
CONTAE NA MÍ

Moyglare
Stud Farm

Vault   Grave
Yard

Rye Water

Anne's
Bridge

Pound
Hill

1

COUNTY KILDARE
CONTAE CHILL DARA

TIMARD

CREWHILL

Moyglare
Hall

MARIAVILLA

Nursing
Home

Moyglare
Abbey

THE PADDOCK

Moyglare
Village

Maria
Villa

St Columbans
Religious House

2

Moyglare
Abbey

THE LAWN

THE GREEN

THE STEEPLE

Maynooth
GAA Club

MOYGLARE ROAD

St Pauls
Religious House

LARAGHBRYAN WEST

LARAGHBRYAN EAST

University Village
Apartments

MOYGLARE
MEADOWS

Sewage
Treatment
Plant

66   R148

Society of
African Missions

Sports
Ground

Sch

Convent

Carton
Square

Dillon's Row

ROYAL CANAL

N.U.I. Maynooth

Sch

Divine Word
Missionaries

Cross
Lane

Convent Lane

7

Parish
Hall

Pound
Park

Back
Lane

6

5

Pound La

Church
(In Ruins)   Grave Yard

R148

KILCOCK ROAD

66

Main Street

Doctors La

Jackson's
Bridge

Lyreen River

Weirs

F.B.

Manor
Court

Leinster St

Sports
Ground

3

Aqueduct

Royal Canal Way

**St Patrick's College
Maynooth**

Playing
Fields

66X

Lyreen Court

Treadstown
House

Community
Hall

Health
Centre

66

Parson St

Parson Court

Silken Vale

The Arches

Silken Vale

Treadstown

ROYAL CANAL

Castle-
Dawson

Woodlands

NEWTOWN ROAD

NEWTOWN GROVE

Old Greenfield

Old Greenfield

Stella Maris
Apts

M4

Ashleigh
Grove

Parsons
Hall

LAWN

Beaufield

AVE   CRES   LAWNS   CLOSE

GREENFIELD
CLOSE

66
66X

Cluain
Aoibhinn

DR   GRO   CLO

NEWTOWN
COURT

Meadowbrook

Kingsbury

Newtown
Court

GDNS

GREEN   AVE   DRIVE

MEADOWBROOK AVE

Carton
Court

Straffan Road

4

Sports
Ground

College
Green

STRAFFAN COURT   GREEN   GROVE   CLOSE

STRAFFAN
WAY

R408

BROOKFIELD PARK

MEADOWBROOK CRESCENT

STRAFFAN DRIVE

WAY

LAWN   GROVE   CLOSE

66   66X

CRINSTOWN

BROOKFIELD AVENUE

LAWN   CRES   PLACE

AVENUE

Straffan Wood

M4

Crinstown
House

Rowanstown
House

211

Cormickstown

A   B   C

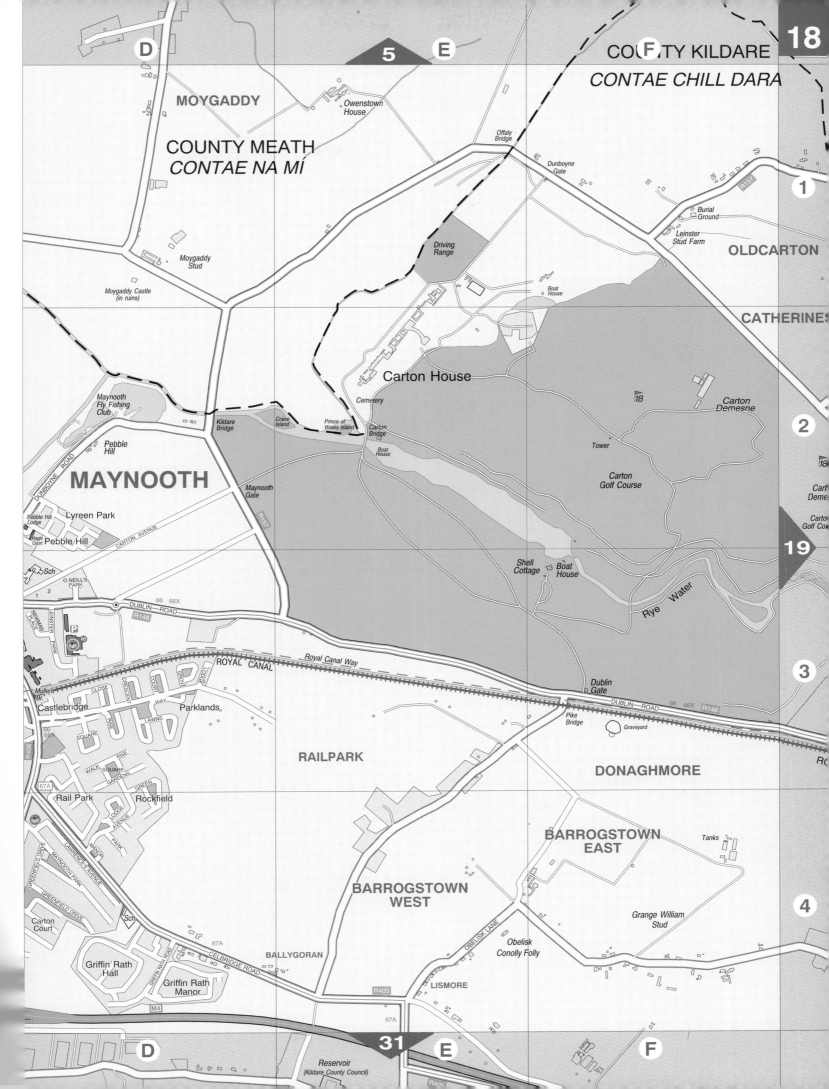

MOYGADDY

Owenstown
House

COUNTY MEATH
CONTAE NA MÍ

Offaly
Bridge

Dunboyne
Gate

R157

Burial
Ground

Leinster
Stud Farm

OLDCARTON

Driving
Range

Moygaddy
Stud

Boat
House

CATHERINES

Moygaddy Castle
(in ruins)

Carton House

Maynooth
Fly Fishing
Club

Cemetery

18

Carton
Demesne

Pebble
Hill

Kildare
Bridge

Crane
Island

Prince of
Wales Island

Carton
Bridge

Tower

18

MAYNOOTH

Maynooth
Gate

Boat
House

Carton
Golf Course

Cart

Pebble Hill
Lodge

Lyreen Park

R157

Nagle
Court

Pebble Hill

CARTON AVENUE

Shell
Cottage

Boat
House

Cart
Deme

Cart
Golf Co

Sch

O'NEILL'S
PARK

1 2

DUBLIN   ROAD

66 66X

R148

Rye   Water

NEWMAN
PLACE

LEINSTER PARK

P

PO

Royal Canal Way

ROYAL   CANAL

Mullen
Br.

CLOSE

COURT

GROVE

LODGE

Dublin
Gate

DUBLIN   ROAD

66 66X

R148

Castlebridge

CRESCENT

RISE

WAY

LAWNS

Parklands

Pike
Bridge

Graveyard

66
66X

SQUARE

R405

WALK

RISE

SQUARE

GARDENS

GREEN

RAILPARK

DONAGHMORE

R

67A

Rail Park

Rockfield

LODGE
AVENUE

PARK

MANOR

**BARROGSTOWN
EAST**

Tanks

GREENFIELD DRIVE

MAYNOOTH PARK

LAWRENCE'S AVENUE

GREENFIELD DRIVE

**BARROGSTOWN
WEST**

Grange William
Stud

Carton
Court

Sch

GRIFFIN RATH ROAD

67A

OBELISK LANE

Obelisk
Conolly Folly

Griffin Rath
Hall

Griffin Rath
Manor

CELBRIDGE ROAD

BALLYGORAN

R405

LISMORE

M4

Reservoir
(Kildare County Council)

R405

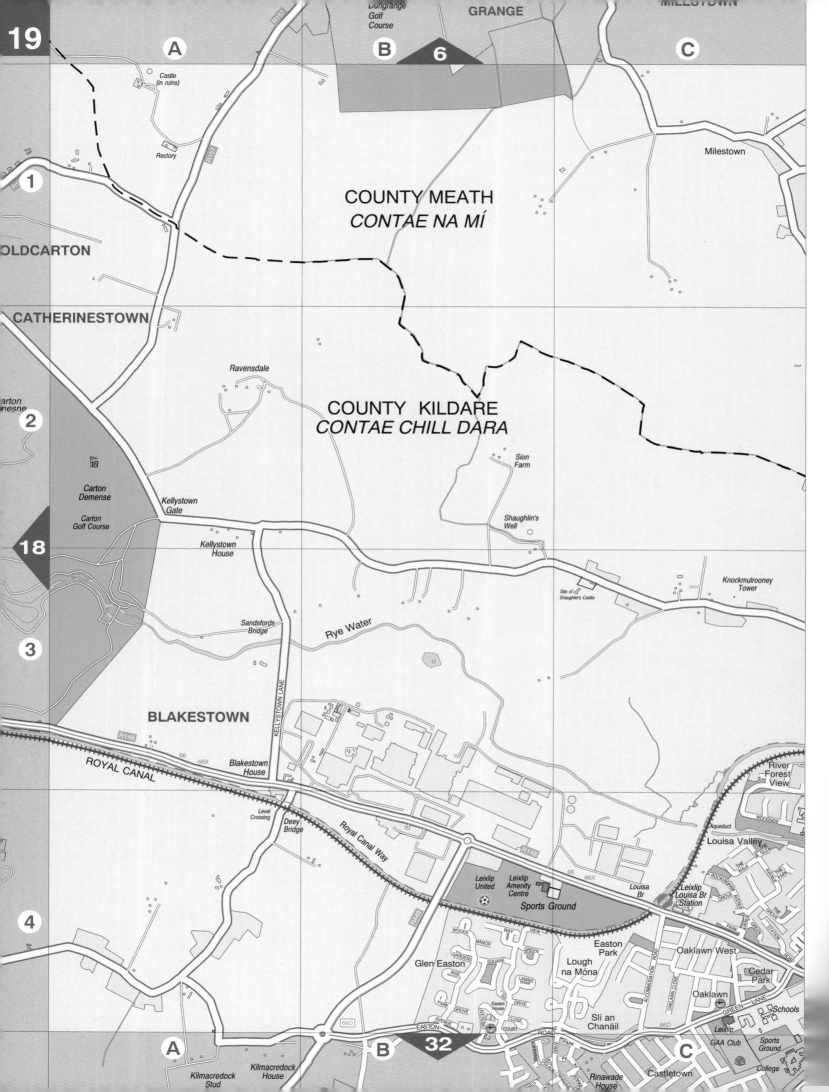

A   **B**   6   **C**

GRANGE

MILESTOWN

Dungrange
Golf Course

R157

Castle
(in ruins)

Rectory

R157

1

OLDCARTON

COUNTY MEATH
CONTAE NA MÍ

Milestown

CATHERINESTOWN

Ravensdale

2

arton
emesne

COUNTY KILDARE
CONTAE CHILL DARA

Sion
Farm

18

Carton
Demense

Kellystown
Gate

Shaughlin's
Well

Carton
Golf Course

18

Kellystown
House

Knockmulrooney
Tower

Site of
Shaughlin's Castle

3

Sandsfords
Bridge

Rye Water

KELLYSTOWN LANE

BLAKESTOWN

R148

ROYAL CANAL

66 66X

92

River
Forest
View

Blakestown
House

WOODSIDE

Level
Crossing

Deey
Bridge

Royal Canal Way

R148

Aqueduct

Louisa Valley

Louisa
Br

Leixlip
United

Leixlip
Amenity
Centre

66 66X

Leixlip
Louisa Br
Station

THE WALK

ROCKINGHAM

AVENUE

THE GLEN

THE AVENUE

GROVE

Sports Ground

R148

THE GROVE

STATION

GREEN LANE

PARK

AVENUE

4

WOODS

MANOR

WAY

GREEN

VIEW

Easton
Park

Oaklawn West

Cedar
Park

GARDENS

SQUARE

LAWNS

ACCOMMODATION ROAD

OAKLAWN CLOSE

ROAD

Glen Easton

RISE

Lough
na Móna

Oaklawn

Schools

PARK

GROVE

DRIVE

CLOSE

COURT

Leixlip

66D

AVENUE

Easton
House

CRESCENT

Slí an Chanáil

66D

GAA Club

Sports
Ground

A   **B**   32   **C**

EASTON

ROAD

College

Kilmacredock
Stud

Kilmacredock
House

RINAWADE

Rinawade
House

Castletown

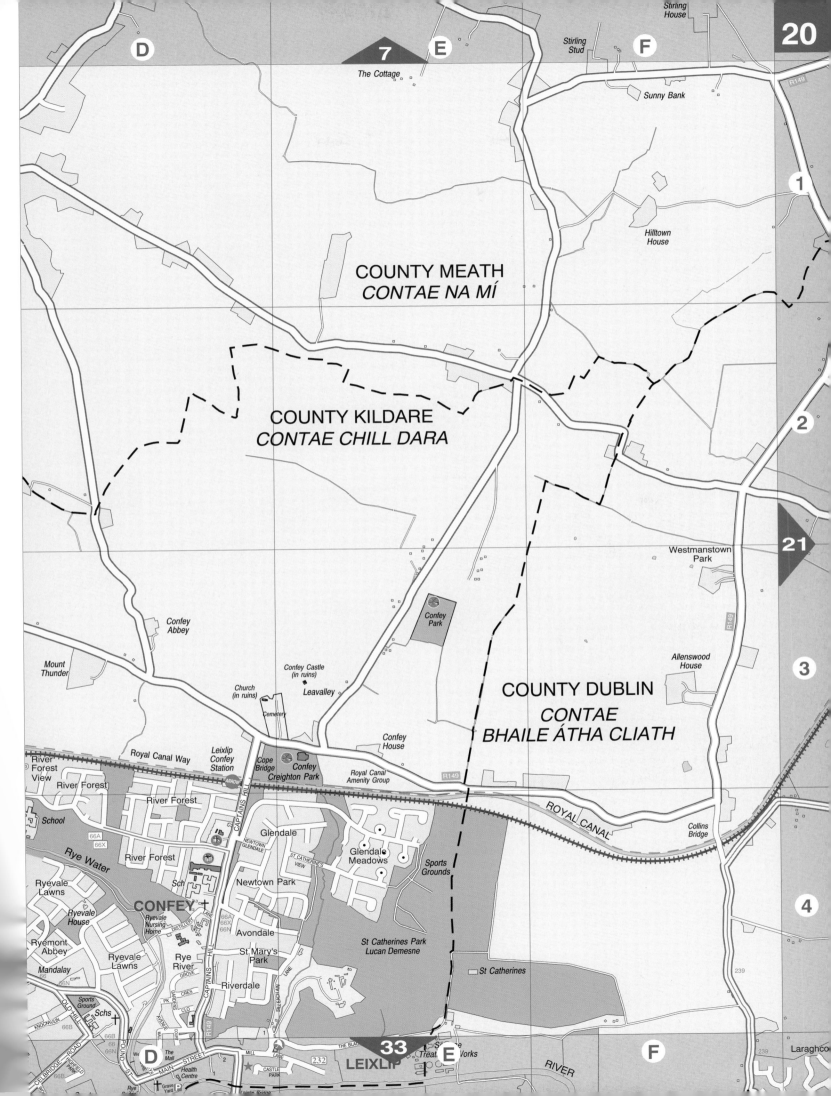

D

7

E

F

Stirling House

Stirling Stud

The Cottage

Sunny Bank

R149

1

COUNTY MEATH
CONTAE NA MÍ

Hilltown House

2

COUNTY KILDARE
CONTAE CHILL DARA

21

Westmanstown Park

R149

Confey Park

Confey Abbey

Allenswood House

3

Mount Thunder

Confey Castle (in ruins)

Church (in ruins)

Leavalley

COUNTY DUBLIN
CONTAE BHAILE ÁTHA CLIATH

Cemetery

Confey House

Royal Canal Way

Leixlip Confey Station

Cope Bridge

Confey Creighton Park

Royal Canal Amenity Group

R149

ROYAL CANAL

Collins Bridge

River Forest View

River Forest

River Forest

School

66A
66X

River Forest

Glendale

Newtown Glendale

St.Catherines View

Glendale Meadows

Sports Grounds

Rye Water

Ryevale Lawns

Ryevale House

Sch

Newtown Park

4

Ryemont Abbey

Mandalay

66

66N

Ryevale Lawns

Ryevale Nursing Home

DISTILLERY

Avondale

St Catherines Park Lucan Demesne

66A
66X
66N

St.Mary's Park

Rye River

St Catherines

239

Sports Ground

Schs

66B

OLD HILL

66B
66
66N

CELBRIDGE ROAD

HIGHFIELD PARK

66B

KNOCKAULIN

Riverdale

R149

The Mall

MAIN STREET

POUND ST

232

MILL LANE

THE BLACK

D

33

E

LEIXLIP

Health Centre

Sewage Treatment Works

239

RIVER

F

Laragh...

CONFEY

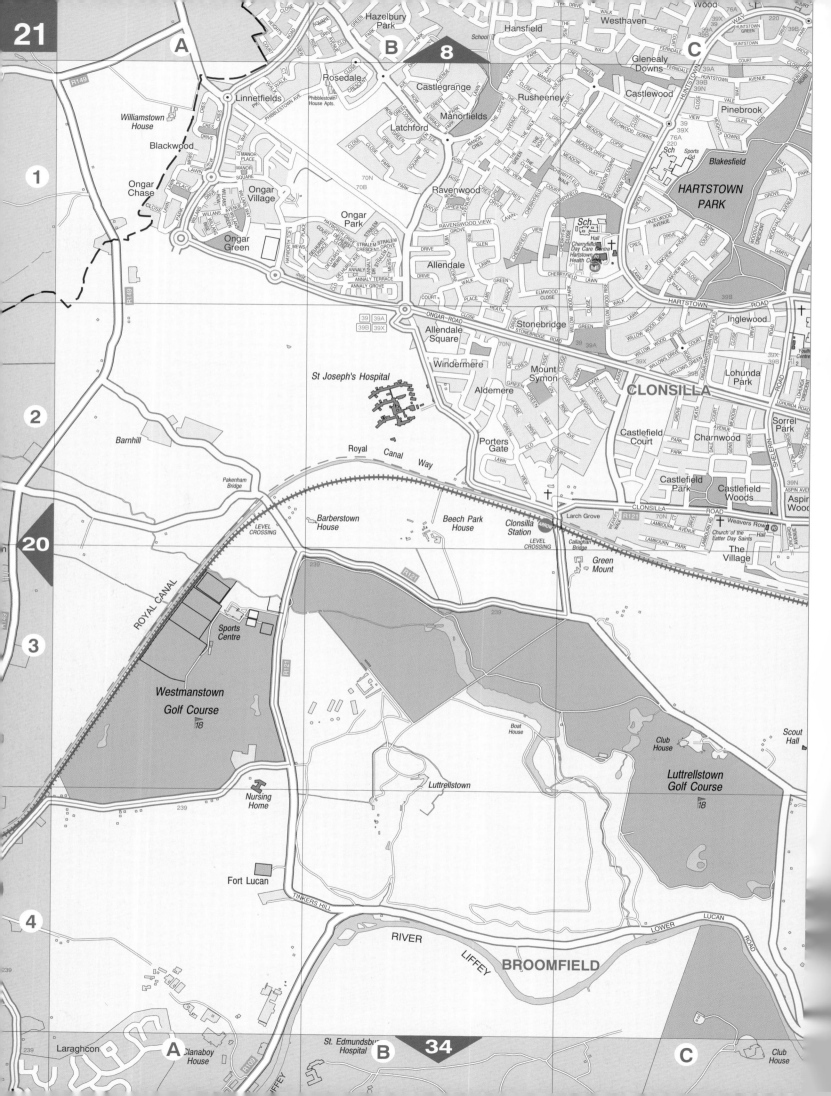

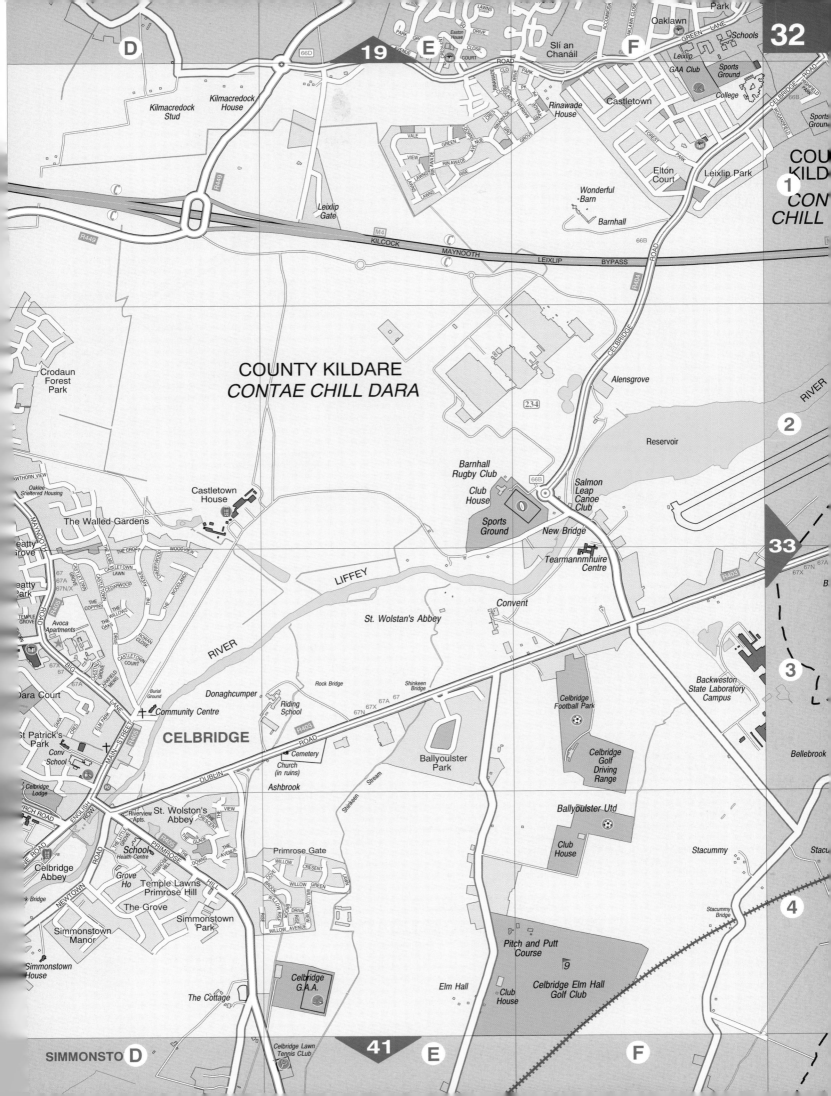

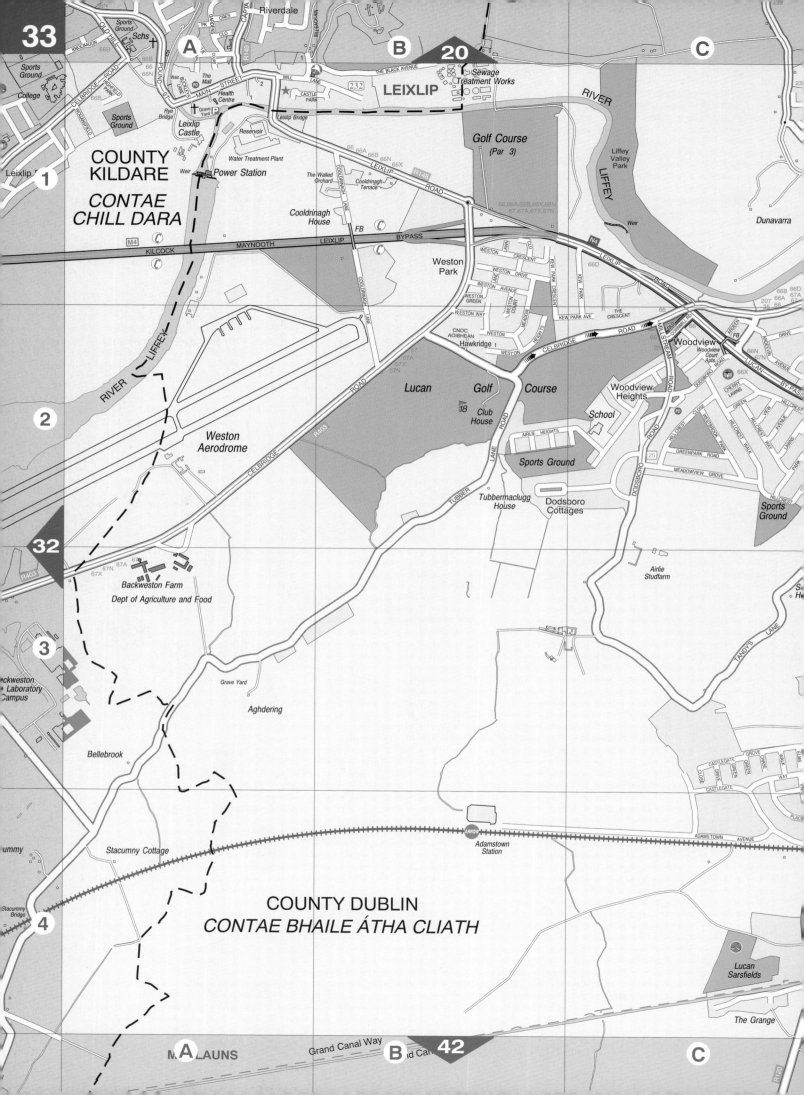

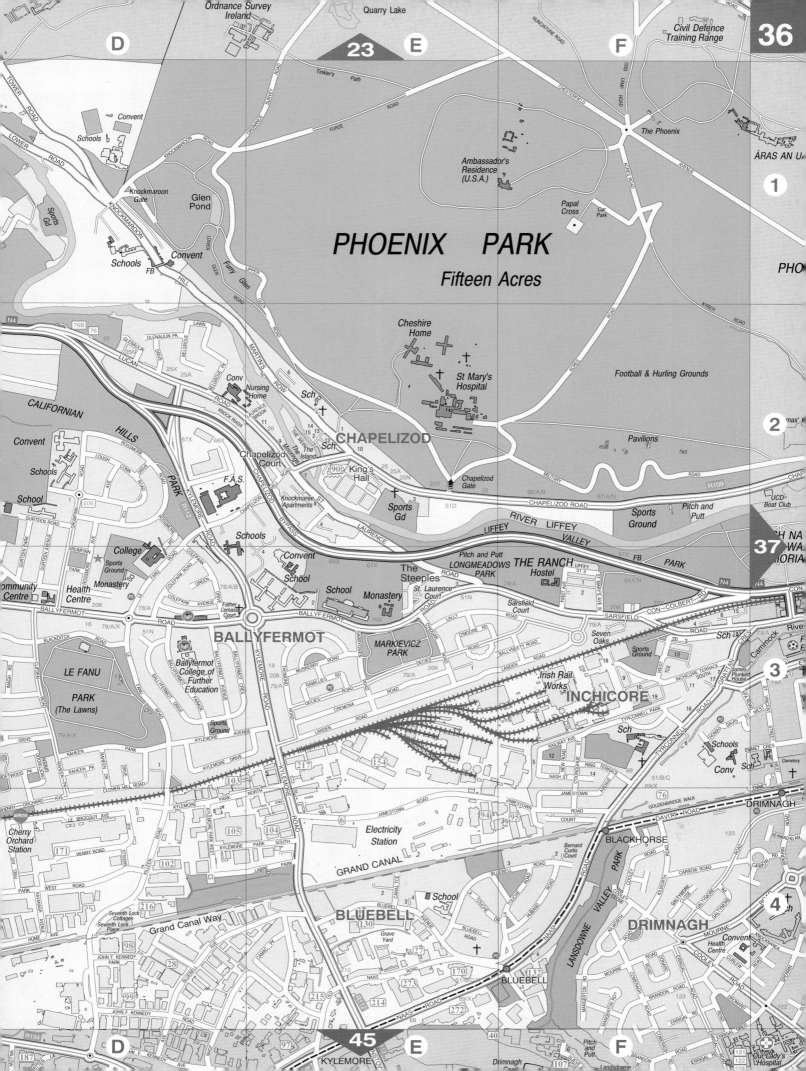

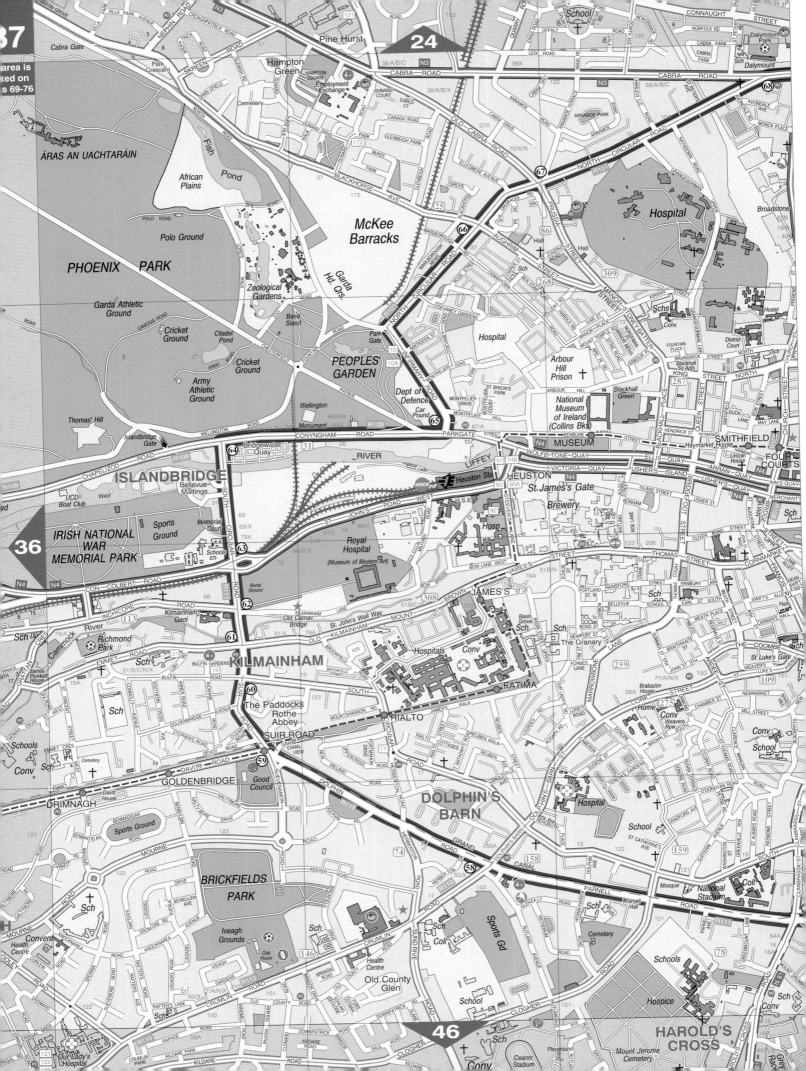

Wooden
Bridge

Seascout Den
Bull Wall Cottages

18

Royal
Dublin
Golf
Links

Club
House

Dollymount Beach

Bull Wall

Bathing Place

Statue

Breakwater

Lighthouse

North Bull
Lighthouse

Poolbeg
Lighthouse

SOUTH   BULL

DUBLIN   BAY

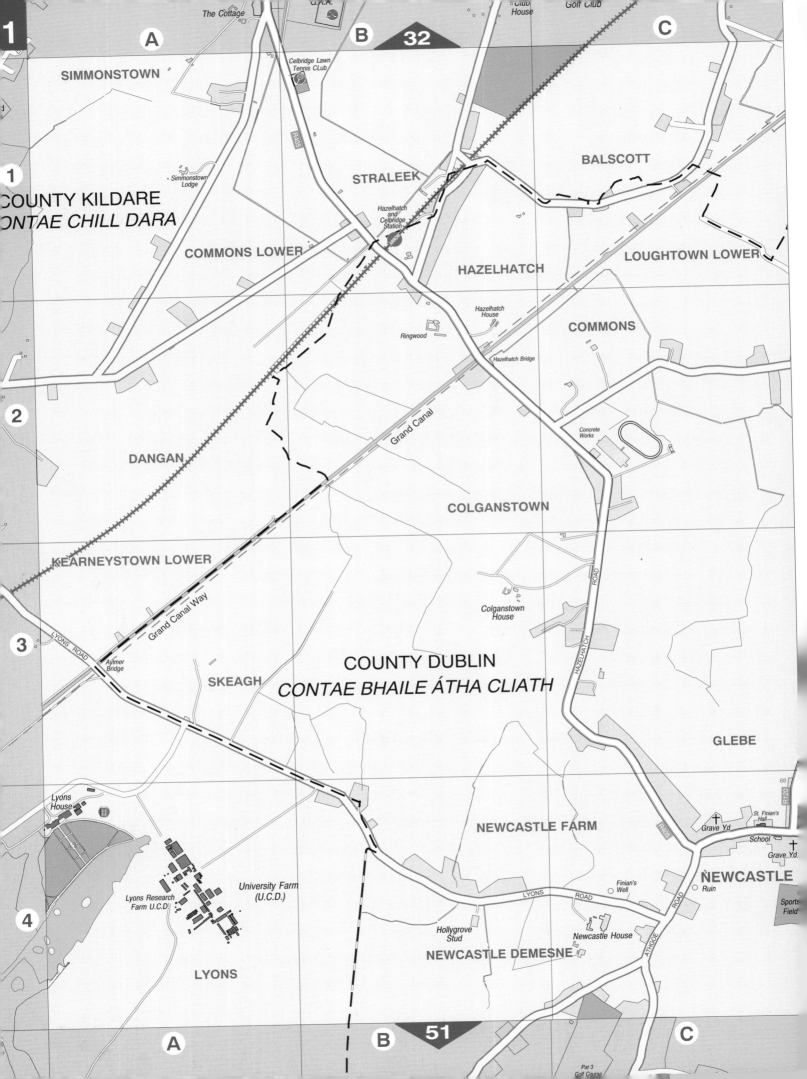

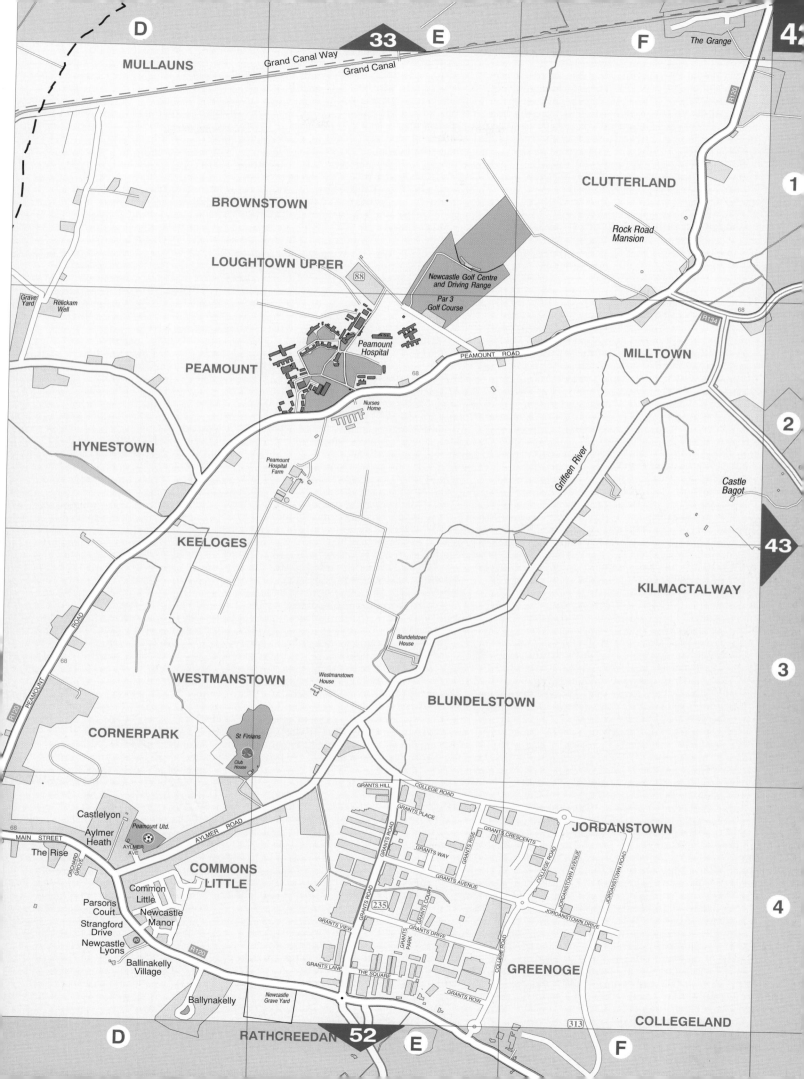

The Grange

MULLAUNS

Grand Canal Way

Grand Canal

CLUTTERLAND

BROWNSTOWN

Rock Road
Mansion

R120

LOUGHTOWN UPPER

88

Newcastle Golf Centre
and Driving Range

Par 3
Golf Course

R134

68

Grave
Yard

Relickam
Well

Peamount
Hospital

MILLTOWN

PEAMOUNT

PEAMOUNT ROAD

68

Nurses
Home

HYNESTOWN

Griffeen River

Castle
Bagot

Peamount
Hospital
Farm

KEELOGES

KILMACTALWAY

ROAD

68

Blundelstown
House

WESTMANSTOWN

Westmanstown
House

BLUNDELSTOWN

R120

PEAMOUNT

CORNERPARK

St Finians

Club
House

COLLEGE ROAD

GRANTS HILL

GRANTS PLACE

JORDANSTOWN

GRANTS ROAD

GRANTS CRESCENTS

Castlelyon

Peamount Utd.

AYLMER ROAD

GRANTS RISE

COLLEGE ROAD

JORDANSTOWN AVENUE

JORDANSTOWN ROAD

68

MAIN STREET

Aylmer
Heath

AYLMER AVE

GRANTS WAY

GRANTS AVENUE

The Rise

ORCHARD GROVE

COMMONS
LITTLE

GRANTS COURT

JORDANSTOWN DRIVE

Common
Little

Newcastle
Manor

235

GRANTS VIEW

GRANTS ROAD

GRANTS DRIVE

Parsons
Court

Strangford
Drive

Newcastle
Lyons

R120

GRANTS PARK

GREENOGE

Ballinakelly
Village

GRANTS LANE

THE SQUARE

GRANTS ROW

Ballynakelly

Newcastle
Grave Yard

313

COLLEGELAND

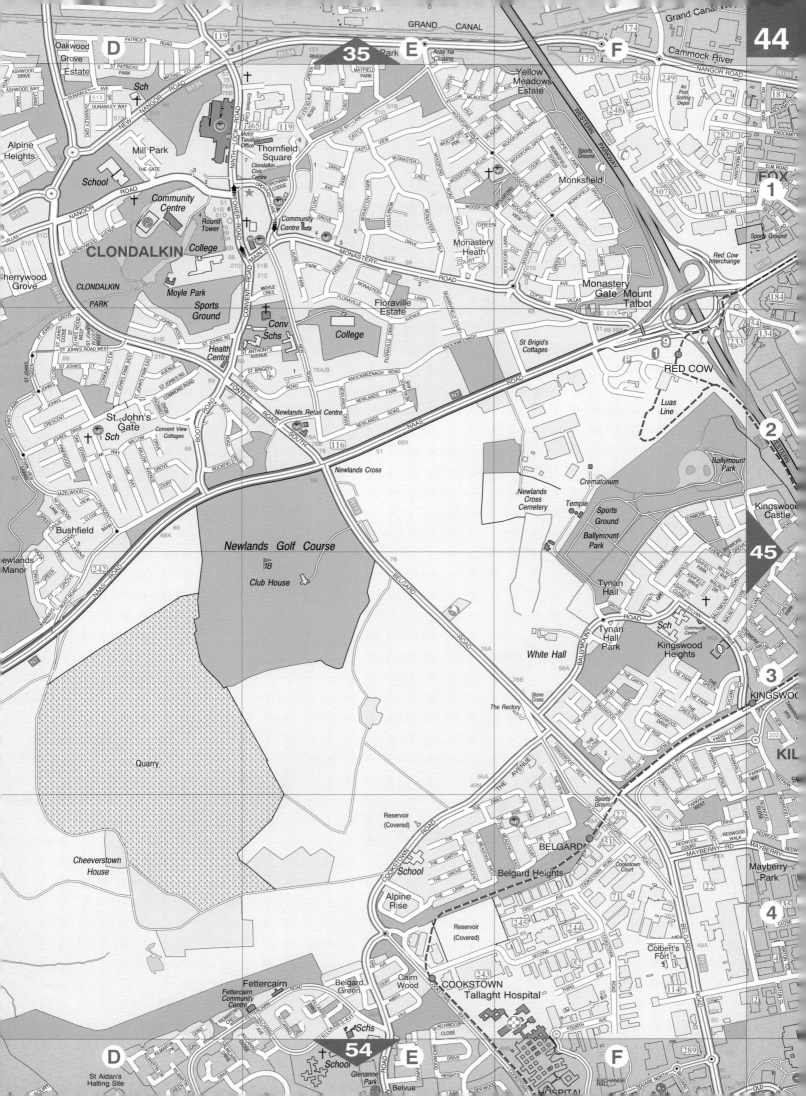

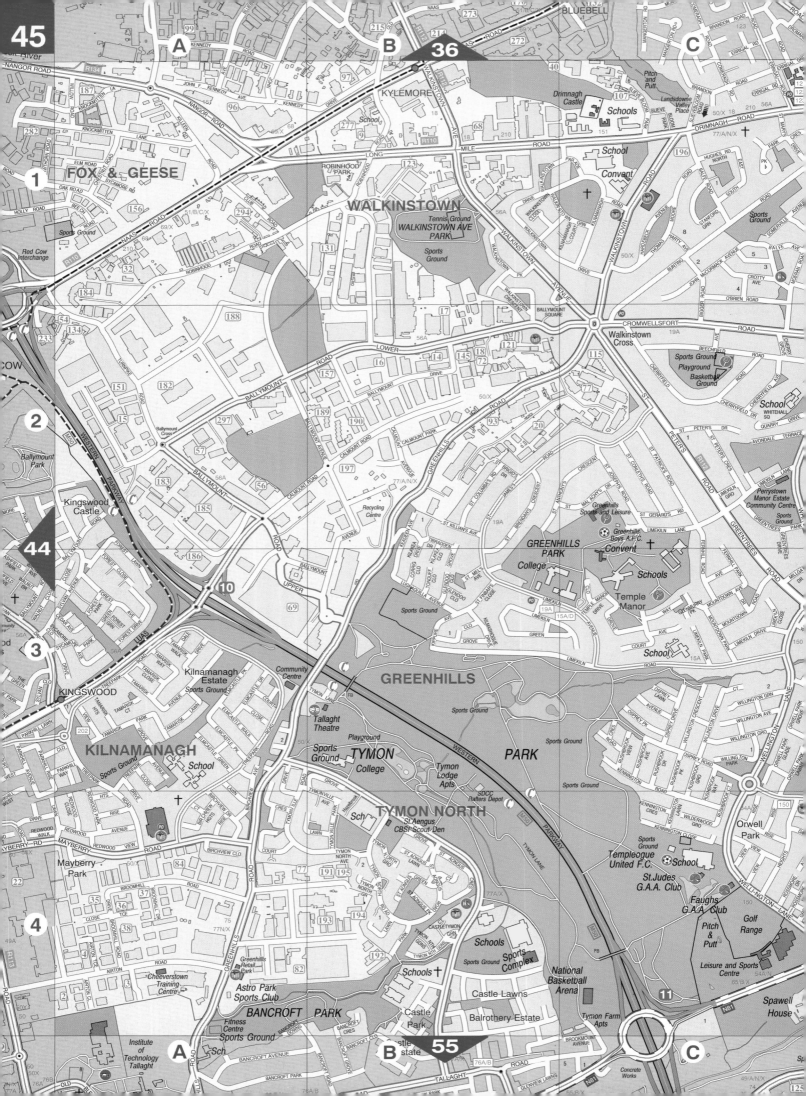

Lighthouse

Lighthouse

Harbour

EAST PIER

Car Ferry
Terminal

7B | 746
45A | 46A
46X | 59
75 | 111

Yacht Club

HARBOUR ROAD

CROFTON ROAD

N31

Car Ferry
Terminal

Band Stand

Dún Laoghaire
Station

Harbour
View
Harbour
Square

Yacht Club

Dun-Laoghaire/Rathdown
Co. Council

Town
Hall

Yacht Club

Geographical Pointer
Toilets

GEORGE'S PLACE

QUEEN'S ROAD

Hosp

GEORGE'S STREET-LOWER

Sch

MARINE RD

MORAN
PARK

DÚN LAOGHAIRE

Maritime
Museum

Baths

DOMINICK
ST
CROSS
AVENUE

Health
Centre

GEORGE'S STREET-UPPER

PEOPLES
PARK

Scotsman's Bay

WINDSOR TCE

NEWTOWNSMITH

Forty Foot
Bathing Place

TIVOLI TERRACE EAST

Nursing
Home

PATRICK

MULGRAVE

NORTHUMBER LAND

CORRIG AVENUE

CLARINDA PARK WEST

CLARINDA PK NORTH

PARK ROAD

Sandycove/
Glastule
Station

SUMMERHILL

LINK RD

MARINE
PARADE

Harbour

SANDYCOVE POINT

Tower

Baths

SANDYCOVE AVE W

SANDYCOVE AVE EAST

E.H.B.
Nursing
Home

CORRIG

Children's
Home

D   *Clarinda
Manor*

Sch

EDEN RD UPR

GLENAGEARY RD

ROSMEEN GDNS

CLARINDA PARK EAST

Coll
Schs

EDEN RD LR

GLAST-HULE ROAD

SANDYCOVE ROAD

60

E SANDYCOVE LANE E

SANDYCOVE AVE N

*Bullock
Harbour*

F

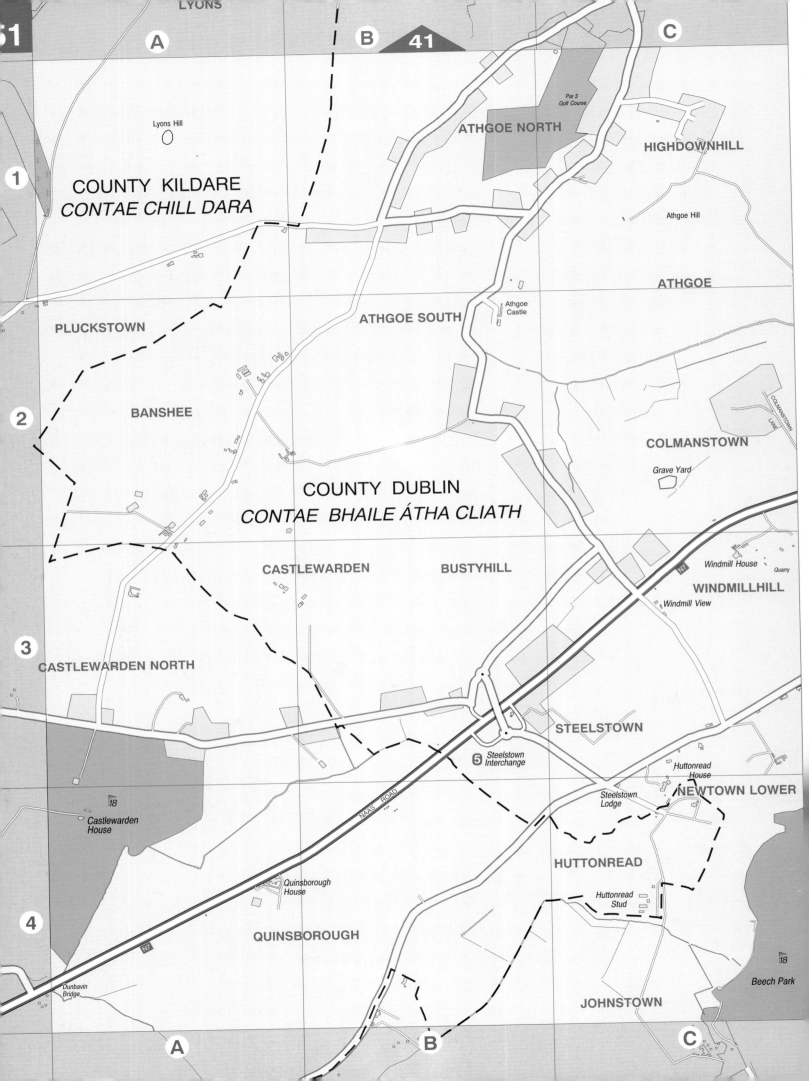

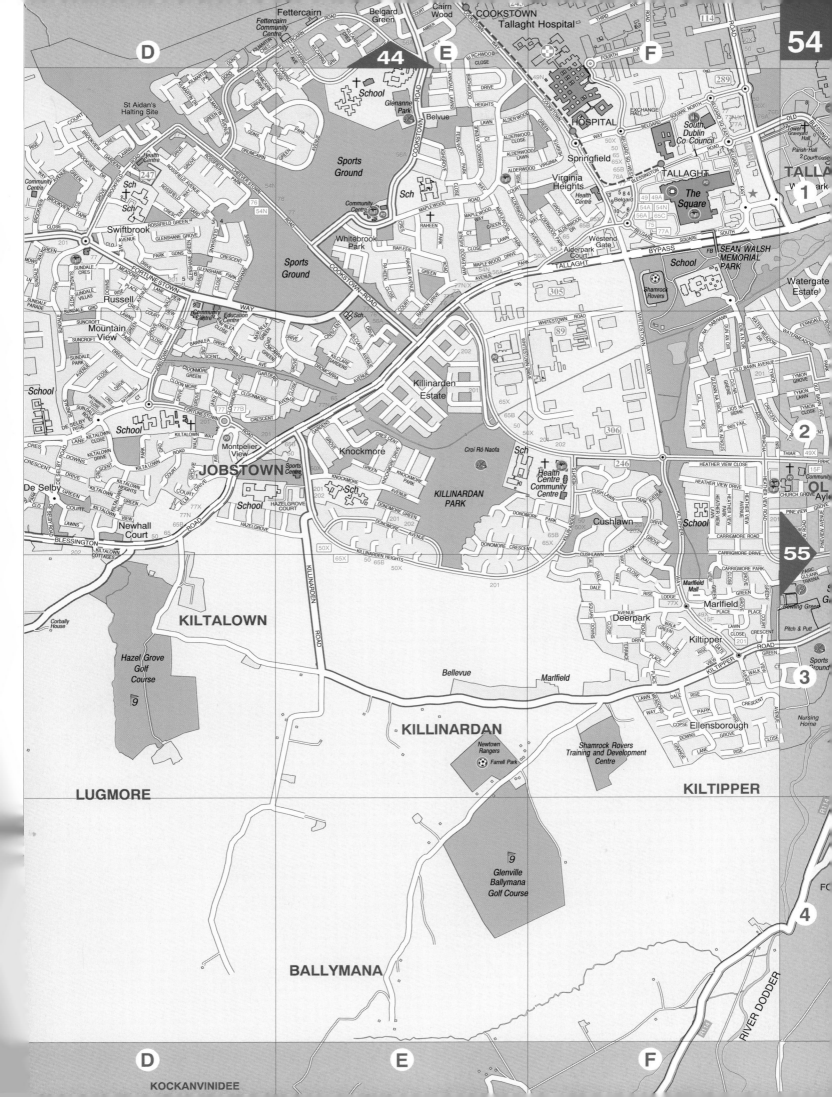

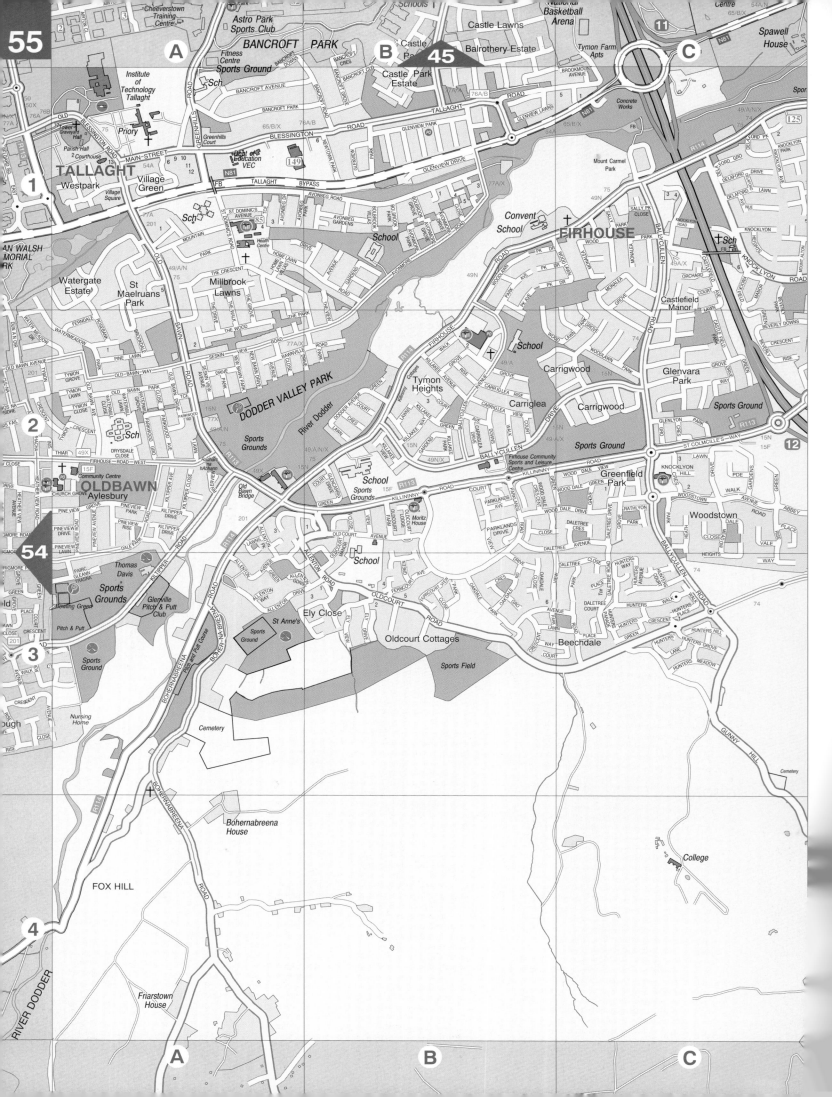

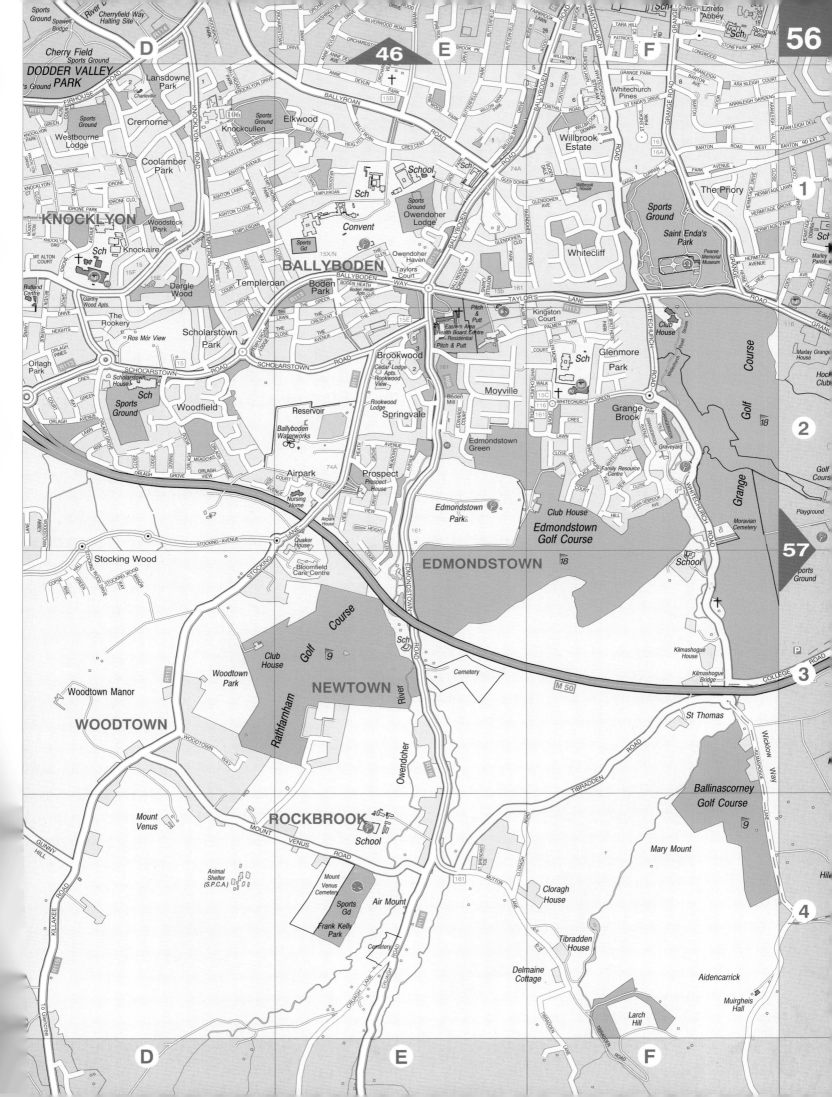

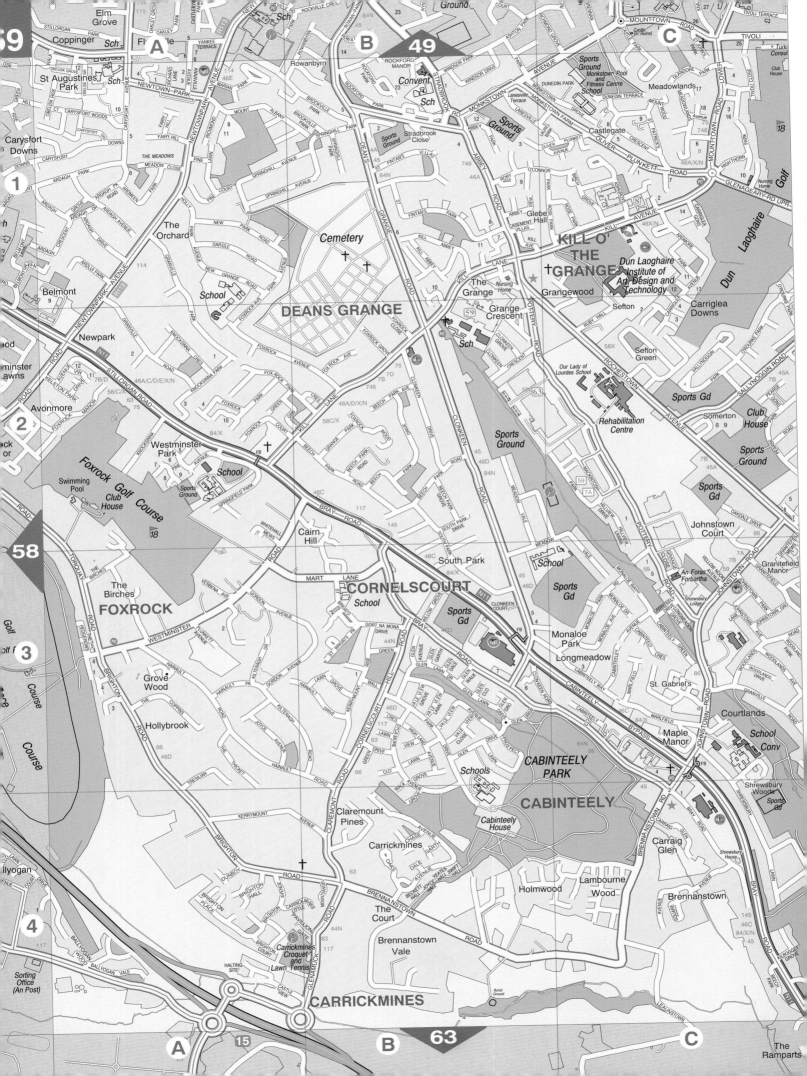

Stepaside
Village
Par 3
Golf Course
Kilgobbin Lawn
Waste Disposal
Site (Land Fill)
Office
(An Post)

Cruagh
Wood
Wingfield
Cairnfort
Stepaside
Public Golf Course
18

STEPASIDE

Quarry
BALLYEDMONDUFF ROAD
BURROW ROAD

Jamestown
Cottages

JAMESTOWN

Sports
Ground

Jamestown Par 3
Golf Course

Club
House

De la salle
Palmerston F.C.

Ballyedmonduff

Quarry

Driving
Range

Jamestown
House

Club
House

Sch

GLENAMUCK
NORTH

Stepaside
Golf Centre

Pinecroft

Bridon

Grave
Yard

Shaldon Grange

GLENAMUCK ROAD

Glenamuck

Quarry
Brackloon
House

Glebe

Sch

Rectory

Long
Meadow

Greenmount
Lodge

Cruagh

Golden Ball

Cromlech
Close

Rockville

63

Filter
Weir

Barnacullia
Water Works

Taylors
Folly

Knockbracken

Water Works

Wayside
Cottages

44

Sports
Gd

Sports
Gd

Cromlech
Lodge

Kilternan
Abbey

KILTERNAN

2

Cartowkeel
Stud

Ballyedmonduff
House

Newtown
House

BISHOP'S LANE

Grave
Yard

Kilternan
Lodge

Sch

Adult
Education
School

118

63

BALLYCORUS ROAD

R116

Mill
House

Cuckoo Field

Kilternan
Bridge

63

Pinefield
House

Giants' Grave

Kestrel
Lodge

Evesham

Verny
House

44

3

Glencullen
Pitch & Putt

NEWTOWN

Stone

Sunnyside

R116 BALLYBETAGH ROAD

Ballybetagh
House

9

Glencullen
Golf Course

Old
Grave Yard

Ballybetagh Wood

Grave
Yard

Dinish

18

Sch

GLENCULLEN

Glenacre

BALLYBETAGH

4

Par 3
Golf Course

The
Moors

Butter
Well

Glencullen
House

FIERY LANE

BALLYEDMONDUFF ROAD

R116

Eagle
Lodge

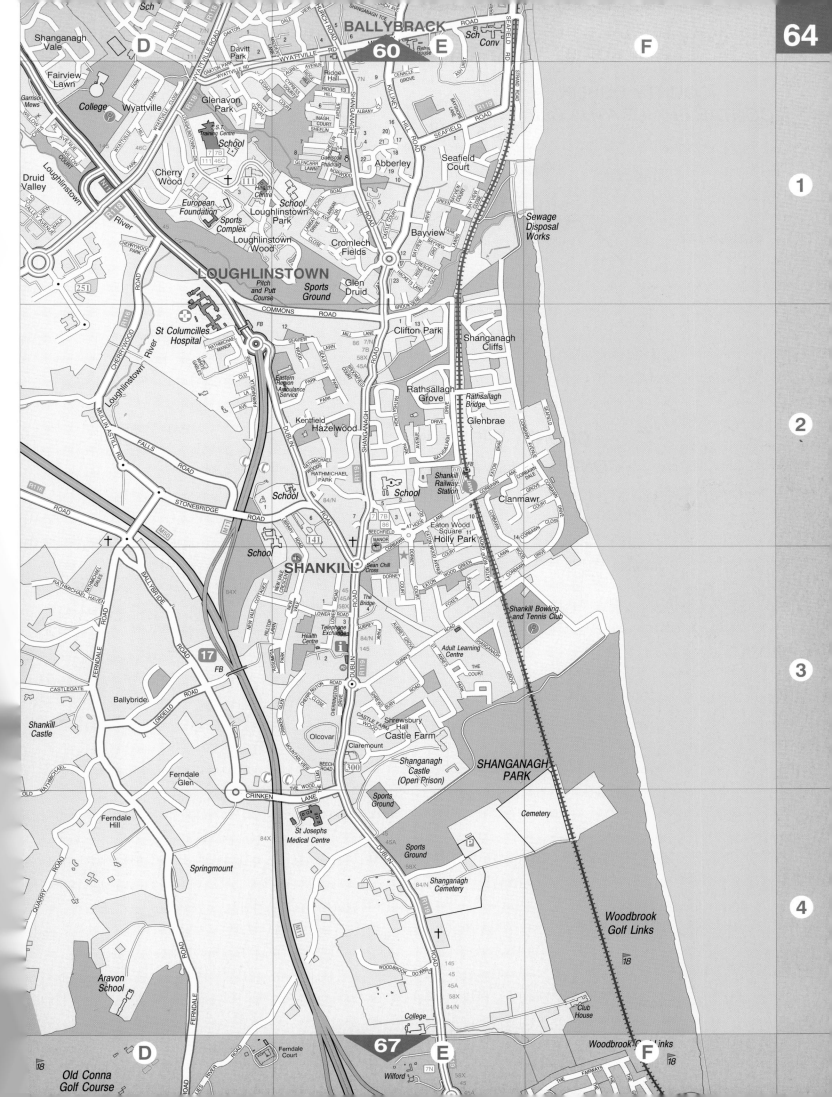

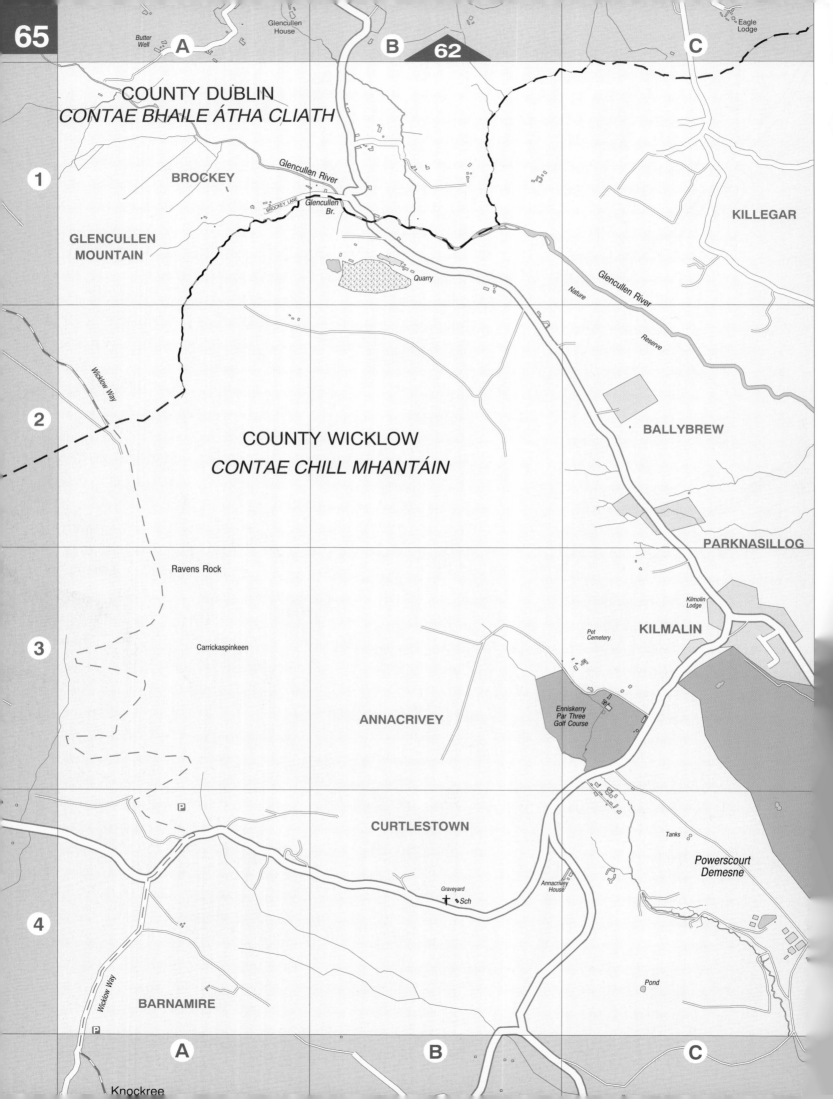

A

B

C

Butter
Well

Glencullen
House

Eagle
Lodge

Glencullen River

1

COUNTY DUBLIN
CONTAE BHAILE ÁTHA CLIATH

BROCKEY

BROCKEY LANE
Glencullen
Br.

KILLEGAR

GLENCULLEN
MOUNTAIN

Quarry

Nature

Glencullen River

Reserve

Wicklow Way

2

COUNTY WICKLOW
CONTAE CHILL MHANTÁIN

BALLYBREW

PARKNASILLOG

Ravens Rock

Kilmolin
Lodge

Pet
Cemetery

KILMALIN

3

Carrickaspinkeen

ANNACRIVEY

Enniskerry
Par Three
Golf Course

P

CURTLESTOWN

Tanks

Powerscourt
Demesne

Graveyard
† ⚲ Sch

Annacrivey
House

4

Pond

Wicklow Way

BARNAMIRE

P

A

B

C

Knockree

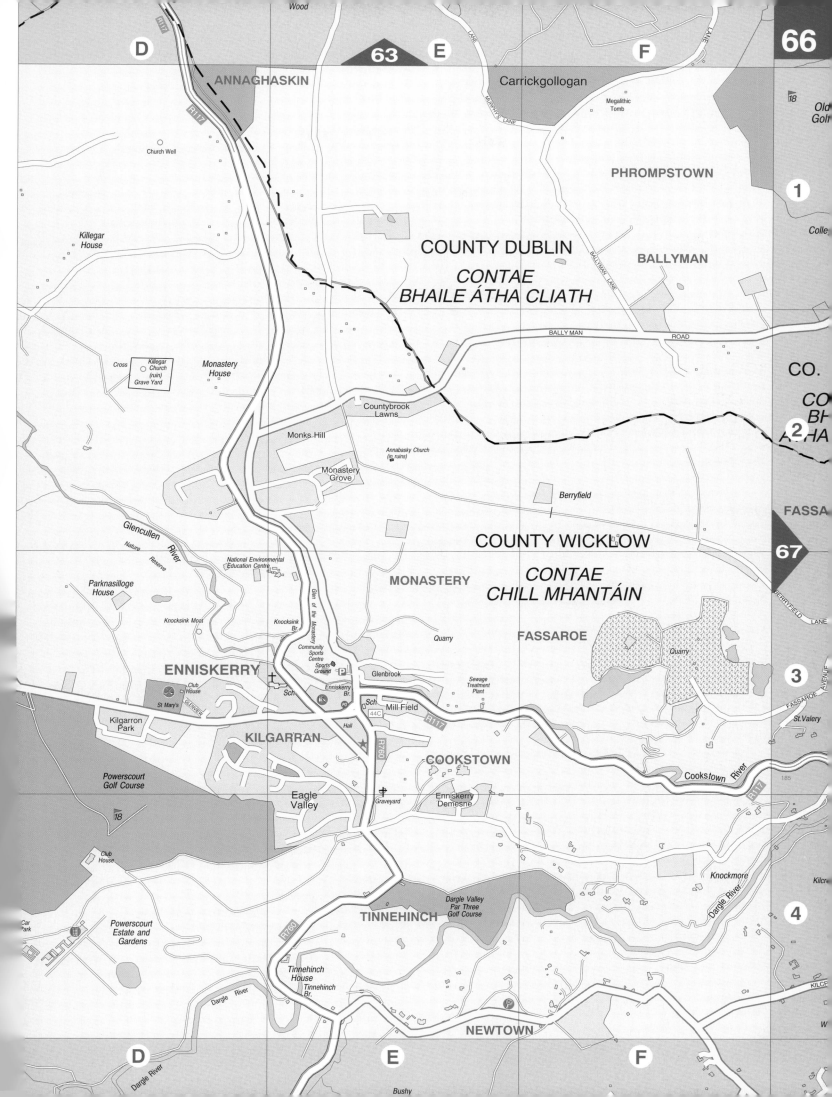

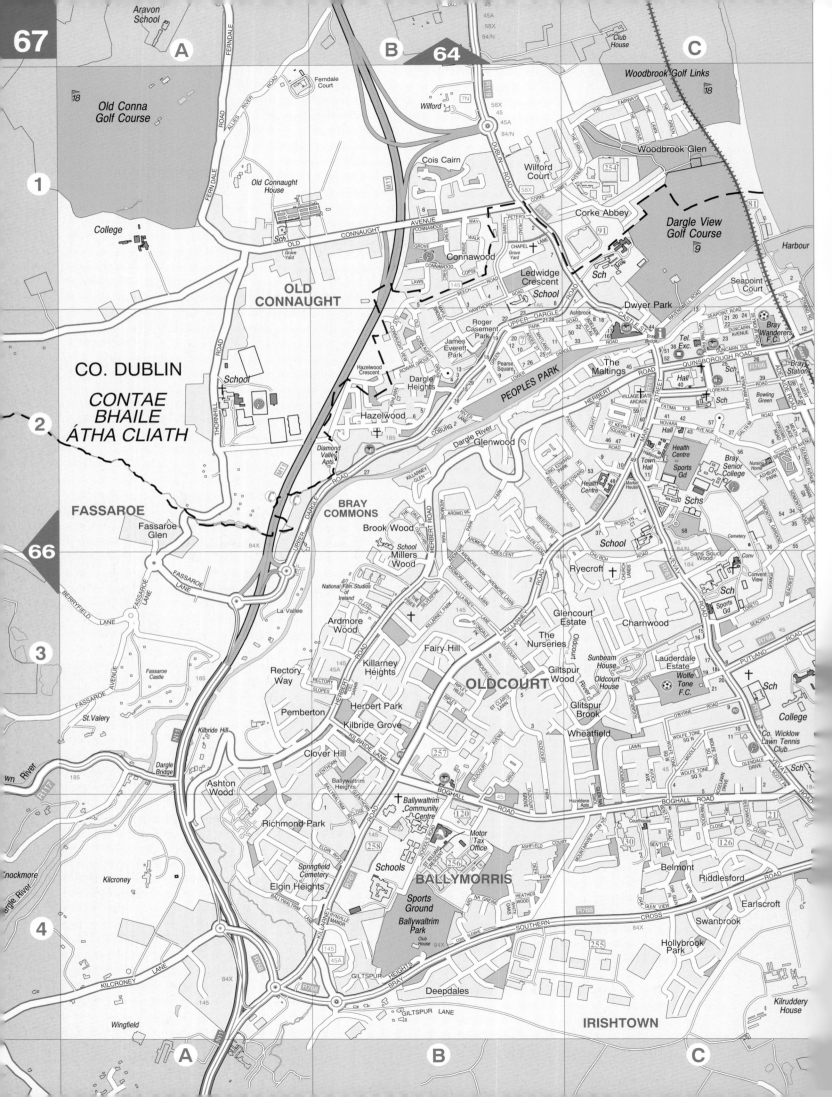

D E F

1

2

3

4

BRAY

National Sea Life Aquarium

Esplanade

South Esplanade

STRAND ROAD

VICTORIA AVE

CONVENT AVENUE

Hall

R766

ROAD

NEWCOURT ROAD

EDWARD RD

CAMADERRY RD

CUALA ROAD

RAHEEN PARK

AVENUE

Naylor's Cove

Fontenoy Terrace

Raheenacluig Church (in Ruins)

Golf Course

CUALA GROVE

NEWCOURT ROAD

NEWCOURT ROAD

Briar Wood

NEWCOURT

R761

Tunnel

Bray Head

COUNTY WICKLOW

Golf Course

CONTAE CHILL MHANTÁIN

84/X/N 184

Tunnel

Tunnel
Tunnel

D E F

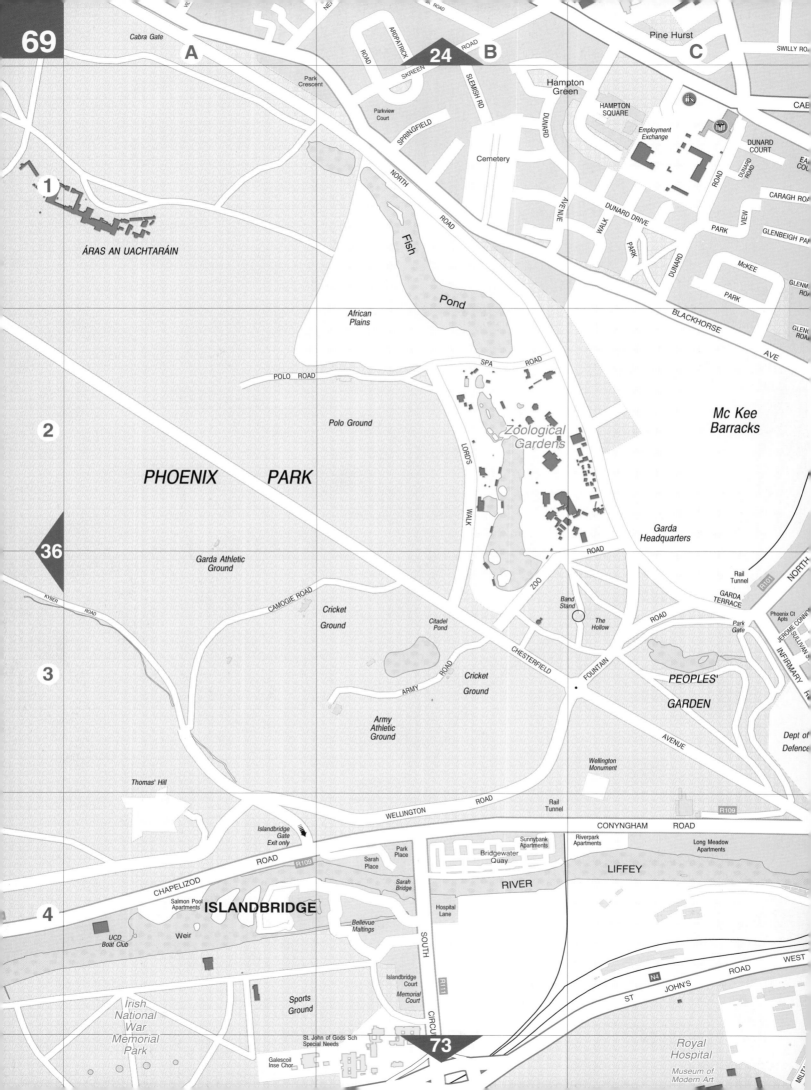

Cabra Gate

A

B

Pine Hurst

SWILLY RO

Park
Crescent

NEI

K ROAD

ROAD

ROAD

ARDPATRICK

SKREEN

SLEMISH RD

Hampton
Green

HAMPTON
SQUARE

Hampton
Green

SPRINGFIELD

Parkview
Court

Springfield

NORTH

ROAD

DUNARD

AVENUE

Cemetery

Employment
Exchange

DUNARD DRIVE

DUNARD COURT

EA
CO

DUNARD ROAD

CARAGH ROA

1

ÁRAS AN UACHTARÁIN

Fish

Pond

African
Plains

WALK

PARK

DUNARD

GLENBEIGH PAR

McKEE

PARK

GLENM
RO

GLENC
RO

SPA   ROAD

BLACKHORSE

AVE

POLO   ROAD

2

PHOENIX   PARK

Polo Ground

LORD'S

WALK

Zoological
Gardens

Mc Kee
Barracks

ROAD

Garda
Headquarters

NORTH

36

Garda Athletic
Ground

KYBER

ROAD

CAMOGIE ROAD

Cricket
Ground

ARMY

ROAD

Citadel
Pond

ZOO

ROAD

Band
Stand

The
Hollow

ROAD

Rail
Tunnel

R101

GARDA
TERRACE

Phoenix Ct
Apts

JEROME CONNO

3

Cricket
Ground

CHESTERFIELD

FOUNTAIN

Park
Gate

PEOPLES'

GARDEN

INFIRMARY

Army
Athletic
Ground

AVENUE

Dept of
Defence

Thomas' Hill

Wellington
Monument

WELLINGTON   ROAD

Rail
Tunnel

R109

CONYNGHAM   ROAD

Islandbridge
Gate
Exit only

ROAD

R109

Park
Place

Sarah
Place

CHAPELIZOD

Sarah
Bridge

Salmon Pool
Apartments

Sunnybank
Apartments

Bridgewater
Quay

Riverpark
Apartments

Long Meadow
Apartments

RIVER

LIFFEY

4

ISLANDBRIDGE

UCD
Boat Club

Weir

Bellevue
Maltings

Hospital
Lane

SOUTH

Islandbridge
Court

Memorial
Court

R111

ST JOHN'S

ROAD

WEST

N4

ST

Irish
National
War
Memorial
Park

Sports
Ground

CIRCULAR

St. John of Gods Sch
Special Needs

Royal
Hospital

Museum of
Modern Art

Galescoil
Inse Chor

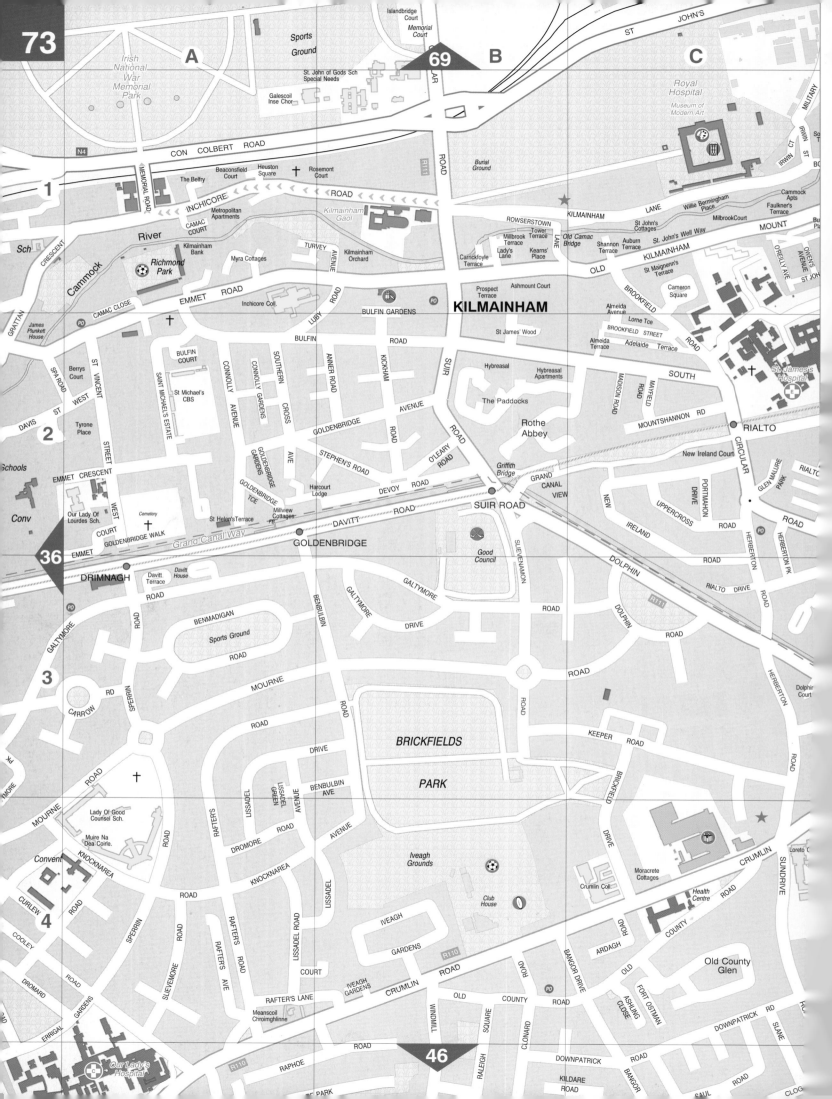

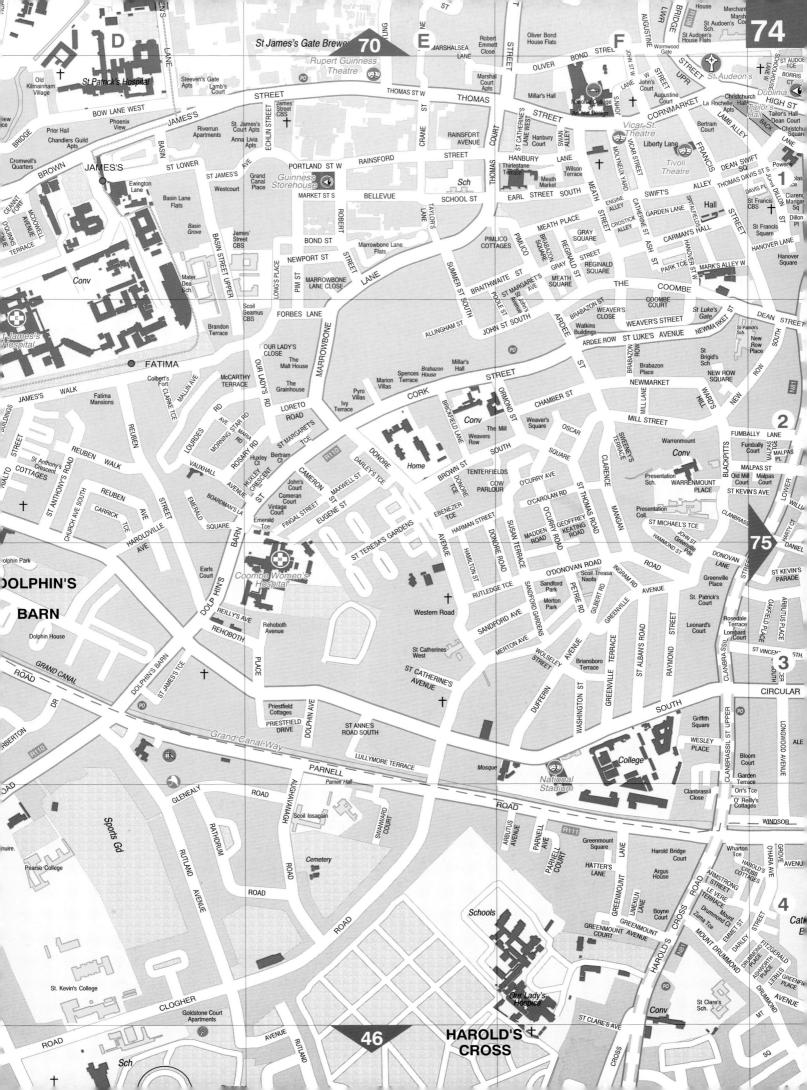

ASHBOURNE

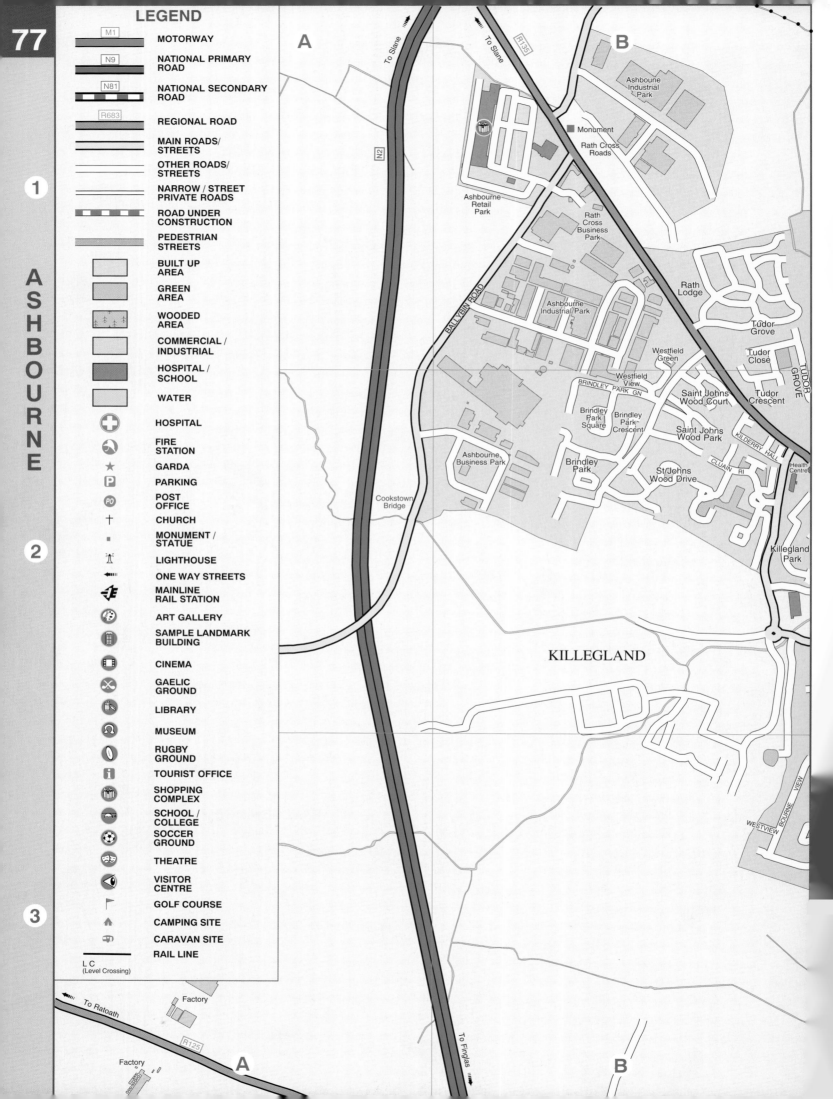

LEGEND

M1	MOTORWAY
N9	NATIONAL PRIMARY ROAD
N81	NATIONAL SECONDARY ROAD
R683	REGIONAL ROAD
	MAIN ROADS/ STREETS
	OTHER ROADS/ STREETS
	NARROW / STREET PRIVATE ROADS
	ROAD UNDER CONSTRUCTION
	PEDESTRIAN STREETS
	BUILT UP AREA
	GREEN AREA
	WOODED AREA
	COMMERCIAL / INDUSTRIAL
	HOSPITAL / SCHOOL
	WATER
	HOSPITAL
	FIRE STATION
★	GARDA
P	PARKING
PO	POST OFFICE
†	CHURCH
▪	MONUMENT / STATUE
	LIGHTHOUSE
	ONE WAY STREETS
	MAINLINE RAIL STATION
	ART GALLERY
	SAMPLE LANDMARK BUILDING
	CINEMA
	GAELIC GROUND
	LIBRARY
	MUSEUM
	RUGBY GROUND
	TOURIST OFFICE
	SHOPPING COMPLEX
	SCHOOL / COLLEGE
	SOCCER GROUND
	THEATRE
	VISITOR CENTRE
⚑	GOLF COURSE
	CAMPING SITE
	CARAVAN SITE
	RAIL LINE
L C (Level Crossing)	

A

B

1

2

3

To Slane

To Slane

R135

N2

Ashbourne Industrial Park

Monument

Rath Cross Roads

Ashbourne Retail Park

Rath Cross Business Park

Rath Lodge

Tudor Grove

BALLYBIN ROAD

Ashbourne Industrial Park

Westfield Green

Tudor Close

Tudor Crescent

TUDOR GROVE

Westfield View

BRINDLEY PARK GN

Saint Johns Wood Court

Brindley Park Square

Brindley Park Crescent

Saint Johns Wood Park

KILDERRY HALL

Ashbourne Business Park

Brindley Park

CLUAIN RI

St Johns Wood Drive

Health Centre

Cookstown Bridge

Killegland Park

KILLEGLAND

BOURNE VIEW

WESTVIEW

To Ratoath

Factory

R125

Factory

To Finglas

Alderbrook Downs	C3	Brookville	C2	Milltown Estate	C2
Alderbrook Glen	C3	Brookville Apts	C2	Milltown Road	C2
Alderbrook Park	C3	Castle Close	C2	Pinewood Court	C3
Alderbrook Rise	C3	Castle Crescent	C2	Race Hill	C1
Alderbrook Road	C3	Castle Park	C2	Race Lane	C1
Alderbrook Vale	C3	Castle Street	C2	Racehill Close	C1
Archerstown Road	D2	Castle Way	C3	Racehill Crescent	C1
Arkle Hill	C3	Castle Park	C3	Racehill Park	C1
Ashbourne Business Pk.	B2	Cherry Court	C3	Racehill Road	C1
Ashbourne Industrial Pk.	B2	Cherry Lane	C3	Racehill View	C1
Ashbourne Retail Park	B1	Cluain Rí	B2	Rath Cross Business Pk.	B1
Ashdale Crescent	C2	Cookstown Bridge	B2	Rath Cross Roads	B1
Ashwood	C2	Crestwood	C2	Rath Lodge	B1
Ashwood Close	C2	Crestwood Avenue	C2	Saint Johns Wood Court	B2
Ashwood Court	C2	Crestwood Green	C2	Saint Johns Wood Drive	B2
Ashwood Drive	C2	Crestwood Park	C3	Saint Johns Wood Park	B2
Ashwood Glen	C2	Crestwood Road	C2	Tara Close	C3
Ashwood Green	C2	Deerpark	C3	Tara Court	C3
Ashwood Heath	C2	Dublin Road	C3	Tara Lawns	C3
Ashwood Meadow	C2	Frederick Street	C2	Tara Place	C2
Ashwood Walk	C2	Frederick Court	C2	The Bailey	C3
Bachelors Walk	C2	Greenfield Grove	C3	The Briars	C3
Baldara Court	D3	Hickey's Lane	C3	The Green	C3
Ballybin Road	B1	Hunters Lane	C3	The Hawthorns	C2
Bourne Avenue	C3	Huntsgrove	C3	Tudor Close	B1
Bourne Court	C3	Kilderry Hall	B2	Tudor Crescent	B2
Bourne View	B3	Killegland Court	B2	Tudor Grove	B1
Bridge Street	C3	Killegland Hall	C2	Tudor Grove	C2
Brindley Park	B2	Killegland Park	B2	Tudor Heights	C1
Brindley Park Crescent	B2	Killegland Rise	C3	Westfield Green	B1
Brindley Park Green	B2	Killegland Road	C3	Westfield View	B2
Brindley Park Square	B2	Lindsay Mews	C3	Westview	B3
Broad Meadow Castle	C2	Maple Grove	C2	White Ash Park	D2
Broadmeadow Green	C2	Meadow Brook Court	C2		
Broadmeadow Road	C3	Milltown Bridge	D3		

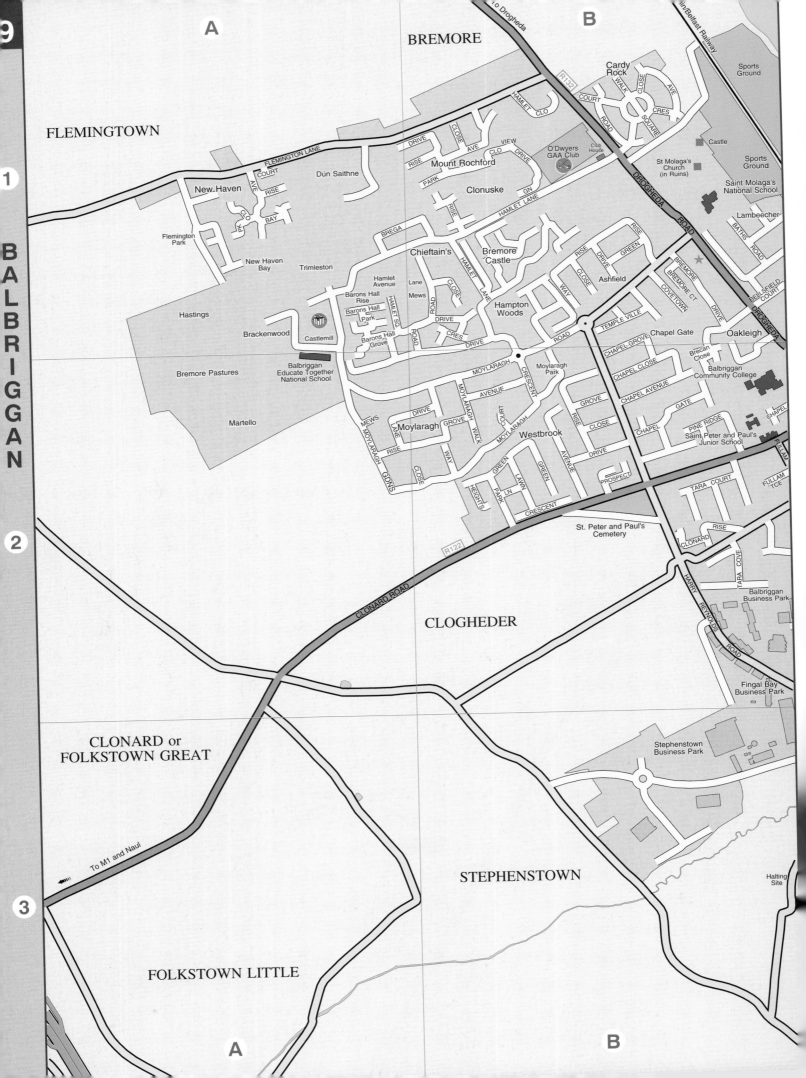

Street	Grid
Ardgillen Close	C3
Ardgillen Drive	C3
Ardgillen Lawn	C3
Ardgillen Road	C3
Ashfield Close	B1
Ashfield Drive	B1
Ashfield Green	B1
Ashfield Rise	B1
Ashfield Way	B1
Balbriggan Business Park	B2
Balbriggan Retail Park	B2
Baron's Hall Grove	A1
Baron's Hall Park	A1
Baron's Hall Rise	A1
Baths Road	B1
Baths Road	C1
Bellsfield Court	B1
Brackenwood	A1
Brecan Close	B2
Brega	B1
Bremore Castle	B1
Bremore Court	B1
Bremore Drive	B1
Bremore Pastures	A2
Brick Lane	C2
Bridge Street	C2

Street	Grid
Cardy Rock Avenue	B1
Cardy Rock Close	B1
Cardy Rock Court	B1
Cardy Rock Crescent	B1
Cardy Rock Road	B1
Cardy Rock Square	B1
Cardy Rock Walk	B1
Castleland Court	C2
Castleland Park View	C3
Castleland	C3
Castlemill	A1
Chapel Avenue	B2
Chapel Close	B2
Chapel Court	C2
Chapel Gate	B2
Chapel Grove	B2
Chapel Street	C2
Chapel Street Crescent	B2
Chieftain's Close	B1
Chieftain's Crescent	B1
Chieftain's Drive	B1
Chieftain's Lane	B1
Chieftain's Mews	B1
Chieftan's Road	B1
Church Street	C2
Cloch Choirneal	C4
Clonard Court	C2
Clonard Rise	B2
Clonard Road	A2
Clonard Street	C2
Clonuske Close	B1
Clonuske Drive	B1
Clonuske Green	B1
Clonuske Park	B1
Clonuske Rise	B1
Clonuske View	B1
Convent Lane	C2
Cornmill Apartments	C2

Street	Grid
Covetown	B1
Craobhin Close	C2
Craobhin Park	C2
Curran Park	C2
Derham Park	D2
Drogheda Road	B1
Drogheda Street	B1
Dublin Street	C2
Dún Saithne	A1
Fancourt	C2
Fancourt Heights	D2
Fingal Bay Business Pk.	B2
Flemington Lane	A1
Flemington Park	A1
Fullam Terrace	B2
George's Court	C2
George's Hill	C2
Gibbons Terrace	C2
Glover Court	C2
Haniliton	C3
Hamlet Avenue	A1
Hamlet Close	B1
Hamlet Lane	B1
Hamlet Square	A1
Hampton Court	C2
Hampton Cove	D2
Hampton Green	C2
Hampton Place	B2
Hampton Street	C2
Hampton Woods	B1
Harbour Road	C2
Harry Reynolds Road	B2
Hastings	A1
High Street	C2
Lambeecher	B1
Laragh	C2
Lawless Terrace	C2
Linnen Hall	C2[1]

Street	Grid
Martello	A2
McWeill Hall	C2[2]
Mill Race	C2
Mill Street	C2
Mill Walk	C2
Mount Rochford Avenue	B1
Mount Rochford Close	B1
Mount Rochford Drive	B1
Mount Rochford Rise	B1
Moylaragh Avenue	B2
Moylaragh Close	B2
Moylaragh Court	B2
Moylaragh Crescent	B2
Moylaragh Drive	B2
Moylaragh Gardens	A2
Moylaragh Grove	B2
Moylaragh Lane	C2
Moylaragh Mews	A2
Moylaragh Park	B2
Moylaragh Rise	A2
Moylaragh Road	B2
Moylaragh Walk	B2
Moylaragh Way	B2
New Haven Avenue	A1
New Haven Bay	A1
New Haven Close	A1
New Haven Court	A1
New Haven Park	A1
New Haven Rise	A1
New Market Green	C2
Oakleigh	B2
Old Market Green	C2
Papworth Hall	C2[3]
Pine Ridge	B2
Pinewood Green Avenue	D3
Pinewood Green Close	C3
Pinewood Green Court	D3
Pinewood Green Hill	D2

Street	Grid
Pinewood Green Lawn	C3
Pinewood Green Road	D3
Prospect	B2
Pump Lane	C2
Quay Street	C2
Railway Street	C2
Seapoint Lane	C2
Skerries Road	C2
St. Molagha's Terrace	C2
St. Paul's Crescent	C2
St. Peter's Terrace	C2
Stephenstown Bus. Pk.	B3
Tanners Water Lane	C3
Tara Court	B2
Tara Cove	B2
Templeville	B1
The Chantries	C3
The Square	C2
Trimelston	A1
Vauxhall Street	C2
Westbrook Avenue	B2
Westbrook Close	B2
Westbrook Crescent	B2
Westbrook Drive	B2
Westbrook Green	B2
Westbrook Grove	B2
Westbrook Height	B2
Westbrook Lawn	B2
Westbrook Park	B2
Westbrook Rise	B2

Streets not named but shown as small numbers:

C2	1	Linnen Hall
	2	McWeill Hall
	3	Papworth Hall

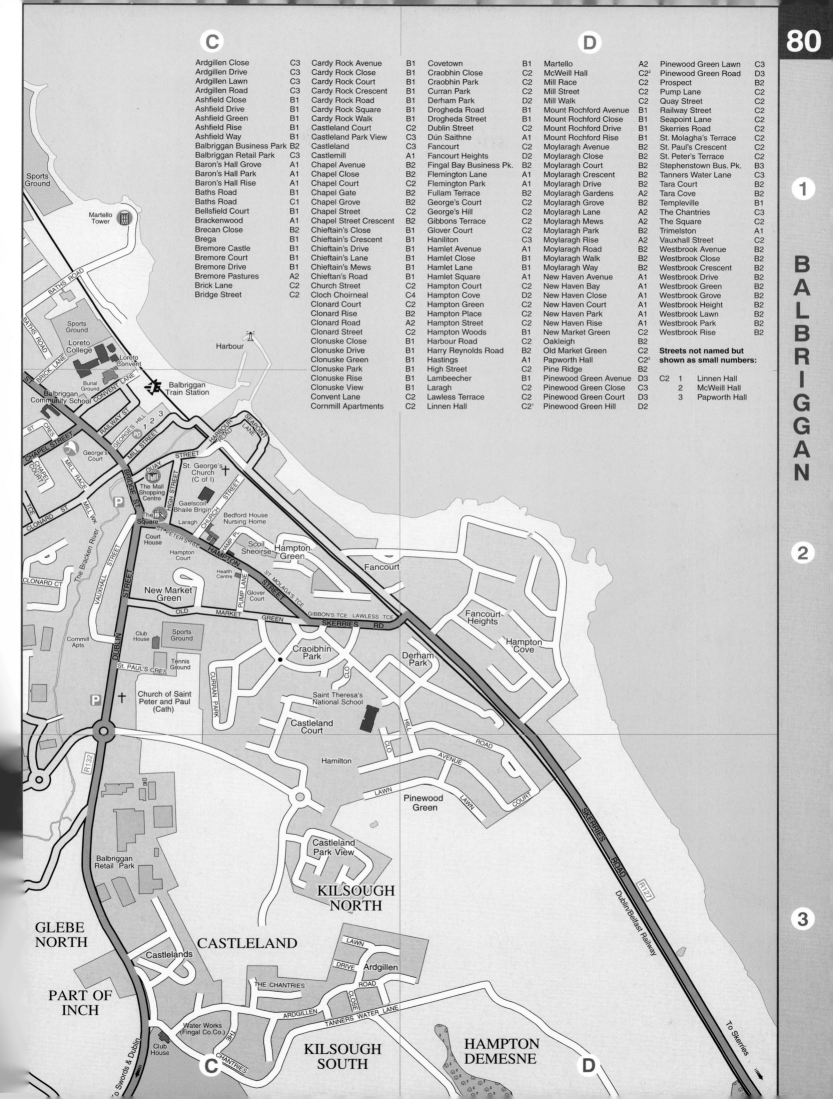

BLESSINGTON

Ashton	A2	Glenview Court	A2	Rocky Pool Villas	B2
Beechdale Close	A2	Glenview	A2	St. Joseph's Road	B2
Beechdale Garden	A2	Haywood	A2	The Close B. Abbey	A3
Beechdale Grove	A2	Kilbride Road	B2	The Glen B.Abbey	A3
Beechdale Lawn	A2	Kilmalum Avenue	A3	The Green B.Abbey	A3
Beechdale View	A2	Kilmalum Close	A3	The Park B.Abbey	A3
Beechdale Way	A2	Kilmalum Crescent	A3	The Avenue D. Park	A2
Blessington Abbey	A3	Kilmalum Drive	A3	The Close D. Park	A2
Blessington Ind. Estate	A3	Kilmalum Green	A3	The Dale D. Park	A2
Blessington Newtown Cen.	B2	Kilmalum View	A3	The Green D. Park	A2
Blessington Orchard	A3	Kilmalum Way	A3	The Grove D. Park	A2
Blessington Retail Park	A3	Lakeshore Holiday Village	B3	The Walk D. Park	A2
Burgage Manor	A3	Lakeside Downs	B2	The Way D. Park	A2
Carrig Glen	B3	Lakeview	B2	Troopersfield	A3
Deerpark Close	A2	Main Street	B2	Westpark	A2
Deerpark Court	A2	Mountain View	B3	Woodleigh	B1
Deerpark Drive	A2	Naas Road	A2	Woodleigh Avenue	B1
Deerpark Green	A2	Oak Drive	B2	Woodleigh Close	B1
Deerpark Road	A2	Old Ballymore Road	A3	Woodleigh Grove	B1
Deerpark View	A2	Old Lakeview	B2	Woodleigh Park	B1
Deerpark Walk	A2	Park View Villas	A3	Woodleigh Way	B1
Downshire Park	A2	Rocky Pool Crescent	B2		

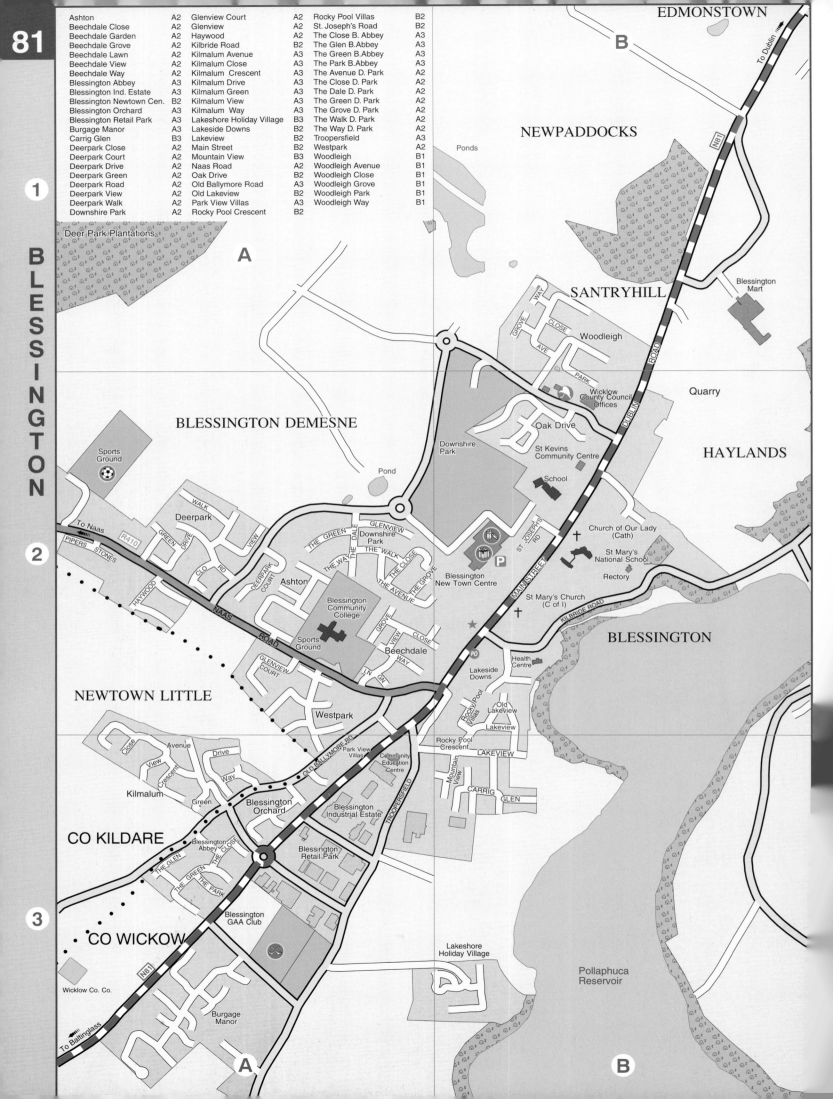

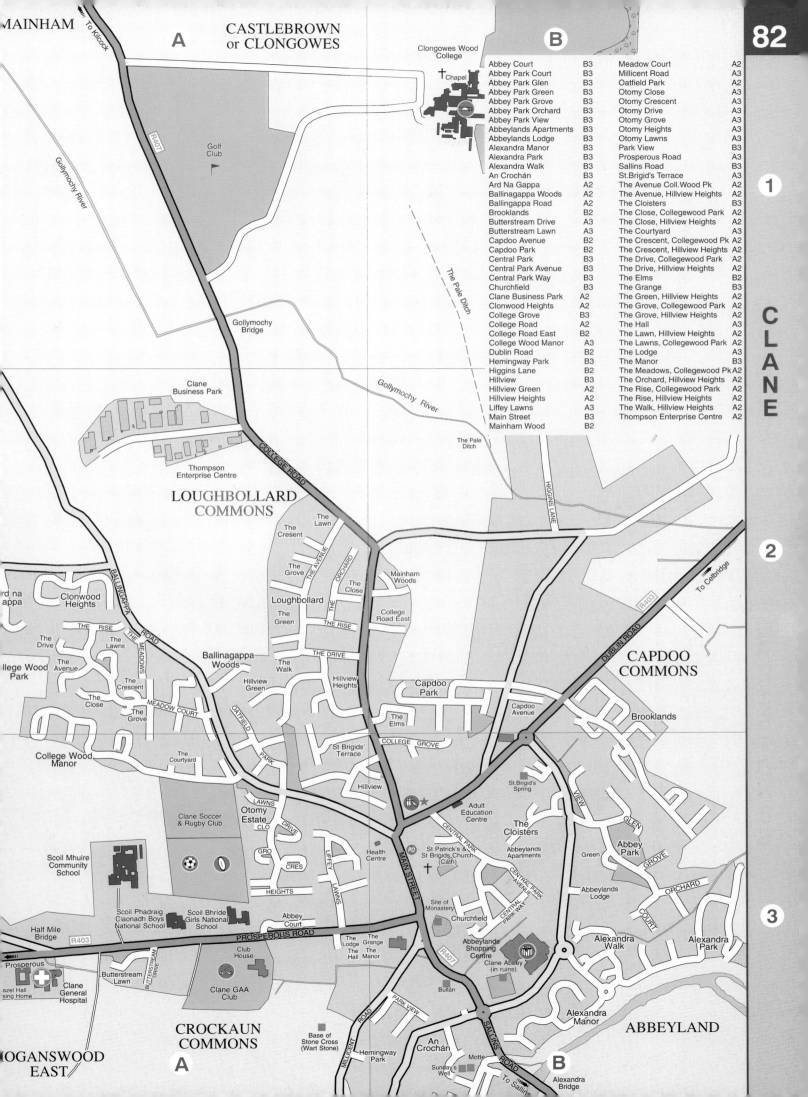

MAINHAM

CASTLEBROWN or CLONGOWES

A

B

Clongowes Wood College

† Chapel

Golf Club

Gollymochy River

To Kilcock

R407

Gollymochy Bridge

The Pale Ditch

Gollymochy River

Clane Business Park

Thompson Enterprise Centre

LOUGHBOLLARD COMMONS

COLLEGE ROAD

The Pale Ditch

1

2

3

C L A N E

Higgins Lane

To Celbridge

R403

Dublin Road

CAPDOO COMMONS

The Lawn

The Cresent

The Grove

THE AVENUE

THE ORCHARD

The Close

Mainham Woods

Loughbollard

The Green

THE RISE

College Road East

Brooklands

THE RISE

THE DRIVE

Capdoo Park

Capdoo Avenue

Ballingappa Woods

Hillview Green

Hillview Heights

The Walk

The Elms

St Brigids' Terrace

COLLEGE GROVE

VIEW

GLEN

St.Brigid's Spring

Abbey Park

GROVE

Clonwood Heights

BALLINGAPPA ROAD

THE MEADOWS

MEADOW COURT

THE RISE

The Drive

The Lawns

The Avenue

The Crescent

The Close

The Grove

OATFIELD PARK

DRIVE

The Cloisters

Green

ORCHARD

COURT

Ard na Gappa

College Wood Park

College Wood Manor

The Courtyard

Clane Soccer & Rugby Club

Otomy Estate

CLO

GRO

CRES

LIFFEY LAWNS

Health Centre

Adult Education Centre

Abbeylands Apartments

Abbeylands Lodge

Scoil Mhuire Community School

LAWNS

HEIGHTS

MAIN STREET

PO

St Patrick's & St Brigids Church (Cath)

†

Site of Monastery

Churchfield

CENTRAL PARK AVENUE

CENTRAL PARK WAY

Abbey Park

Half Mile Bridge

R403

Scoil Phadraig Claonadh Boys National School

Scoil Bhride Girls National School

Abbey Court

Prosperous

Prosperous Road

Butterstream Lawn

BUTTERSTREAM DRIVE

Club House

Clane GAA Club

The Lodge

The Hall

The Grange

The Manor

R407

Abbeylands Shopping Centre

Clane Abbey (in ruins)

Bullán

Alexandra Walk

Alexandra Park

Hazel Hall Nursing Home

Clane General Hospital

Base of Stone Cross (Wart Stone)

MILLICENT ROAD

PARK VIEW

Hemingway Park

An Crochán

Motte

Sunday's Well

SALLINS ROAD

Alexandra Manor

Alexandra Bridge

ABBEYLAND

HOGANSWOOD EAST

CROCKAUN COMMONS

A

B

To Sallins

INSET
FOR
PAGE 84

B

KINDLESTOWN UPPER

DELGANY

GREYSTONES

To Bray

R761

Saint Crispins

Church (In Ruins)

Rathdown Castle (Site of)

Redford

Redford Court

Sports Ground

RATHDOWN ROAD

SEA VIEW

Redford Park

Mount Haven

Willowmere

Redford Rise

Kindlestown Rise

Kindlestown Heights

Dromont

Kindlestown Castle (In Ruins)

CONVENT ROAD

Bellevue Cottages

St Mary's Church (Cath)

Meadow Court

Bellevue Lawns

Monastery

Bellevue Court

Convent Court

Church (in Ruins)

Cross

Hunter's Brook

PO

Christ Church (C of I)

Priory Gate

PRIORY ROAD

Valley View

Delgany Golf Course

Club House

Reservoir

A

Woodlands Church (In Ruins)

Fair Green

Glen of the Downs

R762

N11

DRUMMIN WEST

To Wicklow Town & Arklow

R762

BLACKBERRY LANE

STILEBAWN

Reservoir

B

Adare Close	C2	Cherry Green	C2	Kindlestown Park	C2	Rathdown Park	C1
Applewood Drive	C1	Cherry Grove	C2	Kindlestown Rise	B1	Rathdown Road	INSET
Applewood Heights	C1	Cherry Orchard	C2	Kinlen Road	D2	Rathdown Road	C1
Bayswater Terrace	D1	Cherry Rise	C2	La Touche Close	D1	Redford	INSET
Beechbrook Park	C1	Church Gate	D1	La Touche Park	C1	Redford Court	INSET
Belleview Demesne	C1	Church Lane	C1	La Touche Place	C1	Redford Park	INSET
Bellevue Cottages	B2	Church Road	D1	La Touche Road	D1	Redford Rise	INSET
Bellevue Court	B3	Churchfields	C2	Lower Grattan Park	C1	Rivendell Grove	C2
Bellevue Heights	C2	Cliff Road	D1	Manor Avenue	D2	Riverfield	C2
Bellevue Lawns	B2	Convent Court	B3	Marine Road	D1	Saint Crispins	INSET
Bellevue Park	D1	Convent Road	B2	Marine Terrace	D1	Saint Vincent Road	D2
Bellevue Road	D1	Delgany Glen	C2	Meadow Court	B3	Salem Vale	C3
Blackberry Lane	B3	Delgany Park	C3	Mill Road	D2	Sea View	INSET
Blacklion Manor	C1	Delgany Wood	C3	Mill Road	D3	Sidmonton Place	D1
Burnaby Avenue	D3	Dromont	B2	Millbrook	D3	Somerby Road	D1
Burnaby Court	D3	Drummin Rise	C3	Millgrove	C3	South Place	D2
Burnaby Heights	C2	Eden Gate	C3	Millgrove Close	C3	St. Bridget's Park	C1
Burnaby Lawns	D3	Eden Road	D1	Mount Haven	INSET	The Arch	D1
Burnaby Manor	D1	Elsinore	C3	Mountain View Park	C1	The Bawn	D1
Burnaby Mews	D1	Erskine Avenue	D2	New Road	C3	The Manor	D1
Burnaby Mill	D3	Fair Green	A3	New Road	D1	The Nurseries	C2
Burnaby Park	D2	Fairfield Park	D1	Oaklands	C1	The Poplars	C2
Burnaby Road	D2	Glen of the Downs	A3	Oaklands Court	C1	Thornbury	D3
Burnaby Woods	D2	Glenair Manor	C3	Old Mill Road	D2	Trafalgar Court	D1
Carraig Orchard	C2	Glenbrook Park	C3	Orchard View	C2	Trafalgar Road	D1
Carrick Villas	C2	Harbour Court	D1	Park Lane	D2	Turn Pike Lane	D1
Carrig Villas	C3	Hawkins Lane	D2	Pavilion Road	D2	Upper Grattan Park	C1
Castle Villas	C1	Hethervue	D1	Portland Place	D2	Valley View	B3
Castlefield Terrace	C2	Hillcrest Avenue	C2	Portland Road	D2	Victoria Road	D1
Chapel Road	C1	Hillside	D1	Portland Road North	D2	Wendon Brook	C3
Chapel Road	D1	Hillside Road	D1	Priory Gate	B2	Wendon Drive	C3
Chapel View	C1	Hunter's Brook	B3	Priory Rise	C2	Wendon Park	C3
Charlesland Court	D3	Kenmare Heights	C2	Priory Road	B3	Whitshed Road	D2
Charlesland Grove	D3	Killincarrick Road	D1	Priory Way	C2	Willow Bank	C1
Charlesland Park	D3	Kimberley Court	D1	Quarry Road	D2	Willowmere	INSET
Charlesland Wood	D3	Kimberley Road	D1	Rathdown Close	D1	Woodlands	D2
Cherry Court	C2	Kindlestown Heights	B2	Rathdown Court	C1		
Cherry Drive	C2	Kindlestown Lower	C2	Rathdown Lawn	C1		

C

D

Sailing Club

Fairfield Park

The Arch

Bayswater Tce

Blacklion Manor

Rathdown Park

La Touche Park

NEW ROAD

VICTORIA ROAD

Harbour Court

Willow Bank

St Killian's Church

Rathdown Lawn

Mountain View Park

Clinic

St. Patrick's NS

Sports Ground

TRAFALGAR ROAD

Sidmonton Place

Belleview Demesne

RATHDOWN ROAD

CHURCH GATE

Trafalgar Court

Marine Terrace

CLIFF ROAD

St Bridget's Park

Rathdown Court

Oaklands Court

Rathdown Close

The Manor

R762

Nursing Home

Church (Presb)

Saint Brigid's NS

MARINE ROAD

Saint David's Secondary School

Chapel View

APPLEWOOD DRIVE

Oaklands

CHURCH LANE

St Patrick's Church (C of I)

TURN PIKE LANE

LA TOUCHE CLOSE

Church Of The Holy Rosary (Cath)

KIMBERLEY ROAD

The Grey Stones

Applewood Heights

Nursing Home

CHURCH ROAD

La Touche Place

Parish Hall

Kimberley Court

CHAPEL ROAD

Lower Grattan Park

Hillside

Bellevue Park

EDEN ROAD

LA TOUCHE ROAD

PO

Beechbrook Park

Upper Grattan Park

RIVENDELL GROVE

Kindlestown Park

BELLEVUE ROAD

Hethervue

Hillside Evangelical Church

HILLSIDE ROAD

Burnaby Manor

Burnaby Mews

KILLINCARRICK RD

Greystones Rail Station

Bellevue Heights

KINDLESTOWN LOWER

R761

Greystones Golf Course

SAINT VINCENT ROAD

BURNABY ROAD

Burnaby Park

Bowling Green

MILL ROAD

Park Lane

Kenmare Heights

Saint Laurence's School

Club House

PAVILION ROAD

WHITSHED ROAD

PORTLAND RD NORTH

SOMERBY ROAD

PORTLAND ROAD

SOUTH PLACE

Portland Place

Burnaby Woods

The Poplars

CHAPEL ROAD

PORTLAND ROAD

HAWKINS LANE

ERSKINE AVENUE

QUARRY ROAD

Delgany Glen

The Nurseries

Cherry Drive

Carraig Orchard

Burnaby Heights

KINLEN ROAD

MILL ROAD

Woodlands

Riverfield

Priory Way

Cherry Risé

Cherry Green

Castle (In Ruins)

Castlefield Tce

MANOR AVENUE

OLD MILL ROAD

KILLINCARRIG

Hillcrest Ave

Priory Rise

Cherry Court

Cherry Orchard

Castle Villas

Orchard View

Cherry Grove

Adare Close

Burnaby Park

Greystones Rugby Club

Churchfields

Carrick Villas

P

Drummin Rise

Delgany Wood

Thornbury

Carrig Villas

Wendon Park

Salem Vale

R762

Burnaby Mill

Elsinore

Delgany NS

Wendon Drive

Wendon Brook

NEW ROAD

MILL ROAD

R762

Greystones Lawn Tennis Club

Sports Grounds

Burnaby Lawns

To Wicklow & N11

Delgany Park

Millgrove

Millgrove Close

Millbrook

BURNABY AVENUE

Burnaby Court

Glenair Manor

R761

To Kilcoole & Wicklow Town

Charlesland Court

Charlesland Wood

FARRANKELLY

Glenbrook Park

Eden Gate

Charlesland

Charlesland Grove

Charlesland Park

CHARLESLAND

C

D

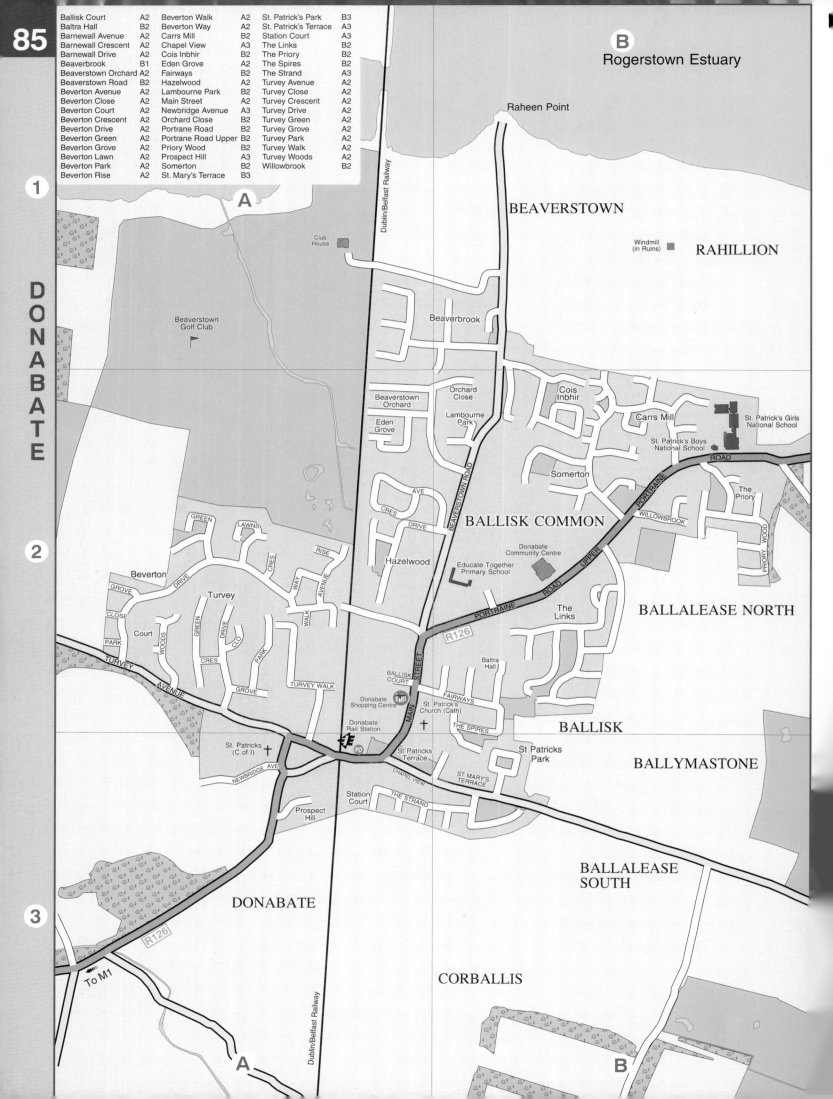

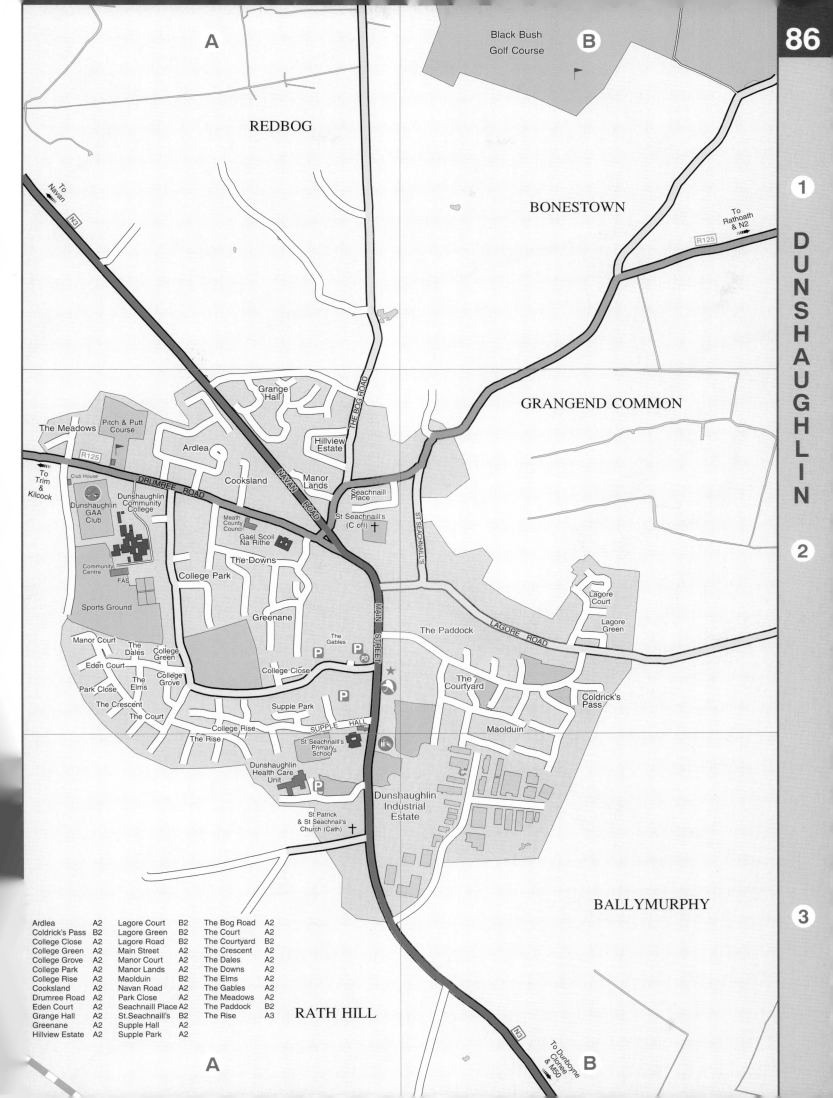

A
B
1
2
3

REDBOG

Black Bush
Golf Course

To Navan

N3

BONESTOWN

To Rathoath
& N2

R125

GRANGEND COMMON

The Meadows

Pitch & Putt
Course

R125

Grange
Hall

Ardlea

To Trim &
Kilcock

Club House

Cooksland

DRUMREE ROAD

NAVAN ROAD

THE BOG ROAD

Hillview
Estate

Manor
Lands

Dunshaughlin
GAA Club

Dunshaughlin
Community
College

Meath
County
Council

Gael Scoil
Na Rithe

Seachnaill
Place

ST SEACHNAILL'S

St Seachnaill's
(C of I)

Community
Centre

FÁS

The Downs

Sports Ground

College Park

Greenane

Lagore
Court

Manor Court

The
Dales

College
Green

The Gables

P

P
PO

The Paddock

LAGORE ROAD

Lagore
Green

Eden Court

College
Grove

College Close

Park Close

The Elms

MAIN STREET

The
Courtyard

Coldrick's
Pass

The Crescent

The Court

College Rise

Supple Park

P

SUPPLE HALL

Maolduin

The Rise

St Seachnaill's
Primary School

Dunshaughlin
Health Care
Unit

P

Dunshaughlin
Industrial
Estate

St Patrick
& St Seachnail's
Church (Cath)

BALLYMURPHY

RATH HILL

To Dunboyne
& Clonee
& M50

N3

Ardlea	A2	Lagore Court	B2	The Bog Road	A2
Coldrick's Pass	B2	Lagore Green	B2	The Court	A2
College Close	A2	Lagore Road	B2	The Courtyard	B2
College Green	A2	Main Street	A2	The Crescent	A2
College Grove	A2	Manor Court	A2	The Dales	A2
College Park	A2	Manor Lands	A2	The Downs	A2
College Rise	A2	Maolduin	B2	The Elms	A2
Cooksland	A2	Navan Road	A2	The Gables	A2
Drumree Road	A2	Park Close	A2	The Meadows	A2
Eden Court	A2	Seachnaill Place	A2	The Paddock	B2
Grange Hall	A2	St. Seachnaill's	B2	The Rise	A3
Greenane	A2	Supple Hall	A2		
Hillview Estate	A2	Supple Park	A2		

A
B

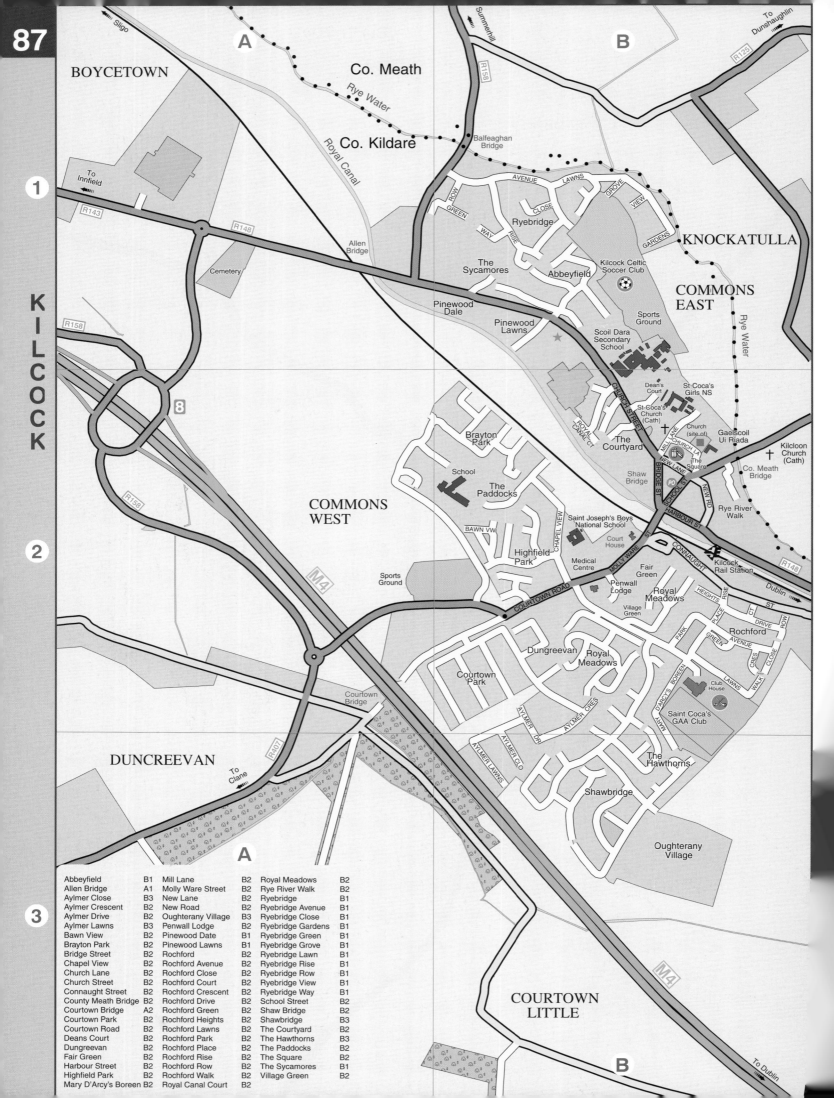

KILCOCK

BOYCETOWN

Co. Meath

Rye Water

Co. Kildare

Royal Canal

To Sligo

To Dunshaughlin

To Innfield

R143

R148

R158

R125

Allen Bridge

Balfeaghan Bridge

Cemetery

Summerhill

KNOCKATULLA

COMMONS EAST

Ryebridge

The Sycamores

Abbeyfield

Kilcock Celtic Soccer Club

Sports Ground

AVENUE LAWNS GROVE VIEW GARDENS ROW GREEN CLOSE WAY RISE

Pinewood Dale

Pinewood Lawns

Scoil Dara Secondary School

Dean's Court

St Coca's Girls NS

St Coca's Church (Cath)

Church (site of)

Gaelscoil Ui Riada

Kilcloon Church (Cath)

Co. Meath Bridge

Rye Water

Brayton Park

School

The Paddocks

CHURCH STREET

ROYAL CANAL CT

COMMONS WEST

BAWN VW

The Courtyard

Shaw Bridge

MILL LANE

CHURCH LA

The Square

NEW LANE

BRIDGE ST

SCHOOL ST

PO

Highfield Park

CHAPEL VIEW

Saint Joseph's Boys National School

Court House

Medical Centre

Penwall Lodge

Village Green

MOLLY WARE ST

Fair Green

CONNAUGHT

HARBOUR ST

NEW RD

Rye River Walk

Kilcock Rail Station

R148

To Dublin

M4

Sports Ground

COURTOWN ROAD

Royal Meadows

Dungreevan

Royal Meadows

Courtown Park

Courtown Bridge

To Clane

R407

DUNCREEVAN

Rochford

HEIGHTS PLACE RISE PARK GREEN CRES CLOSE ROW DRIVE AVENUE

CT ST

LAWNS WALK

MARY DARCY'S BOREEN

AYLMER CRES

AYLMER DR

AYLMER CLO

AYLMER LAWNS

Club House

Saint Coca's GAA Club

The Hawthorns

Shawbridge

Oughterany Village

COURTOWN LITTLE

To Dublin

M4

Abbeyfield	B1	Mill Lane	B2	Royal Meadows	B2
Allen Bridge	A1	Molly Ware Street	B2	Rye River Walk	B2
Aylmer Close	B3	New Lane	B2	Ryebridge	B1
Aylmer Crescent	B2	New Road	B2	Ryebridge Avenue	B1
Aylmer Drive	B2	Oughterany Village	B3	Ryebridge Close	B1
Aylmer Lawns	B3	Penwall Lodge	B2	Ryebridge Gardens	B1
Bawn View	B2	Pinewood Date	B1	Ryebridge Green	B1
Brayton Park	B2	Pinewood Lawns	B1	Ryebridge Grove	B1
Bridge Street	B2	Rochford	B2	Ryebridge Lawn	B1
Chapel View	B2	Rochford Avenue	B2	Ryebridge Rise	B1
Church Lane	B2	Rochford Close	B2	Ryebridge Row	B1
Church Street	B2	Rochford Court	B2	Ryebridge View	B1
Connaught Street	B2	Rochford Crescent	B2	Ryebridge Way	B1
County Meath Bridge	B2	Rochford Drive	B2	School Street	B2
Courtown Bridge	A2	Rochford Green	B2	Shaw Bridge	B2
Courtown Park	B2	Rochford Heights	B2	Shawbridge	B3
Courtown Road	B2	Rochford Lawns	B2	The Courtyard	B2
Deans Court	B2	Rochford Park	B2	The Hawthorns	B3
Dungreevan	B2	Rochford Place	B2	The Paddocks	B2
Fair Green	B2	Rochford Rise	B2	The Square	B2
Harbour Street	B2	Rochford Row	B2	The Sycamores	B1
Highfield Park	B2	Rochford Walk	B2	Village Green	B2
Mary D'Arcy's Boreen	B2	Royal Canal Court	B2		

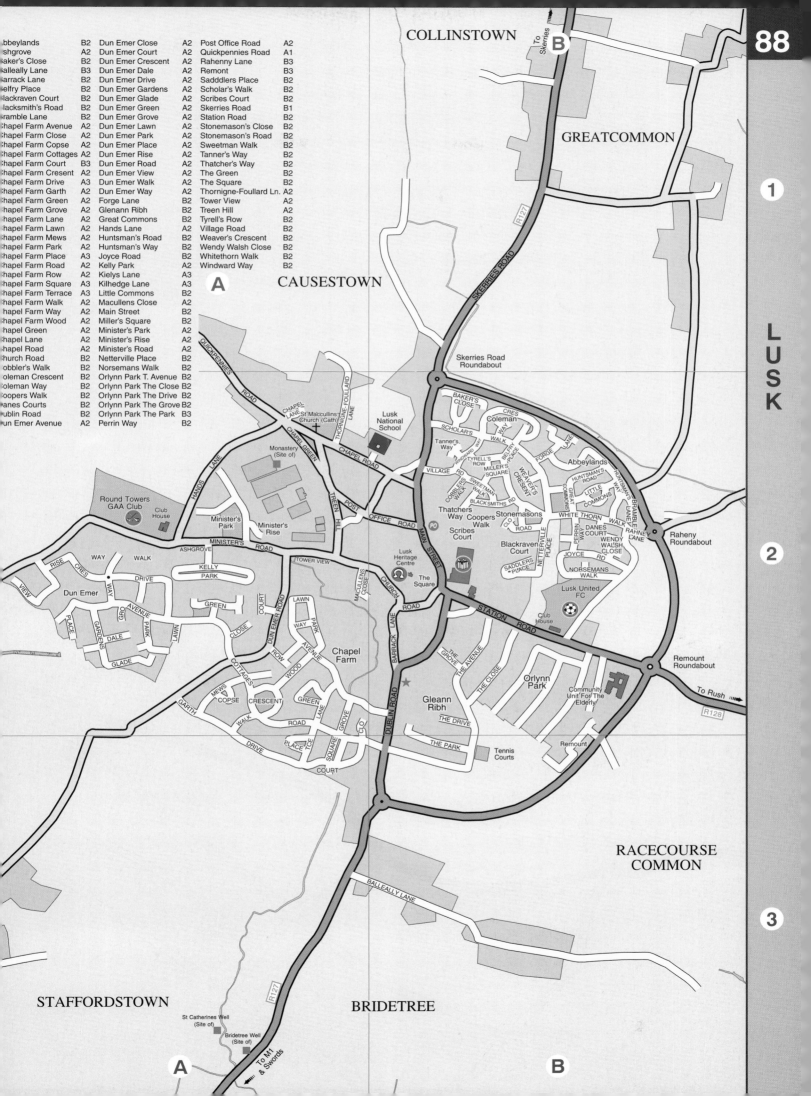

bbeylands B2	Dun Emer Close A2	Post Office Road A2
shgrove A2	Dun Emer Court A2	Quickpennies Road A1
aker's Close B2	Dun Emer Crescent A2	Rahenny Lane B3
alleally Lane B3	Dun Emer Dale A2	Remont B3
arrack Lane B2	Dun Emer Drive A2	Sadddlers Place B2
elfry Place B2	Dun Emer Gardens A2	Scholar's Walk B2
lackraven Court B2	Dun Emer Glade A2	Scribes Court B2
lacksmith's Road B2	Dun Emer Green A2	Skerries Road B1
ramble Lane B2	Dun Emer Grove A2	Station Road B2
hapel Farm Avenue A2	Dun Emer Lawn A2	Stonemason's Close B2
hapel Farm Close A2	Dun Emer Park A2	Stonemason's Road B2
hapel Farm Copse A2	Dun Emer Place A2	Sweetman Walk B2
hapel Farm Cottages A2	Dun Emer Rise A2	Tanner's Way B2
hapel Farm Court B3	Dun Emer Road A2	Thatcher's Way B2
hapel Farm Cresent A2	Dun Emer View A2	The Green B2
hapel Farm Drive A3	Dun Emer Walk A2	The Square B2
hapel Farm Garth A2	Dun Emer Way A2	Thornigne-Foullard Ln. A2
hapel Farm Green A2	Forge Lane B2	Tower View A2
hapel Farm Grove A2	Glenann Ribh B2	Treen Hill A2
hapel Farm Lane A2	Great Commons B2	Tyrell's Row B2
hapel Farm Lawn A2	Hands Lane A2	Village Road B2
hapel Farm Mews A2	Huntsman's Road B2	Weaver's Crescent B2
hapel Farm Park A2	Huntsman's Way B2	Wendy Walsh Close B2
hapel Farm Place A3	Joyce Road B2	Whitethorn Walk B2
hapel Farm Road A2	Kelly Park A2	Windward Way B2
hapel Farm Row A2	Kielys Lane A3	
hapel Farm Square A2	Kilhedge Lane A3	
hapel Farm Terrace A3	Little Commons B2	
hapel Farm Walk A2	Macullens Close A2	
hapel Farm Way A2	Main Street B2	
hapel Farm Wood A2	Miller's Square B2	
hapel Green A2	Minister's Park A2	
hapel Lane A2	Minister's Rise A2	
hapel Road A2	Minister's Road A2	
hurch Road B2	Netterville Place B2	
obbler's Walk B2	Norsemans Walk B2	
oleman Crescent B2	Orlynn Park T. Avenue B2	
oleman Way B2	Orlynn Park The Close B2	
oopers Walk B2	Orlynn Park The Drive B2	
anes Courts B2	Orlynn Park The Grove B2	
ublin Road B2	Orlynn Park The Park B3	
un Emer Avenue A2	Perrin Way B2	

RUSH

An Tearmann	B3	Eden Terrace	C2	Melbourne Gardens	C3	St Catherines Drive	C1
Barrack Lane	C2	Farran's Lane	C2	Mill Bank	B2	St Catherines Green	C1
Bawn Road	C2	Finistere	D2	Mill Bank Court	B2	St Catherines Grove	C1
Bayview Villas	C2	Golden Ridge	C2	Old Barrack Road	D3	St Catherines Lawn	C1
Bollum Lane	C2	Golf Road	B3	Old Haystown	B2	St Catherines Park	C1
Brookfield Park	C2	Hand Park	D2	Old Road	B2	St Catherines View	C1
Brookfield	B2	Hands Lane	C3	Old Road Court	B2	St Catherines Way	C1
Brookside Gardens	B2	Harbour Road	D2	Old Road Grove	B2	St. Joseph's Road	C3
Carthy's Lane	A3	Haystown	B2	Palmer Court	C1	St. Maur's Park	C2
Ceol na Mara	C2	Haystown Road	B2	Palmer Road	C1	Sundrive Road	B3
Channel Road	A3	Healy's Lane	B3	Park Road	C2	Sundrive Road	C3
Chapel Green	B2	Kenure Crescent	C2	Quay Road	D2	Sunlock Court	C2
Clifflands	C1	Kenure Lawns	C1	Ravenswell	C1	Sunset Court	C2
Clifflands Court	C1	Kenure Park	C2	Rogerstown Court	B3	Tayleurs Point	D3
Clifflands Rise	C1	Kilbush Lane	C2	Rogerstown Park	B3	The Cairn	C1
Cois Tra	C2	Kilbush View	C2	Sandy Lane	C3	The Forge	D2
Congress Gardens	C3	Knockabawn	D2	Sandy Road	C2	The Mall	C2
Convent Lane	C3	Lady Cove	C1	Seafield Court	D2	Thorn Chase	C1
Cooper's Bank	C2	Lambay View	C1	Skerries Road	C1	Thornleigh	C2
Cooper's Lane	C2	Linkside	INSET	South Shore Road	C3	Tower Street	D2
Coopersfield	C2	Linn Ban	B2	South Strand	C3	Upper Main Street	C2
Crescent Road	B3	Linn Beag	B2	Spout Road	A3	Whitestown Road	A3
Daly's Lane	B3	Linn Cuin	B2	St Catherines Avenue	C1	Woodbury	C2
Doctor's Lane	B2	Linn Dubh	B2	St Catherines Close	C1	Woodland Park	C2
Echlin Court	C2	Lower Main Street	C2	St Catherines Crescent	C1	Woodvale Road	C1

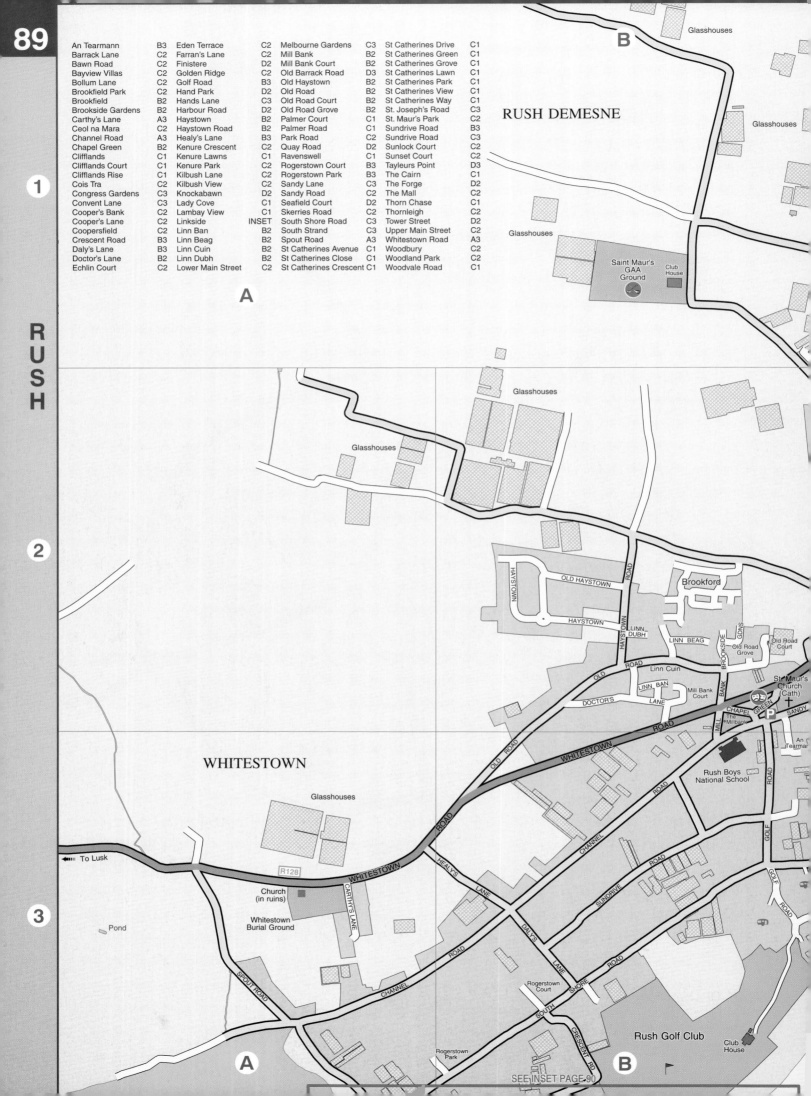

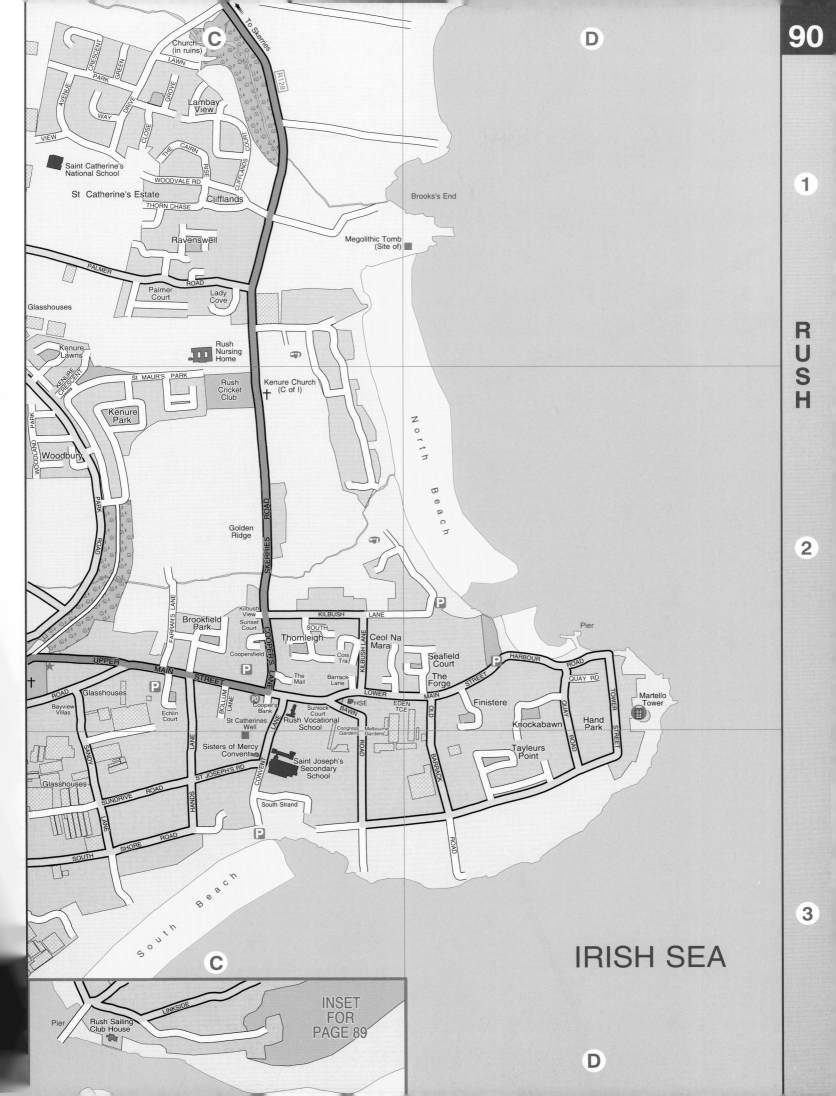

C

To Skerries

D

1

Church
(in ruins)

R128

CRESCENT

PARK

GREEN

LAWN

GROVE

AVENUE

WAY

DRIVE

CLOSE

Lambay
View

CLIFFLANDS COURT

VIEW

THE CAIRN

RISE

Saint Catherine's
National School

WOODVALE RD

St Catherine's Estate

THORN CHASE

Clifflands

Brooks's End

Ravenswell

Megolithic Tomb
(Site of)

PALMER

ROAD

Glasshouses

Palmer
Court

Lady
Cove

Kenure
Lawns

Rush
Nursing
Home

KENURE CRESCENT

St MAUR'S PARK

Rush Cricket
Club

Kenure Church
(C of I)

North Beach

WOODLAND PARK

Kenure
Park

2

PARK ROAD

Woodbury

Golden
Ridge

SKERRIES ROAD

Pier

P

FARRAN'S LANE

Brookfield
Park

Kilbush
View
Sunset
Court

KILBUSH LANE

SOUTH

Ceol Na
Mara

COOPERS LANE

Thornleigh

KILBUSH LANE

P

Coopersfield

Cois
Tra

Seafield
Court

HARBOUR ROAD

P

QUAY RD

UPPER

MAIN

STREET

The Mall

Barrack
Lane

The Forge

STREET

Martello
Tower

ROAD

Glasshouses

P

BOLLUM LANE

PO

LOWER

MAIN

QUAY

TOWER STREET

Bayview
Villas

Echlin
Court

Cooper's
Bank

HSE

EDEN
TCE

OLD

Finistere

ROAD

St Catherines
Well

Sunlock
Court

BAWN

Knockabawn

Hand
Park

SAND

CONVENT LANE

Rush Vocational
School

Congress
Gardens

Melbourne
Gardens

Sisters of Mercy
Convent

Saint Joseph's
Secondary
School

BARRACK

Tayleurs
Point

Glasshouses

ST JOSEPH'S RD

LANE

SUNDRIVE

ROAD

HANDS

South Strand

ROAD

P

SHORE ROAD

SOUTH

South Beach

3

IRISH SEA

C

Pier

LINKSIDE

Rush Sailing
Club House

INSET
FOR
PAGE 89

D

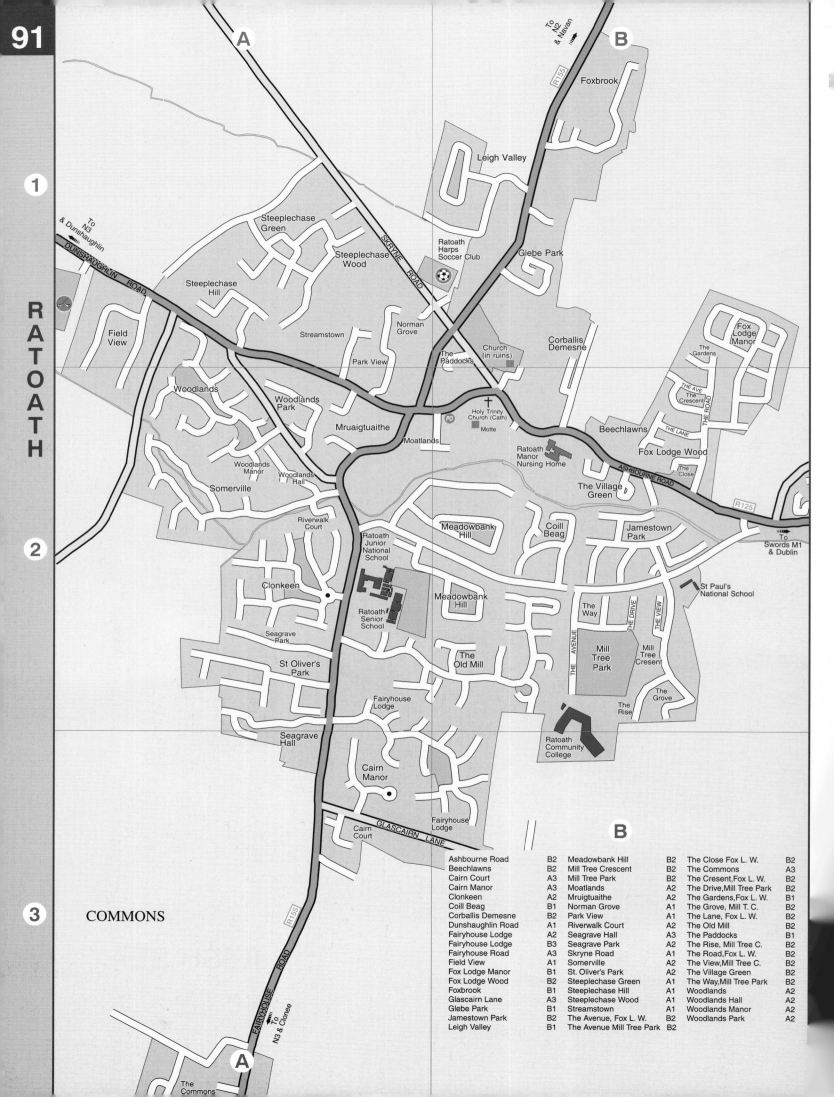

RATOATH

A 1

Steeplechase Green

Steeplechase Wood

Steeplechase Hill

Field View

SKRYNE ROAD

Streamstown

Norman Grove

Park View

Woodlands

Woodlands Park

Mruaigtuaithe

Moatlands

The Paddocks

Church (in ruins)

Ratoath Harps Soccer Club

To N2 & Navan

B

Foxbrook

Leigh Valley

Glebe Park

Corballis Demesne

Fox Lodge Manor

The Gardens

THE AVE
The Crescent

THE ROAD

THE LANE

Beechlawns

Fox Lodge Wood

The Close

ASHBOURNE ROAD

R125

Holy Trinity Church (Cath)

PO

Motte

Ratoath Manor Nursing Home

The Village Green

Woodlands Manor

Woodlands Hall

Somerville

Riverwalk Court

Ratoath Junior National School

Meadowbank Hill

Coill Beag

Jamestown Park

To Swords M1 & Dublin

Clonkeen

Meadowbank Hill

Ratoath Senior School

The Way

THE DRIVE

THE VIEW

St Paul's National School

Seagrave Park

St Oliver's Park

The Old Mill

THE AVENUE

Mill Tree Park

Mill Tree Cresent

Fairyhouse Lodge

Seagrave Hall

The Rise

The Grove

Ratoath Community College

Cairn Manor

Fairyhouse Lodge

GLASCAIRN LANE

R155

COMMONS

Cairn Court

FAIRYHOUSE ROAD

To N3 & Clonee

The Commons

To N3 & Dunshaughlin

DUNSHAUGHLIN ROAD

A

2

3

Ashbourne Road	B2	Meadowbank Hill	B2	The Close Fox L. W.	B2
Beechlawns	B2	Mill Tree Crescent	B2	The Commons	A3
Cairn Court	A3	Mill Tree Park	B2	The Cresent, Fox L. W.	B2
Cairn Manor	A3	Moatlands	A2	The Drive, Mill Tree Park	B2
Clonkeen	A2	Mruigtuaithe	A2	The Gardens, Fox L. W.	B1
Coill Beag	B1	Norman Grove	A1	The Grove, Mill T. C.	B2
Corballis Demesne	B2	Park View	A1	The Lane, Fox L. W.	B2
Dunshaughlin Road	A1	Riverwalk Court	A2	The Old Mill	B2
Fairyhouse Lodge	A2	Seagrave Hall	A3	The Paddocks	B1
Fairyhouse Lodge	B3	Seagrave Park	A2	The Rise, Mill Tree C.	B2
Fairyhouse Road	A3	Skryne Road	A1	The Road, Fox L. W.	B2
Field View	A1	Somerville	A2	The View, Mill Tree C.	B2
Fox Lodge Manor	B1	St. Oliver's Park	A2	The Village Green	B2
Fox Lodge Wood	B2	Steeplechase Green	A1	The Way, Mill Tree Park	B2
Foxbrook	B1	Steeplechase Hill	A1	Woodlands	A2
Glascairn Lane	A3	Steeplechase Wood	A1	Woodlands Hall	A2
Glebe Park	B1	Streamstown	A1	Woodlands Manor	A2
Jamestown Park	B2	The Avenue, Fox L. W.	B2	Woodlands Park	A2
Leigh Valley	B1	The Avenue Mill Tree Park	B2		

An Claddagh	A2	Kelly's Bay Parade	INSET	Shalloch Hill Grove	A2	The Haven	B2
Arcadia Court	B2	Kelly's Bay Pier	INSET	Shenick Avenue	B3	The Heights, Skerries Rk.	A2
Ardgillan View	A2	Kelly's Bay Promenade	INSET	Shenick Drive	B3	The Hoar Rock	A2
Balbriggan Road	A2	Kelly's Bay Rise	INSET	Shenick Grove	B3	The Kybe	B2
Balbriggan Street	A2	Kelly's Bay Rocks	INSET	Shenick Park	B3	The Lawn, Skerries Rock	A2
Beau-Piers Lane	B2	Kelly's Bay Shore	A2	Shenick Road	B3	The Maltings	B3
Brookville Lane	B2	Kelly's Bay Strand	INSET	Sherlock Park	B3	The Park	A2
Cabra Hill	B3	Kelly's Bay Tide	INSET	Sherlock Terrace	B3	The Park, Skerries Rock	A2
Callaghan's Lane	B2	Kelly's Bay Tower	INSET	South Strand	B2	The Rise, Skerries Rock	A2
Chapel Lane	B2	Kelly's Bay View	A1	St. Patrick's Close	A3	The Square	B2
Church Street	B2	Kelly's Bay Weir	INSET	Station Road	A3	The Vale, Skerries Rock	A2
Churchfield Close	B3	Little Strand Street	B2	Strand Street	B2	The View, Skerries Rock	A2
Churchfield Lawns	B3	Manning's Opening	B2	Tennis Courts Lane	B2	The Walk, Skerries Rock	A2
College Court	B2	Martine Court	B2	The Avenue,Skerries Rock	A2	The Way, Skerries Rock	A2
Convent Lane	B2	Marywell	B3	The Brambles	A2	Thomas Hand Street	B2
Downside Heights	B3	McLoughlin's Lane	B2	The Close, Skerries Rock	A2	Townparks	A2
Downside Park	B3	Miller's Lane	B3	The Court, Skerries Rock	A2	Weldon's Lane	B3
Dublin Road	A3	Millhill Park	B2	The Crescent, Skerries RK.	A2	Windmill Lane	B3
Friar's Lane	B2	Millview	B2	The Cross	B2		
Fox Grove	A2	Mooring Cove	A2	The Drive, Skerries Rock	A2		
Golf Links Road	B3	Mourne Close	A2	The Green	A2		
Greenlawns	A3	Mourne Court	A2	The Grove, Skerries Rock	A2		
Hacketstown Park	C4	Mourne Drive	A2				
Harbour Road	B2	Mourne Grove	A2				
Harrison's Cove	A2	Mourne Park	A2				
Heeney's Lane	B2	Mourne View	A2				
Hillside Close	B3	New Street	B2				
Hillside Gardens	A3	New Townparks	A2				
Holmpatrick	B2	North Strand	A2				
Holmpatrick Terrace	B3	Northcliffe Heights	A2				
Kelly's Bay Beach	INSET	Quay Street	B2				
Kelly's Bay Cliffs	INSET	Red Island	B1				
Kelly's Bay Cove	INSET	Rush Road	B3				
Kelly's Bay Drive	INSET	Sandy Banks	B2				
Kelly's Bay Harbour	INSET	Seacrest	A2				
Kelly's Bay Heights	INSET	Selskar Avenue	A2				
Kelly's Bay Inlet	INSET	Selskar Court	A2				
Kelly's Bay Jetty	INSET	Selskar Rise	A2				
Kelly's Bay Moorings	INSET	Selskar Road	A2				

SKERRIES

A B 1 2 3

Book of Kells
The Book of Kells was written around the year 800 AD and is one of the most beautifully illuminated manuscripts in the world. **71 C4**

Chimney Viewing Tower
Jameson Distillery Chimney is topped with a two-tiered glass enclosed viewing platform which provides a 360 degree panoramic view of Dublin city. **70 F4**

Christ Church Cathedral
The Cathedral was founded in the year c.1030 by Sitriuc, King of the Dublin Norsemen.

75 A1

Croke Park Experience
A must for anyone interested in the history and development of Ireland's national games of hurling and gaelic football. **71 C1**

Dublin Castle
Dublin Castle is the heart of historic Dublin. In fact the city gets its name from the Black Pool, Dubh Linn which was on the site of the present Castle garden. **75 A1**

The Hugh Lane Dublin City Gallery
The Hugh Lane Dublin City Gallery, is a gallery of modern art and it is the municipal gallery for the city of Dublin. **71 B2**

Dublin City Hall
The Story of the Capital Exhibition in the atmospheric vaults of Dublin City Hall is an exciting multimedia exhibition which traces the evolution of Dublin city. **75 A1**

Dublinia and the Medieval Viking World
The Dublinia and Viking World exhibitions are amongst Dublin's most popular visitor attractions.

75 A1

Dublin Zoo
Visit Dublin Zoo for a unique, fun, wild experience close to the city centre! In doing so, you are contributing directly to the continued care of the animals. **69 B2**

General Post Office
Dublin's GPO is a landmark building, situated prominently in the middle of O'Connell Street.

71 B3

Government Buildings
Undertaken by the British administration in Ireland was available immediately to be occupied by the new Irish government in 1922. **71 C3**

Guinness Storehouse
Located in the heart of the St James's Gate Brewery, this has been home to the black stuff since 1759. **74 E1**

Irish Museum of Modern Art
The Irish Museum of Modern Art is Ireland's leading institution for the collection and presentation of modern and contemporary art. **73 C1**

Kilmainham Gaol
Kilmainham Gaol gives the visitor a dramatic and realistic insight into what is was like to have been confined in one of these forbidding bastions of punishment and correction between 1796 and 1924. **73 B1**

Mansion House
The Mansion House is the residence of the Lord Mayor of Dublin and has been since 1715.

75 C1

Marsh's Library
Marsh's Library, built in 1701 by Archbishop Narcissus Marsh (1638 - 1713) is the oldest public library in Ireland.

75 A2

Molly Malone Statue
The Molly Malone statue is located at the end of Grafton Street Molly Malone was a semi historical/legendary figure commerated in song. **75 B1**

National Botanic Gardens
The Gardens contain many attractive features including an arboretum, sensory garden, rock garden large pond and extensive herbaceous borders. **24 F3**

National Gallery of Ireland
The National Gallery of Ireland was established by an Act of Parliament in 1854 and first opened its doors to the public in January 1864. **75 C1**

National Library of Ireland
Established in 1877, National Library's holdings of books, and manuscripts, comprise a comprehensive collection of Irish documentary heritage. **75 C1**

National Museum of Ireland - Archaeology
The Museum first opened its doors in 1890 and since then it has been filling in the blanks for us through its extensive archeological collections. **75 C1**

National Museum of Ireland Decorative Arts & History
Formerly Collins Barracks has been completely renovated and now charts Ireland's progress through the ages. **70 E4**

National Museum of Ireland - Natural History
This zoological museum encompasses outstanding examples of wildlife from Ireland and the far corners of the globe. **75 C1**

Phoenix Park
One of the largest and most magnificent city parks in Europe. an exhibition on the history and wildlife of the Phoenix Park is on display in the Visitor Centre. **69 A2**

St. Mary's Pro Cathedral
Dublin has not possessed a Catholic cathedral since the Reformation, St. Mary's Pro Cathedral has served as the 'mother-church' of Dublin. **71 B3**

Saint Patrick's Cathedral
Saint Patrick's Cathedral has contributed much to Irish life throughout its long history (it was founded in 1191). **75 A1**

St Stephen's Green
Probably Ireland's best known Victorian Public Park is a sanctuary from the bustle of the city streets. **75 B2**

Smithfield
Smithfield village has been developed into a sophisticated residential, commercial and cultural district, a village within the city. **70 F4**

The Spire
The Spire of Dublin, a 120 metre high landmark in the heart of Dublin City, was unveiled in 2002. **71 B3**

Trinity College
Trinity College is the oldest college in Ireland. Founded in 1592 by Queen Elizabeth I. **71 C4**

Malahide Castle
Set on 250 acres of parkland. The castle was the home of the Talbot family from 1185 to 1973.
The house contains period furniture and Irish portrait paintings. **3 B3**

Dublin Tourism located in the restored former church of St. Andrew in Suffolk Street is the official tourist board for Dublin. For further tourist interest information visit http://www.visitdublin.com **71 C4**

Apostolic Nunciature
183 Navan Road
Dublin 7
Tel: 838 0577
24 D4

Argentine Embassy
15 Ailesbury Drive
Dublin 4
Tel: 269 1546
48 D1

Australian Embassy
7th Floor,
Fitzwilton House
Wilton Terrace, Dublin 2
Tel: 664 5300
38 E4

Austrian Embassy
15 Ailesbury Court Apts.
93 Ailesbury Road
Dublin 4
Tel: 269 4577
48 D1

Belgian Embassy
2 Shrewsbury Road
Dublin 4
Tel: 269 2082
48 D1

Embassy of the Federative Republic of Brazil
HSB House
Fifth Floor
41-54 Harcourt House,
Dublin 2.
Tel: 475 6000
38 D4

British Embassy
29 Merrion Road
Dublin 4
Tel: 205 3700
48 D1

Bulgarian Embassy
22 Burlington Road
Dublin 4
Tel: 660 3293
38 E4

Canadian Embassy
7/8 Wilton Place.
Dublin 2
Tel: 234 4001
38 E4

Chilean Embassy
44 Wellington Road
Ballsbridge
Dublin 4
Tel: 667 5094
38 F4

Embassy of the People's Republic of China
40 Ailesbury Road
Ballsbridge, Dublin 4
Tel: 260 1119
48 D1

Embassy of the Republic of Croatia
Adelaide Chambers
Peter Street
Dublin 8
Tel: 476 7181
38 D3

Embassy of the Republic of Cuba
2 Adelaide Court,
Adelaide Road,
Dublin 2
Tel: 475 0899
38 D4

Embassy of Republic of Cyprus
71 Lower Leeson Street
Dublin 2
Tel: 676 3060
38 E3

Embassy of Czech Republic
57 Northumberland Road
Dublin 4
Tel: 668 1135
38 F4

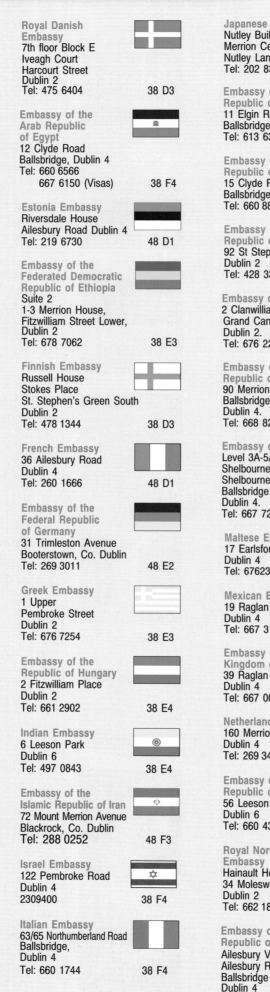

Royal Danish Embassy
7th floor Block E
Iveagh Court
Harcourt Street
Dublin 2
Tel: 475 6404
38 D3

Embassy of the Arab Republic of Egypt
12 Clyde Road
Ballsbridge, Dublin 4
Tel: 660 6566
667 6150 (Visas)
38 F4

Estonia Embassy
Riversdale House
Ailesbury Road Dublin 4
Tel: 219 6730
48 D1

Embassy of the Federated Democratic Republic of Ethiopia
Suite 2
1-3 Merrion House,
Fitzwilliam Street Lower,
Dublin 2
Tel: 678 7062
38 E3

Finnish Embassy
Russell House
Stokes Place
St. Stephen's Green South
Dublin 2
Tel: 478 1344
38 D3

French Embassy
36 Ailesbury Road
Dublin 4
Tel: 260 1666
48 D1

Embassy of the Federal Republic of Germany
31 Trimleston Avenue
Booterstown, Co. Dublin
Tel: 269 3011
48 E2

Greek Embassy
1 Upper
Pembroke Street
Dublin 2
Tel: 676 7254
38 E3

Embassy of the Republic of Hungary
2 Fitzwilliam Place
Dublin 2
Tel: 661 2902
38 E4

Indian Embassy
6 Leeson Park
Dublin 6
Tel: 497 0843
38 E4

Embassy of the Islamic Republic of Iran
72 Mount Merrion Avenue
Blackrock, Co. Dublin
Tel: 288 0252
48 F3

Israel Embassy
122 Pembroke Road
Dublin 4
2309400
38 F4

Italian Embassy
63/65 Northumberland Road
Ballsbridge,
Dublin 4
Tel: 660 1744
38 F4

Japanese Embassy
Nutley Building
Merrion Centre
Nutley Lane, Dublin 4
Tel: 202 8300
48 E1

Embassy of the Republic of Kenya
11 Elgin Road
Ballsbridge, Dublin 4
Tel: 613 6380 / 668 3506
38 F4

Embassy of the Republic of Korea
15 Clyde Road
Ballsbridge, Dublin 4
Tel: 660 8800
38 F4

Embassy of the Republic of Latvia
92 St Stephen's Green
Dublin 2
Tel: 428 3320
38 E4

Embassy of Lesotho
2 Clanwilliam Square,
Grand Canal Quay,
Dublin 2.
Tel: 676 2233
38 F3[41]

Embassy of the Republic of Lithuania
90 Merrion Road,
Ballsbridge,
Dublin 4.
Tel: 668 8292
48 E1

Embassy of Malaysia
Level 3A-5A
Shelbourne House
Shelbourne Road
Ballsbridge
Dublin 4.
Tel: 667 7280
38 F3

Maltese Embassy
17 Earlsfort Terrace
Dublin 4
Tel: 6762340
38 E4

Mexican Embassy
19 Raglan Road
Dublin 4
Tel: 667 3105
38 F4

Embassy of the Kingdom of Morocco
39 Raglan Road
Dublin 4
Tel: 667 0020
38 F4

Netherlands Embassy
160 Merrion Road
Dublin 4
Tel: 269 3444
48 D1

Embassy of the Federal Republic of Nigeria
56 Leeson Park
Dublin 6
Tel: 660 4366
38 E4

Royal Norwegian Embassy
Hainault House
34 Molesworth Street,
Dublin 2
Tel: 662 1800
38 E3

Embassy of the Islamic Republic of Pakistan
Ailesbury Villa
Ailesbury Road
Ballsbridge
Dublin 4
Tel: 261 3032
48 D1

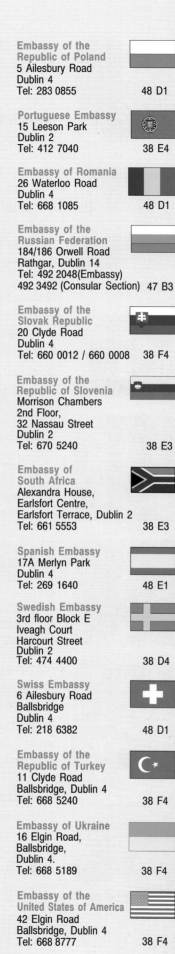

Embassy of the Republic of Poland
5 Ailesbury Road
Dublin 4
Tel: 283 0855
48 D1

Portuguese Embassy
15 Leeson Park
Dublin 2
Tel: 412 7040
38 E4

Embassy of Romania
26 Waterloo Road
Dublin 4
Tel: 668 1085
48 D1

Embassy of the Russian Federation
184/186 Orwell Road
Rathgar, Dublin 14
Tel: 492 2048(Embassy)
492 3492 (Consular Section)
47 B3

Embassy of the Slovak Republic
20 Clyde Road
Dublin 4
Tel: 660 0012 / 660 0008
38 F4

Embassy of the Republic of Slovenia
Morrison Chambers
2nd Floor,
32 Nassau Street
Dublin 2
Tel: 670 5240
38 E3

Embassy of South Africa
Alexandra House,
Earlsfort Centre,
Earlsfort Terrace, Dublin 2
Tel: 661 5553
38 E3

Spanish Embassy
17A Merlyn Park
Dublin 4
Tel: 269 1640
48 E1

Swedish Embassy
3rd floor Block E
Iveagh Court
Harcourt Street
Dublin 2
Tel: 474 4400
38 D4

Swiss Embassy
6 Ailesbury Road
Ballsbridge
Dublin 4
Tel: 218 6382
48 D1

Embassy of the Republic of Turkey
11 Clyde Road
Ballsbridge, Dublin 4
Tel: 668 5240
38 F4

Embassy of Ukraine
16 Elgin Road,
Ballsbridge,
Dublin 4.
Tel: 668 5189
38 F4

Embassy of the United States of America
42 Elgin Road
Ballsbridge, Dublin 4
Tel: 668 8777
38 F4

For further information contact:
Dept of Foreign Affairs,
80 St. Stephen's Green, Dublin 2.
Tel: 478 0822 / www.foreignaffairs.gov.ie

Adelaide & Meath (A&E)
Hospital & The National
Childrens Hospital
Tallaght
Dublin 24
Tel: 01-414 2000 **54 F1**

Beaumont Hospital (A&E)
Beaumont Road
Beaumont Dublin 9
Tel: 01-809 3000 **26 D1**

Cherry Orchard Hospital
Ballyfermot
Dublin 10.
Tel: 01-620 6000 **35 C3**

Cheeverstown House
Kilvare
Templeogue
Dublin 12 Tel:
01-490 4681 **46 D4**

City Of Dublin
Skin & Cancer Hospital
Hume St.
Dublin
Tel: 01-676 6935 **38 E3**

Connolly Hospital (A&E)
Blanchardstown
Dublin 15.
Tel: 01-646 5000 **22 F2**

Dublin Dental
School & Hospital
Lincon Place
Dublin 2
Tel: 01-612 7200 **38 E3**

National Orthopaedic
Hospital
Cappagh
Finglas
Dublin 11
Tel: 01-814 0400 **23 C1**

National Rehabilitation
Hospital
Dun Laoghaire
Co.Dublin
Tel: 01-235 5000 **59 C2**

Orthopaedic Hospital
Of Ireland
Castle Ave.
Clontarf
Dublin 3.
Tel: 01-833 2521 **26 E4**

Peamount Hospital
Newcastle
Co. Dublin
Tel: 01-628 0685 **42 E2**

Royal Hospital
Donnybrook
off Morehampton Rd.
Dublin 4
Tel: 01-497 2844 **47 B1**

Royal Victoria
Eye & Ear Hospital
Adelaide Road
Dublin 2.
Tel: 01-664 4600 **38 E4**

St. Bricins Military Hospital
Infirmary Road
Dublin
Tel: 01-677 6112 **37 B2**

St.Columcilles Hospital (A&E)
Loughlinstown
Co . Dublin
Tel: 01-282 5800 **64 D2**

St. James's Hospital (A&E)
James's St.
Dublin 8.
Tel: 01-410 3100 **37 B3**

St. Joseph's Hospital
Clonsilla
Dublin 15
Tel: 01-821 7177 **21 B2**

St. Joseph's Hospital
Springdale Road
Raheny
Dublin 5
Tel: 01 877 4900 **27 A2**

St. Luke's Hospital
Highfield Road.
Rathgar
Dublin 6.
Tel: 01-406 5314 **47 A2**

St. Mary's Hospital
Phoenix Park
Dublin 20
Tel: 01-625 0300 **36 E2**

St. Michael's Hospital (A&E)
Lower George's St.
Dun Laoghaire
Co. Dublin.
Tel: 01-280 6901 **50 D4**

St. Vincent's Hospital (A&E)
Elm Park
Dublin 4.
Tel: 01-277 4000 **48 E1**

Stewart's Hospital
Palmerston
Dublin
Tel: 01-626 4444 **35 C1**

The Mater Hospital (A&E)
Eccles St.
Dublin 7.
Tel: 01-803 2000 **38 D1**

MATERNITY HOSPITALS

Coombe Women's Hospital
Dolphin's Barn
Dublin 8
Tel: 01-408 5200 **37 C4**

National Maternity Hospital
Holles Street
Dublin 2.
Tel: 01-637 3100 **38 E3**

Rotunda Hospital
Parnell St.
Dublin 1
Tel: 01-873 0700 **38 D1**

CHILDRENS HOSPITALS

Childrens University
Hospital (A&E)
Temple Street
Dublin 1
Tel: 01-878 4200 **38 D1**

National Childrens
Hospital
Tallaght
Dublin 24
Tel: 01-414 2000 **54 F1**

Our Lady's Hospital
for Sick Children (A&E)
Crumlin
Dublin 12
Tel: 01-409 6100 **46 D1**

PSYCHIATRIC HOSPITALS

Central Mental Hospital
Dundrum
Dublin 14
Tel: 01-298 9266 **47 C3**

St. Brendan's Hospital
Rathdown Road
Dublin 7
Tel: 01-869 3000 **37 C1**

St. Ita's Hospital
Portrane
Donabate
Co. Dublin
Tel: 01-843 6337

St. John of God Hospital
Stillorgan
Co. Dublin
Tel: 01-288 1781 **58 F1**

St. Vincent's Hospital
Richmond Road
Fairview
Dublin 3
Tel: 01-837 5101 **25 B4**

St. Patrick's Hospital
James's St.
Dublin 8
Tel: 01-249 3200 **37 B3**

PRIVATE HOSPITALS

Beacon Hospital
Sandyford
Dublin 18
Tel: 01-293 6600 **58 D2**

Blackrock Clinic
Rock Road
Blackrock
Co. Dublin
Tel: 01-283 2222 **48 F3**

Bon Secours Hospital
Glasnevin
Dublin 9
Tel: 01-837 5111 **25 A3**

Hermitage Medical Clinic
Old Lucan Road
Dublin 20.
Tel: 01-645 9000 **35 A1**

Clane General Hospital
Prosperous Road
Clane
Co. Kildare
Tel: 045-982 300 **82 A3**

Name	Page	Grid/Ref.	No.
Abbey Business Park	14	F4	112
Advance Business Park	12	F3	179
Aerodrome Business Park	52	F1	60
Airport Business Park	13	A1	213
Airport Industrial Campus	12	E4	1
Airside Business Park	2	D3	266
Airside Retail Park	1	C3	295
Airton Business Park	45	A4	2
Airton Business Park	45	A4	3
Airton Business Park	45	A4	4
Airton Coporate Park	45	A4	38
Airways Industrial Estate	12	F4	5
Allied Industrial Estate	36	E4	6
Alltech Technology Park	6	E2	307
Ardee Court	67	B2	7
Ashgrove Industrial Estate	59	C1	8
Aughrim Lane Ind Est	37	C1	268
Avonbeg Enterprise Centre	55	A1	85
Avonbeg Ind Est	45	B1	277
Avondale	49	A4	167
Baldonnel Business Park	43	A4	241
Baldoyle Ind Est	27	C1	10
Balfe Road Ind Est	45	C1	196
Balheary Ind Park	2	D1	11
Ballyboggan Ind Est	24	D3	12
Ballycoolin Business Park	10	D4	13
Ballymount Business Centre	45	B2	14
Ballymount Court Business Centre	45	B2	72
Ballymount Cross Ind. Est.	45	A2	15
Ballymount Ind Est	45	B2	16
Ballymount Road Ind. Est.	45	B2	17
Ballymount Trading Centre	45	B2	18
Ballymun Ind Est	12	D4	19
Barbeque Poultry Business Park	64	E3	300
Base Enterprise Centre	9	A4	301
Beech Hill Office Campus	47	C2	228
Beechlawn Industrial Complex	45	B2	20
Beechwood Close Ind Est	67	C4	21
Belfield Office Park	47	C2	229
Belgard Ind Est	44	F4	22
Bellevue Industrial Park	24	E3	86
Benson Street Enterprise Centre	38	F2	24
Blackhorse Ind Est	37	B1	25
Blackrock Business Park	49	A3	169
Blanchardstown Corporate Park	9	C3	165
Blanchardstown Ind Park	9	C4	26
Bluebell Business Centre	36	E4	273
Bluebell Business Park	36	E4	27
Bluebell Ind Est	36	D4	28
Bow Bridge Business Centre	37	B3	308
Bracetown Business Park	7	C1	29

Name	Page	Grid/Ref.	No.
Bray Business Park	67	C4	255
Bray Ind Est	67	C4	30
Bridges Ind Est	45	A1	32
Bridgewater Business Centre	37	B2	31
Brookfield Enterprise Centre	54	D1	247
Broombridge Ind Est	24	E3	33
Broomfield Business Park	3	B4	271
Broomhill Bus Pk Close	45	A4	35
Broomhill Bus Pk Drive	45	A4	36
Broomhill Bus Pk Road	45	A4	37
Broomhill Business Park	45	A4	84
Burton Hall Campus	58	E2	39
Butterly Business Park	26	D2	66
Calmount Business Park	45	B2	197
Carrigalea Ind Est	45	B1	40
Cashel Business Centre	46	E2	293
Castleforbes Business Park	38	F2	41
Cedar Ind Park	67	B4	258
Celbridge Ind Est	31	C3	238
Central Park Business Park	58	E2	253
Century Business Park	11	B4	206
Chapelizod Ind Est	36	E2	90
Charlestown Centre	11	A4	160
Cherry Orchard Ind Est	35	C2	42
Cherrywood Business Park	64	D1	251
Churchtown Business Park	47	B4	225
Cian Park Ind Est	25	B4	43
City Junction Business Park	13	C4	212
City Link Business Park	36	E4	215
City West Business Campus	53	B1	44
Clondalkin Business Centre	35	B4	46
Clondalkin Commercial Park	35	B4	45
Clondalkin Enterprise Centre	35	A3	177
Clonshaugh Business & Technology Park	13	A4	311
Clonshaugh Ind Est	13	A4	47
Clonskeagh House Office Park	47	C2	226
Clonskeagh Square Office Park	47	C2	227
Cloverhill Ind Est	35	B4	48
College Business & Technology Park	9	C4	200
Collinstown Cross Ind Est	12	F2	49
Collinstown Ind Est	12	F3	50
Collinstown Ind Park (Intel)	19	B3	92
Concord Ind Est, Naas Road	36	E4	272
Cookstown Business Centre	44	F4	245
Cookstown Enterprise Park	44	F4	51
Cookstown Ind Est	44	F4	52
Cookstown Ind Est The Extension	44	E4	243
Cookstown Square	44	F4	244
Coolmine Industrial Est	22	D2	53
Courtyard Business Park	43	B2	269
Crag Avenue Ind Centre	35	B4	219

Name	Page	Grid/Ref.	No.
Cranford Centre, Stillorgan	48	D2	274
Croke Park Ind Est	38	E1	55
Crosbie Business Centre	38	F1	262
Crossbeg Ind Est	45	A2	56
Crosslands Business Park	45	A2	297
Crosslands Ind Park	45	A2	57
Cruiserath Business Park	9	C3	199
Crumlin Business Park	46	E1	292
Damastown Ind Est	8	F3	58
Damastown Ind Park	8	F3	302
Damastown Technology Park	8	E3	166
Dartmouth House Ind Centre	36	E3	217
Deansgrange Business Park	59	B2	59
Docklands Innovation Park	39	A1	155
(The)Donnelly Centre Cork Street	37	C3	275
Dublin Ind Est / Glasnevin/Broombridge	24	E3	61
Dun Laoghaire Ind Est	59	B2	63
Dunboyne Ind Est	7	B2	62
Dundrum Business Park	47	C3	231
Earlscourt Industrial Estate	47	B4	224
Earlsfort Centre	38	E3	276
East Point Business Park	39	A1	263
East Road Ind Est	38	F1	64
Elmfield Ind Est	44	E1	65
Fashion City	45	A3	69
Feltrim Industrial Park	2	E3	67
Finches Industrial Park	45	B1	68
Finglas Business Centre	11	B4	140
Finglas Business Park	24	E3	23
Finglas Business Park	9	C3	210
Fonthill Retail Park	35	A2	176
Frank Fahey Centre	45	B1	9
Furry Park Ind Est, Santry	12	E3	181
Gaywood Ind Est	9	B3	70
Glasnevin Business Centre	24	D3	220
Glasnevin Business Park	24	D3	221
Glen Abbey Complex	44	F4	71
Glen Ind Est	24	E3	73
Glenageary Office Park	60	D2	291
Glenview Ind Est	37	B4	74
Glenville Ind Est	48	E3	75
Goldenbridge Ind Est	36	F4	76
Grange Castle Business Park	34	D4	218
Grange Castle International Business Park	43	B1	239
Great Keppel Business Centre	15	A1	296
Green Isle Business Park	44	D3	242
Greenhills Business Centre	45	B4	193
Greenhills Business Park	45	B4	192
Greenhills Centre	45	B4	191
Greenhills Ind Est	45	A4	77
Greenmount Ind Est	37	C4	78
Greenogue Business Park	42	E4	235

Name	Page	Grid/Ref.	No.
Grove Ind Est Dubber Cross	11	B3	79
Grove Ind Est, Finglas	24	E1	80
Harbour Ind Est	67	C1	81
(The) Harcourt Centre,	38	D4	278
Hewlett Packard Ind Park	32	F2	234
Hibernian Industrial Estate	45	A4	82
Hillcrest Industrial Estate	45	B2	93
Hills Ind Est	34	D1	83
Hollywood Business Park	9	C3	303
Horizon Logistics	11	B2	204
Howth Junction Business Park	27	B1	270
I.D.A.Tallaght Business Park	54	F2	89
Industrial Yarns Complex	67	C1	91
International Financial Services Centre (IFSC)	38	E2	279
Irish Life Centre	38	E2	280
J.F.K. Ave	45	A1	96
J.F.K. Drive	45	B1	97
J.F.K. Park	36	D4	98
J.F.K. Road	36	D4	99
Jamestown Business Park	11	A4	208
Jamestown Ind Centre	36	F4	95
Jamestown Ind Estate	36	E4	94
Jamestown Little Ind Estate	11	A4	298
KCR Ind Est	46	E2	100
Kilbarrack Ind Est	27	B1	101
Kilcarberry Ind Park	43	A1	283
Kileen Ind Park	36	D4	216
Killarney Road Business Park	67	B3	257
Killinardin Enterprise Park	54	F2	246
Kinsealy Business Park	14	D1	281
Knockmitten Business Park	44	F1	282
Kylemore Ind Est	36	D4	102
Kylemore Park North	36	D3	103
Kylemore Park South	36	E4	104
Kylemore Park West	36	D4	105
Landys Ind Est	56	D1	106
Lansdown Valley	45	C1	107
Leopardstown Office Park	58	E2	261
Leopardstown Retail Park	58	E2	108
Liberties Craft & Small Industries Centre	37	C3	109
(The)Liffey Trust Enterprise Centre	38	F2	150
Lilmar Ind Est	12	F4	110
Loughlinstown Ind Est	64	D1	111
(The)Maltings Business Park	37	C3	259
Manor Street Business Park	37	C1	309
Maynooth Business Campus	17	C4	211
Merrywell Business Park	45	A2	188
Merrywell Ind Est	45	A2	182
Metropolitan Ind Est	37	A3	113
Mill Lane Business Park	33	B1	232
Millbank Business Park	34	D1	87
Millenium Business Park	10	E3	202
Monarch Ind Est	44	F4	114
Montone Business Park	44	F1	248
Mount Pleasant Ind Est	47	A1	284
Mulcahy Keane Est	45	C2	115
Mygan Industrial Estate	11	B4	207
Naas Road Business Park	36	E4	132
Naas Road Ind Park	36	F4	170
Nangor Road Business Centre	35	C4	174
Newcastle Business Centre	42	E1	88
Newcourt Business Park	11	A2	205
Newlands Business Centre	44	E2	116
Newtown Ind Est	13	C4	117
North Park Business & Office Park	11	A4	209
North Richmond Ind Est	38	E1	118
North Ring Business Park	12	F3	180
Northern Cross Business Park	11	A4	285
Northwest Business Park	10	D3	201
Nutgrove Enterprise Park	57	A1	252
Nutgrove Office Park	47	A4	223
Oak Road Business Park	44	F1	250
Oakfield Ind Est	35	A4	119
Old Court Ind Est	67	B4	120
Old Sawmills Ind Est	45	B2	121
Ossory Ind Est	38	F1	122
Palmgrove Ind Est	25	B2	265
Park West Business Park	35	C4	173
Park West Enterprise Centre	35	C4	172
Park West Ind Park	36	D4	171
Parkmore Ind Est	45	B1	123
Parkway Business Centre	45	A2	183
Phoenix Ind Est	23	B3	124
Pineview Ind Est	55	C1	125
Pinewood Close Ind Est	67	C4	126
Plato Business Park	9	A3	198
Poppintree Ind Est	11	B4	127
Port Tunnel Business Park	13	A4	310
Portside Business Centre	38	F1	128
Red Cow Business Park	45	A1	184
(The)Red Cow Interchange Est	44	F2	233
Richmond Road Ind Est	25	B4	129
Richview Park	47	C2	230
Riversdale Ind Est	36	E4	130
Riverview Business Centre	35	C4	175
Robinhood Business Park	45	A1	294
Robinhood Ind Est	45	B1	131
Rock Enterprise Centre	43	B3	240
Rosemount Business Park	10	D4	133
Royal Liver Retail Park	36	E4	214
Sandyford Business Centre	58	E2	137
Sandyford Ind Est	58	E2	135
Sandyford Office Park	58	E2	136
Sandyford Park	58	E2	163
Santry Avenue Ind Est	12	E4	138
Santry Hall Ind Est	25	B1	139
Shankhill Business Centre	64	E2	141
Shanowen Ind Est, Santry	25	B1	142
Sitecast Ind Est	45	B4	194
Solus Retail Park, Bray	67	C1	254
South City Business Park	54	F2	306
South City Executive Park	46	E1	288
South County Business Park	58	F2	143
Southern Cross Business Park	67	B4	256
S.P.A.D.E. Unemployment Enterprise Centre	37	C2	287
(The)Square Industrial Complex	54	F1	289
St. Joans Ind Est	45	A2	134
St. John's Court Office Park	25	B1	264
St. Margaret's Business Park	11	A4	286
St. Anthony's Business Park	45	A2	54
Stadium Ind Est	10	E4	203
Stillorgan Ind Park	58	D2	144
Sunbury Ind Est	45	B2	145
Sunshine Ind Est	37	A4/B4	146
Swanward Business Centre	45	A2	185
Swiftbrook Ind Est	53	A2	147
Swords Business Campus	2	D1	267
Swords Business Park	2	E1	148
Tallaght Enterprise Centre	55	A1	149
Taurus Business Park	45	B4	195
Terenure Business Park	46	F2	290
Terenure Enterprise Centre	46	F2	304
Tolka Ind Park	24	D3	34
Tolka Valley Business Park	24	D3	222
Turnpike Ind Est see Ballymount Cross	45	A2	151
Unidare/Jamestown Business Park	24	E1	152
Weatherwell Ind Est	35	A4	153
West Pier Business Campus	49	C4	168
Westend Retail Park	22	E2	237
Western Business Park	44	F1	249
Western Ind Est	45	A1	156
Western Office Park	22	E1	236
Western Parkway Business Centre, Ballymount Road	45	B2	157
Western Parkway Business Park	45	B2	190
Westgate Business Park	45	A3	186
Westland Square Business Park	38	E2	260
Westlink Ind Est	36	E3	154
Westpoint Buisness Park	8	F4	164
Westway Centre	45	B2	189
White Heather Ind Est	37	B4	158
White Swan Business Park	37	C4	159
Whitestown Ind Est	54	F1	305
Willow Business Park	45	A1	187
Woodford Business Park	12	F3	178
Woodlawn Ind Est	12	F3	162

Due to the limitations imposed by scale it has not been possible to include all street names on the maps. Unnamed streets have been given small numbers which appear after their grid reference in this index. A list of such streets, by grid reference, is given on page 140.

Streets not named or indicated by number on map pages are prefixed by * and are given their approximate location and grid reference.

STREET NAME	PAGE/GRID REFERENCE
A	
1 Branch Road North	39 A2
1 Branch Road South	39 A2
2 Branch Road North	39 B2
2 Branch Road North Extension	39 B1
2 Branch Road South	39 A2
3 Branch Road Sth.	39 A2
4 Branch Road South	39 B2
A.W. Pugin House	46 F4 [19]
Abberley	64 E1
Abberley Square Apts.	54 F1 [2]
Abbey Cottages	71 B4
Abbey Court (Celbridge)	31 C4
Abbey Court (Killester)	26 E3
Abbey Court (Monkstown)	59 B1 [7]
Abbey Drive	24 D4
Abbey Green	31 C4
Abbey House	8 D3
Abbey Lane	31 C4
Abbey Park	31 C4
Abbey Park (Baldoyle)	27 C1
Abbey Park (Kill o' the Grange)	59 B1
Abbey Park (Killester)	26 E3
Abbey Road	59 B1
Abbey Street (Howth)	30 D1
Abbey Street Lower	71 C3
Abbey Street Middle	71 B4
Abbey Street Old	71 C3
Abbey Street Upper	71 B4
Abbey Terrace	30 D1 [11]
Abbey View	59 B1
Abbeydale	34 F3
Abbeydale Close	34 F3
Abbeydale Crescent	34 F3
Abbeydale Gardens	34 F3
Abbeydale Park	34 F3
Abbeydale Rise	34 F3
Abbeydale Walk	34 F3
Abbeyfarm	31 C4
Abbeyfield	26 E3
Abbeyfield (Clonskeagh)	47 B2
Abbeyfield (Killester)	26 E3
Abbeylea Avenue	1 C1
Abbeylea Close	1 C1
Abbeylea Drive	1 C1
Abbeylea Green	1 C1
Abbeyvale Avenue	1 B1
Abbeyvale Close	1 B1
Abbeyvale Court	1 B1
Abbeyvale Crescent	1 B1
Abbeyvale Drive	1 B2
Abbeyvale Green	1 B2
Abbeyvale Grove	1 B1
Abbeyvale Lawn	1 B1
Abbeyvale Place	1 B1
Abbeyvale Rise	1 B1
Abbeyvale View	1 B2
Abbeyvale Way	1 B2
Abbeywood	34 F3
Abbeywood Avenue	34 F3
Abbeywood Close	34 F3
Abbeywood Court	34 E3
Abbeywood Crescent	34 F3
Abbeywood Park	34 F3
Abbeywood Way	34 F3
Abbots Hill	3 C3
Abbotstown Avenue	23 C2
Abbotstown Drive	23 C1
Abbotstown Drive	24 D2
Abbotstown Road	24 D2
Abby Well	14 D1
Abercorn Road	72 E3
Abercorn Square	36 F3 [19]
Abercorn Terrace	36 F3 [10]
Aberdeen Street	70 D3
Abington	2 F3
Accommodation Road	19 C4
Achill Road (Drumcondra)	25 B3
Achill Road (Loughlinstown)	64 E1
Acorn Drive	57 B1
Acorn Road	57 B1
Acres Road	36 F2
Acres Road	36 F2
Adair	39 A4 [14]
*Adair Lane (off Aston Place)	71 B4
*Adair Terrace (on St Joseph's Parade)	71 A1
Adam Court (off Grafton Street)	75 B1
Adams Town Court	34 D2 [2]
Adamstown Avenue	33 C4
Adamstown Road	34 D2
Adare Avenue	26 E1
Adare Drive	26 E1
Adare Green	26 E1
Adare Park	26 E1
Adare Road	26 E1
Addison Avenue	24 F3 [8]
Addison Drive	24 F3
Addison Hall	24 F3 [6]
Addison Lane	24 F3
Addison Park	24 F3
Addison Place	25 A3 [9]
Addison Road	25 C4
Adelaide Court	75 B3
Adelaide Mews	48 E1
Adelaide Road (Bray)	67 C2
Adelaide Road (Dun Laoghaire)	60 E1
Adelaide Road (Leeson Street)	75 B3
Adelaide Street	50 D4
Adelaide Terrace (Dun Laoghaire)	60 E1 [28]
Adelaide Terrace (off Brookfield Road)	73 C2
Adelaide Villas (Bray)	67 C2
Adelaide Villas (Dun Laoghaire)	60 E1 [27]
Admiral Court	15 A4 [9]
Admiral Park	15 A4
Adrian Avenue	46 F1
Aengus Hall (Belgard Square)	54 F1 [3]
Affollus	5 C3
Aideen Avenue	46 E2
Aideen Drive	46 E2
Aideen Place	46 E2
Aikenhead Terrace	39 A3
Aiken's Village	58 D3
Ailesbury	25 B1 [1]
Ailesbury Close	48 D1 [4]
Ailesbury Drive	48 D1
Ailesbury Gardens	48 E1
Ailesbury Grove (Donnybrook)	48 D1
Ailesbury Grove (Dundrum)	57 B1
Ailesbury Lane (off Ailesbury Road)	48 D1
Ailesbury Lawn	57 B1
Ailesbury Mews	48 E1
Ailesbury Park	48 E1
Ailesbury Road	48 D1
Ailesbury Wood	48 D1
Airfield Court	48 D2
Airfield Drive	47 B4 [13]
Airfield Park	48 D2
Airfield Road	46 F2
Airlie Heights	33 B2
Airpark Avenue	56 E2
Airpark Close	56 E2
Airpark Court	56 E2
Airpark House	56 E2
Airpark Rise	56 E2
Airside	2 D3
Airton Close	45 A4
Airton Road	45 A4
*Airton Terrace (off Greenhills Rd)	45 A4
Albany Avenue	49 B4
Albany Court	64 E1
Albany Road	47 B1
Albert Avenue	68 D2
Albert College Avenue	25 A2
Albert College Court	25 A2
Albert College Crescent	25 A2
Albert College Drive	25 A2
Albert College Grove	25 A2
Albert College Lawn	25 A2
Albert College Park	25 A2
Albert Court (Grand Canal St. Lower)	76 E1
Albert Court (off Grand Canal St)	76 E1
Albert Court (Sandycove Road)	60 E1
Albert Park	60 E1 [3]
Albert Place East	76 E1
Albert Place West	75 B3
Albert Road Lower	60 E1
Albert Road Upper	60 E2
Albert Terrace (Charlemont Street)	75 B3
Albert Terrace (Dún Laoghaire)	50 D4 [27]
Albert Walk	67 C2
Aldborough House	72 D2
Aldborough Parade	72 D2
Aldborough Place	72 D2
Aldborough Square (off Aldborough Place)	72 D2
Aldemere	21 B2
Alden Drive	27 C1
Alden Park	27 C1
Alden Road	27 C1
Alder Court	4 D4 [1]
Alder Lodge	23 A4
Alderpark Court	54 F1
Alderwood Avenue	54 E1
Alderwood Close	54 E1
Alderwood Court	54 E1
Alderwood Drive	54 E1
Alderwood Green	54 E1
Alderwood Grove	54 F1
Alderwood Lawn	54 E1
Alderwood Park	54 F1
Alderwood Rise	54 E1
Alderwood Way	54 F1
Aldrin Walk	26 E1
Alen Hall (Belgard Square)	54 F1 [4]
Alensgrove	32 F2
Alexander Court Apts.	76 D1
Alexander Terrace (Bray)	67 C2 [43]
Alexander Terrace (North Wall)	72 F3
Alexandra Court	47 C4
Alexandra Quay	39 A2 [2]
Alexandra Quay	39 A2
Alexandra Road	39 A2
Alexandra Road Extension	39 C2
Alexandra Terrace (Dundrum)	47 C4
Alexandra Terrace (Portobello)	75 A3
Alexandra Terrace (Terenure)	46 F2
Alexandra Villas	47 C4 [3]
Alfie Byrne House	71 B2
Alfie Byrne Road	72 F1
All Hallows Green	25 B3
All Hallows Lane	25 B3 [7]
All Hallows Square	25 B3
All Saint's Close	27 A3
All Saints Drive	27 A3
All Saints Park	27 A3
All Saints Road	26 F3
Allen Park Drive	58 E1
Allen Park Road	58 E1
Allen Terrace (off Avondale Avenue)	70 F1
Allendale Close	21 B2
Allendale Copse	21 B1
Allendale Court	21 B1
Allendale Drive	21 B1
Allendale Elms	21 B1
Allendale Glen	21 B1
Allendale Green	21 B1
Allendale Grove	21 B2
Allendale Heath	21 B1
Allendale Lawn	21 B1
Allendale Place	21 B1
Allendale Rise	21 B1
Allendale Square	21 B2
Allendale Terrace	21 B1
Allendale View	21 B1
Allendale Walk	21 B1
Allenton Avenue	55 A3
Allenton Crescent	55 A2 [3]
Allenton Drive	55 A3
Allenton Gardens	55 A3
Allenton Green	55 A3
Allenton Lawns	55 A3
Allenton Park	55 A2
Allenton Road	55 B3
Allenton Way	55 A3
Allies River Road	67 A1
Allingham Street	74 E2
Alma Park	49 C4 [30]
Alma Place	49 C4 [14]
Alma Road	49 B4
Alma Terrace	47 A1 [13]
Almeida Avenue	73 C1
Almeida Terrace	73 C1
Alone Walk	26 E2
Alpine Heights	44 D1
Alpine Rise	44 E4
Altadore	60 D2
Altamont Hall	47 C4
Alverno	39 B1 [1]
Ambassador Court	76 E3
Amber Vale	44 E4
Amberwood	9 A4
Amiens Street	72 D3
An Crannog	60 D3
Anastasia Lane	60 F2 [3]
Anglers Rest	47 C1
Anglesea Avenue	49 A3
Anglesea House	39 A4 [40]
Anglesea Lane	50 D4 [20]
Anglesea Park	60 E2
Anglesea Row	71 A3
Anglesea Street	71 B4
Anley Court	34 E1
Ann Devlin Avenue	46 E4
Ann Devlin Drive	46 E4
Ann Devlin Park	56 E1
Ann Devlin Road	46 E4
Anna Livia Apts.	74 E1
Anna Villa	47 B1
Annabeg	60 D4 [1]
Annacrivey	65 B3
Annadale	47 B4 [16]
Annadale Avenue	25 C4 [1]
Annadale Crescent	25 C3
Annadale Drive	25 C3
Annagh Court	22 F1
Annaghaskin	66 D1
Annaly Close	21 B1
Annaly Court	21 B1
Annaly Drive	21 B1
Annaly Grove	21 B1
Annaly Road	24 F4
Annaly Terrace	21 B1
Annamoe Drive	70 E1
Annamoe Parade	70 E1
Annamoe Park	70 E1
Annamoe Road	70 D1
Annamoe Terrace	70 E1
Annaville Avenue	59 A1
Annaville Close	47 C4
Annaville Grove	47 C3 [1]
Annaville Lodge	47 C4
Annaville Park	47 C4
Annaville Terrace	47 C3
Anne Street North	71 A3
Anne Street South	75 B1
Anner Road	73 B2
Anne's Bridge	17 C1
Anne's Lane	75 B1
Annesley Avenue	72 E1
Annesley Bridge	72 E1
Annesley Bridge Road	72 E1
Annesley Close	72 E1
Annesley Park	47 B1
Annesley Place	72 E1
Annfield	22 D3
Annfield Court	22 D3
Annfield Crescent	22 D3
Annfield Drive	22 D3
Annfield Lawn	22 D4
Annsbrook	47 C2
Annville Drive	58 E1
Apollo Way	26 D1
*Appian Close (on Leeson Park)	76 D4
Apples Road	58 D2
Applewood Avenue East	1 Inset
Applewood Birch	1 Inset
Applewood Crescent	1 Inset
Applewood Drive	1 Inset
Applewood Main Street	1 Inset
Applewood Mews	1 Inset
Applewood Place	1 Inset
Applewood Square	1 Inset

STREET NAME	PAGE/GRID REFERENCE
Aranleigh Court	56 F1
Aranleigh Dell	57 A1
Aranleigh Gardens	56 F1
Aranleigh Mount	56 F1
Aranleigh Park	57 A1
Aranleigh Vale	56 F1
Arás na Cluaine	35 B4
Aravon Court	68 D2
Arbour Hill	70 E3
Arbour Place	70 E3
Arbour Terrace	70 D3
Arbutus Avenue	74 F4
Arbutus Grove	67 B1 [4]
Arbutus Place	75 A3
Archers Wood	8 F4
Archers Wood	8 F4
Ard Lorcain	58 F1
Ard Lorcain Villas	58 F1 [2]
Ard Mhacha	54 F2
Ard Mhuire Park	60 E2
Ard Mor Avenue	53 C1
Ard Mor Close	53 C1
Ard Mor Court	53 C1
Ard Mor Crescent	53 C1
Ard Mor Dale	53 C1
Ard Mor Drive	53 C1
Ard Mor Green	53 C1
Ard Mor Lawn	53 C1
Ard Mor Park	53 C1
Ard Mor Walk	53 C1
Ard na Glaise	48 F4
Ard Na Gréine	47 A3 [11]
Ard Na Gréine (Ballymorris)	67 B4
Ard na Mara	3 A3
Ard na Meala	12 D4
Ard Ri Road	70 E3
Ard Right Place	70 E3
Ardagh Avenue	59 A1
Ardagh Close	59 A1 [6]
Ardagh Court	58 F1
Ardagh Crescent	59 A1
Ardagh Drive	59 A1
Ardagh Grove	59 A1
Ardagh Park	59 A1
Ardagh Park Road	59 A1
Ardagh Road	73 C4
Ardara Avenue	14 D4
Ardbeg Crescent	26 E2
Ardbeg Drive	26 E2
Ardbeg Park	26 E2
Ardbeg Road	26 E2
Ardbrugh Close	60 F2 [31]
Ardbrugh Road	60 F2
Ardbrugh Villas	60 F2 [21]
Ardcian Park	1 C1
Ardcollum Avenue	26 E2
Ardee Grove	75 B4
Ardee Road	75 B4
Ardee Row	74 F2
Ardee Street (Bray)	67 B2
Ardee Street (The Coombe)	74 F2
Ardeen	33 C2
Ardeevin Avenue	33 C2
Ardeevin Court	33 C2
Ardeevin Drive	33 C2
Ardeevin Road	60 F2
*Ardeevin Terrace (off Ardeevin Road)	60 F2
Ardenza Park	49 B3 [3]
Ardenza Terrace	49 B3 [1]
Ardglas Estate	57 C1
Ardilaun	14 F1
Ardilaun Road	72 D1
*Ardilaun Square (off Sackville Avenue)	72 D1
Ardilea Downs	48 D4
Ardlea Road	26 E2
Ardlui Park	59 A1
Ardmeen Park	59 A1
Ardmore Avenue	70 D1
Ardmore Close	26 D2
Ardmore Crescent (Artane)	26 D2
Ardmore Crescent (Bray)	67 B2
Ardmore Drive	26 D1
Ardmore Grove	26 D1
Ardmore Lawn	67 B3
Ardmore Park (Artane)	26 D2
Ardmore Park (Bray)	67 B2
Ardmore Park (Kill o' the Grange)	59 C1
Ardmore Wood	67 B3
Ardoyne Mews	76 E4
Ardpatrick Road	24 D4
Ardtona Avenue	47 B4 [6]
Arena Road	58 E2
Argus House	74 F4
Argyle House Apts.	39 A4 [37]
Argyle Road	76 E4
Argyle Square	47 C1 [25]
Arkendale Court	60 E1 [26]
Arkendale Road	60 E1
Arkendale Woods	60 E1 [25]
Arkle Road	58 E2
Arkle Square	58 F2 [6]
Arklow Street	70 D2
Armagh Road	46 D1
Armstrong Street	74 F4
Armstrong Street (off Harold's Cross Road)	74 F4
Armstrong Walk	26 E1
Army Road	69 B3
Arnold Grove	60 D2
Arnold Park	60 D2
Arnott Street	75 A2
Arran Avenue	64 E1
Arran Close	64 E1
Arran Court	22 F1
Arran Drive	64 E1
Arran Green	67 C2
Arran Quay	70 F4
Arran Quay Apts.	70 F4
Arran Quay Terrace (Arran Quay)	70 F4
Arran Road	25 B3
Arran Square Apts.	70 F4
Arran Street East	71 A4
Arran Street West	70 F4
Arranmore Avenue	71 A1
Arranmore Road	47 C1
Artane	26 E2
Artane Cottages Lower	26 E2 [2]
Artane Cottages Upper	26 E2 [3]
Arthur Griffith Court	34 D2 [1]
Arthur Griffith Park	34 D3
Arundel	49 B4 [19]
Asdill's Row (off Temple Bar)	71 B4
Asgard Apts.	30 D1
Asgard Park	30 D2
Asgard Road	30 D2
Asgard Road	72 E4
*Ash Grove (Meath Street)	74 F1
Ash Park Avenue	34 E3
Ash Park Court	34 E3
Ash Park Grove	34 E2
Ash Park Heath	34 E2
Ash Street	74 F1
Ashberry	34 D3
Ashbrook (Ashtown)	23 C3
Ashbrook (Bray)	67 C2
Ashbrook (Clontarf)	26 D4
*Ashbrook Terrace (Ranelagh)	47 B1
*Ashbrook Villas (Ranelagh)	47 B1
Ashbury Park	67 C2
Ashcroft	27 A2
Ashcroft Court	22 D1 [5]
Ashcroft Grove	22 D1 [4]
Ashdale Avenue	46 F2
Ashdale Close	2 E3
Ashdale Gardens	46 F2
Ashdale Park	46 F2 [1]
Ashdale Road (Swords)	2 E2
Ashdale Road (Terenure)	46 F2
Ashe Court	2 E2
Ashfield	46 D4
Ashfield Avenue (Clondalkin)	44 F3
Ashfield Avenue (Ranelagh)	47 B1
Ashfield Close (Clondalkin)	44 F3
Ashfield Court (Ballymorris)	67 B4
Ashfield Court (Mulhuddart)	9 A4
Ashfield Drive	44 F3
Ashfield Gardens	9 A4
Ashfield Green	8 F4
Ashfield Grove	9 A4
Ashfield Lawn	8 F4
Ashfield Park (Booterstown)	48 E2
Ashfield Park (Clondalkin)	44 F3
Ashfield Park (Huntstown Way)	9 A4 [2]
Ashfield Park (Terenure)	46 F2
Ashfield Road (Ranelagh)	47 B1
Ashfield Way	8 A4
Ashford Cottages	70 D2
Ashford Place	70 D2
Ashford Street	70 D2
Ashgrove (Baskin Lane)	13 C1
Ashgrove (Celbridge)	31 C2
Ashgrove (Kill o' the Grange)	59 C1
Ashgrove (Tallaght)	54 E1
Ashgrove Court	57 C1 [8]
Ashgrove Terrace	57 C1 [2]
Ashington Avenue	24 D3
Ashington Close	24 D3
Ashington Court	24 D3
Ashington Crescent	23 C3
Ashington Dale	24 D3
Ashington Gardens	24 D3
Ashington Green	24 D3
Ashington Grove	24 D3
Ashington Heath	24 D3
Ashington Mews	24 D3
Ashington North	24 D3
Ashington Park	24 D3
Ashington Rise	23 C3
Ashlawn	57 C1
Ashlawn Court	67 B2
Ashlawn Park	60 D4
Ashleigh Court	22 F3 [3]
Ashleigh Green	22 F3
Ashleigh Grove (Blanchardstown)	22 F3
Ashleigh Grove (Maynooth)	17 B4
Ashleigh Lawn	3 B3
Ashley Avenue	2 D2
Ashley Drive	2 D2
Ashley Grove	2 D2
Ashley Heights	67 B2 [4]
Ashley Rise	4 D4
Ashling Close	73 C4
Ashling Court	47 B1
Ashling Heights	22 E1
Ashmount	9 A4 [1]
Ashmount Court	73 B1
Ashton Avenue	1 Inset
Ashton Avenue	56 D1
Ashton Close	1 Inset
Ashton Close	56 D1
Ashton Court	1 Inset
Ashton Drive	1 Inset
Ashton Green	1 Inset
Ashton Grove	1 Inset
Ashton Grove	56 D1
Ashton Lawn	56 D1
Ashton Lawns	1 Inset
Ashton Park	49 B4
Ashton Rise	1 Inset
Ashton Wood	67 A3
Ashtown	23 C3
Ashtown Court	23 C4
Ashtown Gate (Phoenix Park)	23 B4
Ashtown Gate Road	23 B4
Ashtown Grove	23 C4
Ashtown Lodge	23 C4 [4]
Ashtown Road	23 B3
Ashtowngate	23 C3
Ashurst	60 E4
Ashurst (Ballybrack)	64 E1
Ashurst (Mount Merrion)	48 E4 [3]
Ashville Close	34 E1
Ashwood Avenue	43 C1
Ashwood Close	43 C1
Ashwood Drive	44 D1
Ashwood Lawns	44 D1
Ashwood Park	44 D1
Ashwood Road	44 D1
Ashwood Way	44 D1
Ashworth Place (off Mount Drummond Avenue)	75 A4
Aspen Drive	2 E3
Aspen Park (Kill O'The Grange)	59 C1 [11]
Aspen Park (Kinsealy Court)	2 E3
Aspen Road	2 E3
Aspen Wood	22 D2
Aspin Avenue	21 C2
Aspin Lawns	22 D2
Assumpta Park	64 E3
Aston Place	71 B4
Aston Quay	71 B4
Astor Hall	71 C4
Athgoe	51 C1
Athgoe Drive	64 E2 [4]
Athgoe North	51 B1
Athgoe Road (Newcastle)	41 C4
Athgoe Road (Shankill)	64 E2
Athgoe South	51 B2
Atlumney Villas	75 B4
Atmospheric Road	60 E1 [29]
Aubrey Grove	64 E3
Aubrey Park	64 E3
Auburn	26 D4
Auburn Avenue (Cabinteely)	60 D3
Auburn Avenue (Castleknock)	23 A3
Auburn Avenue (Donnybrook)	47 C1
Auburn Avenue Roundabout	23 A3
Auburn Close (Cabinteely)	60 D3
Auburn Close (Castleknock)	23 A3
Auburn Drive (Cabinteely)	60 D3
Auburn Drive (Castleknock)	23 A3
Auburn Green	23 A3
Auburn Grove	3 A3
Auburn Road (Cabinteely)	60 D3 [1]
Auburn Road (Cabinteely)	60 D3
Auburn Road (Donnybrook)	47 C1 [11]
Auburn Street	71 A2
Auburn Terrace (Old Kilmainham)	73 C1
Auburn Villas (Bray)	67 B2 [1]
Auburn Villas (Rathgar)	47 A2
Auburn Walk	70 D2
Aughavannagh Road	74 E4
Aughrim Court	70 E3
Aughrim Lane	70 E2
Aughrim Place	70 D2
Aughrim Street	70 D2
Aughrim Villas	70 D2
Augustine Court (St Margaret's Tce)	74 F1
Augustine Villas	67 C2 [30]
Aulden Grange	12 F4
Aungier Lane	75 B2
Aungier Place	75 B2
Aungier Street	75 B1
Austin's Cottages	72 E1
Avalon	59 A3 [3]
Avalon Apts.	29 B1 [2]
Ave Maria Road	74 D2
Avenue Road	75 A3
Avila Apts	59 A1 [10]
Avila Park	23 C1
Avila Park Gardens	23 C1
Avoca Apartments	32 D3
Avoca Avenue (Dun Laoghaire)	67 C3
Avoca Avenue (Stillorgan)	48 F4
Avoca Court	48 F4
Avoca Hall	49 A4 [10]
Avoca Park	48 F4
Avoca Place	49 A3
Avoca Road	48 F4
Avoca Terrace	48 F4
Avoca Wood	48 F4
Avonbeg Court	55 A1 [3]
Avonbeg Drive	55 A1
Avonbeg Gardens	55 B1
Avonbeg Park	55 A1
Avonbeg Road	55 B1
Avondale	20 D4
Avondale Avenue	70 F1
Avondale Court (Blackrock)	49 A4
Avondale Court (Dalkey)	60 E1 [31]
Avondale Crescent	60 E2
Avondale House	71 C2
Avondale Lawn	49 A4
Avondale Mews	39 A4 [55]
Avondale Park (Blackrock)	49 A4 [1]
Avondale Park (Dalkey)	60 E2
Avondale Park (Dun Laoghaire)	67 B3

STREET NAME	PAGE/GRID REFERENCE	
Avondale Park (Raheny)	27	A2
Avondale Road (Dalkey)	60	D2
Avondale Road (Phibsborough)	70	F1
Avondale Square	7	B2 [2]
Avondale Terrace	45	C2
Avonmore	59	A2
Avonmore Avenue	55	B1 [5]
Avonmore Close	55	B1
Avonmore Drive	55	B1
Avonmore Grove	55	B1
Avonmore Park	55	B1
Avonmore Road	55	B1
Aylesbury	55	A2
Aylmer Ave	42	D4
Aylmer Heath	42	D4
Aylmer Road	42	D4
Ayrefield Avenue	26	F1
Ayrefield Court	26	F1
Ayrefield Drive	26	F1
Ayrefield Grove	26	F1
Ayrefield Park	26	F1 [2]
Ayrefield Place	26	F1
Ayrefield Road	26	F1
Ayward Green	24	D2

B

STREET NAME	PAGE/GRID REFERENCE	
Bachelor's Walk	71	B4
Bachelors Walk Apartments.	71	B4
Bachelors Way	71	B4
Back Lane (Baldoyle)	15	A4 [3]
Back Lane (High Street)	75	A1
Back Lane (Maynooth)	17	C3
*Back Lane (off Sandwith St Upr)	76	D1
Back Road	3	B4
Baggot Bridge Court	76	D2
Baggot Close	75	C2
Baggot Court	76	D2
Baggot Lane	76	E3
Baggot Rath House	39	A3 [48]
Baggot Road	23	C4
Baggot Street Lower	76	D2
Baggot Street Upper	76	E3
Baggot Terrace	23	C4 [1]
Baggotrath Place	76	D2
Bailey Green	30	E3
Bailey Green Road	30	E3
Bailey View	60	F1 [15]
Bailey's Row	72	D2
Balally Avenue	58	D1
Balally Close	58	D1
Balally Drive	58	D1
Balally Grove	58	D2
Balally Hill	58	D2
Balally Park	58	D1
Balally Road	57	C1
Balally Terrace	58	D2 [1]
Balbutcher Drive	11	C4
Balbutcher Lane	11	C4
Balbutcher Lane Lower	11	C4
Balbutcher Way	11	C4
Balcurris Close	12	D4
Balcurris Gardens	12	D4
Balcurris Park East	12	D4
Balcurris Road	12	D4
Baldoyle	15	A4
Baldoyle Road	28	D1
Balfe Avenue	45	C1
Balfe Road	45	C1
Balfe Road East	46	D1
Balfe Street	75	B1
Balgaddy Road	34	F3
Balglass Road	30	D2
Balgriffin	14	D3
Balgriffin Cottages	14	D3
Balgriffin Park	14	D3
Balgriffin Road	14	D3
Balheary Road	2	D1
Balkill Park	30	D2
Balkill Road	30	D2
Ballawley Court	57	C2
Ballentree	9	B2
Ballentree Avenue	9	B2
Ballentree Close	9	B2
Ballentree Crescent	9	B2
Ballentree Drive	9	B2

STREET NAME	PAGE/GRID REFERENCE	
Ballentree Grove	9	B3
Ballentree Lodge Apts.	9	B2
Ballentree Villa	9	B3
Ballinakelly Village	42	D4
Ballinclea Heights	60	E3
Ballinclea Road	60	D3
Ballinteer	57	B2
Ballinteer Avenue	57	B2
Ballinteer Close	57	B2
Ballinteer Court	57	B2 [2]
Ballinteer Crescent	57	B2
Ballinteer Drive	57	B2
Ballinteer Gardens	57	C2
Ballinteer Grove	57	B2
Ballinteer Park	57	B2
Ballinteer Road	57	C1
Ballinteer Road (Delbrook Park)	57	C2
Ballintrane Wood	1	C2
Ballintyre Demesne	57	B2
Ballintyre Downs	57	B2
Ballintyre Lane	57	B2
Ballintyre Meadows	57	B2
Ballintyre Square	57	B2
Ballintyre Terrace	57	B2
Ballintyre Walk	57	B2
Ballintyre Woods	57	B2
Ball's Lane	71	A3
Ballsbridge	76	F4
Ballsbridge Avenue	39	A4 [26]
Ballsbridge Court	39	A4 [39]
Ballsbridge Gardens	39	A4 [25]
Ballsbridge Park	39	A4 [23]
Ballsbridge Terrace	76	F4
Ballsbridge Wood	39	A4 [27]
Ballybetagh	62	F4
Ballybetagh Road	62	E4
Ballyboden	56	E1
Ballyboden Crescent	56	E1
Ballyboden Road	56	E1
Ballyboden Way	56	E1
Ballyboggan Road	24	E3
Ballybough Avenue	72	D1
Ballybough Court	72	D1
*Ballybough Lane (King's Avenue)	72	D1
Ballybough Road	72	D1
Ballybrack	60	E4
Ballybrack (Two Rock Mountain)	61	B3
Ballybrew	65	C2
Ballybride	64	D3
Ballybride Road	64	D3
Ballycoolin Road	10	D4
Ballycorus	63	B3
Ballycorus Road	62	F2
Ballycorus Road	63	A2
Ballycullen Avenue	55	B2
Ballycullen Drive	55	B2
Ballycullen Road	55	C1
Ballydowd Grove	34	E1
Ballydowd Manor	34	E2
Ballyedmonduff	61	C2
Ballyedmonduff	62	E1
Ballyedmonduff Road	62	D1
Ballyfermot	36	D3
Ballyfermot Avenue	36	D3
Ballyfermot Crescent	36	D3
Ballyfermot Drive	36	D3
Ballyfermot Parade	36	D3
Ballyfermot Road	35	C3
Ballyfermot Road	36	E3
Ballyfermot Road (Cherry Orchard)	36	D3
Ballygall Avenue	24	E1
Ballygall Crescent	24	E2
Ballygall Parade	24	E2
Ballygall Place	24	E2 [1]
Ballygall Road	24	E2
Ballygall Road East	24	F2
Ballygall Road West	24	E1
Ballygihen Avenue	60	E1
Ballygihen Villas	60	E1 [20]
Ballygoran	18	E4
Ballygoran Court	31	C2
Ballygoran View	31	C2
Ballyhoy Avenue	27	A3

STREET NAME	PAGE/GRID REFERENCE	
Ballymacartle	13	C1
Ballymace Green	46	E4
Ballymacoll	6	D3
Ballymadrough Road	2	F1
Ballymakealy Grove	31	C4
Ballymakealy Lawns	31	C4
Ballyman	66	F1
Ballyman Lane	63	C4
Ballyman Lane	66	F1
Ballyman Road	66	F2
Ballymana	54	E4
Ballymanagin Lane	35	A4 [1]
Ballymorris	67	B4 [2]
Ballymorris	67	B4
Ballymoss Parade	58	F2 [5]
Ballymoss Road	58	E2
Ballymount Avenue	45	B2
Ballymount Cottages	45	B2 [2]
Ballymount Drive	45	B2
Ballymount Road	44	F3
Ballymount Road Lower	45	B2
Ballymount Road Upper	45	A2
Ballymount Square	45	B2
Ballymun	25	A1
Ballymun Main Street	12	D4
Ballymun Road	12	D4
Ballymun Road	25	A1
Ballymun Road	25	A3
Ballynakelly	42	D4
Ballyneety Road	36	F3
Ballynoe Court	67	B3 [1]
Ballyogan Avenue	58	F4
Ballyogan Close	58	F4
Ballyogan Court	58	F4
Ballyogan Crescent	58	F4
Ballyogan Drive	58	F4
Ballyogan Estate	58	F4
Ballyogan Green	58	F4
Ballyogan Lawn	58	F4
Ballyogan Park	58	F4 [1]
Ballyogan Road	58	F4
Ballyogen Vale	59	A4
Ballyogen Wood	59	A4
Ballyolaf Manor	57	C1 [6]
Ballyoulster Park	32	E3
Ballyowen Avenue	34	F1
Ballyowen Court	34	F1
Ballyowen Crescent	34	F1
Ballyowen Drive	34	F1
Ballyowen Green	34	F1
Ballyowen Grove	34	F1
Ballyowen Hall	34	F2
Ballyowen Lane	34	F2
Ballyowen Lawn	34	F1
Ballyowen Road	34	F1
Ballyowen Square	34	F2
Ballyowen View	34	F1
Ballyowen Way	34	F1
Ballyroan Court	56	D1 [3]
Ballyroan Crescent	56	E1
Ballyroan Heights	56	E1
Ballyroan Park	56	D1
Ballyroan Road	56	E1
Ballyshannon Avenue	25	C1
Ballyshannon Road	26	D1
Ballytore Road	46	F3
Ballywaltrim Cottages	67	B4 [1]
Ballywaltrim Heights	67	B3
Ballywaltrim Lane	67	A4
Ballywaltrim Road	67	B4
Ballywilliam Close	67	B4
Balnagowan	47	B2 [4]
Balrothery Cottages	55	C1 [5]
Balrothery Estate	45	B4
Balscadden Road	30	E1
Balscott	41	C1
Bancroft Avenue	55	A1
Bancroft Close	55	B1
Bancroft Crescent	45	B4
Bancroft Downs	45	A4
Bancroft Grove	55	B1
Bancroft Park	55	A1
Bancroft Road	55	B1
Bangor Circle	46	E1
Bangor Drive	73	C4
Bangor Road	46	E1

STREET NAME	PAGE/GRID REFERENCE	
Bankside Cottages	47	B2
Bann Road	24	E3
Bannaville	75	B4
Bannow Road	24	E4
Banshee	51	A2
Bantry Road	25	A3
Bantry Square	22	F1
Banville Avenue	36	D4
Barberstown Lane	1	A4
Barclay Court	49	A3
Bargy Road	72	F2
Barnacoille Park	60	F1
Barnamire	65	A4
Barnamore Crescent	24	D3
Barnamore Grove	24	D3
Barnamore Park	24	D3
Barnaslingan Lane	63	A3
Barneville Green	35	C3
Barneville Walk	35	C4
Barnhall	32	F1
Barnhall Drive	32	F1
Barnhill Avenue	60	E2
Barnhill Cross Road	34	D1
Barnhill Grove	60	F2 [7]
Barnhill Lawn	60	E2 [1]
Barnhill Park	60	E2 [3]
Barnhill Road	60	E2
*Barnhill Villas (on Barnhill Road)	60	F2
Barnville Park	35	C4
Barnwell Drive	24	F1
Baroma	46	E2 [10]
Barrack Bridge	3	A2
Barrack Court	52	F2
*Barrack Lane (off Irishtown Road)	39	A3
Barrett Street	49	C4 [2]
Barrogstown East	18	F4
Barrogstown West	18	E4
Barron Place	25	A3 [4]
Barrow Road	24	E3
Barrow Street	76	F1
Barry Avenue	24	D1
Barry Close (off Barry Drive)	24	D1
Barry Drive	24	D1
Barry Green	24	D1
Barry Park	24	D1
Barry Road	24	D1
Barry's Park	2	D2
Barryscourt Road	26	E1
Barton Avenue	56	F1
Barton Court	57	A1 [3]
Barton Drive	56	F1
Barton Road East	57	B1
Barton Road East Extension	57	A1
Barton Road Extension	57	A1
Barton Road West	56	F1
Bartra Rock Apts.	60	F1 [18]
Basin Grove	74	D1
Basin Lane Flats	74	D1
Basin Street Lower	74	D1
Basin Street Upper	74	D1
*Basin View (off Basin Street Upper)	74	D1
Baskin Cottages	13	C1
Baskin Lane	13	B1
Bass Place	76	D1
Bath Avenue (Malahide)	3	C2
Bath Avenue (Sandymount)	76	F2
Bath Avenue Gardens	76	F2
Bath Avenue Place	76	F2
Bath Lane	71	B2
Bath Place	49	A3 [8]
Bath Street	39	A3
Bawnlea Avenue	54	D2
Bawnlea Close	54	D2
Bawnlea Crescent	54	D2
Bawnlea Drive	54	D2
Bawnlea Green	54	D2
Bawnogue Cottages	43	C1 [1]
Bawnogue Road	43	C1
Bawnville Avenue	55	A2
Bawnville Close	55	A2
Bawnville Drive	55	B2
Bawnville Park	55	B2
Bawnville Road	55	A2

STREET NAME	PAGE/GRID REFERENCE	STREET NAME	PAGE/GRID REFERENCE	STREET NAME	PAGE/GRID REFERENCE	STREET NAME	PAGE/GRID REFERENCE
Baymount Park	27 A4	Beaupark Row	14 D4	Beechlawn Green	26 E1	Belgard Green	44 E4
Bayshore Lane	64 E1	Beaupark Street	14 D4	Beechlawn Grove	26 E1	Belgard Heights	44 F4
Bayside Boulevard North	27 C1	Beaupark Tce	14 D4	Beechlawn Manor	46 F2 [20]	Belgard Road	44 E3
Bayside Boulevard South	27 C1	Beauvale Park	26 D2	Beechlawn Mews	46 F2 [21]	Belgard Square	54 F1
Bayside Crescent	27 C1 [1]	Beaver Close	72 D2	Beechmount Drive	47 C3	Belgard Square East	54 F1
Bayside Park	27 C1	Beaver Row	47 C1	(Windy Arbour)		Belgard Square North	54 F1
Bayside Square East	27 C1	Beaver Street	72 D2	Beechpark Avenue	26 E1	Belgard Square South	54 F1
Bayside Square North	27 C1	Beckett Hall	59 B4	Beechpark Close	23 A3 [3]	Belgard Square West	54 F1
Bayside Square South	27 C1	Beckett Way	35 C4	Beechpark Court	26 E1	Belgrave Avenue	47 B1
Bayside Square West	27 C1	Bective Square	70 F1	Beechpark Orchard	23 A3	Belgrave Place (Monkstown)	49 B4 [10]
Bayside Walk	27 C1	Bedford Court	46 E1 [5]	Beechurst	67 B2	Belgrave Place (Rathmines)	47 A1 [15]
Bayswater Terrace	60 F1 [7]	Bedford Lane (off Aston Quay)	71 B4	Beechview	56 E2 [1]	Belgrave Road (Monkstown)	49 B4
Baytownpark	6 E1	Bedford Row (off Aston Quay)	71 B4	Beechwood	14 F1	Belgrave Road (Rathmines)	47 A1
Bayview (Bray)	67 C2 [51]	Beech Drive	57 B1	Beechwood Avenue Lower	47 B1	Belgrave Square (Monkstown)	49 B4
Bayview (Loughlinstown)	64 E1	Beech Grove (Blackrock)	48 F2	Beechwood Avenue Upper	47 B1	Belgrave Square (Rathmines)	47 A1
*Bayview (On Seapoint Road)	67 C2	Beech Grove (Lucan)	34 E2	Beechwood Close	67 C4	Belgrave Square East	49 B4
Bayview Avenue	72 D1	Beech Hill	47 C2	(Boghall Road)		(Monkstown)	
Bayview Close	64 E1	Beech Hill Avenue	47 C2	Beechwood Close (Hartstown)	21 C1	Belgrave Square East	47 A1
Bayview Court	64 E1	Beech Hill Court	47 C1	Beechwood Court	58 F1	(Rathmines)	
Bayview Crescent	64 E1	Beech Hill Crescent	47 C2 [3]	Beechwood Downs	21 C1	Belgrave Square North	49 B4
Bayview Drive	64 E1	Beech Hill Drive	47 C2	Beechwood Grove	60 D1 [11]	(Monkstown)	
Bayview Glade	64 E1 [12]	Beech Hill Road	47 C2	Beechwood House	64 E2 [10]	Belgrave Square North	47 A1
Bayview Glen	64 E1	Beech Hill Terrace	47 C2 [4]	Beechwood Lawn	60 D2	(Rathmines)	
Bayview Green	64 E1	Beech Hill Villas	47 C2 [2]	Beechwood Lawns	52 F2	Belgrave Square South	49 B4
Bayview Grove	64 E1	Beech House	76 D3	Beechwood Park	60 D1	(Monkstown)	
Bayview Lawn	64 E1	Beech House (Swords)	1 Inset	(Dun Laoghaire)		Belgrave Square South	47 A1
Bayview Rise	64 E1	Beech Lawn	57 B1	Beechwood Park (Rathmines)	47 B1 [7]	(Rathmines)	
Beach Avenue	39 A3	Beech Lodge	23 A4	Beechwood Road	47 B1	Belgrave Square West	49 B4
Beach Drive	39 A3	Beech Park (Cabinteely)	59 C4	Beggar's Bush Buildings	76 F2	(Monkstown)	
Beach Park	15 A1	Beech Park (Castleknock)	22 F3	Beggars Bush Court	76 F2	Belgrave Square West	47 A1
Beach Road	39 A3	Beech Park (Lucan)	34 E1	Belarmine	58 D4	(Rathmines)	
Beach View	27 C2	Beech Park Avenue	23 A3	Belarmine Avenue	58 D4	Belgrave Terrace (Bray)	68 D2 [10]
Beacon Court	58 D2	(Castleknock)		Belarmine Close	58 D4	Belgrave Terrace (Monkstown)	49 B4 [11]
*Beacon Hill (off Nerano Road)	60 F2	Beech Park Avenue	59 B2	Belarmine Court	58 D4	Belgrave Villas (Bray)	68 D2 [9]
Beaconsfield Court	73 A1	(Deans Grange)		Belarmine Drive	58 D4	Belgrave Villas (Rathmines)	47 B1 [16]
Bealing	9 B2	Beech Park Crescent	23 A3 [1]	Belarmine Grange	58 D4	Belgree	9 B2
Bealing Avenue	9 B2	Beech Park Drive	59 B2	Belarmine Heath	58 D4	Belgree Avenue	9 B2
Bealing Close	9 B3	Beech Park Grove	59 B2	Belarmine Park	58 D4	Belgree Close	9 B2
Bealing Crescent	9 B2	Beech Park Lawn	23 A3	Belarmine Place	58 D4	Belgree Court	9 B2
Bealing Grove	9 B2	Beech Park Road	59 B2	Belarmine Square	58 D4	Belgree Drive	9 B2
Bealing Mews	9 B2	Beech Road	64 E3	Belarmine Vale	58 D4	Belgree Green	9 B2
Bealing View	9 B2	Beech Road (Bray)	67 B1	Belarmine Way	58 D4	Belgree Grove	9 B2
Bealing Walk	9 B2	Beech Road (Fox & Geese)	45 A1	Belcamp Avenue	13 B4	Belgree Heights	9 B2
Bealing Wood	9 B3	Beech Row (Nangor Road)	44 D1 [3]	Belcamp Crescent	13 B4	Belgree Lawns	9 B2
Bearna Park	58 D3	Beech Row (Newlands Road)	35 A4	Belcamp Gardens	13 B4	Belgree Rise	9 B2
Beatty Grove	32 D2	Beech Walk	56 E2 [4]	Belcamp Green	13 B4	Belgree Square	9 B2
Beatty Park	32 D3	Beechbrook Grove	14 D4 [4]	Belcamp Grove	13 B4	Belgree Walk	9 B2
Beatty's Avenue	76 F3	Beechcourt	60 D3	Belcamp Lane	13 C4	Belgree Woods	9 B2
Beaucourt	25 B3 [4]	Beechdale	7 B3	Belcamp Park	13 A3	Belgrove Lawn	36 D2
Beaufield	17 C4	Beechdale Avenue	55 B3	Belclare Avenue	11 C4	Belgrove Park (Chapelizod)	36 D2
Beaufield Ave	17 C4	Beechdale Close	55 B3 [6]	Belclare Crescent	11 C4	Belgrove Park (Vernon Avenue)	26 F4
Beaufield Close	17 C4	Beechdale Court	55 B3	Belclare Drive	11 C4	Belgrove Road	26 F4
Beaufield Crescent	17 C4	Beechdale Crescent	55 B3	Belclare Green	11 C4	*Bella Avenue (off Bella St)	72 D2
Beaufield Drive	17 C4	Beechdale Lawn	55 B3	Belclare Grove	11 C4	Bella Place (off Bella St)	72 D2
Beaufield Gardens	17 C4	Beechdale Mews	47 B1 [19]	Belclare Lawns	11 C4	Bella Street	71 C2
Beaufield Green	17 C4	Beechdale Park	55 B3	Belclare Park	11 C4	Belleview Maltings	69 B4
Beaufield Grove	17 C4	Beechdale Place	55 C3	Belclare Terrace	11 C4	Belleville	23 C4
Beaufield Lawn	17 C4	Beechdale Road	55 C3	Belclare View	11 C4	Belleville Avenue	47 A2
Beaufield Manor	48 E4	Beechdale Way	55 B3	Belclare Way	11 C4	Bellevue	74 E1
Beaufield Mews	48 E4 [2]	Beeches Park	60 E1	Belfield Close	47 C3 [8]	Bellevue Ave (Merrion)	48 E2
Beaufield Park	48 E4	Beeches Road	58 D1	Belfield Court	48 D2	Bellevue Avenue (Dalkey)	60 E2
Beaufort	60 E1 [19]	Beechfield	8 D4	Belfield Downs	47 C4	Bellevue Copse	48 E2
Beaufort Court	46 F4 [10]	Beechfield Avenue (Clonee)	8 D4	Belfield Park Apts.	48 E3	Bellevue Cottages	24 F3 [4]
Beaufort Downs	46 F4	Beechfield Avenue	45 C2	Belfry Avenue	53 C2	Bellevue Court	48 E2 [2]
Beaufort Villas	46 F4 [3]	(Walkinstown)		Belfry Close	53 C2	Bellevue Park	48 E2
Beaumont	26 D1	Beechfield Close (Clonee)	8 D4	Belfry Court	53 C2	Bellevue Park Avenue	48 E2
Beaumont Avenue	47 B4	Beechfield Close (Walkinstown)	46 D2	Belfry Crescent	53 C2	Bellevue Road	60 D2
Beaumont Close	47 B4 [3]	Beechfield Court	8 D4	Belfry Dale	53 C2	Bellman's Walk	72 E3
Beaumont Cottages	34 D2	Beechfield Drive	8 D4	Belfry Downs	53 C2	Bell's Lane	1 C2
Beaumont Court	25 C1 [2]	Beechfield Green	8 D4	Belfry Drive	53 C2	Bell's Lane	75 C2
Beaumont Crescent	26 D2	Beechfield Haven	64 E2 [3]	Belfry Gardens	53 C2	Belmont (Irishtown)	67 C4
Beaumont Drive	47 B4	Beechfield Heights	8 D4	Belfry Green	53 C2	Belmont (Stillorgan)	59 A1
Beaumont Gardens	48 F4	Beechfield Lawn	8 E4	Belfry Hall	53 C2	Belmont Avenue	47 C1
Beaumont Grove	25 C2	Beechfield Manor	64 E2	Belfry Lawn	53 C2	*Belmont Court	47 C1
Beaumont Hall	25 C2 [7]	Beechfield Meadows	8 E4	Belfry Lodge	53 C2	(off Belmont Ave)	
Beaumont House	46 F2 [25]	Beechfield Mews	46 D2 [4]	Belfry Manor	53 C2	Belmont Gardens	47 C1
Beaumont Road	25 C2	Beechfield Place	8 E4	Belfry Meadows	53 C2	Belmont Green	58 F1
Beaumont Wood	25 C1 [3]	Beechfield Rise	8 E4	Belfry Park	53 C2	Belmont Grove	58 F1
Beaumont Wood	25 C2	Beechfield Road (Clonee)	8 D4	Belfry Place	53 C2	Belmont Lawn	58 F1
Beaupark Downs	49 B4 [15]	Beechfield Road (Walkinstown)	45 C2	Belfry Rise	53 C2	Belmont Park (Donnybrook)	47 C1 [3]
Beaupark Avenue	14 D4	Beechfield View	8 E4	Belfry Road	53 C2	Belmont Park (Raheny)	27 A2
Beaupark Close	14 D4	Beechfield Way	8 E4	Belfry Square	53 C2	Belmont Place	71 C2
Beaupark Cresc	14 D4	Beechlawn	48 F3	Belfry Terrace	53 C2	(off Gardiner St Middle)	
Beaupark Mews	14 D4	Beechlawn Avenue (Ballinteer)	57 B1	Belfry Walk	53 C2	Belmont Square	27 A2
Beaupark Place	14 D4	Beechlawn Avenue (Coolock)	26 E1	Belfry Way	53 C2	*Belmont Terrace	58 F1
Beaupark Road	14 D4	Beechlawn Close	26 E1	Belgard Close	44 F3 [2]	(off Stillorgan Road)	

Street Name	Page/Grid Reference
Belmont Villas	47 C1
Belmount Court	25 C4 [18]
Belton Park Avenue	26 D3
Belton Park Gardens	26 D3
Belton Park Road	26 D3
Belton Park Villas	26 D3
Belton Terrace	67 C2 [44]
Belvedere Court	71 B2
Belvedere Square	71 B1
Belvidere Avenue	71 C1
Belvidere Court	71 B1
Belvidere Place	71 C1
Belvidere Road	71 B1
Ben Edar Road	70 D2
Ben Inagh Park	49 A3 [3]
Ben Of Howth	30 D3
Benbulbin Avenue	73 B3
Benbulbin Road	73 B3
Benburb Street	70 E3
Beneavin Court	24 F2
Beneavin Drive	24 F2
Beneavin Park	24 F1
Beneavin Road	24 F2
Bengal Terrace	24 F4 [4]
Benmadigan Road	73 A3
Benson Street	72 F4
Bentley Avenue	67 C4 [3]
Bentley Park	67 C4
Bentley Road	67 C4
Bentley Villas	49 C4 [17]
Beresford	25 B3
Beresford Avenue	25 B3
Beresford Green	25 B3
Beresford Lane	71 C3
Beresford Lawn	25 B3
Beresford Place	71 C3
Beresford Street	71 A3
Berkeley Avenue	71 A1
Berkeley Place	71 A1
Berkeley Road	71 A1
Berkeley Street	71 A1
Berkeley Terrace	76 F2
Bernard Curtis Court	36 F4
Bernard Curtis House	36 F4 [2]
Berryfield	34 D3
Berryfield Crescent	24 D2
Berryfield Drive	24 D2
Berryfield Lane	67 A3
Berryfield Lane	67 A3
Berryfield Road	24 D2
Berrys Court	73 A2
Bertram Court	74 E2
Berwick Avenue	1 B2
Berwick Court	1 B1
Berwick Crescent	1 B1
Berwick Drive	1 B1
Berwick Grove	1 B1
Berwick Hall	47 A4
Berwick Lawn	1 B1
Berwick Place	1 B1
Berwick Rise	1 B1
Berwick View	1 B1
Berwick Walk	1 B2
Berwick Way	1 B1
Berystede	75 C4
Bessborough Avenue	72 E1
Bessborough Court	75 B4
Bessborough Parade	75 B4
Besser Drive	35 B4
Bethany House	39 B4 [4]
Bethesda Place	71 B2
Bettyglen	27 B2
Bettysford	44 E1 [3]
Bettystown Avenue	26 F3
Beverly Avenue	56 D1
Beverly Court	26 F4
Beverly Crescent	55 C2
Beverly Downs	55 C2
Beverly Drive	56 D2
Beverly Green	55 C2
Beverly Grove	56 D1
Beverly Heights	56 D2
Beverly Lawns	56 D2
Beverly Park	55 C1
Beverly Rise	55 C2
Bewley	34 E2
Bewley Avenue	34 E2
Bewley Drive	34 E2
Bewley Grove	34 E2
Bewley Lawn	34 E2
Bianconi Ave	53 B1
Big Lane	32 D3
Bigger Road	45 C2
Bill Shelly Park	23 C2
Binn Eadair	29 A1
Binn Eadair Court	29 A1
Binn Eadair Crescent	29 A1
Binn Eadair View	29 A1
Birch Avenue	58 D2
Birch Dale (Foxrock)	59 A2 [9]
Birch Dale (Kill O'The Grange)	59 C1 [12]
Birch Grove	59 C1
Birchdale Close	2 E3
Birchdale Drive	2 E3
Birchdale Park	2 E3
Birchdale Road	2 E3
Birches Road	58 D1
Birchfield Avenue	47 C4
Birchfield Court	47 C4
Birchfield Heights	47 C4
Birchfield Lawn	47 C4
Birchfield Park	47 C4
Birch's Lane	47 C4
Birchview Avenue	45 A4
Birchview Close	45 A4
Birchview Court	45 A4
Birchview Drive	45 A4
Birchview Heights	45 A4
Birchview Lawn	45 A4
Birchview Rise	45 A4
Birchwood Close	44 E4
Birchwood Drive	54 E1
Birchwood Heights	54 E1
Bird Avenue	47 C3
Biscayne	3 C3
Bishop Street	75 A2
Bishops Lane	62 F2
Bishop's Orchard	9 B2
Bishop's Orchard Boulevard	9 B2
Bishop's Orchard House Apts.	9 B2
Bishop's Square	75 A2
Bissett's Loft Apts.	3 B2
Bissett's Strand	3 B2
Black Street	69 C3
Blackberry Lane (Portmarnock)	15 A1
Blackberry Lane (Rathmines)	75 B4
Blackberry Rise	15 A1
Blackburn Square	46 F4 [15]
Blackcourt Road	22 E1
Blackditch Drive	35 C3
Blackditch Road	35 C3
Blackditch Road	36 D3
Blackglen Court	58 D3
Blackglen Road	57 C3
Blackhall Court	70 E3
Blackhall Green	70 E3
Blackhall Little	5 B1
Blackhall Parade	70 F3
(Blackhall Street)	
Blackhall Place	70 E4
Blackhall Place Apts.	70 E3
Blackhall Street	70 F4
Blackhall View	70 E3
Blackhall Walk	70 F4
Blackheath Avenue	26 F4
Blackheath Court	26 F4
Blackheath Drive	26 E4
Blackheath Gardens	26 E4
Blackheath Grove	26 E4
Blackheath Park	26 E4
Blackhorse Avenue	23 C4
Blackhorse Avenue	69 C2
Blackhorse Grove	70 D2
Blackpitts	74 F2
Blackrock	49 A3
Blackthorn Avenue	58 E2
Blackthorn Close (Portmarnock)	4 D4
Blackthorn Close (Sandyford)	58 D2 [7]
Blackthorn Court	58 D2 [4]
Blackthorn Drive	58 D2
Blackthorn Green	58 D2 [6]
Blackthorn Grove	58 D2 [3]
Blackthorn Hall	57 C3
Blackthorn Hill Avenue	52 E2
Blackthorn Hill Close	52 E2
Blackthorn Hill Crescent	52 E2
Blackthorn Hill Drive	52 E2
Blackthorn Hill View	52 E2
Blackthorn Road	58 D2
Blackwater Road	24 E3
Blackwood Close	21 A1
Blackwood Crescent	21 A1
Blackwood Drive	21 A1
Blackwood Lane	3 C4
Blackwood Lawn	21 A1
Blackwood Mews	21 A1
Blackwood Park	21 A1
Blackwood Place	21 A1
Blackwoods	3 B4
Blakeney House	2 E2
Blakeney House (Mews)	30 E3
Blake's Court	22 D1 [7]
Blakes Villas	70 F2
(on Grangegorman Lower)	
Blakesfield	21 C1
Blakestown Cottages	22 D1
Blakestown Drive	22 D1
Blakestown Road	9 A4
Blakestown Road	22 D1
Blakestown Way	22 D1
Blanchardstown	22 F2
Blanchardstown ByPass	22 F2
Blanchardstown Interchange	23 A2
Blanchardstown Road North	9 B4
Blanchardstown Road South	22 D2
Blanchardstown Roundabout	22 F2
Blarney Park	46 E1
Blasket Square	22 F1
Blessington Court	71 A2
Blessington Lane	71 A2
Blessington Place	71 A2
(off St Joseph's Parade)	
Blessington Road	53 C2
Blessington Street	71 A2
Blizzard Apts.	2 F3 [1]
Blood Stoney Road	72 F4
Bloom Court	74 F3
Bloomfield Avenue	76 D4
(Donnybrook)	
Bloomfield Avenue (Portobello)	75 A3
Bloomfield Cottages	75 A3
Bloomfield Park (Ballsbridge)	76 E4
Bloomfield Park (Rathmines)	75 A3
Bluebell	36 E4
Bluebell Avenue	36 E4
Bluebell Road	36 E4
Blundelstown	42 E3
Blunden Drive	13 C4
Blythe Avenue	72 E3
Boardman's Lane	74 D2
(off Cork Street)	
Boden Dale	56 F1
Boden Heath	56 E1
Boden Heath Apts.	56 E1
Boden Mill	56 E2
Boden Park	56 E1
Boden Wood	46 F4
Boeing Road	12 F4
Boghall Road	67 B4
Boghall Road (off Vevay road)	67 C4
Bohammer	13 C2
Boherboy	53 B2
Boherboy Road	53 B2
Bohernabreena Road	55 A3
Bolbrook Avenue	55 B1 [3]
Bolbrook Close	55 B1 [4]
Bolbrook Drive	55 B1 [1]
Bolbrook Grove	55 B1
Bolbrook Park	55 B1
Bolbrook Villas	55 B1
Bolton Green	1 A2
Bolton Street	71 A3
Bond Drive	39 A1
Bond Road	39 A1
Bond Street	74 E1
Bonham Street	70 E4
Boolavogue Road	72 F2
Boot Road	44 D2
Booterstown	48 E2
Booterstown Avenue	48 F3
*Booterstown Grove	48 F2
(off Booterstown Avenue)	
Booterstown Park	48 F3
Boranaraltry	61 B4
Boranaraltry Bridge	61 B4
Boranaraltry Lane	61 C4
Boroimhe Alder	1 C3
Boroimhe Ash	1 C3
Boroimhe Aspen	1 C3
Boroimhe Beech	1 C3
Boroimhe Birches	1 C3
Boroimhe Blackthorn	1 C3
Boroimhe Cedars	1 C3
Boroimhe Cherry	1 C3
Boroimhe Elms	1 C3
Boroimhe Hawthorns	1 C3
Boroimhe Hazel	1 C3
Boroimhe Laurels	1 C3
Boroimhe Maples	1 C3
Boroimhe Oaks	1 C3
Boroimhe Pines	1 C3
Boroimhe Poplars	1 C3
Boroimhe Rowan	1 B3
Boroimhe Willows	1 C3
Botanic Avenue	25 A4
Botanic Hall	24 F3
Botanic Hall	24 F3 [7]
Botanic Mews	25 A4 [18]
Botanic Park	25 A4 [14]
Botanic Road	25 A4
Botanic Square	25 A4 [17]
Botanic Villas	25 A4 [10]
Bottle Works	39 A3
Boundary Road	39 A1
Bow Bridge	74 D1
Bow Bridge Court (Bow Bridge)	74 D1
*Bow Bridge Place	74 D1
Bow Lane East	75 B1
Bow Lane West	74 D1
Bow Street	70 F4
Bowbridge House	74 D1
(Mount Brown)	
Boyne Court	74 F4
Boyne Lane	76 D1
Boyne Road	24 E3
Boyne Street	76 D1
Brabazon Cottages	67 C2 [16]
Brabazon House	74 E2
Brabazon Place	74 F2
Brabazon Row	74 F2
Brabazon Square	74 F1
Brabazon Street	74 F2
Bracken Drive	4 D4
Bracken Hill	57 C3
Bracken Road	58 D2
Brackenbush Park	60 D4
Brackenbush Road	60 D4
Bracken's Lane	71 C4
Brackenstown Avenue	1 C2
Brackenstown Road	1 C2
Braeburn Terrace	1 Inset
Braemor Avenue	47 A3
Braemor Drive	47 A3
Braemor Grove	47 A3
Braemor Park	47 A3
Braemor Road	47 A3
Braithwaite Street	74 E1
Bramblefield	8 F4
Bramblefield Court	8 F4
Bramblefield Crescent	8 F4
Bramblefield Drive	8 F4
Bramblefield Park	8 F4
Bramblefield View	8 F4
Bramblefield Walk	8 F4
Bramley Avenue	22 E3
Bramley Court	22 E3
Bramley Crescent	22 E3
Bramley Garth	22 E3
Bramley Green	22 E3
Bramley Grove	22 E3
Bramley Heath	22 E3
Bramley Park	22 E3
Bramley Road	22 E3

STREET NAME	PAGE/GRID REFERENCE		STREET NAME	PAGE/GRID REFERENCE		STREET NAME	PAGE/GRID REFERENCE		STREET NAME	PAGE/GRID REFERENCE	
Bramley View	22	E3	Brighton Terrace	60	E1 [13]	Brooklawn (Clontarf)	26	D4	Bunratty Drive	26	E1
Bramley Walk	22	E3	(Dun Laoghaire)			Brooklawn (Lucan)	34	D3	Bunratty Road	26	E1
Bramley Way	22	E3	Brighton Terrace (Monkstown)	49	B4 [9]	Brooklawn Avenue	49	B4 [12]	Bunting Road	45	C1
Brandon Road	36	F4	Brighton Vale	49	B3	Brooklawn Wood	49	B4 [13]	Burdett Avenue	60	E1
Brandon Road	45	C1	Britain Place	71	B2	Brookmount Avenue	55	C1	Burg an Rí Glen	34	F3
*Brandon Terrace	74	D2	Britain Quay	72	F4	Brookmount Court	46	E4 [2]	Burg an Rí Terrace	34	F3
Bray	68	D1	Broadfield Avenue	52	E2	Brookmount Lawns	55	C1 [1]	Burgage	13	C3
Bray Commons	67	B2	Broadfield Close	52	E2	Brookpark	34	D3	Burgess Lane	70	F4
Bray Head Terrace	67	C3 [20]	Broadfield Court	52	E2	Brookstone Lane	15	A4 [6]	Burgh Quay	71	C4
Bray Road	59	B2	Broadfield Heath	52	E2	Brookstone Road	15	A4	Burke Place	74	D1
Bray Road	59	C4	Broadfield Manor	52	E2	Brookvale	34	D1 [8]	Burke Place (off Mount Brown)	74	D1
Bray Southern Cross Road	67	B4	Broadfield Meadows	52	E2	Brookvale Downs	46	F3	Burleigh Court	76	D3
Breakwater Road North	39	B2	Broadfield Park	52	E2	Brookvale Road (Donnybrook)	47	C1 [8]	Burleigh Mews	76	D3
Breakwater Road South	39	B2	Broadford Avenue	57	B2	Brookvale Road (Rathfarnham)	46	F3	Burlington Gardens	76	D3
Breffini Terrace	60	E1	Broadford Close	57	B2	Brookview Avenue	54	D1	Burlington Mews	76	D3
Breffni Gardens	15	A4 [5]	Broadford Crescent	57	B2	Brookview Close	54	D1	Burlington Road	76	D3
Breffni Road	60	E1	Broadford Drive	57	B2	Brookview Court	54	D1	Burmah Close	60	F2 [22]
Bregia Road	24	F4	Broadford Hill	57	B2	Brookview Crescent	54	D1	Burnell Park Avenue	22	E4
Brehon Field Road	57	B2	Broadford Lawn	57	B2	Brookview Drive	54	D1	Burnell Park Green	22	E4
Brehon's Chair	57	A3	Broadford Park	57	B2	Brookview Gardens	54	D1	Burnell Square	14	D4
Bremen Avenue	39	A3	Broadford Rise	57	B2	Brookview Green	54	D1	Burnside	25	B1
Bremen Grove	39	A3	Broadford Road	57	B2	Brookview Grove	54	D1	Burren Court	11	C4
Bremen Road	39	A3	Broadford Walk	57	B2	Brookview Lawns	54	D1	Burris Court (off High Street)	75	A1
Brendan Behan Court	71	C1	Broadmeadow	1	C1	Brookview Park	54	D1	Burrow Court (Poppintree)	11	C4
Brendan Road	47	C1	Broadmeadow Mews	3	B2 [7]	Brookview Rise	54	D1	Burrow Court (Portmarnock)	15	A1
Brennans Parade	68	D2 [14]	Broadstone	70	F2	Brookview Terrace	54	D1	Burrow Road (Stepaside)	58	D4
Brennans Terrace	68	D2 [4]	Broadstone Avenue	71	A2	Brookview Way	54	D1	Burrow Road (Stepaside)	62	D1
Brennanstown Avenue	59	C4	(off Royal Canal Bank)			Brookville	24	D1	Burrow Road (Sutton)	29	B1
Brennanstown Road	59	B4	*Broadstone Place	71	A2	Brookville Crescent	26	E1 [2]	Burrowfield Road	28	D1
Brennanstown Square	59	C4	(off Royal Canal Bank)			Brookville Park (Artane)	26	E2	Burton Court	58	E2
Brennanstown Vale	59	B4	Broadway Drive	22	E2	Brookville Park (Coolock)	26	E1	Burton Hall Avenue	58	E2
Brewery Road	58	F2	Broadway Grove	22	E2	Brookville Park (Dean's Grange)	59	B1	Burton Hall Road	58	E2
Brian Avenue	25	C4	Broadway Park	22	E2	Brookwood	56	E2	Burton Road	60	F2
Brian Boru Avenue	39	C1	Broadway Road	22	E2	Brookwood Abbey	26	E2 [4]	Bushfield Avenue	47	B1 [8]
Brian Boru Street	39	C1	Brockey	61	C4	Brookwood Avenue	26	E2	Bushfield Drive	44	D2
Brian Road	25	C4	Brockey	65	A1	Brookwood Crescent	26	F2	Bushfield Green	44	D2
Brian Terrace	25	C4	Brockey Lane	65	A1	Brookwood Drive	26	E2	Bushfield Grove	44	D3
Briansboro Terrace	74	F3	Brodin Row	70	D3	Brookwood Glen	26	F3	Bushfield Lawns	44	D2
Briar Walk	4	D4	Brompton Court	22	E3	Brookwood Grove	26	E2	Bushfield Place	47	B1 [17]
Briar Wood	68	D3	Brompton Green	22	E2	Brookwood Hall	26	E3	Bushfield Square	25	C4 [15]
Briarfield Grove	27	B1	Brompton Grove	22	E3	Brookwood Heights	26	F2	Bushfield Terrace	47	B1
Briarfield Road	27	B2	Brompton Lawn	22	E2	Brookwood Lawn	26	F2	Bushy Park Gardens	46	F3
Briarfield Villas	27	B1 [5]	Brook Court	49	B4	Brookwood Meadow	26	E2	Bushy Park House	46	E3
Briarly Court	47	B4 [4]	Brook House	25	B4 [14]	Brookwood Park	26	E3	Bushy Park Road	46	F3
Briarsfield Walk	27	B1 [4]	Brook Wood	67	B2	Brookwood Rise	26	F3	Bustyhill	51	B3
Briarwood Avenue	22	D1	Brookdale	55	A2	Brookwood Road	26	E2	Butlerstown	5	C3
Briarwood Close	9	A4	Brookdale Avenue	1	B3	Broombridge Road	24	E4	Butt Bridge	71	C4
Briarwood Gardens	22	D1	Brookdale Close	1	B2	Broomfield	21	B4	Buttercup Close	13	C4
Briarwood Green	22	D1	Brookdale Court	1	B3	Broomfield (Malahide)	3	B4	Buttercup Drive	13	C4
Briarwood Lawn	22	D1	Brookdale Drive	1	B2	Broomfield Court	64	D2	Buttercup Park	13	C4
Briarwood Park	22	D1 [1]	Brookdale Green	1	B2	Broomfield Mews	3	B4	Buttercup Square	13	C4
Briarwood Road	22	D1 [3]	Brookdale Grove	1	B2	Broomhill Close	45	A4	Buttercup Terrace	13	C4
Brickfield	67	B3	Brookdale Lawns	1	B2	Broomhill Drive	45	A4	Butterfield Avenue	46	E4
Brickfield Drive	73	C3	Brookdale Park	1	B2	Broomhill Road	45	A4	Butterfield Close	46	E4
Brickfield Lane	74	E2	Brookdale Road	1	B2	Broomhill Terrace	45	A4	Butterfield Court	46	E4
Brickfield Lane	67	B3 [8]	Brookdale Walk	1	B2	(Off Broomhill Road)			Butterfield Crescent	46	E4
Bride Close	75	A1	Brookdale Way	1	B2	Brown Street North	70	F3	Butterfield Drive	46	E4
Bride Road	75	A1	Brookdene	64	E2	Brown Street South	74	E2	Butterfield Grove	46	E4
Bride Street	75	A1	Brookfield (Blackrock)	48	F3	Brownrath	5	B1	Butterfield Meadow	46	E4 [1]
Brides Glen	63	C2	Brookfield (Coolock)	26	F2	Brownsbarn	43	C4	Butterfield Orchard	46	E4
Bride's Glen Avenue	1	Inset	Brookfield (Donnybrook)	47	C1 [19]	Brownsbarn Court	43	C4	Butterfield Park	46	E4
Brides Glen Park	1	C1	Brookfield (Lucan)	34	D3	Brownsbarn Garden	43	C4	*Byrne's Cottages (Francis Street)	74	E2
Bride's Glen Park	1	Inset	Brookfield (Milltown)	47	B2	Brownsbarn Orchard	43	C4	Byrne's Lane (Jervis St)	71	B4
Bridge Street (Ringsend)	39	A3	Brookfield Avenue (Blackrock)	49	A4	Brownstown	42	D1	Byrnes Lane (Pearse Sq West)	72	E4
Bridge Street (Swords)	2	D2	Brookfield Avenue (Bray)	68	D3 [4]	Brownstown (Kilcloon)	5	A2	Byrne's Terrace	47	C2 [12]
Bridge Street Lower	70	F4	Brookfield Avenue (Maynooth)	17	C4	Bruce's Terrace	67	B2 [29]			
*Bridge Street Upper	74	F1	Brookfield Court (Blackrock)	49	A4 [12]	Brug Chroimlinn	46	D1 [6]			
Bridgefoot Street	70	F4	Brookfield Court (Kimmage)	46	E2 [6]	Brunswick Place	76	E1	C		
Bridgeview	35	B3	Brookfield Court (Tallaght)	54	D1 [1]	Brunswick Street North	70	F3			
Bridgewater Quay	69	B4	Brookfield Estate	46	E2	Brunswick Villas (Pearse Street)	71	C4	Cabinteely	59	C4
Bridon	62	F1	Brookfield Green	46	E2 [5]	Brusna Cottages	49	A3 [12]	Cabinteely Avenue	59	C3
Brighton Avenue (Carrickmines)	59	A4	Brookfield Grove	49	A4 [11]	Buckingham St Lower	72	D2	Cabinteely Bypass	59	C3
Brighton Avenue (Clontarf)	26	D4 [1]	Brookfield Park	17	C4	Buckingham St Upper	72	D2	Cabinteely Close	59	C3
Brighton Avenue (Monkstown)	49	B4	Brookfield Place	49	A4	Buckingham Village	71	C2	Cabinteely Court	59	C3 [2]
Brighton Avenue (Rathgar)	46	F2	Brookfield Road (Kilmainham)	73	C1	Buckleys Lane	33	A1	Cabinteely Crescent	59	C3
Brighton Cottages	59	A3 [1]	Brookfield Road (Tallaght)	54	D1	Bulfin Court	73	A2	Cabinteely Drive	59	C3
Brighton Court	59	A4	Brookfield Street	73	C2	Bulfin Gardens	73	B1	Cabinteely Green	59	C3
Brighton Gardens	46	F2	Brookfield Terrace	49	A4	Bulfin Road	73	A2	Cabinteely Park	59	C3 [3]
Brighton Green	46	F2 [13]	Brookhaven Drive	22	E1	Bull Alley Street	75	A1	Cabinteely Way	59	C3
Brighton Hall	59	A4	Brookhaven Grove	22	E1	Bull Lane (Off Main Street)	67	C2 [59]	Cabra	24	E4
Brighton Lane	49	B4 [22]	Brookhaven Lawn	22	E1	Bull Wall	40	D1	Cabra Drive	70	D1
Brighton Lodge	59	A3 [4]	Brookhaven Park	22	E1	Bull Wall Cottages	40	D1	Cabra Grove	70	D1
Brighton Place	59	A4	Brookhaven Rise	22	E1	Bullock Steps	60	F1 [8]	Cabra Park	24	F4
Brighton Road (Foxrock)	59	A3	Brooklands	48	E1	Bunbury Gate Avenue	1	Inset	Cabra Road	70	D1
Brighton Road (Terenure)	46	F2	Brooklawn	35	B1	Bunbury Gate Crescent	1	Inset	Caddell	14	F2
Brighton Square	46	F2	Brooklawn (Blackrock)	48	F3	Bunratty Avenue	26	E1	Cadogan Road	25	C4
									Cairn Brook	63	A1

STREET NAME	PAGE	GRID
Cairn Brook Hall	63	A1
Cairn Brook Manor	63	A1
Cairn Brook View	63	A1
Cairn Brook Way	63	A1
Cairn Court	12	D4
Cairn Hill	59	B2
Cairnfort	62	E1
Cairnwood Avenue	44	E4
Cairnwood Court	44	E4
Cairnwood Green	44	E4
Calderwood Avenue	25	C3
Calderwood Grove	25	C3 [3]
Calderwood Road	25	C3
Caledon Court	72	F2
Caledon Road	72	F2
Callaghan Bridge	21	C2
Callary Road	48	D3
Calmount Avenue	45	B2
Calmount Park	45	B2
Calmount Road	45	B2
Camac Close	73	A1
Camac Court	73	A1
Camac Park	36	E4
Camaderry Road	68	D3
Camberley Elms	47	B4 [20]
Camberley Oaks	47	B4 [19]
Cambridge Avenue	39	A3 [7]
Cambridge Court	39	A3 [24]
Cambridge Park	39	A3
Cambridge Road (Rathmines)	47	A1
Cambridge Road (Ringsend)	39	A3
*Cambridge Square (off Thorncastle St.)	39	A3
Cambridge Street	39	A3 [1]
Cambridge Terrace (Dun Laoghaire)	49	C4 [24]
Cambridge Terrace (Ranelagh)	75	C4
Cambridge Villas	47	A1 [16]
Camden Avenue	23	C3
Camden Buildings	75	B2
Camden Court	75	B3
Camden Lock	76	F1
Camden Market	75	B3
Camden Place	75	B2
Camden Row	75	A2
Camden Street Lower	75	B2
Camden Street Upper	75	B3
Camden Villas	75	B2
Cameron Square	73	C1
Cameron Street	74	E2
Cammock Apts.	73	C1
Camogie Road	69	A3
Campbell Court	30	D2 [16]
Campbell's Court	71	A3
Campbell's Lane (off Belvidere Ave)	71	C1
Campbell's Row (off Portland Street N)	71	C1
Campfield Terrace	57	C1
Campshire Hall	72	D4
Campshire Mews	72	D4
Canal Road	75	B4
Canal Terrace	36	E4
Canal Turn	35	B4
Cannon Mews	39	A4 [29]
Cannon Mews East	76	F2
Cannon Mews West	76	F2
Cannon Place	39	A4 [30]
Cannon Rock Estate	30	E2
Cannon Rock View	30	E2 [1]
Cannonbrook	34	D2
Cannonbrook Avenue	34	D2
Cannonbrook Court	34	D2
Cannonbrook Lawn	34	D2
Cannonbrook Park	34	D2
Canon Lillis Avenue	72	E2
Canon Mooney Gardens	39	A3 [15]
Capel Street	71	A3
Cappagh Avenue	24	D1
Cappagh Drive	24	D2
Cappagh Green	24	D1
Cappagh Road	10	E4
Cappagh Road	24	D1
Cappaghmore Estate	35	A4
Cappoge	10	F4
Cappoge Cottages	10	E4
Captain's Avenue	46	D1
Captain's Drive	46	D2
Captain's Hill	20	D4
Captain's Road	46	D2
Cara Park	13	B3
Caragh Court	25	C4 [12]
Caragh Road	69	C1
Carberry Road	25	C3
Carbury Place	49	A3 [20]
Carbury Terrace	72	F3
Cardiff Castle Road	24	D2
Cardiff Lane	72	E4
Cardiffs Bridge	24	D3
Cardiffsbridge Avenue	24	D2
Cardiffsbridge Grove	24	D1 [1]
Cardiffsbridge Road	24	D2
Card's Lane (Pearse St)	71	C4
Carleton Road	25	C4
Carlingford Court	76	E1
Carlingford Parade	76	E1
Carlingford Road	25	A4
Carlisle Avenue	47	B1
Carlisle Court	46	F2 [23]
Carlisle Street	75	A3
Carlisle Terrace (Dún Laoghaire)	60	D1 [17]
Carlisle Terrace (Malahide)	3	B3
*Carlisle Terrace (Off N C Rd)	70	F1
*Carlisle Terrace (On Seymour Road)	67	C2
*Carlisle Terrace (on Tivoli Road)	60	D1
Carlton Court (Clontarf)	26	D4
Carlton Court (Swords)	2	D2
Carlton Terrace	67	C2 [41]
Carlton Villas (Ballsbridge)	76	F3
Carlton Villas (Clontarf)	67	C2 [42]
Carmanhall Court	58	E2
Carmanhall Road	58	E2
Carman's Hall	74	F1
Carna Road	35	C3
Carndonagh Drive	27	B1
Carndonagh Lawn	27	B1
Carndonagh Park	27	B1
Carndonagh Road	27	B1
Carne Court	8	F4
Carnegie Court	2	D1
Carnew Street	70	D2
Carnlough Road	24	E4
Caroline Court	76	E3
Caroline Row	39	A3 [16]
Caroline Row	39	A3 [35]
Carpenterstown	22	D3
Carpenterstown Avenue	22	E3
Carpenterstown Manor	22	E3
Carpenterstown Park East	22	E3
Carpenterstown Road	22	E4
Carraig Close	11	C4
Carraig Glen	59	C4
Carraig Grennane	60	E4
Carraroe Avenue	27	A1
Carrick Court	14	F1
Carrick Lawn	58	D1 [2]
Carrick Terrace	74	D2
Carrickaspinkeen	65	A3
Carrickbrack Heath	29	B2
Carrickbrack Hill	29	B2
Carrickbrack Lawn	29	B2
Carrickbrack Park	29	B2
Carrickbrack Road	29	B2
Carrickbrack Road	30	D4
Carrickbrennan Lawn	49	C4
Carrickbrennan Road	49	C4
Carrickfoyle Terrace	73	B1
Carrickhill Close	4	D4
Carrickhill Drive	15	A1
Carrickhill Heights	15	A1
Carrickhill Rise	4	D4
Carrickhill Road	15	A1
Carrickhill Road Middle	15	A1
Carrickhill Road Upper	3	C4
Carrickhill Walk	4	D4
Carrickmines	59	B4
Carrickmines Avenue	59	B4
Carrickmines Chase	59	B4
Carrickmines Dale	59	B4
Carrickmines Garth	59	B4
Carrickmines Green	63	A1
Carrickmines Little	59	A4
Carrickmines Manor	63	A1
Carrickmines Oaks	59	B4
Carrickmount Avenue	57	B1
Carrickmount Drive	57	A1
Carrig Road	11	C4
Carrigallen Drive	24	E3
Carrigallen Park	24	E3
Carrigallen Road	24	E3
Carrigeen	52	D3
Carriglea	55	B2
Carriglea Avenue (Kill O'The Grange)	59	C2
Carriglea Avenue (Tallaght)	55	B2
Carriglea Court (Kill O'The Grange)	59	C1 [14]
Carriglea Court (Tallaght)	55	B2
Carriglea Downs (Kill O'The Grange)	59	C2
Carriglea Downs (Tallaght)	55	B2
Carriglea Drive	55	B2
Carriglea Gardens	59	C1
Carriglea Grove	55	B2
Carriglea Rise	55	B2
Carriglea View	55	B2
Carriglea Walk	55	B2
Carrigmore Avenue	53	B2
Carrigmore Close (Oldbawn)	54	F3
Carrigmore Close (Saggart)	53	B2
Carrigmore Court	53	C2
Carrigmore Crescent	53	C1
Carrigmore Dale	53	B2
Carrigmore Downs	53	B1
Carrigmore Drive	54	F2
Carrigmore Elms	53	B2
Carrigmore Gardens	53	B1
Carrigmore Glen	53	B1
Carrigmore Green	53	C2
Carrigmore Grove (Oldbawn)	54	F3
Carrigmore Grove (Saggart)	53	B2
Carrigmore Lawns	53	B1
Carrigmore Manor	53	B2
Carrigmore Meadows	53	B2
Carrigmore Oak	53	B2
Carrigmore Park	54	F3
Carrigmore Place	53	B2
Carrigmore Road	54	F2
Carrigmore Terrace	53	B2
Carrigmore View	54	F3
Carrigmore Way	53	C2
Carrigwood	55	C2
Carrow Road	36	F4
Carton Avenue	18	D2
Carton Bridge	18	E3
Carton Court	17	C4
Carton Court	18	D4
Carton Demesne	18	F2
Carton Square	17	C2
Carton Square	17	C2
Carwell Court	2	E2
Carysfort Avenue	49	A4
Carysfort Downs	58	F1
Carysfort Downs	59	A1
Carysfort Drive	60	F1 [1]
Carysfort Grove	59	A1
Carysfort Hall	49	A4
Carysfort Park	49	A4
Carysfort Road	60	F1
Carysfort Woods	59	A1
Casana View	30	E2
Casement Close (off Barry Road)	24	D1 [2]
Casement Drive	24	D1
Casement Green	24	D1
Casement Grove	24	D1
Casement Park	24	D1
Casement Road	24	D1
Casement Road	24	D2
Casement Villas	59	B1
Cashel Avenue	46	E2
Cashel Road	46	D1
Casimir Avenue	46	F1
Casimir Court	46	F1 [17]
Casimir Road	46	F1
Casino Drive	3	B2
Casino Park	26	D3
Casino Road	25	C4
Cassian Court	24	D3 [2]
Castaheany	8	E4
Castilla Park	26	F4
Castle Avenue (Clondalkin)	44	E1
Castle Avenue (Clontarf)	26	E4
Castle Avenue (Swords)	2	D2
Castle Close (Clondalkin)	44	E1
Castle Close (Dalkey)	60	F1
Castle Court	58	E4
Castle Court (Booterstown)	48	F2
Castle Court (Clontarf)	26	D4
Castle Court (Dundrum)	57	C1 [4]
Castle Court (Loughlinstown)	64	E1
*Castle Court (off Cypress Lawn)	46	D4
Castle Court (Rathfarnham)	46	F4 [18]
Castle Court (Rathfarnham)	47	A4 [1]
Castle Court Apts.	3	B3 [1]
Castle Court Apts.	75	A1
Castle Cove (Dalkey)	60	F2 [32]
Castle Cove (Malahide)	3	A2
Castle Crescent	44	E1 [4]
Castle Dawson	17	B3
Castle Down Croft	2	F2
Castle Down Grove	2	F2
Castle Down Road	2	F2
Castle Drive	58	E4
Castle Drive (Clondalkin)	44	E1
Castle Drive (Swords)	2	D2
Castle Elms	26	E1
Castle Farm	64	E3
Castle Farm Wood	64	E3
Castle Gate Apartments.	75	A1
Castle Grove (Clondalkin)	44	E1
Castle Grove (Clontarf)	26	E4
Castle Grove (Swords)	2	D2
Castle Lawn	58	E4
Castle Lawns (Malahide)	2	F2
Castle Lawns (Tallaght)	45	B4
Castle Market (off Drury Street)	75	B1
Castle Oaks	3	A3 [1]
Castle Park (Clondalkin)	44	E1
Castle Park (Leixlip)	33	A1
Castle Park (Monkstown)	49	C4
Castle Park (Swords) (Swords)	2	D2
Castle Park (Tallaght)	45	B4
Castle Park Estate (Tallaght)	55	B1
*Castle Place (on Breffni Road)	60	F1
Castle Riada Avenue	34	E2
Castle Riada Crescent	34	E2
Castle Riada Drive	34	E3
Castle Riada Grove	34	E2
Castle Road (Clontarf)	26	E4
Castle Road (Lucan)	34	E2
Castle Rosse	14	F4
Castle Side	55	C1 [7]
Castle Steps (off Castle Street)	75	A1
Castle Street (Bray)	67	C2
Castle Street (Cork Hill)	75	A1
Castle Street (Dalkey)	60	F2
Castle Terrace (Malahide)	3	B2
*Castle Terrace (off Ulverton Road)	60	F1
Castle Terrace (Phibsborough Ave)	70	F1
Castle View (Carrickmines)	59	A4
Castle View (Clondalkin)	44	E1
Castle Village	31	C2
Castle Village Avenue	31	C2
Castle Village Close	31	C2
Castle Village Court	31	C2
Castle Village Crescent	31	C2
Castle Village Drive	31	C2
Castle Village Green	31	C2
Castle Village Lawns	31	C2
Castle Village Park	31	C2
Castle Village Place	31	C2
Castle Village Rise	31	C2
Castle Village Walk	31	C2
Castle Village Way	31	C2
Castle Village Woods	31	C2
Castle Villas	60	F2
Castlebridge	18	D3
Castlebrook	57	C1

STREET NAME	PAGE/GRID REFERENCE
Castlebyrne Park	49 A4
Castlecurragh Heath	9 A4
Castlecurragh Park	9 B4
Castlecurragh Vale	9 A4
Castledawson Avenue	48 F3
Castlefarm	1 C1
Castlefield Avenue	55 C1
Castlefield Court (Clonsilla)	21 C2
Castlefield Court (Firhouse)	55 C1
Castlefield Drive	55 C2
Castlefield Green	55 C2
Castlefield Grove	55 C2
Castlefield Lawn	55 C1
Castlefield Manor (Firhouse)	55 C1
Castlefield Manor (Malahide)	3 B3
Castlefield Orchard	55 C1
Castlefield Park ((Firhouse)	55 C2
Castlefield Park (Clonsilla)	21 C2
Castlefield Way	55 C2
Castlefield Woods	21 C2
Castleforbes Road	72 F3
Castleforbes Square	72 F3
Castlegate (Monkstown)	59 C1
Castlegate (Shankill)	64 D3
Castlegate Chase	33 C3
Castlegate Chase	33 C3
Castlegate Close	33 C3
Castlegate Close	33 C3
Castlegate Crescent	33 C3
Castlegate Crescent	33 C3
Castlegate Dene	33 C3
Castlegate Dene	33 C4
Castlegate Drive	33 C3
Castlegate Drive	33 C3
Castlegate Elms	33 C3
Castlegate Elms	33 C3
Castlegate Green	33 C3
Castlegate Green	33 C3
Castlegate Grove	33 C3
Castlegate Grove	33 C3
Castlegate Park	33 C3
Castlegate Park	33 C3
Castlegate Place	33 C3
Castlegate Place	33 C4
Castlegate Square	34 D3
Castlegate Walk	33 C3
Castlegate Walk	33 C3
Castlegate Way	33 C3
Castlegate Way	33 C3
Castlegrange	21 B1
Castlegrange Avenue (Clonsilla)	21 B1
Castlegrange Avenue (Swords)	2 D1
Castlegrange Close (Clondalkin)	43 B1
Castlegrange Close (Swords)	2 D1
Castlegrange Court (Clondalkin)	43 B1
Castlegrange Court (Clonsilla)	21 B1
Castlegrange Dale	21 B1
Castlegrange Drive (Clondalkin)	43 B1
Castlegrange Drive (Clonsilla)	21 B1
Castlegrange Gardens	21 B1
Castlegrange Green (Clondalkin)	43 B1
Castlegrange Green (Clonsilla)	21 B1
Castlegrange Green (Swords)	2 D1
Castlegrange Grove	21 B1
Castlegrange Heights	2 D1
Castlegrange Hill	2 D1
Castlegrange Lawn (Clondalkin)	43 C1
Castlegrange Lawn (Clonsilla)	21 B1
Castlegrange Park	21 B1
Castlegrange Road (Clondalkin)	43 C1
Castlegrange Road (Swords)	2 D1
Castlegrange Row	21 B1
Castlegrange Square (Clondalkin)	43 C1
Castlegrange Square (Clonsilla)	21 B1
Castlegrange Terrace	21 B1
Castlegrange Way	2 D1
Castleheath	3 A3
Castlekevin Road	26 D1
Castleknock	22 F3
Castleknock Avenue	22 F3
Castleknock Brook	22 F3
Castleknock Close	22 E3
Castleknock Court	22 F3 [2]
Castleknock Crescent	22 F3
Castleknock Dale	22 F3
Castleknock Downs	22 E3
Castleknock Drive	22 F3
Castleknock Elms	22 F3
Castleknock Gate	23 B4 [1]
Castleknock Glade	22 F3
Castleknock Grange	22 F3
Castleknock Green	23 A3
Castleknock Grove	22 F3
Castleknock Laurels	22 F3
Castleknock Lodge	23 A4
Castleknock Manor	23 A3 [5]
Castleknock Meadows	22 F3
Castleknock Oaks	22 F3
Castleknock Park	23 A3
Castleknock Rise	22 E3
Castleknock Road	22 F3
Castleknock Road	23 A4
Castleknock Vale	22 F3
Castleknock View	22 F3
Castleknock Walk	22 E3
Castleknock Way	22 F3
Castleknock Wood	22 F3
Castlelands	60 F1 [16]
Castlelands Grove	60 F1 [12]
Castlelyons	42 D4
Castlemoyne	14 D3
Castlepark Court	60 E2 [9]
Castlepark Road	60 E1
Castlerosse Crescent	14 F4
Castlerosse Drive	14 F4
Castlerosse View	14 F4
Castleside Drive	46 F3
Castletimon Avenue	25 C1
Castletimon Drive	25 C1
Castletimon Gardens	25 C1
Castletimon Green	25 C1
Castletimon Park	25 C1
Castletimon Road	25 C1
Castletown	32 F1
Castletown Court	32 D3
Castletown Drive	32 D3
Castletown Grove	32 D3
Castletown Lawn	32 D3
Castletymon Court	45 B4
Castletymon Gardens	45 B4
Castletymon Green	45 B4
Castleview	26 E4
Castleview Court	1 Inset
Castleview (Artane)	26 E2
Castleview (Dunboyne)	7 B3
Castleview (Dundrum)	57 C1 [7]
Castleview Avenue	1 Inset
Castleview Close	1 Inset
Castleview Crescent	1 Inset
Castleview Drive	1 Inset
Castleview Green	1 Inset
Castleview Grove	1 Inset
Castleview Heights	1 Inset
Castleview Lawns	1 Inset
Castleview Meadows	1 Inset
Castleview Park	1 Inset
Castleview Park	3 A3
Castleview Place	1 Inset
Castleview Rise	1 Inset
Castleview Row	1 Inset
Castleview Walk	1 Inset
Castleview Way	1 Inset
Castlewarden	51 A3
Castlewarden North	51 A3
Castlewood	21 C1
Castlewood Avenue	47 A1
Castlewood Close	47 A1 [24]
Castlewood Court	47 B1 [26]
Castlewood Park	47 A1
Castlewood Place	47 A1 [6]
Castlewood Terrace	47 A1 [5]
Cathal Brugha Street	71 B3
Cathedral Lane	75 A2
Cathedral Street	71 B3
Cathedral View Court	75 A2
Cathedral View Walk	75 A2
Catherine Court (off William Street North)	72 D1
Catherine Lane	70 F3
Catherine Street (Swift's Alley)	74 F1
Catherine's Well	22 F2 [3]
Cats Ladder	60 F2 [5]
Causeway Road	27 B3
Cavendish Row	71 B2
Caves Strand	3 A2
Ceanchor Road	30 D4
Ceannt Fort (off Mount Brown)	74 D1
Cecil Avenue	26 D4
Cecilia Street (off Temple Bar)	71 B4
Cedar Avenue	45 A3
Cedar Brook	35 C4
Cedar Brook Avenue	35 B3
Cedar Brook Place	35 B3
Cedar Brook Walk	35 B3
Cedar Court (Loughlinstown)	64 D1
Cedar Court (Terenure)	46 F2
Cedar Drive (Dunboyne)	7 B2
Cedar Drive (Palmerstown)	35 B2
Cedar Grove	21 C2 [2]
Cedar Hall	47 C1 [16]
Cedar House	76 D3
Cedar Lodge	23 A4
Cedar Lodge Apts	56 E2
Cedar Park (Donaghmede)	27 A1
Cedar Park (Leixlip)	19 C4
Cedar Square (Stillorgan)	48 F4 [4]
Cedar Square (Swords)	1 B3
Cedar Walk	27 B2
Cedarhurst Green	23 B3
Cedarhurst Road	23 B3
Cedarmount Road	48 E4
Cedarwood	32 D3
Cedarwood Avenue	24 F1
Cedarwood Close	24 F1
Cedarwood Green	24 F1
Cedarwood Grove	24 F1
Cedarwood Park	24 F1
Cedarwood Rise	24 F1
Cedarwood Road	24 F1
Ceder Park	1 B3
Ceder View	1 B3
Celbridge	32 D3
Celbridge Abbey	31 C4
Celbridge Road (Leixlip)	32 F2
Celbridge Road (Lucan)	33 B2
Celbridge Road (Maynooth)	18 D4
Celestine Avenue	39 A3 [42]
*Celestine Avenue (off Dermot O'Hurley Ave)	39 A3
Celtic Park Avenue	25 C2
Celtic Park Road	25 C2
Cenecle Grove	64 E1
Chalet Gardens	34 E1
Chalfont Avenue	3 B2
Chalfont Park	3 B2
Chalfont Place	3 B2
Chalfont Road	3 A2
*Chamber Court (off Chamber St)	74 F2
Chamber Street	74 F2
Chamley Gardens	2 F3
Chamley Park	2 F3
Champions Avenue	71 C3
Chancel Mews	24 D4
Chancery Hall Apts.	70 F3
Chancery Hall Apts. (Ellis Quay)	70 E4
Chancery Lane	75 A1
Chancery Place	71 A4
Chancery Street	71 A4
Chandlers Guild Apts.	74 D1
Chanel Avenue	26 E2
Chanel Grove	26 E1
Chanel Road	26 E2
*Chapel Avenue (off Bath St)	39 A3
Chapel Crescent	24 D3
Chapel Hill	34 D1
Chapel Lane (Bray)	67 B1
Chapel Lane (Parnell Street)	71 B3
Chapel Lane (Swords) (Swords)	2 D2
Chapel Road	14 D1
Chapel View Apts.	34 D1
Chapelizod	36 E2
Chapelizod Bypass	36 E2
Chapelizod Court	36 E2
Chapelizod Hill Road	36 E2
Chapelizod Road	36 E2
Chaplegate	25 A4
Chaplewood Avenue	9 C1
Chaplewood Crescent	9 C1
Chaplewood View	9 C1
Charlemont	25 C3
Charlemont Avenue	50 D4 [5]
Charlemont Court	75 B3
Charlemont Gardens	75 B3
Charlemont Mall	75 B4
Charlemont Parade	72 D1
Charlemont Place	75 C3
Charlemont Road	26 D4
Charlemont Street	75 B3
Charlemont Terrace	50 D4 [18]
Charles Lane	71 C1
Charles Sheils Houses	58 F2
Charles Street Great	71 C2
Charles Street West (off Ormond Quay Upper)	71 A4
Charleston Avenue	47 B1
Charleston Court Flats	47 B1 [9]
Charleston Road	47 B1
Charlestown Avenue	11 B4
Charlestown Court	11 B4
Charlestown Drive	11 B4
Charlestown Green	11 B4
Charlestown Mews	11 B4
Charlestown Park	11 B4
Charlestown Place	11 A4
Charlestown Way	11 B4
Charleville	47 B4
Charleville Avenue	72 D1
Charleville Close	47 A1
Charleville Mall	72 D1
Charleville Road (Phibsborough)	70 E1
Charleville Road (Rathmines)	47 A1
Charleville Square	46 E4
Charleville Terrace (on Charleville Rd)	70 E1
Charlotte Quay	76 F1
Charlotte Terrace	60 F2 [18]
Charlotte Way	75 B3
Charlton Lawn	48 D4
Charnwood (Bray)	67 C3
Charnwood (Clonsilla)	21 C2
Charnwood Avenue	21 C2
Charnwood Court	21 C2
Charnwood Dale	21 C2
Charnwood Gardens	21 C2
Charnwood Green	21 C2
Charnwood Grove	21 C2
Charnwood Heath	21 C2
Charnwood Meadows	21 C2
Charnwood Park	21 C2
Charter House	17 C3 [7]
Chatham Court (on Chatham Street)	75 B1
Chatham Lane (off Chatham Street)	75 B1
Chatham Row	75 B1
Chatham Street	75 B1
*Chaworth Terrace (Hanbury Lane)	74 F1
Cheeverstown Road	54 D1
Chelmsford Avenue	75 C4
Chelmsford Lane	47 B1 [15]
Chelmsford Road	47 B1
Chelsea Gardens	26 F4
Cheltenham Place	75 B4
Cherbury Court	48 F3
Cherbury Gardens	48 F3
Cherbury Mews	48 F3 [4]
Cherbury Park Avenue	34 D2
Cherbury Park Road	34 D2
Cherries Road	58 D2
Cherrington Close	64 E3
Cherrington Drive	64 E3
Cherrington Road	64 E3
Cherry Avenue (Carpenterstown)	22 E3
Cherry Avenue (Swords)	1 C3
Cherry Court (Loughlinstown)	64 D1 [1]
Cherry Court (Terenure)	46 F2
Cherry Drive	22 E3
Cherry Garth (Stillorgan)	48 E4
Cherry Garth (Swords)	1 C2
Cherry Grove (Crumlin)	45 C2

STREET NAME	PAGE/GRID REFERENCE
Cherry Grove (Swords)	1 B3
Cherry House	76 D3
Cherry Lawn	22 E3
Cherry Lawns	33 C2
Cherry Lodge	23 A4
Cherry Orchard Ave	36 D4
Cherry Orchard Avenue	35 C3
Cherry Orchard Court	35 C4
Cherry Orchard Crescent	35 C4
Cherry Orchard Drive	35 C4
Cherry Orchard Green	35 C4
Cherry Orchard Grove	35 C4
Cherry Orchard Parade	35 C4
Cherry Orchard Way	35 C4 [1]
Cherry Park (Carpenterstown)	22 E3
Cherry Park (Swords)	1 B3
Cherry Tree Drive	67 C3 [1]
Cherry Wood	64 D1
Cherryfield Avenue	45 C2
Cherryfield Avenue Lr	47 B1
Cherryfield Avenue Upr	47 B1
Cherryfield Close	21 C1
Cherryfield Court	21 B1
Cherryfield Drive	45 C2
Cherryfield Lawn	21 C1
Cherryfield Park	21 C1
Cherryfield Road	45 C2
Cherryfield View	21 B1
Cherryfield Walk	21 C1
Cherryfield Way	46 D4
Cherrymount Crescent	26 D3 [1]
Cherrymount Grove	26 D3 [2]
Cherrymount Park	70 F1
Cherrywood	32 D3
Cherrywood Avenue	44 D1
Cherrywood Crescent	43 C1
Cherrywood Drive	43 C1
Cherrywood Grove	44 D1
Cherrywood Lawn	43 C2
Cherrywood Park (Clondalkin)	43 C2
Cherrywood Park (Loughlinstown)	64 D1
Cherrywood Road	64 D2
Cherrywood Villas	43 C1
Cherrywood Villas	44 D1 [6]
Chester Downs	60 D1
Chester Road	47 B1
Chester Square	60 E1 [23]
Chesterfield Avenue (Castleknock)	23 B4
Chesterfield Avenue (Phoenix Park)	23 B4
Chesterfield Avenue (Phoenix Park)	36 F1
Chesterfield Close	23 B4
Chesterfield Copse	23 B4
Chesterfield Grove	23 B4
Chesterfield Park	23 B3
Chesterfield View	23 B3
Chestnut Court	25 C2 [1]
Chestnut Grove (Ballinteer)	57 B2
Chestnut Grove (Celbridge)	32 D3
Chestnut Grove (Clondalkin)	44 F3
Chestnut Grove (Dunboyne)	7 B3
Chestnut House (Swords)	1 Inset
Chestnut Park	59 A2 [5]
Chestnut Road (Clondalkin)	45 A1
Chestnut Road (Mount Merrion)	48 E3
Christchurch Hall	74 F1
Christchurch Place	75 A1
Christchurch Square	75 A1
Christchurch Square	75 A1
Church Avenue (Blanchardstown)	22 F2
Church Avenue (Drumcondra)	25 B3
Church Avenue (Glasnevin)	25 A3 [2]
Church Avenue (Irishtown)	39 A3
Church Avenue (Killiney)	60 E4
Church Avenue (Portmarnock)	14 F2 [2]
Church Avenue (Rathmines)	47 A1
Church Avenue South (Dolphin's Barn)	74 D2
Church Avenue West (Church Street)	70 F4
Church Court (Castleknock)	22 F3
Church Court (East Wall)	72 F2
Church Gardens	47 A1
Church Green	46 F1
Church Grove	55 A2
Church Lands	67 C3
Church Lane (College Green)	71 B4
Church Lane (Rathfarnham)	46 F3
Church Lane South	75 A2
Church Park	46 F1
Church Park Avenue	46 F1
Church Park Court	46 F1
Church Park Drive	46 F1
Church Park Lawn	46 F1
Church Park Way	46 F1
Church Place (off Irvine Terrace)	72 F3
Church Road (Ballybrack)	60 E4
Church Road (Bray)	67 C3
Church Road (Celbridge)	32 D4
Church Road (Dalkey)	60 F1
Church Road (East Wall)	72 F2
Church Road (Finglas)	24 D2
Church Road (Killiney)	60 D3
Church Road (Malahide)	3 B3
Church Road (Mulhuddart)	9 A4
Church Road (Rathcoole)	52 E2
Church Road (Sutton)	29 B1
Church Road (Swords) (Swords)	2 D2
*Church Row (off Irvine Terrace)	72 F3
Church Street (Finglas)	24 E2
Church Street (Four Courts)	70 F4
Church Street (Howth)	30 D1
Church Street East	72 F3
Church Street New	70 F4
Church Street Upper	70 F3
Church Terrace (Bray)	67 C2 [45]
Church Terrace (Finglas)	24 E2
Church Terrace (off Church Street)	70 F3
Church View (Clondalkin)	44 D2 [1]
Church View (Drumcondra)	25 B3
Church View (Finglas)	24 D2 [7]
Church Villas	59 C4 [2]
Church Walk	24 D4
Churchfields	47 C2
Churchgate Avenue	39 C1 [1]
Churchill Mews	60 F1 [17]
Churchill Terrace	39 A4 [6]
Churchlands	58 D3 [1]
Churchtown	47 B4
Churchtown Avenue	47 B3
Churchtown Close	47 B3
Churchtown Drive	47 B3
Churchtown Road Lower	47 B3
Churchtown Road Upper	47 A4
Churchtown Road Upper	47 B4
Churchview Avenue	60 D3
Churchview Drive	60 D3
Churchview Park	60 D3
Churchview Road	60 D3
Cian Park	25 B4
Cianlea	1 B1
Cill Cais	54 F2
Cill Eanna	26 F2
Cill Manntan Park	67 C2 [9]
Cill Sarain	67 B3
City Quay	72 D4
Citywest Bridge	42 B4
Citywest Avenue	53 C1
Citywest Interchange	42 B4
Citywest Road	53 C1
Claddagh Green	35 C3
Claddagh Road	35 C3
Claddagh Terrace	68 D2 [15]
*Claddagh Terrace (On Strand Road)	67 C2
Clanawley Road	26 E3
Clanboy Road	26 E3
Clanbrassil Close	74 F4
Clanbrassil Street Lower	74 F3
Clanbrassil Street Upper	74 F3
Clanbrassil terrace	74 F2
Clancarthy Road	26 D3
Clancy Avenue	24 E1
Clancy Road	24 E1
Clandonagh Road	26 D3
Clane Road	31 B4
Clanfadda Wood	48 F3
Clanhugh Road	26 E3
Clanmahon Road	26 E3
Clanmaurice Road	26 D3
Clanmawr	64 E2
Clanmoyle Road	26 D3
Clanranald Road	26 D3
Clanree Road	26 D3
Clanwilliam Court	76 E2
Clanwilliam Place	76 E2
Clanwilliam Square	76 E1
Clanwilliam Terrace	76 E1
Clare Hall	14 D4
Clare Lane	75 C1
Clare Park Villas	25 B3 [3]
Clare Road	25 B3
Clare Street	75 C1
Claremont Avenue	25 A3 [1]
Claremont Close	24 F4
Claremont Court	39 A4 [36]
Claremont Court (Finglas)	24 F4
Claremont Court (Sandymount)	39 A4 [21]
Claremont Crescent	24 F4
Claremont Drive	24 F2
Claremont Grove	60 E3
Claremont Lawn	24 F4
Claremont Mews	29 C1
Claremont Park	39 A4
Claremont Road (Carrickmines)	59 B4
Claremont Road (Killiney)	60 E3
Claremont Road (Sandymount)	39 A4
Claremont Road (Sutton)	29 B1
Claremont Terrace	47 C4 [7]
Claremont Villas	60 E1 [4]
Claremount	64 E3
Claremount Pines	59 B4
Claremount Terrace	68 D2 [11]
Clarence Mangan Road	74 F2
Clarence Mangan Square (off John Dillon Street)	75 A1
Clarence Place Great	76 E1
Clarence St Great North	72 D2
Clarence Street	49 C4
Clarendon Market (off William Street South)	75 B1
Clarendon Row (off King St South)	75 B1
Clarendon Street	75 B1
Clareville Court	24 F4 [7]
Clareville Grove	24 F4
Clareville Road	46 F1
Clarinda Manor	60 D1
Clarinda Park East	60 D1
Clarinda Park East	50 D4
Clarinda Park East (Dun Laoghaire)	50 D4
Clarinda Park North	50 D4
Clarinda Park West	50 D4
Clarion Quay	72 D3
Clarke Terrace	74 D2
Clarke's Bridge	72 D1
Clarkeville Terrace	35 C1 [3]
Classon's Bridge	47 B2
Claude Road	25 A4
Clayton Terrace	36 E2 [8]
Clearwater Apts.	3 C2 [2]
Clearwater Court	24 D3 [1]
Clearwater Cove	49 C4 [31]
Cleggan Avenue	35 C3
Cleggan Park	35 C3
Cleggan Road	35 C3
Clifden Drive	35 C3
Clifden Road	36 D3
Cliff Terrace	60 E1 [18]
Clifford's Lane	2 E2
Clifton Avenue	49 C4 [11]
Clifton Court Apts.	70 E4
Clifton Lane	49 C4 [10]
Clifton Park	64 E2
Clifton Terrace	49 C4 [13]
Cliftonville Road	25 A4
Clinch's Court	72 D1
Clipper Court Apts. (off Liffey Street West)	70 E4
Clipper View Apts. (off Liffey Street West)	70 E4
Clogher Road	46 E1
Cloghran	1 C4
Cloghran	13 A1
Cloghran Roundabout	1 C4
Cloister Avenue	49 A4
Cloister Close	48 F4
Cloister Court	24 D3
Cloister Gate	49 A4
Cloister Green	49 A4
Cloister Grove	49 A4
Cloister Park	49 A4
Cloister Square	49 A4
Cloister Way	49 A4
Clon Burgh	58 D3
Clonallen	46 E2 [11]
Clonard Avenue	57 C2
Clonard Close	57 C2
Clonard Court	46 E2 [8]
Clonard Drive	57 C2
Clonard Grove	57 C2
Clonard Lawn	57 C2
Clonard Park	57 C2
Clonard Road (Crumlin)	46 D1
Clonard Road (Sandyford)	57 C2
Clonasleigh	64 E2 [2]
Cloncourt Apts.	8 D3
Clondalkin	44 D1
Clonee	8 D3
Clonee Bridge	8 D3
Clonee Bypass	8 D3
Clonfert Road	46 E1
Clongriffin	14 D4
Clonkeen Court	59 B3
Clonkeen Crescent	59 B2
Clonkeen Drive	59 B2
Clonkeen Grove	59 B2
Clonkeen Lawn	59 B3 [5]
Clonkeen Road	59 B2
Clonkeen Road	59 B3
Clonlara Avenue	43 A4
Clonlara Road (Naas Road)	43 A4
Clonlara Road (Ringsend)	39 A3 [12]
Clonlea	57 C2
Clonlea Wood	57 C2 [1]
Clonliffe Avenue	72 D1
Clonliffe Gardens	25 B4
Clonliffe Road	25 B4
Clonliffe Square	25 B4 [16]
Clonmacnoise Grove	46 E1 [4]
Clonmacnoise Road	46 E1
Clonmel Road	25 A2
Clonmel Street	75 B2
Clonmellon Grove	14 D4 [3]
Clonmore Court	25 A3 [11]
Clonmore Road (Ballybough)	72 D1
Clonmore Road (Goatstown)	48 E4
Clonmore Terrace	72 D1
*Clonmore Villas (Clonmore Road)	72 D1
Clonrosse Court	26 F1
Clonrosse Drive	26 F1
Clonrosse Park	26 F1
Clonshaugh	13 B3
Clonshaugh Avenue	13 A4
Clonshaugh Close	13 B4
Clonshaugh Court	13 B4 [4]
Clonshaugh Crescent	13 A4
Clonshaugh Drive	13 B4
Clonshaugh Glen	13 B4
Clonshaugh Green	13 B4
Clonshaugh Grove	13 B4
Clonshaugh Heights	13 A4
Clonshaugh Lawns	13 B4
Clonshaugh Meadow	13 A4
Clonshaugh Park	13 B4
Clonshaugh Rise	13 B4 [2]
Clonshaugh Road	13 A3
Clonshaugh Road	13 A4
Clonshaugh Walk	13 B4
Clonsilla	21 C2
Clonsilla Close	22 E2
Clonsilla Park	22 E2
Clonsilla Road	22 E2
Clonskeagh	47 C2
Clonskeagh Drive	47 C2 [6]
Clonskeagh Road	47 C2
Clonskeagh Square	47 C2 [7]

STREET NAME	PAGE/GRID REFERENCE
Clontarf	39 C1
Clontarf Park	39 C1
Clontarf Road	26 D4
Clonturk Avenue	25 B3 [1]
Clonturk Court	25 B3 [6]
Clonturk Gardens	25 B4 [3]
Clonturk Park	25 B4
Cloonlara Crescent	24 E3
Cloonlara Drive	24 E2
Cloonlara Road	24 E3
Cloonlara Square	23 B3
Cloonmore Avenue	54 E2
Cloonmore Close	54 E2
Cloonmore Crescent	54 D2
Cloonmore Drive	54 D2
Cloonmore Gardens	54 D2
Cloonmore Green	54 D2
Cloonmore Grove	54 D2
Cloonmore Lawn	54 D2
Cloonmore Park	54 D2
Cloonmore Road	54 D2
Cloragh Road	56 E4
Clover Hill	67 A3
Clover Hill Drive	36 D3
Clover Hill Road	36 D4
Cloverhill Road	35 A4
Cloverhill Road	35 B3
Cloyne Road	46 E1 [2]
Cluain Aoibhinn	17 C4
Cluain Mhuire	60 D1
Cluain na Greine Court	64 E3 [4]
Cluain Rí	34 F2
Cluain Shee	58 D3
Club Road	45 A1
Clune Road	24 E1
Cluny Grove	60 D3
Cluny Park	60 E2
Clutterland	42 F1
Clyde Court	76 E4
Clyde House	39 A4 [43]
Clyde Lane	76 F4
Clyde Road	76 E4
Cnoc Aoibhean	33 B2
Coast Road (Baldoyle)	15 A4
Coast Road (Malahide)	3 C2
Coates Lane	17 C3 [3]
Coburg	67 B2
Coburg Place	72 D2
*Coghill's Court (off Dame Street)	71 B4
Cois Cairn	67 B1
Cois Coillte	64 D1 [3]
Cois Eala	75 A4
Cois Na hAbhann	54 F2
Cois Sleibhe	67 B4
Coke Lane	70 F4
Coke Ovens Cottages	24 F4
Colbert's Fort (off St James Walk)	74 D2
Colbert's Fort (Tallaght)	44 F4
Coldcut Road	35 B2
Coldwater Lakes	53 B2
Coldwell Street	60 D1
Colepark Avenue	36 D3
Colepark Drive	36 D3
Colepark Green	36 D3
Colepark Road	36 D3
Coleraine Street	71 A3
Colganstown	41 B2
Coliemore Road	60 F2
Coliemore Villas	60 F2 [14]
College Crescent	46 D3
College Drive	46 E3
College Fort	22 F4
College Gate	22 F3
College Green	71 B4
College Green (Maynooth)	17 C4
College Grove	22 F4
College Lane (Rathcoole)	52 F1
College Lane (Trinity College)	76 D1
College Manor	25 B4 [8]
College Mews	25 B4 [11]
College Park (Castleknock)	23 A4
College Park (Kimmage)	46 E3
College Park Avenue	57 C2
College Park Close	57 C2
College Park Court	57 C2 [2]
College Park Drive	57 C2 [3]
College Park Grove	57 C2
College Park House	75 C1
College Park Way	57 C2
College Road (Castleknock)	22 F4
College Road (Greenogue Ind Est)	42 E4
College Road (Whitechurch Road)	57 A3
College Street (Baldoyle)	15 A4 [8]
College Street (Baldoyle)	15 A4
College Street (Trinity College)	71 C4
College View (Drumcondra)	25 B3
College View (Tallaght)	55 A1 [6]
College Wood	22 F4
Collegeland	42 F4
Collier's Avenue	47 B1 [3]
Colliersland	6 F2
Collindale	25 C2 [6]
Collins Avenue	25 C2
Collins Avenue East	26 D3
Collins Avenue Extension	25 A2
Collins Avenue West	25 B2
Collins Bridge	20 F4
Collins Close	25 C3 [8]
Collins Court (Blackrock)	49 A3 [13]
Collins Court (Collins Avenue)	25 C3 [6]
Collins Drive	24 E1
Collins Green	24 E1
Collins Park	26 D3
Collins Place	24 E1
Collins Row	24 E2 [6]
Collinstown Crescent	35 A3 [3]
Collinstown Grove	35 B3
Collinstown Road	35 A3
Collinswood	25 C2
Colmanstown	51 C2
Colmanstown Lane	51 C2
Colmcille Court	2 D2 [3]
Colthurst Close	34 F2
Colthurst Crescent	34 F2
Colthurst Gardens	34 F2
Colthurst Green	34 F2
Colthurst Mews	34 F2
Colthurst Park	34 F2
Colthurst Rise	34 F2
Colthurst Road	34 F2
Colthurst Way	34 F2
Comeragh Road	36 F4
Comeran Court	74 E2
Common Little	42 D4
Commons (Hazelhatch)	41 C2
Commons (Rathcoole)	52 E1
Commons East	2 D3
Commons Little	42 D4
Commons Lower	41 A1
Commons Road (Loughlinstown)	64 E2
Commons Road (St. John's Gate)	44 D2
Commons Street	72 D3
Compass Court	23 C3
Compass Court Apts.	24 D3 [4]
Comyn Place	25 A3 [5]
Con Colbert Road	36 F3
Con Colbert Road	73 A1
Confey	20 D4
Congress Gardens	60 E1 [2]
Congress Hall	7 B3
Congress Park	7 B3 [1]
Connaught Parade	24 F4 [6]
Connaught Place	50 D4 [26]
Connaught Street	24 F4
Connawood	67 B1
Connawood Copse	67 B1
Connawood Crescent	67 B1
Connawood Drive	67 B1
Connawood Green	67 B1
Connawood Grove	67 B1
Connawood Lawn	67 B1
Connawood Walk	67 B1
Connawood Way	67 B1
Connolly Avenue (Kilmainham)	73 A2
Connolly Avenue (Malahide)	3 A4
Connolly Gardens	73 A2
Connolly's Folly	18 E4
Conor Clune Road	23 C4
Conquer Hill Avenue	39 C1
Conquer Hill Road	39 C1
Constellation Road	12 F4
Constitution Hill	71 A3
Convent Avenue (Bray)	68 D2
Convent Avenue (Marino)	25 B4
Convent Close	76 D2
Convent Court	58 E1 [4]
Convent Lane (Maynooth)	17 C3
Convent Lane (Portmarnock)	4 D4
Convent Lane (Willbrook)	46 F4
Convent Lawns	36 E3 [4]
Convent Lodge	26 F2
Convent Place	75 C3
Convent Road (Blackrock)	49 A4
Convent Road (Clondalkin)	44 E2
Convent Road (Dalkey)	60 F2
Convent Road (Dun Laoghaire)	50 D4
Convent View (Bray)	68 D2 [23]
Convent View (Oldcourt)	67 C3
Convent View Cottages (Cabra)	24 D4 [2]
Convent View Cottages (St. John's Gate)	44 D2
Convent View Crescent	24 D4 [3]
Convent Way	24 D4
Conway Court	76 E1
Conyngham Road	69 C4
Cook Street	71 A4
Cooks Road	1 A4
Cookstown	66 E3
Cookstown Court	44 F4
Cookstown Road	44 E4
Cookstown Road	44 F4
Cookstown Way	44 E4
Coolamber Court	56 D1 [1]
Coolamber Drive	52 F2
Coolamber Park	56 D1
Coolamber Road	52 F2
Coolatree Close	25 C2
Coolatree Park	25 C2
Coolatree Road	25 C2
Cooldrinagh Lane	33 B1
Cooldrinagh Terrace	33 B1
Cooldríona Court	2 D2
Cooleen Avenue	25 C1
Coolevin (Ballybrack)	60 D4
Coolevin Road	75 A2
Cooley Close	36 F4
Cooley Road	36 F4
Coolgariff Road	25 C1
Coolgreena Close	25 C2
Coolgreena Road	25 C1
Coolkill	58 D3
Coolmine	52 F3
Coolmine Boulevard	22 E2
Coolmine Close	22 D2
Coolmine Cottages	9 A4
Coolmine Court	22 E2
Coolmine Green	22 D3
Coolmine Lawn	22 D2
Coolmine Mews	22 D2 [1]
Coolmine Park	22 E2
Coolmine Road	22 E3
Coolmine Woods	22 E2
Coolnevaun	58 E1
Coolock	26 E1
Coolock Drive	26 E1
Coolock Lane (Santry)	12 F4
Coolock Village	26 E1
Coolock Village Close	26 E1 [3]
Coolrua Drive	25 C1
Coombe Court	74 F1
Coopers Way	70 F3
Coopers Yard (Smithfield)	70 F3
Coopers Yard Apts.	70 F3
Cope Bridge	20 D3
Cope Street	71 B4
Copeland Avenue	26 D4
Copeland Grove	26 D4
Copper Alley(Eustace Street)	71 A4
Copper Beech Grove	67 B2 [6]
Coppinger	49 A4
Coppinger Close	48 F4
Coppinger Glade	48 F4
Coppinger Row	75 B1
Coppinger Walk	49 A4
Coppinger Wood	48 F4
Corbally	53 C3
Corbally Avenue	53 C2
Corbally Close	53 C2
Corbally Downs	53 C2
Corbally Drive	53 C2
Corbally Glade	53 C2
Corbally Green	53 C2
Corbally Heath	53 C2
Corbally Lawn	53 C2
Corbally Park	53 C2
Corbally Rise	53 C2
Corbally Square	53 C2
Corbally Vale	53 C2
Corbally Way	53 C2
Corbawn Avenue	64 E2
Corbawn Close	64 F2
Corbawn Court	64 F2
Corbawn Dale	64 F2
Corbawn Drive	64 F2
Corbawn Glade	64 E2 [14]
Corbawn Grove	64 F2
Corbawn Lane	64 E2
Corbawn Lawn	64 E3
Corbawn Wood	64 F2
Corduff	22 F1
Corduff Avenue	22 F1
Corduff Close	22 F1
Corduff Cottages	22 F1
Corduff Crescent	22 F1
Corduff Gardens	22 F1
Corduff Green	22 F1
Corduff Grove	9 B4
Corduff Park	9 B4
Corduff Place	22 F1
Corduff Way	22 F1
Cork Hill (off Dame St)	71 A4
Cork Street	74 E2
Corkagh View	44 D2
Corke Abbey	67 C1
Corke Abbey Avenue	67 B1
Cormac Terrace	46 F2
Corn Exchange Apts.	71 C4
Corn Exchange Place	71 C4
Cornelscourt	59 B3
Cornelscourt Hill Road	59 B3
Cornelstown	6 D2
Cornerpark	42 D3
Cornmarket	74 F1
Corr Castle	29 B1
Corr Castle Apts	29 B1 [3]
Corrbridge Terrace (off Claremont Road)	29 B1 [1]
Corrib Road	46 E2
Corrig Avenue	50 D4
Corrig Close	45 B3
Corrig Hall	57 C3
Corrig Park	50 D4
Corrig Road (Dalkey)	60 F1
Corrig Road (Dun Laoghaire)	60 D1
Corrig Road (Stillorgan)	58 E2
Corrybeg	46 D4
Cosy Lodge	47 A1 [26]
Coulson Avenue	46 F2
Coultry Avenue	25 B1
Coultry Close	25 A1
Coultry Court	12 D4
Coultry Crescent	12 D4
Coultry Drive	12 D4
Coultry Gardens	12 D4
Coultry Green	12 D4
Coultry Grove	12 E4
Coultry Lawn	12 E4
Coultry Park	12 E4
Coultry Road	12 D4
Coultry Terrace	12 D4
Coultry Way	25 B1
Coundon Court	60 E4
Countess Markievicz House	72 D4
Countybrook Lawns	66 E2
Court House Square	17 C3 [5]
Courthill Drive	7 B2
Courthouse Square Apts.	55 A1 [13]
Courtlands	59 C3

STREET NAME	PAGE/GRID REFERENCE
Courtney Place	72 E1
Courtview	23 C3
Cow Parlour	74 E2
Cowbooter Lane	30 E2
Cowper Downs	47 A1
Cowper Drive	47 B2
Cowper Gardens	47 B2
Cowper Mews	47 A2 [4]
Cowper Road	47 B2
Cowper Street	70 D2
Cowper Village	47 A2
Cows Lane	71 A4
Crag Avenue	35 B4
Crag Crescent	35 B4
Crag Terrace	35 B4
Craigford Avenue	26 E3
Craigford Drive	26 E3
Craiglands	60 F2 [26]
Craigmore Gardens	49 A3 [5]
Crampton Avenue	76 F3
Crampton Court (off Dame St)	71 B4
Crampton Quay	71 B4
Crane Lane (off Dame Street)	71 A4
Crane Street	74 E1
Cranfield Place	39 A3
Cranford Court (Kimmage)	46 E2 [12]
Cranford Court (Stillorgan Road)	48 D2
Cranmer Lane	76 E2
Crannagh	47 C2 [9]
Crannagh Castle	46 F3 [9]
Crannagh Court	46 F3 [10]
Crannagh Grove	47 A3
Crannagh Hall	47 A3
Crannagh Park	46 F3
Crannagh Road	46 F3
Crannagh Way	47 A3 [8]
Crannogue Close	11 C4
Crannogue Road	11 C4
Crawford Avenue	25 A4
Crawford Terrace (off Kings Avenue)	72 D1
Creighton Street	72 D4
Cremona Road	36 E3
Cremore Avenue	24 F3
Cremore Crescent	24 F3
Cremore Drive	24 F3
Cremore Heights	24 F2
Cremore Lawn	24 F3
Cremore Park	25 A3
Cremore Road	24 F3
Cremore Villas	24 F3 [5]
Cremorne (Knocklyon)	56 D1
Cremorne (Terenure Road East)	46 F2
Crescent Gardens	72 E1
Crescent House	26 D4 [6]
Crescent Place	26 D4
Crescent Villas	25 A4
Crestfield Avenue	25 B2
Crestfield Close	25 B2
Crestfield Drive	25 B2
Crestfield Park	25 B2
Crestfield Road	25 B2
Crewhill	17 B1
Crinan Strand	72 D3
Crinken Glen	64 E3
Crinken Lane	64 D4
Crinstown	17 A4
Croaghpatrick Road	24 D4
Crockshane	52 E3
Crodaun Court	31 C2 [1]
Crodaun Forest Park	32 D2
Crofton Avenue	50 D4
Crofton Mansions	50 D4 [28]
Crofton Road	50 D4
Crofton Terrace	50 D4 [25]
Croftwood Crescent	35 C3
Croftwood Drive	35 C3
Croftwood Gardens	35 C3
Croftwood Green	36 D3
Croftwood Grove	35 C3
Croftwood Park	36 D3
Croke Villas	72 D1
Cromcastle Avenue	26 D1
Cromcastle Close	26 D1 [2]
Cromcastle Court	26 D1 [6]
Cromcastle Drive	26 D1
Cromcastle Green	26 D1
Cromcastle Park	26 D1
Cromcastle Road	26 D1
Cromlech Close	62 F2
Cromlech Court	11 C4
Cromlech Fields	64 E1
Cromwell's Quarters	74 A3
Cromwellsfort Road	45 C2
Crooksling	53 B4
Crosbie House	75 C4
Cross Avenue (Booterstown)	48 F3
Cross Avenue (Dun Laoghaire)	50 D4
Cross Lane	17 C3
Crosstrees Court	30 D2 [13]
Crosthwaite Park East	60 D1
Crosthwaite Park South	60 D1
Crosthwaite Park West	60 D1
Crosthwaite Terrace	50 D4 [15]
Crostick Alley (off Meath St)	74 F1
Crotty Avenue	45 C1
Crow Street (off Dame St)	71 B4
Crown Alley (Off Temple Bar)	71 B4
Croydon Gardens	25 C4
Croydon Green	25 C4
Croydon Park Avenue	25 C4
Croydon Terrace	25 C3 [4]
Cruagh Avenue	62 E1
Cruagh Close	62 E1
Cruagh Court	62 E1
Cruagh Green	62 E1
Cruagh Lane	56 E4
Cruagh Rise	62 E1
Cruagh Road	56 E4
Cruagh Wood	62 E1
Cruise Park	9 A2
Cruise Park Avenue	9 A2
Cruise Park Close	9 A2
Cruise Park Court	9 A2
Cruise Park Crescent	9 A2
Cruise Park Drive	9 A2
Cruise Park Hall	9 A2
Cruise Park Rise	9 A2
Cruise Park Square	9 A2
Cruise Park Walk	9 A2
Crumlin	46 D1
*Crumlin Park(off Crumlin Road)	46 D1
Crumlin Road	73 C4
Cuala Grove	68 D3
Cuala Road (Bray)	68 D3
Cuala Road (Cabra)	24 F4
Cuan na Mara	30 D1 [13]
Cuckoo Lane	71 A3
Cuffe Lane	75 B2
Cuffe Street	75 B2
Cuilenn Park	24 F1
Cul na Greine	54 F2
Cullen's Cottages	49 A4 [7]
Cullen's Wood House	75 C4
*Cullenswood Court (off Cullenswood Park)	47 B1
Cullenswood Gardens	47 B1
Cullenswood Park	47 B1
Cullenswood Road	47 B1 [11]
Culmore Park	35 C2 [1]
Culmore Road	35 C2
*Cumberland Place North (on North Circular Road)	70 F1
Cumberland Road	76 D3
Cumberland Street	49 C4
Cumberland Street North	71 C2
Cumberland Street South	76 D1
Cunningham Drive	60 F2
Cunningham Road	60 F2
Curlew Road	36 F4
Curracloe Drive	27 A1 [4]
Curragh Hall	9 B3
Curragh Hall Avenue	9 B3
Curragh Hall Close	9 B3
Curragh Hall Court	9 B3
Curragh Hall Crescent	9 B3
Curragh Hall Drive	9 B3
Curragh Hall Gate	9 B3
Curragh Hall Green	9 B3
Curragh Hall Grove	9 B3
Curragh Hall House	9 B3
Curragh Hall Lane	9 B3
Curragh Hall Lodge	9 B3
Curragh Hall Road	9 B3
Curragh Hall View	9 B3
Curragh Hall Way	9 B3
Curragh Hall Wood	9 B3
Curtlestown	65 B4
Curzon Street	75 A3
Cushinstown	6 F1
Cushlawn Avenue	54 F2
Cushlawn Close	54 F3
Cushlawn Dale	54 F3
Cushlawn Drive	54 F2
Cushlawn Grove	54 F2
Cushlawn Park	54 F2
Cushlawn Walk	54 F3
Cushlawn Way	54 F3
Custom Hall	71 C3
Custom House Harbour	72 D3
Custom House Quay	71 C3
Custom House Square	72 E3
Cymric Road	39 A3
Cypress Avenue	56 E2 [2]
Cypress Court	64 E1
Cypress Drive	46 D3
Cypress Garth	46 D4
Cypress Grove North	46 D3
Cypress Grove Road	46 D3
Cypress Grove South	46 D4
Cypress House	28 D1
Cypress Lawn	46 D4
Cypress Park	46 D4
Cypress Road	48 E3
Cypress Springs	20 D4 [1]

D

STREET NAME	PAGE/GRID REFERENCE
*Daisy Market (off Arran Street)	71 A4
Dakota Avenue	12 F4
Dakota Court	25 A4
Dal Riada	3 C4
Dalcassian Downs	24 F4
Dale Close	58 E1 [1]
Dale Drive	58 E1
Dale Road	58 E1
Dale View	60 E4
Dale View Park	60 E4 [2]
Dalepark Road	55 A2
Daletree Avenue	55 B2
Daletree Close	55 C3
Daletree Court	55 C2
Daletree Crescent	55 C2
Daletree Drive	55 C2
Daletree Park	55 C3
Daletree Place	55 C3
Daletree Road	55 C3
Daletree Terrace	55 C3
Daletree View	55 B3
Daleview Road	1 C1
Dalkey	60 F1
Dalkey Avenue	60 F2
Dalkey Court	60 F2 [23]
Dalkey Grove	60 F2 [6]
Dalkey Park	60 E2
Dalkey Rock	60 F2
Dalton Mews	3 B3
Dalymount	70 F1
Damastown Avenue	8 F3
Damastown Close	8 F3
Damastown Court	9 A3
Damastown Drive	8 E3
Damastown Green	8 F3
Damastown Road	8 F3
Damastown Walk	8 E3
Damastown Way	8 F3
Damastown Way	9 A3
Dame Court	75 B1
*Dame Lane	75 B3
Dame Lane	71 B4
Dame Street	71 B4
Damer Court	71 A2
Damer House	2 E2
Dane Close	11 C4
Dane Road	11 C4
Danes Court	27 A4
Danesfort	39 B1
Daneswell Road	25 A4
Danewood Castleknock	23 A3
Dangan	41 A2
Dangan Avenue	46 D2
Dangan Drive	46 D2
Dangan Park	46 D2
Daniel Street	75 A3
Danieli Drive	26 E2
Danieli Road	26 E2
Dara Court	32 D3
Dara Crescent	32 D3
Dargan Court	68 D2 [6]
Dargan Street	67 B2 [10]
Dargle Bridge	67 A4
Dargle Court	67 B2 [3]
Dargle Crescent	67 B2 [5]
Dargle Drive	57 A1
Dargle Heights	67 B2
Dargle Road (Dean's Grange)	59 A1
Dargle Road (Drumcondra)	25 A4
*Dargle Terrace (On Lower Dargle Road)	67 B2
Dargle Valley	57 A1
Dargle View	57 A1
Dargle Wood	56 D1
Darley Cottages	67 C2 [15]
Darley Street	74 F4
Darley's Terrace	74 E2
Darling Estate	23 C4
Darndale	13 C4
Dartmouth Lane	75 C4
Dartmouth Place	75 C4
Dartmouth Road	75 C4
Dartmouth Square	75 C3
Dartmouth Square East	75 C3
Dartmouth Square North	75 C3
Dartmouth Square South	75 C4
Dartmouth Square West	75 C4
Dartmouth Terrace	75 C4
Dartry Cottages	47 B2 [1]
Dartry Park	47 B2
Dartry Road	47 A2
David Park	25 A4
David Road	25 A4
Davis Place (off Thomas Davis St Sth)	74 F1
Davitt House	73 A3
Davitt Park	60 D4
Davitt Road (Bray)	67 C2
Davitt Road (Inchicore)	36 F4
Davitt Terrace	73 A3
*Dawson Court	75 B1
Dawson Court	48 F3
Dawson Court (off Stephen St Lower)	75 B1
Dawson Lane	75 C1
Dawson Street	75 C1
De Bret House	46 F4 [24]
De Burgh Road	70 D4
De Courcy Square	25 A4 [2]
De Selby	54 D2
De Selby Close	54 D2
De Selby Court	54 D2
De Selby Crescent	54 D2
De Selby Downs	54 D2
De Selby Drive	54 D2
De Selby Green	54 D2
De Selby Lane	54 D2
De Selby Lawns	54 D2
De Selby Park	53 C2
De Selby Rise	54 T4
De Selby Road	54 D2
De Velara Place	71 B1
*De Vesci Court (off Sloperton)	49 C4
De Vesci Terrace	49 C4
Dean Court	75 A1
Dean Street	75 A2
Dean Swift Green	25 A2
Dean Swift Road	25 A2
Dean Swift Square	74 F1
Deans Court	59 B1 [10]
Deans Grange	59 B2
Dean's Grange Road	59 B1
Deansrath Avenue	34 F4
Deansrath Crescent	43 C1
Deansrath Green	43 C1

STREET NAME	PAGE/GRID REFERENCE
Deansrath Grove	34 F4
Deansrath Lawn	34 F4
Deansrath Park	43 C1
Deansrath Road	43 C1
Deanstown Avenue	24 D2
Deanstown Drive	24 D2
Deanstown Green	24 D2
Deanstown Park	24 D2
Deanstown Road	24 D2
Decies Road	36 E3
Deepdales	67 B4
Deerhaven	8 F4
Deerhaven Avenue	8 F4
Deerhaven Close	8 F4
Deerhaven Crescent	8 F4
Deerhaven Green	8 F4
Deerhaven Park	8 F4
Deerhaven View	8 F4
Deerhaven Walk	8 F4
Deerpark	67 B4
Deerpark Avenue (Castleknock)	23 A4
Deerpark Avenue (Kiltipper)	54 F3
Deerpark Close (Castleknock)	23 A3
Deerpark Close (Kiltipper)	54 F3
Deerpark Downs	54 F3
Deerpark Drive (Castleknock)	23 A3
Deerpark Drive (Kiltipper)	54 F3
Deerpark Green	54 F3
Deerpark Lawn	23 B3
Deerpark Lodge	54 F3
Deerpark Place	54 F3
Deerpark Rise	54 F3
Deerpark Road (Castleknock Road)	23 A3
Deerpark Road (Kiltipper)	54 F3
Deerpark Road (Mount Merrion)	48 D4
Deerpark Square	54 F3
Deerpark Terrace	54 F3
Deerpark Walk	54 F3
Deerpark Way	54 F3
Del Val Avenue	27 C2
Del Val Court	27 C2 [2]
Delaford Avenue	55 C1
Delaford Drive	55 C1
Delaford Grove	55 C1
Delaford Lawn	55 C1
Delaford Park	55 C1
Delbrook Manor	57 C2
Delbrook Park	57 C2
Delhurst Avenue	21 B1
Delhurst Close	21 B1
Delhurst Mews	21 B1
Delhurst Terrace	21 B1
Delville Road	25 A2
Delvin Road	24 F4 [3]
Delwood Close	22 E3
Delwood Drive	22 E3
Delwood Grove	22 E3
Delwood Lawn	22 E3
Delwood Park	22 E3
Delwood Road	22 E3
Delwood Walk	22 E3
Demesne	26 E3
Denmark Street Great	71 B2
Denville Court	60 D4
Denzille Lane	76 D1
*Derby Square (off Werburgh Street)	75 A1
Dermot O'Hurley Avenue	39 A3
Derravaragh Road	46 E2
Derry Drive	46 D1
Derry Park	46 D1
Derry Road	46 D1
Derrynane Gardens	39 A3
Derrynane Parade	71 B1
Derrynane Square	71 B1
Desmond Avenue	50 D4 [3]
Desmond Cottages	60 F2 [20]
Desmond Street	75 A3
Devenish Road	46 E1
Deverell Place	71 C3
Devery's Lane	25 A4 [4]
Devitt Villas	60 E1 [8]
Devlin's Place	76 D1
Devon Close	59 B1 [11]
Devoy Road	73 B2
Dewberry Park	4 D4
Dexter Terrace	75 C4
Diamond Terrace	67 B2 [15]
Diamond Valley Apts.	67 B2
*"Digges Lane (Longford St, Little)"	75 B1
Digges Street Upper	75 B2
*Dillon Place South (off John Dillon Street)	75 A1
Dillon's Row	17 C2
Dingle Glen	63 A2
Dingle Road	24 E4
Dispensary Lane (Lucan)	34 D1 [6]
Dispensary Lane (Willbrook)	46 F4
Distillery House Apts.	36 E2 [14]
Distillery Lane	20 D4
Distillery Loft Apts.	25 B4 [15]
Distillery Road	25 B4
Diswellstown Cottages	22 E4
Diswellstown Road	22 D3
Dixon Villas	60 E1 [9]
Doctor's Lane	17 C3
Dodder Avenue	55 B2
Dodder Bank	47 B2 [10]
Dodder Court	55 B2
Dodder Crescent	55 B2
Dodder Dale	46 F4
Dodder Green	55 B2
Dodder Lawn	55 B2
Dodder Park Drive	46 F3 [3]
Dodder Park Grove	46 F3
Dodder Park Road	46 F3
Dodder Road Lower	47 A3
Dodder Terrace	39 A3 [18]
Dodder Vale	47 A3 [13]
Dodder View Cottages	76 F3
Dodsboro Cottages	33 B2
Dodsboro Road	33 C2
D'Olier Street	71 C4
Dollymount	27 A4
Dollymount Avenue	27 A4
Dollymount Grove	26 F4
Dollymount Park	27 A4
Dollymount Rise	27 A4
Dolly's Grove	5 C2
Dolmen Court	12 D4
Dolphin Avenue	74 E3
Dolphin Court	73 C3
Dolphin House	74 D3
*Dolphin Market (off Dolphin's Barn St)	74 D3
Dolphin Park	74 D3
Dolphin Road	73 C3
Dolphin's Barn	74 D3
Dolphin's Barn Street	74 D3
Dominick Lane	71 A3
Dominick Place	71 B3
Dominick Street	50 D4
Dominick Street Lower	71 A3
Dominick Street Upper	71 A2
Domville Court	12 E4 [1]
Domville Drive	46 D4
Domville Green	46 D4
Domville Grove	64 E1 [9]
Domville Road	46 D4
Donaghmede	14 F4
Donaghmede Avenue	27 B1
Donaghmede Drive	27 B1
Donaghmede Park	27 B1
Donaghmede Road	27 B1
Donaghmore	18 F3
Donard Road	36 F4
Donnellan Avenue (St Johns Terrace)	73 C1
Donnybrook	47 C1
Donnybrook Castle	47 C1 [24]
Donnybrook Close	48 D2 [2]
Donnybrook Court	47 C2
Donnybrook Green	48 D2 [3]
Donnybrook Manor	47 C1
Donnybrook Mews	47 C1
Donnybrook Road	47 C1
Donnycarney	26 D3
Donnycarney Road	26 D3
Donomore Avenue	54 E2
Donomore Crescent	54 E2
Donomore Green	54 E2
Donomore Park	54 E2
Donore Avenue	74 E2
Donore Road	74 E2
Donore Terrace	74 E2
Donovan Lane	74 F3
Doon Avenue	70 D1
Doon Court	11 C4
Doonamana Road	60 D3
Doonanore Park	60 D3
Doonsalla Drive	60 D3
Doonsalla Park	60 D3
Doreen House Apts.	24 D4 [8]
Doris Street	76 F1
Dornden Park	48 E2
Dorney Court	64 E3
Dorset Lane	71 B1
Dorset Place	71 B1
Dorset Square	71 B1
Dorset Street Lower	71 B1
Dorset Street Upper	71 A2
Double Lane	17 C3
Dowland Road	46 D1
Dowling's Court	72 D4
Downpatrick Road	73 C4
Downpatrick Road	46 E1
Dowth Avenue	24 F4
Doyles Lane	27 A4 [6]
Drapier Green	24 F2 [1]
Drapier Road	24 F2
Drayton Close	49 B4 [16]
Drimnagh	36 F4
Drimnagh Road	45 C1
Drinagh Park	58 F4
Drinaghmore	58 F4
Drinaghmore Avenue	58 F4
Drinaghmore Close	58 F4
Drinaghmore Court	58 F4
Droim na Coille Avenue	34 F2
Droim na Coille Court	34 F2
Droim na Coille Place	34 F2
Dromard Road	36 F4
Dromard Terrace	39 A4 [17]
Dromawling Road	25 C2
Drombawn Avenue	25 C2
Dromcarra Avenue	54 E2
Dromcarra Drive	54 E2
Dromcarra Green	54 D2
Dromcarra Grove	54 E2
Dromeen Avenue	25 C2
Dromheath Avenue	9 B4
Dromheath Drive	9 B4
Dromheath Gardens	9 B4
Dromheath Grove	9 B4
Dromheath Park	9 B4
Dromlee Crescent	25 C2
Dromnanane Park	25 C2 [3]
Dromnanane Road	25 C2 [2]
Dromore Road	73 A4
Druid Court	11 C4
Druid Valley	63 C1
Druid Valley	64 D1
Drumahill	58 D1
Drumalee Avenue	70 D2
Drumalee Court	70 D2
Drumalee Drive	70 D2
Drumalee Grove	70 D2
Drumalee Park	70 D2
Drumalee Road	70 D2
Drumcairn Avenue	54 E1
Drumcairn Drive	54 D1
Drumcairn Gardens	54 D1
Drumcairn Green	54 E1
Drumcairn Park	54 E1
Drumcliffe Drive	24 E4
Drumcliffe Road	24 E4
Drumcondra	25 A4
Drumcondra Park	71 C1
Drumcondra Road Lower	25 B4
Drumcondra Road Upper	25 B3
Drumderg Court	25 C4
Drumfinn Avenue	35 C2
Drumfinn Park	36 D3
Drumfinn Road	36 D2
Drumkeen Manor	60 D3
Drummartin Close	48 D4
Drummartin Crescent	58 D1 [1]
Drummartin Link Road	58 D1
Drummartin Park	58 D1
Drummartin Road	48 D4
Drummartin Terrace	48 D4
Drummond Place (off Mount Drummond Ave)	75 A4
Drumnigh	14 E3
Drumnigh Road	14 E3
Drumnigh Wood	14 E2
*Drury Hall Apts. (Stephen Street Lwr)	75 B1
Drury Street	75 B1
Drynam Avenue	2 E3
Drynam Close	2 E3
Drynam Copse	2 E3
Drynam Court	2 D2
Drynam Crescent	2 E3
Drynam Drive	2 E3
Drynam Glen	2 E3
Drynam Green	2 E3
Drynam Grove	2 E3
Drynam Hall	2 E3
Drynam Mews	2 E3
Drynam Place	2 E4
Drynam Rise	2 E4
Drynam Road	2 D2
Drynam Square	2 E3
Drynam View	2 E3
Drynam Walk	2 E3
Drynam Way	2 E3
Drysdale Close	55 A2
Dualla Court	48 E4
Dubber Cross	11 B3
Dublin Airport	12 E1
Dublin Road (Bray)	67 B1
Dublin Road (Celbridge)	32 D3
Dublin Road (Donaghmore)	18 F3
Dublin Road (Dunboyne)	7 C3
Dublin Road (Kilbarrack)	27 C2
Dublin Road (Malahide)	3 A3
Dublin Road (Maynooth)	18 D3
Dublin Road (Shankill)	64 E3
Dublin Road (Sutton)	29 A1
Dublin Road (Swords)	1 C3
Dublin Street (Baldoyle)	15 A4
Dublin Street (Swords)	15 A4
Duck Lane	70 E4
Dufferin Avenue	74 F3
Duke Lane Lower	75 C1
Duke Lane Upper	75 B1
Duke Row	72 D2
Duke Street	75 B1
Dun Aengus	54 F2
Dun an Oir	54 F2
Dun Emer Drive	57 C1
Dun Emer Park	57 C1
Dun Emer Road	57 C1
Dun Gaoithe	58 E3
Dun Laoghaire	50 D4
Dunard Avenue	69 B1
Dunard Court	69 C1
Dunard Drive	69 C1
Dunard Park	69 C1
Dunard Road	69 C1
Dunard Road	69 C1
Dunard Walk	69 C1
Dunawley Avenue	44 D1
Dunawley Drive	44 D1
Dunawley Grove	44 D1
Dunawley Way	44 D1
Dunbavin Bridge	51 A4
Dunbo Hill	30 D1 [4]
Dunbo Terrace	30 D1 [1]
Dunboy	59 A4
Dunboyne	7 B2
Dunboyne Bridge	7 C3
Dunboyne Road	18 D2
Dunbro Lane	11 C1
Dunbur Terrace	67 C2 [21]
Duncairn Avenue	67 C2
Duncairn Terrace	67 C2
Duncarraig	29 B2
Dundaniel Road	26 D1
Dundela Avenue	60 E1

STREET NAME	PAGE/GRID REFERENCE	STREET NAME	PAGE/GRID REFERENCE	STREET NAME	PAGE/GRID REFERENCE	STREET NAME	PAGE/GRID REFERENCE
Dundela Crescent	60 E1	Earlsfort Way	34 F3	Eglinton Road	47 C1	Elmcastle Court	45 A3
Dundela Haven	60 E1 [24]	East Pier (Dun Laoghaire)	50 E3	Eglinton Square	47 C1 [13]	Elmcastle Drive	45 A3
Dundela Park	60 E1	East Pier (Howth)	30 D1	Eglinton Terrace (Donnybrook)	47 C1	Elmcastle Green	45 A3
Dundrum	57 C1	East Road	72 F3	Eglinton Terrace (Dundrum)	47 C4	Elmcastle Park	45 A3
Dundrum By Pass	57 C1	East Wall	39 A1	*Eglinton Terrace	71 A2	Elmcastle Walk	45 A3
Dundrum Gate Apts	57 C1 [9]	East Wall Road	72 F1	(Royal Canal Bank)		Elmdale Crescent	35 C3
Dundrum Road	47 C3	East Wall Road	39 A2	Eglinton Wood	47 C1 [22]	Elmdale Drive	35 C3
Dundrum Wood	57 B1	(Alexandra Basin)		Eklad Close	13 C4	Elmdale Park	35 C3
Dunedin Court	59 C1	Eastmoreland Court	76 E3	Eklad Park	13 C4	Elmfield Avenue	14 D4
Dunedin Drive	59 C1 [8]	Eastmoreland Lane	76 E3	El Greco Apts.	39 A4 [51]	Elmfield Close	14 D4 [2]
Dunedin Park	59 C1	Eastmoreland Place	76 E3	Elbin House	39 A4 [41]	Elmfield Court	14 D4
Dunedin Terrace	59 C1	Easton Park	19 C4	Elderberry	34 D3	Elmfield Court (Clondalkin)	44 E1
Dungar Terrace	50 D4 [12]	Easton Road	19 B4	Elderwood Road	35 B2	Elmfield Crescent	14 E4
Dungriffan Road	30 D2	Eastwood	23 C2 [1]	*Elford Terrace	74 E2	Elmfield Drive	14 E4
Dungriffan Villas	30 D2 [8]	Eaton Brae (Orwell Road)	47 A3	(off Donore Avenue)		Elmfield Green	14 D4
Dunleary Hill	49 C4	Eaton Brae (Shankill)	64 E2	Elgin Heights	67 A4	Elmfield Grove	14 D4
Dunleary Road	49 C4	Eaton Close	52 F2	Elgin Road	76 E3	Elmfield Lawn	14 E4
Dunluce Road	26 E3	Eaton Court (Bray)	68 D3 [1]	Elgin Wood	67 B4	Elmfield Park	14 E4
Dunmanus Court	24 E4 [4]	Eaton Court (Terenure)	46 F2 [22]	*Elizabeth O'Farrell Park	72 D4	Elmfield Rise	14 D4
Dunmanus Road	24 E4	Eaton Green	52 F2	(Lombard Street East)		Elmfield Vale	14 E4
Dunmore Grove	44 F2	Eaton Hall	46 F2 [18]	Elizabeth Street	25 B4	Elmfield Walk	14 D4
Dunmore Lawn	44 F3	Eaton House	52 F2 [1]	Elkwood	56 E1	Elmfield Way	14 D4
Dunmore Park	44 F2	Eaton Place	49 B4	Ellenfield Road	25 C2	Elmgrove	60 D4
Dunne Street	72 D2	Eaton Road	46 F2	Ellensborough	54 F3	Elmgrove Terrace	67 C2 [22]
Dunree Park	26 F1	Eaton Square (Monkstown)	49 B4	Ellensborough Avenue	54 F3	Elmpark Apts.	48 E2
Dunsandle Court	23 A3	Eaton Square (Terenure)	46 F2	Ellensborough Close	54 F3	Elmpark Avenue	47 B1
Dunsandle Grove	23 A3	Eaton Terrace	52 F2	Ellensborough Copse	54 F3	Elms	48 F3
Dunseverick Road	26 E4	Eaton Way	52 F2	Ellensborough Court	54 F3	Elmwood Avenue Lower	47 B1
Dunsink Avenue	24 D2	Eaton Wood Avenue	64 E3	Ellensborough Crescent	54 F3	Elmwood Avenue Upper	47 B1
Dunsink Drive	24 D2	Eaton Wood Court	64 E3	Ellensborough Dale	54 F3	Elmwood Close	21 B1
Dunsink Gardens	24 D2	Eaton Wood Green	64 E3	Ellensborough Downs	54 F3	Elmwood Court	1 C1 [1]
Dunsink Green	24 D2	Eaton Wood Grove	64 E3	Ellensborough Grange	54 F3	Elmwood Drive	1 C1
Dunsink Lane	23 A2	Eaton Wood Square	64 E2	Ellensborough Green	54 F3	Elmwood Park	1 C1
Dunsink Park	24 D2	Ebenezer Terrace	74 E2	Ellensborough Grove	54 F3	Elmwood Road	1 C1
Dunsink Road	24 D2	Eblana Avenue	50 D4	Ellensborough Lane	54 F3	Elner Court	4 D4
Dunsoghly	23 C1	Eblana Villas	76 E1	Ellensborough Lawn	54 F3	Elton Court (Coolock)	26 F1 [1]
Dunsoghly Avenue	23 C1	(Lr Grand Canal St)		Ellensborough Meadows	54 F3	Elton Court (Dalkey)	60 E1
Dunsoghly Close	23 C1	Eblana Villas (off Arbour Hill)	70 E3	Ellensborough Park	54 F3	Elton Court (Dunboyne)	7 B3
Dunsoghly Court	23 C1	Eccles Court	71 B1	Ellensborough Rise	54 F3	Elton Court (Leixlip)	32 F1
Dunsoghly Drive	23 C1	Eccles Place	71 B1	Ellensborough View	54 F3	Elton Court (Marino)	25 C4 [17]
Dunsoghly Green	23 C1	Eccles Street	71 A1	Ellensborough Walk	54 F3	Elton Drive (Coolock)	27 A1
Dunsoghly Grove	23 C1	Echlin Street	74 E1	Ellensborough Way	54 F3	Elton Drive (Dunboyne)	7 B2
Dunsoghly Park	23 C1	Eden Avenue	57 A1	Ellesmere	58 F2 [4]	Elton Grove (Dunboyne)	7 B3
Dunstaffnage Hall Apts	58 F1 [6]	Eden Court	57 A1	Ellesmere Avenue	70 D1	Elton Park (Coolock)	27 A1
Dunville Avenue	47 B1	Eden Crescent	57 A1	Ellis Court	70 E4	Elton Park (Dalkey)	60 E1
Durham Place	60 D1 [18]	Eden Grove	57 A1	Ellis House Apts.	70 F4	Elton Walk	27 A1 [1]
Durham Road	39 B4	Eden Park	60 D1	Ellis Quay	70 E4	Ely Close	55 B3
Durrow Road	46 E1	Eden Park Avenue	58 D1	Ellis Street	70 E4	Ely Crescent	55 B3 [1]
Dursey Row	22 F1	Eden Park Drive	48 D4	Elm Close	34 E3	Ely Drive	55 B3
Dwyer Park	67 C1	Eden Park Road	58 D1	Elm Court (Jobstown)	54 D2	Ely Green	55 B3 [3]
		Eden Quay	71 C4	Elm Court (Lucan)	34 E3	Ely Grove	55 B3
E		Eden Road Lower	60 D1	Elm Dene	34 E3	Ely Place	75 C2
Eagle Hill	49 A3 [15]	Eden Road Upper	60 D1	Elm Drive (Jobstown)	54 D2	Ely Place Upper	75 C2
Eagle Hill Avenue	46 F2 [4]	Eden Terrace (Botanic Ave)	25 A4	Elm Drive (Lucan)	34 E3	Ely View	55 B3
Eagle Park	26 D1	Eden Terrace (Dun Laoghaire)	60 D1	Elm Green	34 E3	Embassy Lawn	47 C2
*Eagle Terrace (Dalkey)	60 F2	Eden Villas	60 D1 [5]	Elm Grove	49 A4	Emerald Cottages	76 F2
Eagle Terrace (Dundrum)	57 C1 [3]	Edenbrook Court	56 F1 [5]	Elm Grove (Jobstown)	54 D2	Emerald Place	72 D3
Eagle Valley	66 E4	Edenbrook Drive	46 E4	Elm Grove (Lucan)	34 E3	Emerald Square	74 D2
Eaglewood Apts	59 C2 [5]	Edenbrook Park	46 E4	Elm House	76 D3	Emerald Street	72 E3
Eaglewood House	59 C2 [7]	Edenmore	26 F2	Elm House Apartments	54 D2 [1]	Emerald Terrace	74 E2
Eaglewood Mews	59 C2 [8]	Edenmore Avenue	26 F1	Elm Mount Avenue	25 C2	Emily Lawless Court	27 C1 [1]
Earl Place	71 B3	Edenmore Crescent	27 A2	Elm Mount Close	26 D2	Emmet Court	73 A2
Earl Street North	71 B3	Edenmore Drive	26 F2	Elm Mount Court	26 D3	Emmet Crescent	73 A2
Earl Street South	74 F1	Edenmore Gardens	26 F2	Elm Mount Crescent	26 D2	Emmet Place	70 F4
Earls Court	74 D3	Edenmore Green	26 F2	Elm Mount Drive	26 D2	Emmet Road	73 A1
Earls Court (Cabra)	69 C1	Edenmore Grove	26 F2	Elm Mount Grove	26 D2	Emmet Square	48 F3
Earls Court (Terenure)	46 F2 [15]	Edenmore Park	26 F2	Elm Mount Heights	26 D2	Emmet Street (Harold's Cross)	74 F4
Earlscroft	67 C4	Edenvale	57 A2	Elm Mount Lawn	26 D2	Emmet Street (Nth Circular Rd)	71 C1
Earlsfort	34 F3	Edenvale Road	47 B1	Elm Mount Park	26 D2	Emmet Street (Sallynoggin)	60 D1 [4]
Earlsfort Avenue	34 F3	Edenwood (Goatstown)	48 D4 [1]	Elm Mount Rise	26 D2	Emor Street	75 A3
Earlsfort Close	34 F3	Edgewood (Richmond Road)	25 B4 [10]	Elm Mount Road	26 D2	Emorville Avenue	75 A3
Earlsfort Court	34 F3	Edgewood Lawns	22 E1	Elm Mount View	26 D2	Empress Place	72 D2
Earlsfort Drive	34 F3	Edmondsbury Court	34 E1 [1]	Elm Park (Celbridge)	32 D3	Enaville Avenue	72 E1
Earlsfort Gardens	34 F2	Edmondstown	56 E3	Elm Park (Nutley Lane)	48 D1	(off Annesley Place)	
Earlsfort Green	34 F3	Edmondstown Green	56 E2	Elm Park Terrace	46 F2	Enaville Road	72 E1
Earlsfort Grove	34 F3	Edmondstown Road	56 E3	Elm Road (Donnycarney)	26 D3	Engine Alley (off Meath St)	74 F1
Earlsfort Lane	34 F3	Edward Court	76 D4	Elm Road (Fox & Geese)	45 A1	English Row	32 D4
Earlsfort Lawn	34 F2	Edward Road	68 D3	Elm Vale	34 E3	Ennafort Avenue	26 F2
Earlsfort Meadows	34 F2	*Edward Terrace	60 F2	Elm Way (Grange Wood)	57 A2 [3]	Ennafort Court	26 F3
Earlsfort Park	34 F2	(Off Nerano Rd)		Elm Way (Lucan)	34 E3	Ennafort Drive	26 F3
Earlsfort Rise	34 F3	Edwards Court	56 E2	Elm Wood	34 E3	Ennafort Grove	26 F2
Earlsfort Road	34 F2	Edwin Court	60 E2 [5]	Elmbrook	34 E2	Ennafort Park	26 F3
Earlsfort Terrace	75 C3	Effra Road	47 A1	Elmbrook Crescent	34 E2	Ennafort Road	26 F3
Earlsfort Vale	34 F2	Eglington Road	67 C2 [3]	Elmbrook Lawn	34 E2	Ennel Avenue	26 F2
Earlsfort View	34 F3	Eglinton Court	47 C1	Elmbrook Walk	34 E2	Ennel Court	64 E1 [6]
		Eglinton Park (Donnybrook)	47 C1	Elmcastle Close	45 A3	Ennel Drive	26 F2

STREET NAME	PAGE/GRID REFERENCE
Ennel Park	26 F2
Ennis Grove	39 A3 [19]
Enniskerry	66 D3
Enniskerry Bridge	66 E3
Enniskerry Demense	66 E4
Enniskerry Road (Phibsborough)	25 A4 [3]
Enniskerry Road (Sandyford)	58 D4
Erne Place Little	76 D1
Erne Place Lower	72 D4
Erne Place(Lansdowne Park)	76 E1
Erne Street Lower	72 D4
Erne Street Upper	76 D1
Erne Terrace Front	76 D1
Erne Terrace Rere	76 D1
Errigal Gardens	45 C1
Errigal Road	36 F4
Errigal Road	45 C1
Erris Road	24 E4
Erris Square	22 F1
Esker Drive	34 D2
Esker Glebe	34 D2
Esker Lane	34 E2
Esker Lawns	34 D1
Esker Lodge	34 E2
Esker Lodge Avenue	34 E2
Esker Lodge Close	34 E2
Esker Lodge View	34 E2
Esker Manor	34 E2
Esker Meadow	34 E2
Esker Meadow Close	34 E2
Esker Meadow Court	34 E2
Esker Meadow Green	34 E2
Esker Meadow Grove	34 E2
Esker Meadow Lawn	34 E2
Esker Meadow Rise	34 E2
Esker Meadow View	34 E2
Esker Park	34 E2
Esker Pines	34 E1
Esker Road	34 D2
Esker South	34 D3
Esker Villas	47 A1 [11]
Esker Woods	34 E2
Esker Woods Close	34 E2
Esker Woods Court	34 E2
Esker Woods Drive	34 E2
Esker Woods Grove	34 E2
Esker Woods Rise	34 E2
Esker Woods View	34 E2
Esker Woods Walk	34 E2
Esmond Avenue	25 C4
Esmonde Terrace	67 B2 [18]
Esplanade Terrace	68 D2 [3]
Esposito Road	45 C1 [5]
Essex Gate (off Essex Quay)	71 A4
Essex Quay	71 A4
Essex Street East	71 A4
Essex Street West (off Fishamble St)	71 A4
Estate Avenue	48 E1
Estate Cottages	76 E2
Estate Cottages (Northumberland Rd)	76 E2
Estate Cottages (Shelbourne Rd)	76 F3
Estuary Court	2 E1
Estuary Road	2 E1
Estuary Road	2 F2
Estuary Roundabout (Swords)	2 D1
Estuary Row	3 B2
Estuary Walk	2 F2
Eugene Street	74 E2
Eustace Street	71 B4
Everton Avenue	70 D2
Evora Crescent	30 D1 [12]
Evora Park	30 D1
Evora Terrace	30 D1 [2]
Ewington Lane	74 D1
Exchange Court	71 C4
Exchange Street Lower (off Wood Quay)	71 A4
Exchange Street Upper (off Lord Edward St)	71 A4
Exchequer Street	75 B1
Excise Walk	72 E3
Eyre Court	2 E3

F

STREET NAME	PAGE/GRID REFERENCE
Faber Grove	59 B1 [9]
Fade Street	75 B1
Fagan's Lane	17 C3 [2]
Fair Haven	3 B2 [1]
Fairacre	2 F3
Fairbrook Lawn	46 F4
Fairfield Avenue	72 E2
Fairfield Court	39 A3 [47]
Fairfield House	46 F2 [24]
Fairfield Park	47 A2
Fairfield Road	25 A4
Fairgreen	53 A2
Fairgreen Court	67 C2 [50]
Fairgreen Road	67 B2 [11]
Fairgreen Terrace	67 C2 [32]
Fairlawn Park	24 E2
Fairlawn Road	24 E2
Fairlawns	60 E2 [6]
Fairview Avenue (Ringsend)	39 A3 [49]
Fairview Avenue Lower	25 C4
Fairview Avenue Upper	25 C4
Fairview Close	25 C4
Fairview Court	25 C4 [14]
Fairview Green	25 C4 [7]
Fairview Lawn	64 D1
Fairview Passage	25 C4 [10]
Fairview Strand	25 C4
Fairview Terrace	25 C4 [11]
Fairways	46 E4
Fairway's Avenue	24 F2
Fairway's Green	24 F2
Fairways Grove	24 E2
Fairway's Park	24 F2
Fairy Castle	61 B2
Fairyhill (Oldcourt)	67 B3
Fairyhill (Stillorgan)	59 A1
Faith Avenue	72 E1
Falcarragh Road	25 B2
Falls Road	64 D2
Farmhill Drive	47 C4
Farmhill Park	47 C4
Farmhill Road	47 C4
Farmleigh	23 A4
Farmleigh Avenue (Castleknock)	23 A4
Farmleigh Avenue (Stillorgan)	58 F1
Farmleigh Close (Castleknock)	23 A4
Farmleigh Close (Stillorgan)	58 F1
Farmleigh Court	23 A4
Farmleigh Park (Castleknock)	23 A4
Farmleigh Park (Stillorgan)	58 F1
Farmleigh View	23 A4
Farmleigh Woods	23 A4
Farney Park	39 A4
Farnham Crescent	24 E2
Farnham Drive	24 E2
Farrenboley Cottages	47 B3
Farrenboley Park	47 B3
Fassaroe	66 F3
Fassaroe	67 A2
Fassaroe Avenue	67 A3
Fassaroe Glen	67 A2
Fassaroe Lane	67 A3
Father Colohan Terrace	67 C2 [11]
Father Kit Court	46 D1 [3]
Father Lemass Court	36 D3
Father Mathew Square	70 F3
Father Matthew Bridge	70 F4
Father Scully House	71 C2
Fatima Mansions (off James's Walk)	74 D2
Fatima Terrace	67 C2
Faughart Road	46 E1 [3]
Faulkner's Terrace	73 C1
Faussagh Avenue	24 E4
Faussagh Road	24 F4
Fawn Lodge	23 A4
Feltrim	3 A4
Feltrim Hall	2 D3
Feltrim Road	2 F4
Fenian Street	76 D1
Fergus Road	46 F2
Ferguson Road	25 A3
Fernbrook	67 B1 [6]
Ferncarrig Avenue	58 D3
Ferncarrig Court	58 D3
Ferncarrig Rise	58 D3
Ferncourt Avenue	55 B3
Ferncourt Close	55 B3
Ferncourt Crescent	55 B3 [5]
Ferncourt Drive	55 B3 [4]
Ferncourt Green	55 B3
Ferncourt Park	55 B3
Ferncourt View	55 B3
Ferndale (Hartstown)	21 C1
Ferndale (Tallaght)	55 A2
Ferndale Avenue	24 F2
Ferndale Glen	64 D3
Ferndale Hill	64 D4
Ferndale Road (Bray)	67 A1
Ferndale Road (Glasnevin)	24 F2
Ferndale Road (Shankill)	64 D3
Fernhill Avenue	45 C3
Fernhill Park	45 C3
Fernhill Road	45 C2
Fernleigh	22 D3
Fernleigh Close	22 D3
Fernleigh Court	22 D3
Fernleigh Crescent	22 D3
Fernleigh Dale	22 D3
Fernleigh Dene	22 D4
Fernleigh Drive	22 D3
Fernleigh Grange	22 D4
Fernleigh Green	22 D3
Fernleigh Grove	22 D4
Fernleigh Heath	22 D4
Fernleigh Lawn	22 D3
Fernleigh Park	22 D3
Fernleigh Place	22 D3
Fernleigh Vale	22 D3
Fernleigh View	22 D4
Fernley Court	75 A2
Ferns Road	46 E1
Fernvale Drive	46 D1
Fernwood Avenue	54 E1
Fernwood Close	54 E1
Fernwood Court	54 E1
Fernwood Lawn	54 E1
Fernwood Park	54 E1
Fernwood Way	54 E1
Ferrard Road	46 F2
Ferrycarrig Avenue	13 B4
Ferrycarrig Drive	13 B4
Ferrycarrig Green	13 B4 [3]
Ferrycarrig Park	13 B4
Ferrycarrig Road	13 B4
Ferryman's Crossing	72 E3
Fertullagh Road	24 F4 [5]
Fettercairn	44 E4
Fettercairn Road	44 E4
Fey Yerra	58 F2 [8]
Fforester	34 E2
Fforester Close	34 E2
Fforester Court	34 E2
Fforester Drive	34 F2
Fforester Lawn	34 E2
Fforester Park	34 E2
Fforester Walk	34 E2
Fforester Way	34 E2
Fforster Crescent	34 E2
Field Avenue	45 C1 [1]
Field's Terrace	47 B1 [5]
Fieldview Cottages	49 A4 [6]
Fiery Lane	62 D4
Findlater Building Apts.	30 D1 [3]
Findlater Place	71 B3
Findlater Street (Dun Laoghaire)	60 E1 [7]
Findlater Street (Nth Circular Rd)	70 D3
Fingal Place	70 E2
Fingal Street	74 E2
Finglas	24 D1
Finglas East	24 E1
Finglas Park	24 E1
Finglas Place	24 E2
Finglas Road	24 E2
Finglas Road Old	24 F3
Finglas Roundabout (M50 J5)	11 A4
Finglas South	24 D2
Finglas Square	48 D3 [2]
Finglas West	24 D1
Finglaswood Road	24 D1
Finn Street	70 D3
Finneber Fort	24 E2
Finneber Fort Square	24 E2
Finnscourt	34 D3
Finnsgreen	34 D3
Finnsgrove	34 D3
Finnslawn	34 D3
Finnspark	34 D3
Finnstown Cloisters	34 D3
Finnstown Fairways	34 D3
Finnstown Hall	34 D3
Finnsvale	34 D3
Finnsview	34 D3
Finnswalk	34 D3
Finnswood	34 D3
Finsbury Green	47 B4
Finsbury House	76 F3
Finsbury Park	47 B4
Firgrove	60 E4 [7]
Firhouse	55 C1
Firhouse Road	55 B2
Firhouse Road West	55 A2
First Avenue (Belgard Heights)	44 F4
First Avenue (Sarsfield Road)	36 F3
First Avenue (Seville Place)	72 E3
Fishamble Street	71 A4
Fisherman's Green	3 B2 [6]
Fishermans Wharf	39 A2 [1]
Fitzgerald Park	59 C1 [1]
Fitzgerald Street	75 A4
Fitzgibbon Lane	71 C1
Fitzgibbon Street	71 C1
Fitzmaurice Road (Glasnevin)	24 F2
Fitzmaurice Road (Rathcoole)	52 F2
Fitzpatrick's Cottages	46 F1 [6]
Fitzroy Avenue	25 B4
Fitzwilliam Court	76 D4
Fitzwilliam Court (Fitzwilliam Square)	75 C2
Fitzwilliam Court (Stillorgan Road)	48 E3
Fitzwilliam Lane	76 D2
Fitzwilliam Place	75 C3
Fitzwilliam Place North (Grangegorman)	70 F3
Fitzwilliam Point	39 A3 [37]
Fitzwilliam Quay	39 A3
Fitzwilliam Quay	39 A3 [36]
Fitzwilliam Square	75 C2
Fitzwilliam Square East	76 D2
Fitzwilliam Square North	76 D2
Fitzwilliam Square South	75 C2
Fitzwilliam Square West	75 C2
Fitzwilliam Street (Ringsend)	39 A3 [2]
Fitzwilliam Street Lower	76 D2
Fitzwilliam Street Upper	76 D2
Fitzwilliam Terrace	68 D2 [21]
Fleet Street	71 B4
Fleming Road	25 A3
Fleming's Hall Apts.	76 D3
Fleming's Place	76 D3
Flemingstown Park	47 B4
Flemming House	76 D3
Fleurville	49 A4
Floraville Avenue	44 E1
Floraville Drive	44 E2
Floraville Estate	44 E1
Floraville Lawn	44 E1
Florence Road	67 C2
Florence Street	75 A3
Florence Terrace (Bray)	67 C2 [39]
*Florence Terrace (Leeson Park Avenue)	76 D4
Florence Villas (Bray)	67 C2 [40]
Florence Villas (Sandymount)	39 A4
Flower Grove	60 D2
Foley Street	71 C3
Fontenoy Street	71 A2
Fontenoy Terrace	68 D3
Fonthill Abbey	56 F1 [1]
Fonthill Park	56 F1
Fonthill Road (Clondalkin)	35 A2
Fonthill Road (Rathfarnham)	56 F1
Fonthill Road North	35 A3

STREET NAME	PAGE/GRID REFERENCE	STREET NAME	PAGE/GRID REFERENCE	STREET NAME	PAGE/GRID REFERENCE	STREET NAME	PAGE/GRID REFERENCE
Fonthill Road South	44 D2	Foxborough Grove	34 F3	Friarsland Avenue	47 C3 [3]	Gazelle Mews	9 B2
Forbes Lane	74 E2	Foxborough Hall	34 F3 [1]	Friarsland Crescent	47 C3	Gazelle Terrace	9 B2
Forbes Street	72 E4	Foxborough Heights	34 F3	Friarsland Road	47 C3	Gazelle Walk	9 B2
Forest Avenue (Kilnamanagh)	45 A3	Foxborough Hill	34 E3	Friary Avenue	70 F3	Geoffrey Keating Road	74 F2
Forest Avenue (Swords)	1 B3	Foxborough Lane	34 F3	Friary Court	70 F3	George Reynolds Flats	39 A3 [43]
Forest Boulevard	1 B3	Foxborough Lawn	34 F3	Friary Grove	70 F3	*George Reynolds Flats (off	39 A3
Forest Close	45 A3	Foxborough Manor	34 F3	Friel Avenue	36 D4	Oliver Plunkett Ave)	
Forest Court	1 B2	Foxborough Meadows	34 E3	Fumbally Court	75 A2	George's Avenue (Blackrock)	49 A3
Forest Crescent	1 B3	Foxborough Park	34 E3	Fumbally Lane	75 A2	Georges Court	72 D4
Forest Dale	1 B2	Foxborough Place	34 E3	Furry Glen	36 D1	George's Dock	72 D3
Forest Drive (Kilnamanagh)	45 A3	Foxborough Rise	34 E3	Furry Park Court	26 E3	George's Hill	71 A3
Forest Drive (Swords)	1 B3	Foxborough Road	34 E3	Furry Park Road	26 E3	George's Lane	70 F3
Forest Green (Kilnamanagh)	45 A3	Foxborough Row	34 F3	Furze Road (Phoenix Park)	36 E1	George's Place (Blackrock)	49 A3 [6]
Forest Green (Swords)	1 B3	Foxborough Walk	34 F3	Furze Road (Sandyford)	58 E2	George's Place (Dun Laoghaire)	50 D4
Forest Grove	1 B3	Foxborough Way	34 E3			George's Place (Temple Street)	71 B1
Forest Hills (Rathcoole)	52 E2	Foxdene Avenue	34 F3	**G**		George's Quay	71 C4
Forest Hills (Swords)	1 C3	Foxdene Drive	34 F3			Georges Road	24 E1 [1]
Forest Lawn	45 A3	Foxdene Gardens	34 F3	Gables	27 A1 [6]	George's Street Great South	75 B1
Forest Park (Kilnamanagh)	45 A3	Foxdene Green	34 F3	Gaelic Street	72 E2	George's Street Lower	50 D4
Forest Park (Leixlip)	32 F1	Foxdene Grove	34 F3	Gainsborough	2 F3	George's Street Upper	50 D4
Forest Park (Swords)	1 B2	Foxdene Park	34 F3	Gainsborough Avenue	2 F3	Georgian Hamlet	15 A4
Forest Road	1 B4	Foxes Grove	64 E3	Gainsborough Close	2 F3	Georgian Village	23 A4
Forest View	1 B3	Foxe's Lane	27 B2	Gainsborough Court	2 F3	Gerald Street	76 F1
Forest Walk	1 C3	Foxfield	34 D3	Gainsborough Crescent	2 F3	Geraldine Court	17 C3 [4]
Forest Way	1 C3	Foxfield Avenue	27 B2	Gainsborough Downs	2 F3	Geraldine Street	71 A1
Forestfields Road	1 C3	Foxfield Crescent	27 B2	Gainsborough Green	2 F3	Geraldstown Woods Apts	12 D4
Forestwood Avenue	12 D4	Foxfield Drive	27 B2	Gainsborough Lawn	2 F3	Gertrude Terrace	67 B2 [25]
Forestwood Close	12 E4	Foxfield Green	27 B2	Gainsborough Park	2 F3	Gilbert Road	74 F3
Forge Court	30 D2 [15]	Foxfield Grove	27 B2	Gallaun Road	11 C4	Gilford Avenue	39 B4
Forster Way	2 D2	Foxfield Heights	27 B2	Gallery Quay	76 E1	Gilford Court	39 A4 [10]
Fort Ostman	73 C4	Foxfield Lawn	27 B2	Galloping Green	58 F1	Gilford Drive	39 A4
Fortescue Lane	75 B4	Foxfield Park	27 B2	Galloping Green	59 A1 [9]	Gilford Park	39 A4
Fortfield Avenue	46 E3	Foxfield Road	27 B2	Gallows Hill	1 C2	Gilford Pines	39 A4 [46]
Fortfield Court	46 E3 [2]	Foxfield St John	27 B2	Galmoy Road	24 F4	Gilford Place	72 D2
Fortfield Crescent	46 E3	Foxford	34 F2	Galtrim Park	67 C2	Gilford Road	39 A4
Fortfield Drive	46 E3	Foxford Court	34 F2 [2]	Galtrim Road	67 C2	Gilford Terrace	39 B4 [1]
Fortfield Gardens	47 A2	Foxhill Avenue	27 A1	Galtymore Close	36 F4	Giltspur Heights	67 B4
Fortfield Grove	46 E3	Foxhill Close	27 A1	Galtymore Drive	73 B3	Giltspur Lane	67 B4
Fortfield Park	46 E3	Foxhill Court	27 A1	Galtymore Park	36 F4	Giltspur Wood	67 B3
Fortfield Road	46 E2	Foxhill Crescent	27 A1	Galtymore Road	73 B3	Glandore Park	59 C1
Fortfield Road	46 E3	Foxhill Drive	27 A1	Gandon Close	46 F1 [9]	Glandore Road	25 C3
Fortfield Square	46 E3	Foxhill Green	14 D4	Gandon Court	34 D1 [16]	Glasanaon Court	24 E2
Fortfield Terrace	47 A2	Foxhill Grove	27 A1	Gandon Hall	71 C3	Glasanaon Park	24 E2
Forth Road	72 F2	Foxhill Lawn	27 A1	Gandon Mews	34 D1 [10]	Glasanaon Road	24 E2
Forthill Court	56 F1 [6]	Foxhill Park	27 A1	Garda Terrace (Phoenix Park)	69 C3	Glasaree Court	24 E2
Fortlawn Avenue	22 D1	Foxhill Way	27 A1	Garden Lane	74 F1	Glasaree Road	24 E2
Fortlawn Crescent	22 D1	Foxpark	34 D3	Garden Terrace	74 F4	Glasilawn Avenue	24 F2
Fortlawn Drive	22 D1	Foxrock	59 A3	Garden Terrace	74 F3	Glasilawn Road	24 F2
Fortlawn Park	22 D1	Foxrock Avenue	59 B2	(off Clanbrassil St Upper)		Glaslyn	26 D4
Fortlawns	60 E2	Foxrock Close	59 A2	Garden View	75 B4	Glasmeen Road	24 F2
Fortrose Park	46 E4	Foxrock Court	59 B2	Gardiner Lane	71 C2	Glasmore Park	1 C1
Fortunestown	53 C1	Foxrock Crescent	59 B2	Gardiner Place	71 B2	Glasnamana Place	24 F2 [2]
Fortunestown Close	53 C1	Foxrock Green	59 A2	Gardiner Row	71 B2	Glasnamana Road	24 F2
Fortunestown Crescent	53 C1	Foxrock Grove	59 B2	Gardiner St Middle	71 C2	Glasnevin	24 F3
Fortunestown Lane	53 B1	Foxrock Manor	58 F2	Gardiner Street Lower	71 C2	Glasnevin Avenue	24 F1
Fortunestown Road	54 D2	Foxrock Mount	59 A2 [4]	Gardiner Street Upper	71 B1	Glasnevin Court	24 E3
Fortunestown Way	54 D1	Foxrock Park	59 A2	Garnett Hall	7 A2	Glasnevin Downs	24 F3
Fortview Avenue	39 C1	Foxrock Wood	59 B2	Garnett Vale	7 A2	Glasnevin Drive	25 A1
Fortwilliam	48 E4	Foxwood (Lucan)	34 D3	Garnish Square	22 F1	Glasnevin Hill	25 A3
Foster Place North	72 D1	Foxwood (Swords)	2 D2	Garrison Mews	64 D1	Glasnevin North	24 F1
Foster Place South	71 B4	Foyle Road	25 C4	Garrynisk Close	44 F3	Glasnevin Oaks	24 F3 [3]
(College Green)		Frances Ball House	46 F4 [23]	Garrynisk Road	44 F3	Glasnevin Park	24 F1
Foster Terrace	72 D1	Francis Street	74 F1	Garrynure	47 B2	Glasnevin Woods	24 E3
Fosterbrook	48 E2	Frank Sherwin Bridge	70 D4	Garryowen Road	36 E3	Glasson Court	47 B3
Fosters Avenue	48 D3	Frankfort	47 B4 [10]	Gartan Avenue	25 A4	Glasthule Buildings	60 E1 [11]
Fountain Place	70 F3	Frankfort Avenue	47 A2	Gartan Court	2 E1	Glasthule Road	60 E1
Fountain Road	69 C3	Frankfort Cottages	72 D2	Gartan Drive	2 E1	Gleann na Rí	63 C1
Fountain View Apts	74 D1	Frankfort Court	46 F2 [8]	Garter Lane	53 B1	Gleann na Smol (Monkstown)	49 B4
(James's Street)		Frankfort Flats	46 F2 [9]	Garthy Wood Apts.	56 D1	Gleann na Smól (Tallaght)	54 F2
Fourth Avenue (Seville Place)	72 E3	Frankfort Mews	47 B4	Garville Avenue Upper	46 F2	Glebe (Airport)	13 B1
Fourth Avenue (Tallaght)	44 F4	Frankfort Park	47 B4	Garville Court	47 A2 [10]	Glebe (Newcastle)	41 C3
Fownes Street Lower	71 B4	Frascati Court	49 A3 [23]	Garville Drive	47 A2 [6]	Glebe (Rathcoole)	52 D3
(off Temple Bar)		Frascati Hall	49 A3 [24]	Garville Lane	47 A2	Glebe Hall	59 C1
Fownes Street Upper	71 B4	Frascati Park	49 A3	Garville Place	47 A2 [5]	Glebe View (Finglas)	24 E2 [7]
Fox and Geese	45 A1	Frascati Road	49 A3	Garville Road	47 A2	Gledswood Avenue	47 C3
Fox Hill	55 A4	Frederick Court	71 B2	Gas Yard Lane	3 B2	Gledswood Close	47 C3
Foxborough Avenue	34 E3	*Frederick House	75 C1	Gateway Avenue	25 A1	Gledswood Drive	47 C3 [5]
Foxborough Close	34 F2	(Fredrick Street South)		Gateway Court	25 A1	Gledswood Park	47 C3
Foxborough Court	34 F2	Frederick Lane North	71 B2	Gateway Crescent	25 A1	Glen Avenue	59 B3
Foxborough Crescent	34 F3 [2]	Frederick Street North	71 B2	Gateway Gardens	25 A1	Glen Close	59 B3
Foxborough Downes	34 E3	Frederick Street South	75 C1	Gateway Mews	25 A1	Glen Dale	59 B3
Foxborough Drive	34 E3	*French Mullen Flats	75 B3	Gateway Place	25 A1	Glen Drive	59 B3
Foxborough Gardens	34 F3	(Charlemont Street)		Gateway View	25 A1	Glen Druid	64 E1
Foxborough Glade	34 F3	French Park	9 B2	Gaybrook Lawns	3 A3	Glen Ellan Avenue	1 C1
Foxborough Glen	34 F3	Frenchman's Lane	71 C3	Gazelle Avenue	9 B2	Glen Ellan Close	1 C1
Foxborough Green	34 F3	Friar's Walk	44 E1 [5]	Gazelle Lane	9 B2	Glen Ellan Court	1 C1

STREET NAME	PAGE/GRID REFERENCE
Glen Ellan Crescent	1 C1
Glen Ellan Drive	1 C1
Glen Ellan Gardens	1 C1
Glen Ellan Green	1 C1
Glen Ellan Grove	1 C1
Glen Ellan Park	1 C1
Glen Ellan Pines	1 C1
Glen Ellan Walk	1 C1
Glen Garth	59 B3
Glen Grove	59 B3
Glen Lawn Drive	59 B3
Glen na Smol	67 C4
Glen Terrace	60 E1 [10]
Glen Walk	59 B3
Glenaan Road	25 B2
Glenabbey Road	48 E4
Glenacre	62 E4
Glenageary Avenue	60 D2
Glenageary Court	60 D2
Glenageary Hall	60 E2
Glenageary Lodge	60 D2
Glenageary Park	60 D2
Glenageary Road Lower	60 D1
Glenageary Road LR (Dun Laoghaire)	50 D4
Glenageary Road Upper	60 D1
Glenageary Woods	60 D1
Glenalbyn Road	58 F1
Glenalua Heights	60 E3
Glenalua Road	60 E3
Glenalua Terrace	60 E3
Glenamuck Cottages	63 A2
Glenamuck North	62 F1
Glenamuck Road	59 B4
Glenamuck Road	62 F2
Glenamuck Road	63 A1
Glenann	46 F4 [4]
Glenanne	46 E2
Glenard Avenue (Bray)	67 C2
Glenard Avenue (Cabra)	70 D1
Glenard Hall	47 C3 [7]
Glenarm Avenue	25 B4
Glenarriff Road	23 C3
Glenart Avenue	48 F4
Glenaulin	36 D2
Glenaulin Drive	36 D2
Glenaulin Green	35 C2 [2]
Glenaulin Park	36 D2
Glenaulin Road	35 C2
Glenavon Court	25 A3 [18]
Glenavon Park	64 D1
Glenavy Park	46 E2
Glenayle Road	26 F1
Glenayr Road	46 F2
Glenbeigh Park	69 C1
Glenbeigh Road	70 D2
Glenbourne Avenue	58 F4
Glenbourne Close	58 F4
Glenbourne Crescent	58 F4
Glenbourne Drive	58 F4
Glenbourne Green	58 F4
Glenbourne Grove	58 F4
Glenbourne Park	58 F4
Glenbourne Road	58 F4
Glenbourne View	58 F4
Glenbourne Walk	58 F4
Glenbourne Way	58 F4
Glenbower Park	47 B4 [1]
Glenbrae	64 E2
Glenbrian Hall	26 D4 [8]
Glenbrook	66 E3
Glenbrook	67 B3 [6]
Glenbrook Park	46 F4
Glenbrook Road	23 C3
Glenburgh Terrace	67 B2 [2]
Glencairn	58 E3
Glencairn Avenue	58 E3
Glencairn Chase	58 E3
Glencairn Close	58 E3
Glencairn Copse	58 E4
Glencairn Court	58 E4
Glencairn Crescent	58 E4
Glencairn Dale	58 E3
Glencairn Drive	58 E3
Glencairn Garth	58 E3 [1]
Glencairn Glade	58 E4
Glencairn Glen	58 F4
Glencairn Green	58 E3
Glencairn Grove	58 F4
Glencairn Heath	58 E3
Glencairn Heights	58 E3
Glencairn Lawn	58 E3
Glencairn Oaks	58 E4
Glencairn Park	58 E3
Glencairn Place	58 E4
Glencairn Rise	58 E3
Glencairn Road	58 E3
Glencairn Thicket	58 F3
Glencairn View	58 E3
Glencairn Walk	58 E3
Glencairn Way	58 E3
Glencar Road	69 C2
Glencarr Court	64 E1 [8]
Glencarr Lawn	64 E1
Glencarraig	29 B1
Glencarrig Court	55 B2
Glencarrig Drive	55 B2
Glencarrig Green	55 B2
Glencarthy Court Apts.	26 D3
Glencloy Road	25 B2
Glencorp Road	25 C2
Glencourt Estate	67 C3
Glencullen	61 C3
Glencullen	62 E4
Glencullen Bridge	65 B1
Glendale	20 D4
Glendale Drive	67 C3
Glendale Meadows	20 E4
Glendale Park	46 D3
Glendalough Road	25 A4 [6]
Glendenning Lane (off Wicklow Street)	75 B1
Glendhu Park	23 C3
Glendhu Road	23 C3
Glendinning Lane	75 B1
Glendoher Avenue	56 F1
Glendoher Close	56 E1
Glendoher Drive	56 F1
Glendoher Park	56 E1
Glendoher Road	56 E1
Glendoo Close	45 B3
Glendown Avenue	46 D3
Glendown Close	46 D3
Glendown Court	46 D3
Glendown Crescent	46 D3
Glendown Drive	46 D3
Glendown Green	46 D3
Glendown Grove	46 D3
Glendown Lawn	46 D3
Glendown Park	46 D3
Glendown Road	46 D3
Glendun Road	25 B2
Glenealy Downs	8 F4
Glenealy Road	74 D4
Gleneaston	19 B4
Gleneaston Avenue	19 B4
Gleneaston Close	19 B4
Gleneaston Crescent	19 B4
Gleneaston Drive	19 B4
Gleneaston Gardens	19 B4
Gleneaston Green	19 B4
Gleneaston Grove	19 B4
Gleneaston Lawns	19 B4
Gleneaston Manor	19 B4
Gleneaston Park	19 B4
Gleneaston Rise	19 B4
Gleneaston Square	19 B4
Gleneaston View	19 B4
Gleneaston Way	19 B4
Gleneaston Woods	19 B4
Glenesk Court	39 A4 [32]
Glenfarne Road	26 F1
Glenfield Avenue	35 A2
Glenfield Close	35 A2
Glenfield Drive	35 A2
Glenfield Grove	35 A2
Glenfield Park	35 A2
Glengara Close	60 D1 [15]
Glengara Park	60 D1
Glengariff Parade	71 A1
Glengarriff Crescent	71 B1
Glengarriff Parade	71 B1
Glenhill Avenue	24 E2
Glenhill Court	24 E2
Glenhill Drive	24 E2
Glenhill Grove	24 E2
Glenhill Road	24 E2
Glenhill Villas	24 E2 [2]
Glenlucan	67 B2
Glenlyon Crescent	55 C2
Glenlyon Grove	55 C2
Glenlyon Park	55 C2
Glenmalure Park	73 C2
Glenmalure Square	47 B2
*Glenmalure Villas	74 D2
Glenmaroon Park	35 C2
Glenmaroon Road	35 C2
Glenmore	8 E1
Glenmore Court	56 F2
Glenmore Park	56 F2
Glenmore Road	69 C1
Glenmurry Park	45 C3
Glenomena Grove	48 E2
Glenomena Park	48 E2
Glenpark Close	35 B1
Glenpark Drive	35 B1
Glenpark Road	35 B1
Glenshane Close	54 D1
Glenshane Crescent	54 D1
Glenshane Dale	54 D1 [5]
Glenshane Drive	54 D1
Glenshane Gardens	54 D1
Glenshane Green	54 D1
Glenshane Grove	54 D1
Glenshane Lawns	54 D1
Glenshane Park	54 D1
Glenshane Place	54 D1 [6]
Glenshesk Road	25 C2
Glenside Villas	35 C1 [2]
Glenthorn	67 B4
Glenties Drive	24 D2
Glenties Park	24 D2
Glentow Road	25 B2
Glentworth Park	27 A1 [2]
Glenvale	34 E3
Glenvar Park	48 F3
Glenvara Park	55 C2
Glenview (Enniskerry)	66 D3
Glenview (Rochestown Avenue)	60 D3
Glenview Drive	55 B1
Glenview Lawns	55 B1
Glenview Park	55 B1
Glenville Avenue	22 E2
Glenville Court	22 E3
Glenville Drive	22 E3
Glenville Garth	22 E3
Glenville Green	22 E2
Glenville Grove	22 E2
Glenville Lawn	22 E2
Glenville Road	22 E3
Glenville Terrace	47 C4 [8]
Glenville Way	22 E2
Glenwood	67 B2
Glenwood Road	26 F1
Glin Avenue	13 B4
Glin Close	13 B4 [6]
Glin Court	13 B4 [7]
Glin Crescent	13 B4
Glin Drive	13 B4
Glin Grove	13 B4
Glin Park	13 B4
Glin Road	13 B4
Glitspur Brook	67 C3
Gloucester Diamond	71 C2
Gloucester Lane (off Sean McDermott Street Lower)	71 C2
Gloucester Place	71 C2
Gloucester Place Lower	71 C2
Gloucester Place Upper	71 C2
Gloucester Street South	72 D4
Glovers Alley	75 B1
Glovers Court (off York Street)	75 B1
Goatstown	48 D4
Goatstown Avenue	47 C4
Goatstown Road	47 C4
Gobán Saor	58 E4
Godfrey Place (off Oxmanstown Road)	70 D2
Gofton Hall	24 E1 [2]
Golden Ball	62 F2
Golden Lane	75 A1
Goldenbridge Avenue	73 B2
Goldenbridge Gardens	73 A2
Goldenbridge Terrace	73 A2
Goldenbridge Walk	36 F4
Goldenbridge Walk	73 A2
Goldsmith Hall Apts.	72 D4
Goldsmith Street	71 A1
Goldsmith Terrace	67 C2 [25]
Goldstone Court Apts.	74 D4
Golf Links Road	15 A2
Gordon Avenue	59 A3
Gordon Place	75 B3
Gordon Street	76 F1
Gorsefield Court	26 F2 [1]
Gort na Mona Drive	59 B3
Gortbeg Avenue	24 E3
Gortbeg Drive	24 E3
Gortbeg Park	24 E3
Gortbeg Road	24 E3
Gortmore Avenue	24 E2
Gortmore Drive	24 E2
Gortmore Park	24 E3
Gortmore Road	24 E3
Gosworth Park	60 E1
Gowrie Park	60 D1
Grace O'Malley Drive	30 D2
Grace O'Malley Road	30 D2
Grace Park Avenue	25 B4
Grace Park Court	25 C2
Grace Park Gardens	25 B4
Grace Park Heights	25 C3
Grace Park Lawns	25 C2 [9]
Grace Park Manor	25 B3
Grace Park Meadows	25 C3
Grace Park Road	25 C3
Grace Park Terrace	25 C3
Gracefield Avenue	26 F2
Gracefield Road	26 E2
Grafton Street	75 B1
Graham Court	71 B2
Graham's Row	71 A2
Graigue Court	11 C4
Granby Lane	71 A2
Granby Place	71 B3
Granby Row	71 A2
Grand Canal Docks	76 F1
Grand Canal Place	74 E1
Grand Canal Quay	76 E1
Grand Canal Street Lower	76 E1
Grand Canal Street Upper	76 E2
Grand Canal View	73 B2
Grand Parade	75 C3
Grange (Malahide)	14 E1
Grange (Meath)	6 E4
Grange Abbey Crescent	14 E4
Grange Abbey Drive	14 E4
Grange Abbey Grove	14 E4
Grange Abbey Road	14 E4
Grange Avenue	14 F4
Grange Brook	56 F2
Grange Close (Kilbarrack)	27 C1
Grange Close (Pottery Road)	59 C3
Grange Cottages	58 F1 [3]
Grange Court	57 A1
Grange Crescent	59 B2
Grange Downs	57 A1
Grange Drive	27 C1
Grange Grove	59 B1 [3]
Grange Hall	57 B3
Grange Hall Apts.	27 A2
Grange Lodge Avenue	14 D4
Grange Lodge Court	14 D4
Grange Manor	34 D3
Grange Manor Avenue	57 A1
Grange Manor Close	57 A1
Grange Manor Drive	57 A1
Grange Manor Grove	57 A1
Grange Manor Road	57 A1
Grange Parade	27 C1
Grange Park (Baldoyle)	14 F4
Grange Park (Cornelscourt)	59 B2

STREET NAME	PAGE/GRID REFERENCE		STREET NAME	PAGE/GRID REFERENCE		STREET NAME	PAGE/GRID REFERENCE		STREET NAME	PAGE/GRID REFERENCE	
Grange Park (Willbrook)	56	F1	Granville Park	59	A1	Greenore Terrace	76	E1	Grove Avenue (Mount Merrion)	48	F4
Grange Park Avenue	27	A2	Granville Road (Cabinteely)	59	C3	Greenpark Road	33	C2	Grove Court	22	D1
Grange Park Close	27	B2	Granville Road (Deans Grange)	59	A2	Greenridge Court	22	E1	Grove Court (Bluebell)	36	F4 [4]
Grange Park Crescent	27	B2	Grattan Bridge	71	A4	Greentrees Drive	45	C2	Grove Court	1	A2 [1]
Grange Park Drive	27	A2	Grattan Court	31	C4	Greentrees Park	45	C2	(Brackenstown Road)		
Grange Park Green	27	B2	Grattan Court	76	E1	Greentrees Road	45	C2	Grove Court Apts.	22	D1
Grange Park Grove	27	A2	Grattan Court East	76	E1	Greenview	14	E2	Grove House Apts.	59	A3
Grange Park Rise	27	B1	Grattan Crescent	36	F3	Greenville Avenue	74	F3	Grove House Gardens	48	F4 [5]
Grange Park Road	27	A2	Grattan Hall	14	E4	Greenville Parade (Blackpitts)	74	F3	Grove Lane	13	C4
Grange Park View	27	B1	Grattan Lodge	14	E4	Greenville Place	74	F3	Grove Lawn	3	C3
Grange Park Walk	27	A2	Grattan Parade	25	A4	Greenville Road	49	B4	Grove Lawn (Stillorgan)	48	F4
Grange Rise	14	F4	Grattan Place	76	E1	Greenville Terrace	74	F3	Grove Lawns (Malahide)	3	C3
Grange Road (Baldoyle)	14	F4	Grattan Street	76	E1	Greenwood	13	C1	Grove Paddock	48	F4
Grange Road (Marley Park)	57	A2	Gravel Walk Church Apts.	70	E4	Greenwood Avenue	14	D4	Grove Park (Coolock)	13	C4
Grange Road (Rathfarnham)	46	F4	(off Hendrick Street)			Greenwood Close	14	D4	Grove Park (Rathmines)	75	B4
Grange Road (The Priory)	56	F1	Gray Square	74	F1	Greenwood Court	14	D4	Grove Park Avenue	24	F1
Grange Terrace	59	B1 [6]	Gray Street (off Meath St)	74	F1	Greenwood Drive	14	D4	Grove Park Crescent	24	F1
Grange View Close	43	B1	Great Western Avenue	70	F1	Greenwood Park	14	D4	Grove Park Drive	24	F1
Grange View Court	43	B1	Great Western Square	70	F1	Greenwood Walk	14	D4	Grove Park Road	24	F1
Grange View Green	43	B1	Great Western Villas	70	F1	Greenwood Way	14	D4	Grove Road (Blanchardstown)	22	D2
Grange View Grove	43	B1	Greeg Court	71	B3	Grenville Lane	71	B2	Grove Road (Finglas)	24	E1
Grange View Lawn	43	B1	Greek Street	71	A4	Grenville Street	71	B2	Grove Road (Malahide)	3	C3
Grange View Park	43	B1	Green Acre Court	56	D1	Greygates	48	E3	Grove Road (Rathmines)	75	A4
Grange View Road	43	B1	Green Court View Apts.	71	A3	Greygates	48	E4 [1]	Grove Wood (Finglas)	24	E1
Grange View Walk	43	B1	Green Isle Court	44	D2 [2]	Grey's Lane	30	D2	Grove Wood (Foxrock)	59	A3
Grange View Way	43	B1	Green Lane (Celbridge)	31	A2	Greythorn Park	60	D1	Grovedale	63	B2
Grange View Wood	43	B1	Green Lane (Leixlip)	19	C4	Griannan Fidh	58	D3	Guild Street	72	E3
Grange Way	27	C1	Green Lane (Rathcoole)	52	E2	Griffeen	34	E3	Guilford Terrace	64	E3 [1]
Grange Wood (Ballinteer)	57	A2	Green Park (Rathgar)	47	B3	Griffeen Avenue	34	D3	Gulistan Cottages	47	A1
Grangebrook Avenue	56	F2	Green Park Road	67	B2	Griffeen Glen Avenue	34	E3	Gulistan Place	47	A1
Grangebrook Close	56	F2	Green Road (Blackrock)	48	F3	Griffeen Glen Boulevard	34	E3	Gulistan Terrace	47	A1
Grangebrook Park	56	F2	Green Street	71	A3	Griffeen Glen Chase	34	E3	Gunny Hill	55	C3
Grangebrook Vale	56	F2	Green Street East	72	F4	Griffeen Glen Close	34	E3	Gurteen Avenue	36	D3
Grangefield	57	B3	Green Street Little	71	A3	Griffeen Glen Court	34	E3	Gurteen Park	36	D3
Grangegorman Lower	70	F3	Greencastle Avenue	26	E1	Griffeen Glen Court Yard	34	E3	Gurteen Road	36	D2
Grangegorman Upper	70	F2	Greencastle Crescent	26	E1	Griffeen Glen Crescent	34	E3			
Grangegorman Villas	70	F2	Greencastle Drive	13	B4	Griffeen Glen Dene	34	E3			
(Grangegorman Upper)			Greencastle Parade	26	F1	Griffeen Glen Drive	34	E3	**H**		
Grangemore	14	E4	Greencastle Park	13	B4	Griffeen Glen Green	34	E3			
Grangemore Avenue	14	D4	Greencastle Road	13	B4	Griffeen Glen Grove	34	E3	Hacketsland	64	E1
Grangemore Court	14	D4	Greendale Avenue	27	C2	Griffeen Glen Lawn	34	E3	Haddington Lawns	60	E2
Grangemore Crescent	14	D4	Greendale Court	27	B2 [2]	Griffeen Glen Park	34	E3	Haddington Park	60	E2
Grangemore Drive	14	E4	Greendale Road	27	B2	Griffeen Glen Road	34	E3	Haddington Place	76	E2
Grangemore Grove	14	E4	Greenfield Close	17	C4	Griffeen Glen Vale	34	E3	Haddington Road	76	E2
Grangemore Lawn	14	E4	Greenfield Crescent	48	D2	Griffeen Glen View	34	E3	Haddington Terrace	50	D4 [7]
Grangemore Park	14	E4	Greenfield Drive	18	D4	Griffeen Glen Way	34	E3	Haddon Court	39	B1 [2]
Grangemore Rise	14	D4	Greenfield Manor	48	D2 [4]	Griffeen Glen Wood	34	D3	Haddon Park	26	D4 [5]
Grangemore Road	14	D4	Greenfield Park	55	C2	Griffeen Road	34	E3	Haddon Road	26	E4
Grangewood	59	C1	(Ballycullen Road)			Griffeen Way	34	E2	Hadleigh Court	23	A3
Granite Hall	60	D1 [7]	Greenfield Park	48	D2	Griffin Rath Hall	18	D4	Hadleigh Green	23	A3 [2]
Granite Place	76	F4	(Stillorgan Road)			Griffin Rath Manor	18	D4	Hadleigh Park	23	A3
Granite Terrace	36	F3 [11]	Greenfield Place	75	A4	Griffin Rath Road	18	D4	Hagan's Court	76	D2
Granitefield	59	C3	(off Mount Drummond Ave)			Griffith Avenue	25	B3	Haigh Terrace	50	D4
Granitefield	60	D3	Greenfield Road	48	E4	Griffith Bridge	73	B2	Hainault Drive	59	B3
Granitefield Manor	59	C3	(Mount Merrion)			Griffith Close	24	F2	Hainault Grove	59	B3
Granitefield Mews	59	C3	Greenfield Road (Sutton)	29	B1	Griffith Court	25	C4	Hainault Lawn	59	B3
Grantham Place	75	B3	Greenfort Avenue	35	A2	Griffith Crescent	24	F2	Hainault Park	59	A3
Grantham Street	75	A3	Greenfort Close	35	A2	Griffith Downs	25	B3	Hainault Road	59	A3
Grants Avenue	42	E4	Greenfort Crescent	35	A2	Griffith Drive	24	F2	Halfpenny or Liffey Bridge	71	B4
(Greenogue Ind Est)			Greenfort Drive	35	A2	Griffith Hall	25	C3	Halliday Road	70	E3
Grants Court	42	E4	Greenfort Gardens	35	A2	Griffith Heights	24	F2	Halliday Square	70	D3
(Greenogue Ind Est)			Greenfort Lawns	35	A2	Griffith Lawns	25	A3	Hallscourt	67	C2
Grants Cresents	42	E4	Greenfort Park	35	A2	Griffith Parade	24	F2	Halston Street	71	A3
(Greenogue Ind Est)			Greenfort Walk	35	A2	Griffith Road	24	F2	Hamilton Court (Dunboyne)	7	B3 [2]
Grants Drive	42	E4	Greenhills	45	B3	Griffith Square	74	F3	Hamilton Court	71	A4
(Greenogue Ind Est)			Greenhills Court	55	A1	Grosvenor Avenue	68	D3 [3]	(off Strand St Little)		
Grants Hill	42	E4	Greenhills Road	45	A4	Grosvenor Court (Clontarf)	26	E4	Hamilton Hall	7	B3
(Greenogue Ind Est)			Greenisle Road	42	C3	Grosvenor Court	46	D3	Hamilton Street	74	E3
Grants Lane	42	F4	Greenlands	58	D2	(Templeville Road)			Hammond Lane	70	F4
(Greenogue Ind Est)			Greenlawns	13	B4 [1]	Grosvenor Lane	47	A1	Hammond Street	74	F2
Grants Park	42	E4	Greenlea Avenue	46	E2	Grosvenor Lodge	47	A1	Hampstead Avenue	25	A2
(Greenogue Ind Est)			Greenlea Drive	46	E2	Grosvenor Park	47	A1 [7]	Hampstead Court	25	A2
Grants Place	42	E4	Greenlea Grove	46	E2	Grosvenor Place	47	A1	Hampstead Park	25	A3
(Greenogue Ind Est)			Greenlea Park	46	E3	Grosvenor Road	47	A1	Hampton Court	76	E4
Grants Rise	42	E4	Greenlea Place	46	F2 [12]	Grosvenor Square	47	A1	Hampton Court (Clontarf)	26	F4
(Greenogue Ind Est)			Greenlea Road	46	E3	Grosvenor Terrace (Dalkey)	60	F2 [17]	Hampton Court	36	F3 [16]
Grants Road	42	E4	Greenmount Avenue	74	F4	Grosvenor Terrace	49	C4 [9]	(Tyreconnell Road)		
(Greenogue Ind Est)			Greenmount Court	74	F4	(Dun Laoghaire)			Hampton Crescent	48	E3
Grant's Row	76	D1	Greenmount Lane	74	F4	*Grosvenor Villas	60	F2	Hampton Green	69	B1
Grants Row	42	E4	Greenmount Lawns	46	F2	(Off Sorrento Rd)			Hampton Park	48	E3
(Greenogue Ind Est)			Greenmount Lodge	62	F2	Grosvenor Villas (Rathmines)	47	A1	Hampton Square	69	C1
Grants View	42	E4	Greenmount Road	46	F2	Grotto Avenue	48	F2	Hampton Wood	11	C4
(Greenogue Ind Est)			Greenmount Square	74	F4	Grotto Place	48	F2	Hampton Wood Avenue	11	B4
Grants Way	42	E4	Greenoge	42	F4	Grove Avenue (Finglas)	24	E1	Hampton Wood Court	11	C4
(Greenogue Ind Est)			Greenogue Drive	52	F2	Grove Avenue (Harold's Cross)	75	A4	Hampton Wood Crescent	11	B4
Granville Close	60	D3	Greenore Court	76	E1	Grove Avenue (Malahide)	3	C3	Hampton Wood Drive	11	C4
Granville Crescent	60	D3 [2]							Hampton Wood Green	11	B4
									Hampton Wood Lawn	11	C4

STREET NAME	PAGE/GRID REFERENCE	STREET NAME	PAGE/GRID REFERENCE	STREET NAME	PAGE/GRID REFERENCE	STREET NAME	PAGE/GRID REFERENCE
Hampton Wood Park	11 B4	Harty Avenue	45 C1	Hazelwood Court (Beaumont)	26 D1	Hermitage Park (Lucan)	34 F1
Hampton Wood Road	11 B4	Harty Court	45 C1 [8]	Hazelwood Court (Hartstown)	21 C1	Hermitage Place	34 F1
Hampton Wood Square	11 C4	Harty Court (off Daniel Street)	75 A2	Hazelwood Crescent (Bray)	67 B2	Hermitage Road	34 F1
Hampton Wood Way	11 C4	Harty Place	75 A2	Hazelwood Crescent	44 D2	Hermitage Valley	34 F1
Hamwood	6 F3	Harvard	48 D3	(Clondalkin)		Hermitage View	56 F1
Hanbury Court	74 F1	Hastings Street	76 F1	Hazelwood Crescent (Hartstown)	21 C1	Hermitage Way	34 F1
*Hanbury Hall (Hanbury Lane)	74 F1	Hastings Terrace	60 E1 [12]	Hazelwood Drive	26 D2	Heronford Lane	63 C2
Hanbury Lane (Lucan)	34 D1 [3]	Hatch Lane	75 C3	Hazelwood Green	21 C1	Heuston Square	73 A1
Hanbury Lane (The Coombe)	74 F1	Hatch Place	75 C3	Hazelwood Grove	26 E1	Hewardine Terrace	72 D2
*Hanbury Mews (Hanbury Lane)	74 F1	Hatch Street Lower	75 C3	Hazelwood House	75 B4	(off Killarney Street)	
Hanlon's Lane	61 B1	Hatch Street Upper	75 B3	Hazelwood Lane	44 D2	Heytesbury Court	76 E3
Hannaville Park	46 F2	Hatter's Lane	74 F4	Hazelwood Park	26 D1	Heytesbury Lane	76 E4
*Hanover Lane	71 A1	Havelock Square	76 F2	Hazelwood View	44 D2	Heytesbury Street	75 A3
Hanover Quay	72 F4	Havelock Terrace	39 A3 [17]	Hazlebury Park	8 E4	Hibernian Avenue	72 E2
Hanover Square	75 A1	Haven View	3 B2 [2]	Headford Grove	47 B4	Hibernian Terrace	36 E2 [3]
Hanover Street East	72 D4	Haverty Road	25 C4	Healthfield Road	46 F2	High Park	25 C2
Hanover Street West	74 F1	Hawkins Street	71 C4	Healy Street	71 C2	High Street (Christ Church)	75 A1
Hansfield	8 E4	Hawkridge	33 B2	(off Rutland Place North)		High Street (Tallaght)	55 A1 [1]
Hansted Close	34 D4	Hawthorn Avenue	72 E2	Heaney Avenue	35 C4	Highdownhill	51 C1
Hansted Crescent	34 D4	Hawthorn Drive	57 B1 [2]	Heany Avenue	60 F2 [19]	Highfield Avenue (Dundrum)	57 A2
Hansted Dale	34 D4	Hawthorn Lawn	22 F3	Heath Square	24 E1 [3]	Highfield Close	1 C2
Hansted Drive	34 D4	Hawthorn Lodge	22 F3	Heather Close	57 A2	Highfield Court	47 A2 [3]
Hansted Park	34 D4	Hawthorn Lodge	23 A4	Heather Drive	57 A2	Highfield Crescent	1 C2
Hansted Place	34 D4	Hawthorn Manor	59 A1 [4]	Heather Gardens	4 D4	Highfield Downs	1 C2
Hansted Road	34 D4	Hawthorn Park	1 C2	Heather Grove (Ballinteer)	57 B2	Highfield Drive	57 A2
Hansted Way	34 D4	Hawthorn Road (Bray)	67 B1	Heather Grove (Palmerston)	35 B2	Highfield Green	1 C2
Harbour Court	71 C4	Hawthorn Road (Clondalkin)	44 F1	Heather Lawn	57 A2	Highfield Grove	47 A2
Harbour Crescent	60 F1	Hawthorn Terrace	72 E2	Heather Park	57 B2	Highfield Lawn	1 C2
Harbour Master Place	72 D3	Hawthorn View	32 D2	Heather Road (Ballinteer)	57 A2	Highfield Manor	47 A2
Harbour Road (Dalkey)	60 F1	Hawthorns Road	58 D2	Heather Road (Burton Hall)	58 E2	Highfield Park (Celbridge Road)	33 A1
Harbour Road (Dun Laoghaire)	50 D4	Hayden Square	48 D3 [3]	Heather View Avenue	54 F2	Highfield Park (Churchtown)	47 B3
Harbour Road (Howth)	30 D1	Hayden's Lane	34 D3	Heather View Close	54 F2	Highfield Road	47 A2
Harbour Square	50 D4	Haydens Park	34 D3	Heather View Drive	54 F2	Highland Avenue	59 B3
Harbour Terrace	49 C4 [8]	Haydens Park Avenue	34 D3	Heather View Lawn	54 F2	Highland Grove	59 B3
Harbour View (Dún Laoghaire)	50 D4	Haydens Park Close	34 D3	Heather View Park	54 F2	Highland Lawn	59 B3
Harbour View (Howth)	30 D1 [6]	Haydens Park Dale	34 D3	Heather View Road	54 F2	Highland View	59 B3
Harcourt Green	75 B3	Haydens Park Drive	34 D3	Heather Walk	4 D4	Highridge Green	58 E1
Harcourt Hall	75 B3	Haydens Park Glade	34 D3	Heatherwood	67 B4	Highthorn Park	59 C1
Harcourt Lane	75 B3	Haydens Park Green	34 D3	Heathfield	49 B4 [17]	Highthorn Woods	59 C1 [10]
Harcourt Lodge	73 B2	Haydens Park Grove	34 D3	*Heatley Villas (on Pearse Road)	59 C2	Hill Cottages	60 E3 [1]
Harcourt Place	75 B3	Haydens Park Lawn	34 D3	Heidelberg	48 D3	Hill Court	14 F1
Harcourt Road	75 B3	Haydens Park View	34 D3	Hempenstal Terrace	39 B4 [5]	Hill Crest	3 C4
Harcourt Street	75 B2	Haydens Park Walk	34 D3	Hendrick Place	70 E4	Hill Drive	3 B3
Harcourt Terrace	75 C3	Haydens Park Way	34 D3	Hendrick Street	70 F4	Hill Street	71 B2
*Harcourt Villas	47 C3	Haymarket	70 F4	Henley Court	47 B4 [8]	Hill View	57 B1
(off Dundrum Rd/Mulvey Pk)		Haymarket House	70 F4	Henley Park	47 B4	Hillbrook Woods	22 D1
Hardebeck Avenue	45 C1	Haymarket Way	70 F4	Henley Villas	47 B4	Hillcourt	47 A2
Hardiman Road	25 A3	*Hayworth Close	21 B1	Henrietta Lane	71 A2	Hillcourt Park	60 D2
Hardwicke Arch	71 B2	Hayworth Court	21 B1	Henrietta Place	71 A3	Hillcourt Road	60 D2
(off Hardwicke St)		Hayworth Drive	21 B1	Henrietta Street	71 A3	Hillcrest (Lucan)	34 D2
Hardwicke Lane	71 B2	Hayworth Mews	21 A1	Henry Place	71 B3	Hillcrest (Malahide)	3 A2 [1]
Hardwicke Place	71 B2	Hayworth Place	21 A1	Henry Road	36 D4	Hillcrest (Rathgar)	47 A2
Hardwicke Street	71 B2	Hayworth Rise	21 A1	Henry Street	71 B3	Hillcrest (Templeogue)	46 D4 [1]
Harelawn Avenue	35 A3	Hayworth Terrace	21 A1	Herbert Avenue	48 E1	Hillcrest Avenue	33 C2
Harelawn Crescent	35 A3	Hazel Avenue	58 D1	Herbert Cottages	76 F3	Hillcrest Close	33 C2
Harelawn Drive	35 A2	Hazel Court	14 F2 [7]	Herbert Court	39 A4 [48]	Hillcrest Court	25 A3 [19]
Harelawn Green	35 A3	Hazel Grove	14 F2	Herbert Crescent	22 F2 [1]	Hillcrest Court	34 D2
Harelawn Grove	35 A2	Hazel Lawn (Blanchardstown)	22 E2	Herbert House	76 E1	Hillcrest Downs	58 D3
Harelawn Park	35 A2	Hazel Lawn (Kill O'The Grange)	59 C2 [4]	Herbert Lane	76 D2	Hillcrest Drive	33 C2
Harlech Crescent	48 D3	Hazel Park	46 E2 [2]	Herbert Park (Ballsbridge)	76 F4	Hillcrest Green	33 C2
Harlech Downs	47 C3	Hazel Road	26 D3	Herbert Park (Oldcourt)	67 B3	Hillcrest Grove	34 D2
Harlech Grove	48 D3	Hazel Villas	58 D1	Herbert Park Lane	76 F4	Hillcrest Heights	33 C2
Harlech Villas	47 C3 [4]	Hazelbrook (Kilmacud)	58 D1	Herbert Park Mews	47 C1	Hillcrest Lawns	33 C2
Harmac Court	46 F2	Hazelbrook (Malahide)	14 E1	Herbert Place	76 D2	Hillcrest Manor	46 D4 [2]
Harman Street	74 E2	Hazelbrook (Tymon North)	45 B4	(Baggot Street Lower)		Hillcrest Park (Glasnevin)	24 F2
Harmoney Court	76 E1	Hazelbrook Apts.	46 E2 [7]	*Herbert Place (off Bath St)	39 A3	Hillcrest Park (Lucan)	33 C2
Harmonstown Road	26 F2	Hazelbrook Court	46 E2	Herbert Road (Blanchardstown)	22 F2	Hillcrest Road (Lucan)	34 D2
Harmony Avenue	47 C1 [5]	Hazelbrook Drive	46 E2	Herbert Road (Oldcourt)	67 B3	Hillcrest Road (Sandyford)	58 D3
Harmony Court	47 C1 [20]	Hazelbrook Road	46 E2	Herbert Road (Sandymount)	39 A4	Hillcrest View	33 C2
Harmony Row	76 D1	Hazelbury Green	8 E4	Herbert Street	76 D2	Hillcrest Walk	33 C2
Harold Bridge Court	74 F4	Hazelbury Park	8 E4	Herbert View	67 B2 [26]	Hillcrest Way	33 C2
*Harold Crescent	60 E1	Hazelcroft Gardens	24 E2	Herberton Drive	74 D3	Hillsbrook Avenue	46 D2
(off Eden Rd Lower)		Hazelcroft Park	24 E2	Herberton Park	73 C2	Hillsbrook Crescent	46 D2
Harold Road	70 E3	Hazelcroft Road	24 E2	Herberton Road	73 C3	Hillsbrook Drive	46 D2
Harold Ville Avenue	74 D2	Hazeldene	47 C1	Hermitage Avenue	56 F1	Hillsbrook Grove	46 D2
Harold's Cross	46 F1	Hazeldine Apts.	67 C4	Hermitage Close	56 F1	Hillside	60 E2
Harold's Cross Cottages	74 F4	Hazelgrove	54 D2	Hermitage Court	57 A1	Hillside Drive	47 A3
Harold's Cross Cottages	75 A4	Hazelgrove Court	54 E2	Hermitage Crescent	34 F1	Hillside Park	56 E1
Harold's Cross Road	46 F1	Hazelhatch	41 B1	Hermitage Downs	57 A1	Hillside Terrace	30 D2 [7]
Harold's Grange Road	57 B3	Hazelhatch Road	41 C3	Hermitage Drive	56 F1	Hilltop Lawn	64 D3
Harrington Court	75 B3	Hazelwood	12 E4	Hermitage Garden	34 F1	Hilltown	1 B3
Harrington Street	75 A3	Hazelwood (Bray)	67 B2	Hermitage Green	34 F1	Hilltown Close	1 C2
Harrison Row	46 F2	Hazelwood (Shankill)	64 E2	Hermitage Grove	56 F1	Hilltown Court	1 C2
Harristown	5 A2	Hazelwood Avenue	21 C1	Hermitage Lawn	56 F1	Hilltown Crescent	1 A2
Harry Street	75 B1	Hazelwood Bank	44 D2	Hermitage Manor	34 F1	Hilltown Green	1 C2
Hartstown Road	21 C1	Hazelwood Close	44 D2	Hermitage Park (Grange Road)	56 F1	Hilltown Grove	1 C2

STREET NAME	PAGE/GRID REFERENCE	STREET NAME	PAGE/GRID REFERENCE	STREET NAME	PAGE/GRID REFERENCE	STREET NAME	PAGE/GRID REFERENCE
Hilltown Lawn	1 C2	Homelee	39 A4 [11]	Hyde Park Avenue	48 F3	**J**	
Hilltown Park	1 C2	Homeleigh	22 D4	Hyde Park Gardens	48 F3	Jackson's Bridge	17 A3
Hilltown Road	1 C2	Homeville	55 C1 [4]	Hyde Road	60 F1	James Connolly Park	35 A4
Hilltown Way	1 C2	Homeville Court	55 C1 [3]	Hyde Square (Fosters Avenue)	48 D3 [4]	James Connolly Square	67 C2 [5]
Hillview	52 E2	Honey Park	60 D2 [1]	*Hyde Square (Kilmainham)	73 B2	James Everett Park	67 B2
Hillview Cottages	59 C2 [1]	Hope Avenue	72 E1	Hynestown	42 D2	James Joyce Bridge	70 E4
Hillview Court	57 B1 [6]	Hope Street (off Gordon Street)	76 F1			James Joyce Court	25 A3 [21]
Hillview Drive	59 C2	Hopkins Square	48 D3 [1]	**I**		James Joyce Court	27 C1 [5]
Hillview Glade	57 B1 [5]	Horan Hall (Belgard Square)	54 F1 [5]	Idrone Avenue	56 D1	James Joyce St	71 C3
Hillview Grove	57 B1	Horse Fair	72 E4	Idrone Close	56 D1	James Larkin Road	27 B2
Hillview Lawn	59 C2	Horton Court	46 F2	Idrone Drive	56 D1	James McCormack Gardens	29 A1 [1]
Hilton Gardens	57 C2	Hospital Lane	69 B4	Idrone Mews	49 A3 [11]	James Plunkett House	36 F3
Hoey Close	14 D4	Hotel Yard	71 B3	Idrone Park	56 D1	James's Place East	76 D2
Hoey Court	14 D4	Houghton Terrace	70 E3	Idrone Terrace	49 A3	James's Street	74 D1
Hoey Place	14 D4	Howard Street	76 F1	Imaal Road	70 E1	James's Street East	76 D2
*Hoeys Court	75 A1	(off Gordon Street)		Inagh Court	64 E1	James's Street North	72 E1
(off Werburgh Street)		Howth	30 D2	Inagh Road	36 D3	James's Terrace	3 B2
Hogan Avenue	76 E1	Howth Harbour	30 D1	Inbhir Ide	3 A2	James's Terrace Upper	3 B2 [11]
Hogan House	46 F4 [25]	Howth House Apts	30 D1 [10]	Inbhir Ide Close	3 A2	James's Walk	74 D2
Hogan Place	76 D1	Howth Junction Cottages	27 B1 [1]	Inbhir Ide Drive	3 A2	Jamestown	62 F1
Hogan Square	76 E1	Howth Lodge Apts.	29 C1	Inchicore	36 F3	Jamestown Avenue	36 F4
Holles Place	76 D1	Howth Peninsula Apts.	30 D1 [14]	Inchicore Road	73 A1	Jamestown Cottages	62 E1
Holles Row	76 D1	Howth Road (Howth)	29 C1	Inchicore Square	36 F3 [13]	Jamestown Court	36 F4
Holles Street	76 D1	Howth Road (Killester)	26 E3	Inchicore Terrace North	36 F3 [3]	Jamestown Road	11 B4
Holly Avenue	58 D1	Howth Road (Marino)	26 D4	Inchicore Terrace South	36 F3	Jamestown Road (Finglas)	24 E1
Holly Court	64 D1	Howth Road (Raheny)	26 F3	Infirmary Road	69 C3	Jamestown Road (Grand Canal)	36 E4
Holly Park	64 E2	Howth Road (Raheny)	27 B2	Inglewood Close	21 C2	Jamestown Road (Inchicore)	36 F4
Holly Park Avenue	59 A1	Howth Road (Sutton)	29 B1	Inglewood Crescent	21 C2	Jamestown Road (Poppintree)	11 B4
Holly Road (Donnycarney)	26 D3	Howth Road Apts.	26 E3	Inglewood Drive	21 C2	*Jane-Ville (Off Tivoli Road)	50 D4
Holly Road (Fox and Geese)	44 F1	Howth Terrace	30 D1 [5]	Inglewood Road	21 C2	Jerome Connor Place	69 C3
Holly Tree Square	11 C4	Howth View Park	27 B1	Ingram Road	74 F3	Jervis Lane Lower	71 A4
Holly Tree Terrace	11 C4	Huband Road	36 F4	Inis Fáil	54 F2	Jervis Lane Upper	71 A3
Hollybank Avenue Lower	47 B1	Hudson Road	60 E1	Inis Thiar	54 F2	Jervis Street	71 A3
Hollybank Avenue Upper	47 B1	Hughes Road East	45 C1	*Inkerman Cottages	72 D2	Jobstown	54 D2
Hollybank Road	25 A4	Hughes Road North	45 C1	(off Amiens Street)		Jobstown Road	54 D2
Hollybrook	59 A3	Hughes Road South	45 C1	Innisfallen Parade	71 B1	Jobstown Village Square	54 D1 [2]
Hollybrook Court	26 D4 [3]	Hume Ave	36 D4	Innishmaan Road	25 B2	John Dillon Street	75 A1
Hollybrook Court Drive	26 D4 [2]	Hume Avenue	35 C4	Innishmore Terrace	46 D1	John F Kennedy Avenue	45 A1
Hollybrook Grove	26 D4	Hume Street	75 C2	(St Mary's Road)		John F Kennedy Drive	45 A1
Hollybrook Manor	26 D4	Hunters Avenue	55 C3	Innismore	46 D1	John F Kennedy Park	36 D4
Hollybrook Mews	26 D4 [11]	Hunters Court	55 C3	*Inns Court	75 A1	John F Kennedy Road	36 D4
Hollybrook Park (Clontarf)	26 D4	Hunters Crescent	55 C3	(on Winetavern Street)		John Field Road	75 A1
Hollybrook Park (Irishtown)	67 C4	Hunters Green	55 C3	Inns Quay	70 F4	John MacCormack Avenue	45 C1
Hollybrook Road	26 D4	Hunters Grove	55 C3	Inver Road	24 E4	John McCormack Bridge	72 F1
Hollybrook Wood	26 D4	Hunters Hall	55 C3	Invermore Grove	27 A1 [3]	John Street North	70 F4
Hollybrooke	36 E4 [4]	Hunters Hill	55 C3	Inverness Road	25 C4	John Street North	70 E4
Hollyrood Apts	39 A4 [47]	Hunters Lane	55 C3	Iona Avenue	25 A4	(off Ellis Quay)	
Hollystown	9 B1	Hunters Meadow	55 C3	Iona Crescent	25 A4	John Street South	74 F2
Hollystown Park	9 B1	Hunters Parade	55 C3	Iona Drive	25 A4	John Street West	74 F1
Hollyville Lawn	35 C1	Hunters Place	55 C3	Iona Park	25 A4	John's Court	74 E2
Hollywell	11 C4	Hunters Road	55 C3	Iona Road	25 A4	John's Lane East	75 A1
Hollywell Avenue	2 E3	Hunter's Row	26 F4 [2]	Iona Villas	25 A4	John's Lane West	74 F1
Hollywell Close	2 E3	Hunters Run	8 E4	Iris Grove	48 E3	Johnsbridge	34 D3
Hollywell Court	2 D3	Hunters Run The Close	8 E4	Irishtown (Bray)	67 C4	Johnsbridge Avenue	34 D3
Hollywell Gardens	2 D3	Hunters Run The Drive	8 F4	Irishtown (Ringsend)	39 A3	Johnsbridge Close	34 D3
Hollywell Grove	2 E3	Hunters Run The Glade	8 E4	Irishtown Road	39 A3	Johnsbridge Green	34 D3
Hollywell Heath	2 D3	Hunters Run The Grove	8 E4	Irvine Cottages	72 F3	Johnsbridge Grove	34 D3
Hollywell Place	2 D3	Hunters Run The Park	8 E4	Irvine Terrace	72 F3	Johnsbridge Meadows	34 D3
Hollywell Rise	2 D3	Hunters Run The Rise	8 F4	Irwin Court	73 C1	Johnsbridge Park	34 D3
Hollywell Road	2 D3	Hunters Run The View	8 F4	Irwin Street	73 C1	Johnsbridge Walk	34 D3
Hollywell Square	2 E3	Hunters Run The Way	8 F4	Island Street	70 E4	Johnson Place	75 B1
Hollywell View	2 E3	Hunters Walk	55 C3	Island View (Kilbarrack)	27 C2	Johnson's Court	75 B1
Hollywell Walk	2 D3	Hunters Way	55 C3	Island View (Malahide)	3 C3	Johnstown	51 C4
Hollywell Wood	2 D3	Huntstown Avenue	21 C1	Island View Apts.	30 D1 [9]	Johnstown Avenue	59 C3
Hollywood Drive	48 D4	Huntstown Close	8 F4	Island View Court Apts.	27 C2	Johnstown Court	59 C2
Hollywood Park	48 D4	Huntstown Court	8 F4	Island Villa	76 E1	Johnstown Gardens	24 E2 [5]
*Holme's Cottages	47 A1	Huntstown Drive	8 F4	Islandbridge	69 B4	Johnstown Grove	59 C3
(on Church Avenue Rathmines)		Huntstown Glen	8 F4	Islandbridge Court	69 B4	Johnstown House	24 F2 [2]
Holmston Avenue	60 D1	Huntstown Green	8 F4	Islington Avenue	50 E4	Johnstown Lane	59 C3
Holmwood	59 B4	Huntstown Grove	8 F4	Isolda Road	39 A3	Johnstown Park (Cornelscourt)	59 C3
Holycross Avenue	25 B4 [5]	Huntstown Lawn	22 D1	Isolde Gardens	36 E2 [6]	Johnstown Park (Glasnevin)	24 F2
*Holycross Cottages	25 B4	Huntstown Park	8 F4	Isolde House Apts.	36 E2 [13]	Johnstown Road (Cornelscourt)	59 C3
(off Holycross Avenue)		Huntstown Rise	9 A4	Ivar Street	70 E3	Johnstown Road (Rathcoole)	52 E2
Holyrood Park	39 A4	Huntstown Road	21 C1	Iveagh Buildings	75 A2	Jones Terrace	68 D2 [18]
Holywell	58 D1	Huntstown Way	8 F4	Iveagh Court	75 B3	Jones's Road	71 C1
Holywell Avenue	27 B1	Huntstown Way	9 A4	Iveagh Gardens	73 A4	Jordanstown	42 F4
Holywell Crescent	27 B1	Huntstown Wood	8 F4	Iveagh Gardens	73 B4	Jordanstown Avenue	42 F4
Holywell Road	27 B1	Hutchinson's Strand	2 E1	Iveleary Road	25 B2	(Greenogue Ind Est)	
Home Farm Park	25 B3	Huttonread	51 C4	Iveragh Court	76 F3	Jordanstown Drive	42 F4
Home Farm Road	25 A3	Huxley Court	74 E2	Iveragh Road	25 B2	(Greenogue Ind Est)	
Home Villas	47 C1	Huxley Crescent	74 E2	Ivy Cottages	75 C4	Jordanstown Road	42 F4
Homelawn Avenue	55 B1	Hyacinth Street	72 E2	Ivy Court	25 C1 [1]	(Greenogue Ind Est)	
Homelawn Drive	55 B1	Hybreasal	73 B2	Ivy Terrace	74 E2	Josephine Avenue	71 B1
Homelawn Gardens	55 B1	Hybreasal Apts.	73 B2			Joy Street (off Gordon Street)	76 F1
Homelawn Road	55 A1	Hyde Park (Dalkey)	60 E1			Joyce Avenue	59 A3
Homelawn Villas	55 A1	Hyde Park (Templeogue)	46 E3				

STREET NAME	PAGE/GRID REFERENCE
Joyce Hall	59 B4
Joyce Road	25 A3
Joyce Way	35 C4
Jugback Close	1 C1
Jugback Court	1 C1
Jugback Crescent	1 C1
Jugback Green	1 Inset
Jugback Lane	1 C1

K

STREET NAME	PAGE/GRID REFERENCE
Kavanagh Avenue	36 D4
Keadeen Avenue	45 B2
Kearneystown Lower	41 A3
Kearn's Place	73 B2
Keatingspark	52 D2
*Keegan's Cottages (off Merrion Rd)	48 E1
Keeloges	42 D3
Keeper Road	73 C3
Kells Road	46 E1
Kelly's Avenue	50 D4
Kelly's Lane (Maynooth)	17 C3 [1]
Kelly's Lane (Phibsborough)	71 A1
Kelly's Row	71 B1
Kelly's Square	71 B1
Kellystown Lane	19 A3
Kellystown Road	57 B4
Kelston Avenue	59 A2
Kelston Drive	59 A2
Kelston Hall	59 A2 [11]
Kelston Park	59 A2
Kelston View	59 A2
Kelvin Close	4 D4
Kempton	23 C3
Kempton Avenue	23 C3
Kempton Court	23 C3
Kempton Green	23 C3
Kempton Grove	23 C3
Kempton Heath	23 C3
Kempton Lawn	23 C3
Kempton Park	23 C3
Kempton Rise	23 C3
Kempton View	23 C3
Kempton Way	23 C3
Kenah Court	60 E3
Kengar Mews	46 F1 [14]
Kenilworth Lane	46 F1
Kenilworth Manor	46 F1 [11]
Kenilworth Park	46 F1
Kenilworth Road	47 A1
Kenilworth Square	46 F1
Kenilworth Square East	47 A1
Kenilworth Square North	46 F1
Kenilworth Square South	46 F1
Kenilworth Square West	46 F1
Kenmare Parade	71 B1
Kennedy Court	39 A3 [31]
Kennedy Park	67 C3 [5]
Kennelsfort Green	35 B2
Kennelsfort Road Lower	35 C1
Kennelsfort Road Upper	35 C2
Kennilworth Lodge	46 F1 [19]
Kennington Close	45 C4
Kennington Crescent	45 C4
Kennington Lawn	45 C4
Kennington Road	45 C3
*Kent Terrace (on Barnhill Road)	60 F2
Kentfield	64 E2
Kerlogue Road	39 A3
Kerrygold House	46 F1 [18]
Kerrymount Avenue	59 A4
Kerrymount Close	59 B3 [1]
Kerrymount Green	59 B3
Kerrymount Mall	59 B3
Kerrymount Rise	59 B3
Kettles Drive	2 E4
Kettles Lane	2 E4
Kettles Place	2 E4
Kevin Barry Flats (off Church Street Upper)	70 F3
*Kevin Street Cross (on New Bride Street)	75 A2
Kevin Street Lower	75 A2
Kevin Street Upper	75 A2
Kew Park	33 C1
Kew Park Avenue	33 B2
Kew Park Crescent	33 B1
Kickham Road	73 B2
Kilakee Close	45 B3
Kilakee Drive	45 B3
Kilbarrack	27 C1
Kilbarrack Avenue	27 C2
Kilbarrack Gardens	27 C2
Kilbarrack Grove	27 C2
Kilbarrack Parade	27 B1
Kilbarrack Road	27 B1
Kilbarrack Way	27 B1
Kilbarron Avenue	26 D1
Kilbarron Court	26 D1 [1]
Kilbarron Drive	26 D1
Kilbarron Park	26 D1
Kilbarron Road	26 D1
Kilbegnet Close	60 F2 [24]
Kilbogget Grove	59 C4
Kilbogget Villas	59 C4 [1]
Kilbride Grove	67 B3
Kilbride Lane	67 B3
Kilbride Road	26 E3
Kilbrina	7 B2
Kilcarberry Ave	43 C2
Kilcarberry Close	43 C2
Kilcarberry Court	43 C2
Kilcarberry Lawn	43 C2
Kilcarrig Avenue	44 E4
Kilcarrig Close	54 E1
Kilcarrig Crescent	44 E4
Kilcarrig Green	44 E4
Kilclare Avenue	54 E2
Kilclare Crescent	54 E2
Kilclare Drive	54 E2
Kilclare Gardens	54 E2
Kilcloon	5 A2
Kilcloon Lawns	5 A2
Kilcock Maynooth Leixlip ByPass	32 E1
Kilcock Road	17 C3
Kilcock-Maynooth-Leixlip Bypass	33 A1
Kilcolman Court	60 E2 [4]
Kilcronan Avenue	34 E4
Kilcronan Close	34 E4
Kilcronan Court	34 E4
Kilcronan Crescent	34 E4
Kilcronan Grove	34 E4
Kilcronan Lawns	34 E4
Kilcronan View	34 E4
Kilcroney Lane	67 A4
Kilcross Avenue	58 D3
Kilcross Close	58 D3
Kilcross Court	57 C3
Kilcross Crescent	57 C3
Kilcross Drive	57 C3
Kilcross Grove	57 C3
Kilcross Lawn	58 D3
Kilcross Park	57 C3
Kilcross Road	58 D3
Kilcross Square	57 C3
Kilcross Way	57 C3
Kildare Bridge	18 D2
Kildare Park	46 D1
Kildare Place	75 C1
Kildare Road	46 D1
Kildare Street	75 C1
Kildonan Avenue	24 D1
Kildonan Court	24 D1
Kildonan Drive	24 D1
Kildonan Road	24 D1
Kildress House	76 D2
Kilfenora Drive	27 A1
Kilfenora Road	46 E1
Kilgarran	66 D3
Kilgarron Park	66 D3
Kilgobbin Grove	58 E4
Kilgobbin Heights	58 E4
Kilgobbin Lane	58 D4
Kilgobbin Lawn	58 E4
Kilgobbin Road	58 E3
Kilgobbin Wood	58 E4
Kilgraigue	5 B3
Kilgrastor Court	67 B3 [5]
Kilkieran Court	24 E4 [1]
Kilkieran Road	24 E4
Kill Abbey	59 B1
Kill Avenue	59 C1
Kill Lane	59 B2
Kill O' the Grange	59 C1
Killadoon Park	31 C4
Killakee Avenue	55 B2
Killakee Court	55 B2
Killakee Gardens	55 B2
Killakee Green	55 B2
Killakee Grove	55 B2
Killakee Lawns	55 B2
Killakee Park	55 B2
Killakee Rise	55 B2
Killakee Road	56 D4
Killakee View	55 B2
Killakee Walk	55 B2
Killakee Way	55 B2
Killala Road	24 E4
Killan Court	72 F3
Killan Road	72 F3
Killarney Avenue	72 D2
Killarney Court	67 B3 [4]
Killarney Glen	67 B3
Killarney Heights	67 B3
Killarney Lane	67 B3
Killarney Parade	71 B1
Killarney Park	67 B3
Killarney Road	67 B3
Killarney Street	72 D2
Killarney Villas	67 C2 [48]
Killary Grove	27 B1
Killeany	5 A4
Killeck	1 A2
Killeck Lane	1 A3
Killeen	2 F3
Killeen Avenue	2 F3
Killeen Court	2 F3
Killeen Crescent	2 F3
Killeen Mews	3 B3
Killeen Park	2 F3
Killeen Road (Bluebell)	36 D4
Killeen Road (Fox and Geese)	45 A1
Killeen Road (Rathmines)	47 B1
Killeen Terrace	3 B2
Killegar	65 C1
*Killery Terrace (on Upper Dargle Road)	67 B2
Killester	26 E3
Killester Avenue	26 E3
Killester Court	26 E3 [4]
Killester Park	26 E3
Killester Park	26 E3 [5]
Killinarden	54 E3
Killinarden Estate	54 E2
Killinarden Heights	54 E2
Killinarden Road	54 E3
Killiney	60 E3
Killiney Avenue	60 E4
Killiney Court	64 E1 [1]
Killiney Gate	60 E4
Killiney Grove	60 E2
Killiney Heath	60 E4
Killiney Hill Road	60 E3
Killiney Hill Road	64 E1
Killiney Oaks	64 E1 [2]
Killiney Road	60 E2
Killiney Terrace	60 E1 [15]
Killiney Towers	60 E2 [2]
Killiney View	60 E1
Killininny Cottages	55 B2
Killininny Court Apts	55 B2 [2]
Killininny Road	55 B2
Kilmactalway	42 F3
Kilmacud	58 E1
Kilmacud Avenue	58 E1
Kilmacud Park	58 E1
Kilmacud Road Upper	58 E1
Kilmahuddrick Avenue	43 B1
Kilmahuddrick Close	43 B1
Kilmahuddrick Court	43 B1
Kilmahuddrick Crescent	43 B1
Kilmahuddrick Drive	43 B1
Kilmahuddrick Green	43 B1
Kilmahuddrick Grove	43 B1
Kilmahuddrick Lawn	43 B1
Kilmahuddrick Place	43 B1
Kilmahuddrick Road	43 B1
Kilmahuddrick Walk	43 B1
Kilmahuddrick Way	43 B1
Kilmainham	73 B1
Kilmainham Bank	73 A1
Kilmainham Lane	73 C1
Kilmainham Orchard	73 B1
Kilmalin	65 C3
Kilmantain Place	67 C2 [10]
Kilmartin Avenue	54 D1
Kilmartin Crescent	44 D4
Kilmartin Drive	54 D1
Kilmartin Gardens	54 D1
Kilmartin Green	54 D1
Kilmartin Park	54 D1
Kilmashogue Bridge	56 F3
Kilmashogue Close	45 B3
Kilmashogue Drive	45 B3
Kilmashogue Grove	45 B3
Kilmashogue Lane	56 F3
Kilmore	26 D1
Kilmore Avenue (Coolock)	26 E1
Kilmore Avenue (Killiney)	60 E4
Kilmore Close	26 E1
Kilmore Court	26 D1 [5]
Kilmore Crescent	26 E1
Kilmore Drive	26 E1
Kilmore Place Apts.	26 D1
Kilmore Road	26 D1
Kilmorony Close	27 A1
Kilnamanagh	45 A3
Kilnamanagh Court	45 C1
Kilnamanagh Estate	45 A3
Kilnamanagh Road	45 C1
Kilrock Road	30 E2
Kilronan Court	26 D4 [7]
Kilshane	10 E2
Kilshane Avenue	10 D2
Kilshane Cross	10 F2
Kilshane Drive	10 E3
Kilshane Park	10 D2
Kilshane Road (North Road)	10 E3
Kilshane Road (North Road)	10 E3
Kilshane Road (Rathoath Road)	23 C2
Kilshane View	10 D2
Kilshane Way	10 D2
Kiltalown	54 D3
Kiltalown Avenue	54 D2
Kiltalown Close	54 D2
Kiltalown Cottages	54 T4
Kiltalown Court	54 D2
Kiltalown Crescent	54 D2
Kiltalown Drive	54 D2
Kiltalown Green	54 D2
Kiltalown Grove	54 D2
Kiltalown Heights	54 D2
Kiltalown Hill	54 D2
Kiltalown Park	54 D2
Kiltalown Road	54 D2
Kiltalown View	54 D2
Kiltalown Walk	54 D2
Kiltalown Way	54 D2
Kilteel Road	52 E2
Kilteragh Drive	59 A3
Kilteragh Pines	59 A3 [2]
Kilteragh Road	59 A3
Kilternan	62 F2
Kiltiernan Bridge	62 F3
Kiltipper	54 F3
Kiltipper Avenue	55 A2
Kiltipper Close	55 A2
Kiltipper Drive	55 A2
Kiltipper Gate	54 F3
Kiltipper Rise	54 F3
Kiltipper Road	55 A3
Kiltipper View	54 F3
Kiltipper Way	54 F2
Kiltuck Park	64 E4 [1]
Kilvere	46 E4
Kilvere Park	46 D4
Kilwogan Manor	31 C2
Kilworth Road	36 F4
Kimmage	46 D2
Kimmage Court	46 E2 [3]
Kimmage Grove	46 E2
Kimmage Manor Way	46 D2

STREET NAME	PAGE/GRID REFERENCE	STREET NAME	PAGE/GRID REFERENCE	STREET NAME	PAGE/GRID REFERENCE	STREET NAME	PAGE/GRID REFERENCE
Kimmage Road Lower	46 F1	Knockcullen	56 D1	Lakelands Drive	58 E1	Larkfield Close	34 F2
Kimmage Road West	46 D2	Knockcullen Drive	56 D1	Lakelands Grove	58 D1	Larkfield Court	34 F2
Kinahan Street	70 D3	Knockcullen Lawn	56 D1	Lakelands Lawn	58 D1	Larkfield Gardens	46 F1
Kincora Avenue	26 E4	Knockcullen Park	56 D1	Lakelands Park	46 E3	Larkfield Green	34 F2
Kincora Court	39 C1	Knockcullen Rise	56 D1	Lakelands Place	58 D1	Larkfield Grove (Harold's Cross)	46 F1
Kincora Drive	26 E4	Knockdara	3 C3	Lakelands Road	58 E1	Larkfield Grove (Liffey Valley)	34 F2
Kincora Grove	26 E4	Knockfield Manor	55 C1	Lakeshore Drive	2 D3	Larkfield Mews	32 D3
Kincora Park	26 E4	Knocklyon	56 D1	Lakeview Drive	2 D3	Larkfield Park	46 F1
Kincora Road	26 E4	Knocklyon Avenue	55 C1	Lally Road	36 E3	Larkfield Place	34 F2
King Edward Court	67 C2 [53]	Knocklyon Close	56 D1	Lamb Alley	74 F1	Larkfield Rise	34 F2
King Edward Lawn	67 C2	Knocklyon Court	56 D1	Lambay Close	64 E1	Larkfield Square	34 F2
King Edward Park	67 B2	Knocklyon Drive	56 D1	Lambay Court	3 C3	Larkfield View	34 F2
King Edward Road	67 B2	Knocklyon Gate Apts	55 C2 [3]	Lambay Drive	64 E1	Larkfield Way	34 F2
King Street North	70 F3	Knocklyon Green	56 D1	Lambay Road	25 A3	Larkhill Road	25 B2
King Street South	75 B1	Knocklyon Grove	56 D1	Lambourne Avenue	21 C2	Larrisa Court	46 E1 [7]
King William's Rampart	24 D2	Knocklyon Heights	55 C1	Lambourne Court	21 C2	Latchford	21 B1
Kingram Place	75 C3	Knocklyon Mews	55 C1 [2]	Lambourne Drive	21 C2	Latchford Close	21 B1
King's Avenue	72 D1	Knocklyon Park	55 C1	Lambourne Park	21 C2	Latchford Court	21 B1
King's Court	70 E2	Knocklyon Road	55 C1	Lambourne Road	21 C2	Latchford Green	21 B1
King's Hall	36 E2	Knockmaree Apartments	36 E2	Lambourne Village	26 E4 [3]	Latchford Park	21 B1
Kings Inns	71 A3	Knockmaroon Hill	36 D1	Lambourne Wood	59 C4	Latchford Row	21 B1
King's Inn's Court	71 A2	Knockmaroon Road	36 D1	Lamb's Brook	58 D3	Latchford Square	21 B1
King's Inns Street	71 A3	Knockmeenagh Lane	44 E2	Lamb's Court (off James Street)	74 D1	Latchford Terrace	21 B1
Kingsbury	17 C4	Knockmeenagh Road	44 E2	Landen Road	36 E3	Latouka Apts.	34 F1
Kingsland Parade	75 A4	Knockmitten Close	44 F1 [1]	Landore	47 A3 [9]	Latouka Apts.	34 F1 [1]
Kingsland Park Avenue	75 A3	Knockmitten Lane	45 A1	Landscape Avenue	47 A3	Lauderdale Estate	67 C3
Kingsmill Road	67 C2	Knockmitten Lane North	44 F1 [2]	Landscape Crescent	47 A4	Lauderdale Terrace	67 C3 [16]
Kingston	57 B3	Knockmore Avenue	54 E2	Landscape Gardens	47 B4	*Lauderdale Terrace	75 A2
Kingston Avenue	57 B3	Knockmore Crescent	54 E2	Landscape Park	47 A4	(on New Row South)	
Kingston Close	57 B3	Knockmore Drive	54 E2	Landscape Road	47 A3	Lauder's Lane	29 A1
Kingston Court	56 F2	Knockmore Gardens	54 E2	Landsdown Valley Place	45 C1	Laundry Lane	46 F1
Kingston Crescent	57 B3	Knockmore Green	54 E2	Landsdowne Valley	45 C1 [6]	Laurel Avenue (Ballybrack)	64 E1
Kingston Drive	57 C3	Knockmore Grove	54 E2	*Landsdowne Valley Apts	45 C1	Laurel Avenue (Dundrum)	57 B1
Kingston Green	57 B3	Knockmore Park	54 E2	(Landsdowne Valley)		Laurel Bank	59 C1
Kingston Grove	57 B3	Knock-na-Cree Grove	60 F2	Landsdowne Valley Park	36 F4 [5]	Laurel Court	22 E3
Kingston Hall	57 B3	Knock-na-Cree Park	60 F2	Lanesborough Avenue	11 B4	Laurel Drive	57 B1
Kingston Heights	57 C3	Knock-na-Cree Road	60 F2	Lanesborough Court	11 B4	Laurel Hill	60 D1 [6]
Kingston Lawn	57 B3	Knocknagow	49 B4 [23]	Lanesborough Drive	11 B4	Laurel Lodge Road	22 F3
Kingston Lodge	25 B4 [4]	Knocknarea Avenue	73 A4	Lanesborough Gardens	11 B4	Laurel Park	44 E1
Kingston Park	57 B3	Knocknarea Road	73 A4	Lanesborough Grove	11 B4	Laurel Place	46 F2
Kingston Rise	57 B3	Knocknarrow Terrace	73 C1	Lanesborough Mews	11 B4	Laurel Road	57 B1
Kingston View	57 B3	(Kilmainham Lane)		Lanesborough Park	11 B4	Laurelton (Rathbeale Road)	1 C1
Kingston Walk	57 B3	Knocknashee	47 C4	Lanesborough Road	11 B4	Laurelton (Terenure)	46 F3
Kingswood	43 C3	Knocknashee	48 D4	Lanesborough Square	11 B4	Laurence Brook	36 E2
Kingswood Avenue (Citywest)	43 C4	Knocksedan Bridge	1 A2	Lanesborough Terrace	11 B4	Laurence Court	46 F1
Kingswood Avenue	44 F3	Knocksedan Drive	1 A2	Lanesborough View	11 B4	Laurence Place East	72 E3
(Kilnamanagh)		Knocksedan Wood	1 A2	Lanesville	59 B1	Laurleen	58 F1
Kingswood Castle	45 A2	Knocksink Bridge	66 E3	Lanesville Terrace	59 B1	Lavarna Grove	46 E2
Kingswood Drive (Citywest)	43 C4	Knocksinna	59 A2	Lanewood Mews	76 E3	Lavarna Road	46 E2
Kingswood Drive (Kilnamanagh)	44 F3	Knocksinna Court	59 A2 [2]	Langrishe Place	71 C2	Laverna Avenue	22 E3
Kingswood Heights	44 F3	Knocksinna Crescent	59 A2	Lanndale Lawns	54 E1	Laverna Dale	22 E3
Kingswood Interchange	42 C3	Knocksinna Grove	59 A2 [1]	*Lansdowne Court	76 F3	Laverna Grove	22 E3
Kingswood Road	43 C4	Knocksinna Park	59 A2	Lansdowne Crescent	76 F2	Laverna Way	22 E3
Kingswood View	44 F3	Knowth Court	11 C4	Lansdowne Gardens	76 F3	Lavery Avenue	35 C4
Kinsaley	14 D1	Kyber Road	36 F2	Lansdowne Hall	39 A3 [25]	Lavista Avenue	26 E3
Kinsaley Bridge	14 D1	Kyle-Clare Road	39 A3 [13]	Lansdowne Lane	76 F2	Lawnswood Park	58 F1
Kinsaley Lane	3 A4	Kylemore Avenue	36 D3	Lansdowne Park (Ballsbridge)	76 F2	Lawrence Grove	26 D4
Kinsealy Court	2 E3	Kylemore Drive	36 D3	Lansdowne Park (Templeogue)	56 D1	Lawrence's Avenue	18 D4
Kinsealy Downs	2 E3	Kylemore Park North	36 D4	Lansdowne Road	76 F3	Lawson Spinney	3 A3
Kinsealy Lane	14 D1	Kylemore Park South	36 D4	Lansdowne Square	39 A4 [24]	Lawson Terrace	60 E1 [14]
Kinvara Avenue	24 D4	Kylemore Park West	36 D4	Lansdowne Terrace	76 F2	Le Bas Terrace	46 F1 [2]
Kinvara Drive	23 C4	Kylemore Road	36 D2	Lansdowne Village	39 A3	Le Brett Terrace	46 F3 [7]
Kinvara Grove	23 C4	Kylemore Road (Grand Canal)	36 E4	Lansdowne Villas	76 F2	Le Brocquy Avenue	36 D4
Kinvara Park	24 D4			Lansdowne Woods	39 A4 [28]	Le Fanu Drive	36 D3 [1]
Kinvara Road	23 C4			Lapwing Apts.	48 E3	Le Fanu Road	36 D3
Kippure Avenue	45 B3	**L**		Laracor Gardens	27 A1 [5]	Le Vere Terrace	74 F4
Kippure Park	24 D3			Laragh	60 E4	Lea Crescent	39 B4
Kirkfield	22 D2 [2]	La Rochelle Apts.	74 F1	Laragh Close	27 A1	Lea Road	39 B4
Kirkpatrick Avenue	22 D3	La Touche Court (Ballinteer)	57 A2	Laragh Flats	25 C2 [5]	Leahy's Terrace	39 A3
Kirkpatrick Drive	22 D3	La Touche Court (Bluebell)	36 F4 [3]	Laragh Grove	27 A1	Lealand Avenue	43 C1
Kirkwood	39 A4	La Touche Drive	36 E4	Laraghbryan East	17 B2	Lealand Close	43 C1
Kirwan Street	70 E3	La Touche Road	36 F4	Laraghbryan West	17 A2	Lealand Crescent	43 C1
Kirwan Street Cottages	70 E2	La Vallee	67 A3	Laraghon	34 D1	Lealand Drive	43 C1
Kitestown Road	30 E3	La Vista Avenue	29 B2	Larch Drive	56 E2 [3]	Lealand Gardens	43 C1
Knapton Court	49 C4 [21]	Labre Park	36 E4	Larch Grove	21 C2	Lealand Grove	43 C1
Knapton Lawn	49 C4 [22]	Laburnum Road	47 C2	Larch Grove	47 B1	Lealand Road	43 C1
Knapton Road	49 C4	Laburnum Walk	35 B2	Larch Hill	12 F4	Lealand Walk	43 C1
Knapton Terrace	49 C4 [27]	Lad Lane	76 D2	Larch House (Swords)	1 Inset	Leaunstown	59 C4
*Knapton Villas	49 C4	Lad Lane Apts.	76 D3	Larchfield	7 C3	Leda Mews	76 E3
(on Knapton Road)		Lad Lane Upper	76 D3	Larchfield	47 C4	Ledwidge Crescent	67 B1
Knights Bridge	26 E4 [4]	Lady's Lane	73 B1	Larchfield Park	47 C4	Lee Road	24 E3
Knights Wood	12 F4	Lady's Well Road	9 A4	Larchfield Road	47 C4	Leeson Close	75 C3
Knock Riada	36 D2	Lagan Road	24 E3	Larkfield	34 F2	Leeson Court	76 D4
Knockaire	56 D1	Lake Drive	53 C1	Larkfield Avenue	46 F1	Leeson Lane	75 C2
Knockandinny	52 D4	Lakelands Avenue	58 D1	(Harold's Cross)		Leeson Mews	75 C4
Knockaulin	20 D4	Lakelands Close	58 D1	Larkfield Avenue (Liffey Valley)	34 F2	Leeson Park	75 C4
		Lakelands Crescent	58 E1				

STREET NAME	PAGE/GRID REFERENCE
Leeson Park Avenue	76 D4
Leeson Place	75 C3
Leeson Street Lower	75 C2
Leeson Street Upper	76 D4
Leeson Village	76 D4
Leeson Walk	75 C4
Lehaunstown Road	63 C1
Leicester Avenue	47 A1
Leighlin Road	46 E1
Lein Gardens	26 F2
Lein Park	26 F2
Lein Road	26 F2
Leinster Avenue	72 E1
Leinster Cottages	17 C3 [6]
Leinster Court	18 D3 [2]
Leinster Lane	75 C1
Leinster Lawn	47 C3
Leinster Lodge Apts.	18 D3 [1]
Leinster Market	71 C4
Leinster Park (Harold's Cross)	46 F1
Leinster Park (Maynooth)	18 D3
Leinster Place	46 F1
Leinster Road	47 A1
Leinster Road West	46 F1
Leinster Square	47 A1 [2]
Leinster Street	17 C3
Leinster Street East	72 E1
Leinster Street North	24 F4
Leinster Street South	75 C1
Leinster Terrace	44 D1 [2]
Leitrim Place	76 E2
Leix Road	70 D1
Leixlip	33 B1
Leixlip Bridge	33 A1
Leixlip Gate	32 E1
Leixlip Park	32 F1
Leixlip Road	33 B1
Leixlip Road	33 C1
Lemon Street	75 B1
Lennox Place	75 A3
Lennox Street	75 B3
Lennox Terrace	75 B3
Lentisk Lawn	27 A1
Leo Avenue	71 B1
Leo Street	71 B1
Leonard's Court	74 F3
Leopardstown	58 F3
Leopardstown Abbey	58 F4
Leopardstown Avenue	58 F2
Leopardstown Court	58 F2 [1]
Leopardstown Drive	58 F2
Leopardstown Gardens	58 F2
Leopardstown Grove	58 F2
Leopardstown Heights	58 E3
Leopardstown Lawn	58 F2 [2]
Leopardstown Oaks	58 F2
Leopardstown Park	58 F2
Leopardstown Rise	58 E3
Leopardstown Road	58 D3
Leopardstown Road	58 F2
Leopardstown Valley	58 F4
Leslie Avenue	60 F1
Leslie's Buildings	70 F1
Leukos Road	39 A3 [11]
Liberty House	71 C2
Liberty Lane	75 B2
Library Road (Dún Laoghaire)	50 D4
Library Road (Shankill)	64 E2
Library Square	52 F2
Library View Villas	71 A1
Liffey Ave	34 F2
Liffey Close	34 F2
Liffey Court	34 F2
Liffey Crescent	34 F2
Liffey Dale	34 F2
Liffey Downs	34 F2
Liffey Drive	34 F2
Liffey Gardens	34 F2
Liffey Glen	34 F2
Liffey Green	34 F2
Liffey Grove	34 F2
Liffey Hall	34 F2 [1]
Liffey Junction	24 E4
Liffey Lawn	34 F2
Liffey Park	34 F2
Liffey Place	34 F2
Liffey Road	34 F2
Liffey Row	34 F2
Liffey Street Lower	71 B4
Liffey Street South	36 F3
Liffey Street Upper	71 B3
Liffey Street West	70 E4
Liffey Terrace	36 E2 [7]
Liffey Vale	34 F2
Liffey Valley Park	34 F2
Liffey View	34 F2
Liffey View Apts.	33 A1 [2]
Liffey Villas	34 F2
Liffey Walk	34 F2
Liffey Way	34 F2
Liffey Wood	34 F2
Lilys Way	21 A1
Lime Street	72 E4
Limekiln Avenue	45 B3
Limekiln Close	45 C3
Limekiln Drive	45 C3
Limekiln Green	45 B3
Limekiln Grove	45 C2
Limekiln Lane (Harold's Cross)	74 F4
Limekiln Lane (Kimmage)	45 C2
Limekiln Park	45 C3
Limekiln Road	45 C3
Limelawn Court	22 D2
Limelawn Glade	22 D2
Limelawn Green	22 D2
Limelawn Hill	22 D2
Limelawn Park	22 D2
Limelawn Wood	22 D2
Limes Road	58 D2
Limetree Avenue	3 C4
Limetree Avenue	4 D4
Limewood Avenue	26 F1
Limewood Park	26 F1
Limewood Road	27 A1
Lincoln Hall (Swords)	1 Inset
*Lincoln House	70 F4
Lincoln Lane	70 F4
Lincoln Place	76 D1
Linden Court	48 F4
Linden Grove	48 F4
Linden Lea Park	58 F1
Linden Square	48 F4
Lindenvale	49 A4 [4]
Lindisfarne Avenue	43 C1
Lindisfarne Drive	43 C1
Lindisfarne Green	43 C1
Lindisfarne Grove	43 C1
Lindisfarne Lawns	43 C1
Lindisfarne Park	34 F4
Lindisfarne Vale	43 C1
Lindisfarne Walk	43 C1
Lindsay Grove	25 A4 [15]
Lindsay Road	25 A4
Linenhall Parade	71 A3
Linenhall Street	71 A3
(off King Street North)	
Linenhall Terrace	71 A3
Link Road	60 E1
Link Road	49 C4
(Off Monkstown Crescent)	
Linnbhla	12 D4
Linnetfields	21 A1
Linnetfields Avenue	8 E4
Linnetfields Close	8 E4
Linnetfields Court	21 A1
Linnetfields Drive	8 E4
Linnetfields Park	21 A1
Linnetfields Rise	8 E4
Linnetfields Square	8 E4
Linnetfields View	8 D4
Linnetfields Walk	21 A1
Lios na Sídhe	54 F2
Lioscian	1 B1
Lisalea	49 A3 [22]
Lisburn Street	71 A3
Liscannor Road	24 E4
Liscanor	60 F1 [9]
Liscarne Court	35 A3
Liscarne Dale	35 A3 [2]
Liscarne Gardens	35 A3
Lisle Road	46 D1
Lismeen Grove	26 E1 [1]
Lismore	18 E4
Lismore Road	46 E1
Lissadel Avenue	73 B4
Lissadel Court	73 A4
Lissadel Crescent	2 F2
Lissadel Drive	73 A4
Lissadel Green	73 A3
Lissadel Grove	2 F2
Lissadel Park	2 F2
Lissadel Road	73 A4
Lissadel Wood	2 F2
Lissane Apts.	22 E1
Lissen Hall	2 E1
Lissen Hall Drive	2 E1
Lissenfield	75 B4
Lissenhall Avenue	2 D1
Lissenhall Bridge	2 E1
Lissenhall Court	2 D1
Lissenhall Drive	2 D1
Lissenhall Park	2 D1
Little Britain Street	71 A3
Little Fitzwilliam Place	76 D2
Little Meadow	59 C3 [1]
Little Orchard	59 C3 [5]
Littlepace	8 E4
Littlepace Close	8 E4
Littlepace Court	8 E4
Littlepace Crescent	8 E4
Littlepace Drive	8 E4
Littlepace Gallops	8 E4
Littlepace Meadow	8 E4
Littlepace Park	8 E4
Littlepace Road	8 E4
Littlepace View	8 E4
Littlepace Walk	8 E4
Littlepace Way	8 E4
Littlepace Woods	8 E4
Littlewood	58 D4
Litton Lane	71 B4
Llewellyn Close	57 A1
Llewellyn Court	57 A1
Llewellyn Grove	57 A1
Llewellyn Lawn	57 A1
Llewellyn Park	57 A1
Llewellyn Way	57 A1
Llex House	76 D3
Lock Road	34 D3
Lockkeeper's Walk	24 D3
Loftus Hall (Belgard Square)	54 F1 [9]
Loftus Lane	71 A3
Loftus Square	46 F4 [14]
Lohunda Close	22 D2
Lohunda Court	22 D2
Lohunda Crescent	21 C2
Lohunda Dale	22 D2
Lohunda Downs	22 D2
Lohunda Drive	22 D2
Lohunda Grove	22 D2
Lohunda Park	21 C2
Lohunda Road	22 D2
Lombard Court	74 F3
Lombard Court	72 D4
Lombard Street East	72 D4
Lombard Street West	75 A3
Lomond Avenue	25 C4
Londonbridge Drive	39 A3 [20]
Londonbridge Road	39 A3
Long Lane	75 A2
Long Lane Close	75 A2
(off Long Lane)	
Long Meadow Apts.	69 C4
Long Mile Road	45 B1
Longdale Terrace	25 A1
Longdale Way	25 A1
Longford Lane	75 B1
Longford Place	49 C4
Longford Street Great	75 A1
Longford Street Little	75 B1
Longford Terrace	49 C4
Longlands	2 D2
Longmeadow	59 C3
Longmeadow Grove	59 C3
Long's Place	74 E1
Longwood Avenue	75 A3
Longwood Park	46 F4
Looceville Court	46 D1 [7]
Lorcan Avenue	25 C1
Lorcan Crescent	25 C1
Lorcan Drive	25 B1
Lorcan Green	25 C1
Lorcan Grove	25 C1
Lorcan O'Toole Court	46 D2 [2]
Lorcan O'Toole Park	46 D2
Lorcan Park	25 C1
Lorcan Road	25 B1
Lorcan Villas	25 C1
Lord Edward Court	75 A1
Lord Edward Street	75 A1
Lordello Road	64 D3
Lords Walk	69 B2
Loreto Abbey	47 A4
Loreto Avenue (Dalkey)	60 F1
Loreto Avenue	47 A4
(Nutgrove Avenue)	
Loreto Court	47 A4
Loreto Crescent	47 A4
Loreto Grange	67 C3
Loreto Park	47 A4
Loreto Road	74 E2
Loreto Row	47 A4
Loreto Terrace	46 F4
Loretto Avenue	67 C2 [34]
Loretto Terrace	67 C2 [35]
Loretto Villas	67 C2 [54]
Lorne Terrace	73 C2
(off Almeida Avenue)	
Losset Hall (Belgard Square)	54 F1 [6]
Lotts	71 B4
Lough Conn Avenue	36 D2
Lough Conn Drive	36 D2
Lough Conn Road	36 D2
Lough Conn Terrace	36 D2
Lough Derg Road	27 A2
Lough na Mona	19 C4
Loughlinstown	64 D1
Loughlinstown Drive	64 D1
Loughlinstown Park	64 D1
Loughlinstown Wood	64 D1
Loughmorne House	46 F2 [27]
Loughoreen Hills	30 D3
Loughsallagh Bridge	7 C3
Loughtown Lower	41 C1
Loughtown Upper	42 D1
Louis Lane	47 A1 [23]
Louisa Vally	19 C4
Lourdes House	71 C2
Lourdes Road	74 D2
Louvain	48 D3
Louvain Glade	48 D3
Love Lane	76 E2
Love Lane East	76 E2
Lower Dargle Road	67 B2
Lower Glen Road	36 D1
Lower Kilmacud Road	48 D4
(Goatstown)	
Lower Kilmacud Road	58 D1
(Stillorgan)	
Lower Lucan Road	21 C4
Lower Lucan Road	34 D1
Lower Road (Shankill)	64 E3
Lower Road (Strawberry Beds)	35 B1
Luby Road	73 B1
Lucan	34 D2
Lucan Bridge	34 D1
Lucan Bypass	34 D2
Lucan Heights	34 E1
Lucan Newlands Road	34 D2
Lucan Newlands road	35 A4
Lucan Road (Chapelizod)	36 D2
Lucan Road (Lucan)	34 D1
Lucan Road (near Qaurryvale)	35 A1
Lucan Road (Palmerstown)	35 C1
Lucan-Newlands Road	34 F3
Ludford Drive	57 B1
Ludford Park	57 B1
Ludford Road	57 B2
Lugg	52 F4
Lugmore	54 D3
Lugmore Lane	53 C3
Lugnaquilla Avenue	45 B3
Luke Street	71 C4
Lullymore Terrace	74 E3

STREET NAME	PAGE/GRID REFERENCE
Lurgan Street	71 A3
Lutterell Hall	7 A2
Luttrell Park	22 D3
Luttrell Park Close	22 D3
Luttrell Park Court	22 D3
Luttrell Park Crescent	22 E3
Luttrell Park Drive	22 E3
Luttrell Park Green	22 E3
Luttrell Park Grove	22 D3
Luttrell Park Heath	22 E3 [2]
Luttrell Park Lawn	22 D3
Luttrell Park View	22 D3
Luttrellstown Avenue	22 E4
Luttrellstown Chase	22 D4
Luttrellstown Close	22 E4
Luttrellstown Court	22 D4
Luttrellstown Dale	22 D4
Luttrellstown Drive	22 D4
Luttrellstown Glade	22 D4
Luttrellstown Green	22 D4
Luttrellstown Grove	22 D4
Luttrellstown Heath	22 D4
Luttrellstown Heights	22 D4
Luttrellstown Lawn	22 D4
Luttrellstown Oaks	22 D4
Luttrellstown Park	22 D4
Luttrellstown Place	22 D4
Luttrellstown Rise	22 D3
Luttrellstown Thicket	22 D4
Luttrellstown View	22 E4
Luttrellstown Walk	22 D4
Luttrellstown Way	22 D4
Luttrellstown Wood	22 E4
Lymewood Mews	12 E4
Lynches Lane	34 E4
Lynch's Lane	36 E3 [2]
Lynch's Place	71 A1
Lyndon Gate	24 D4 [4]
Lynton Court	39 A4 [12]
Lynwood	57 C1
Lyons	41 A4
Lyons Road	41 B4
Lyreen Court	17 C3
Lyreen Park	18 D2

M

STREET NAME	PAGE/GRID REFERENCE
Ma Tuire Apts.	48 D4
Mabbot House	71 C3
Mabbot Lane	71 C3
Mabel Street	25 B4
Macken Street	76 E1
Macken Villa	76 E1
Mackies Place	75 C2
Mackintosh Park	59 C2
Macroom Avenue	13 B4
Macroom Road	13 B4
Madden Road	74 F2
*Madden's Court (off Thomas Street)	74 E2
Madden's Lane	60 E4
Madison Road	73 C2
Magdalen Terrace	39 A3 [39]
*Magdalen Terrace (off Oliver Plunket Ave)	39 A3
Magenis Place	72 D4
Magenis Square	72 D4
Magenta Crescent	25 B1
Magenta Hall	25 B1
Magenta Place	60 D1 [8]
Magna Drive	53 C2
*Maher's Terrace (on Main Street Dundrum)	47 C4
Maidens Row	36 E2 [2]
Main Street	14 D4
Main Street (Baldoyle)	15 A4
Main Street (Blackrock)	49 A3
Main Street (Blanchardstown)	22 E2
Main Street (Bray)	67 C2
Main Street (Celbridge)	32 D3
Main Street (Clondalkin)	44 E1
Main Street (Dunboyne)	7 B2
Main Street (Dundrum)	47 C4
Main Street (Finglas)	24 E2
Main Street (Howth)	30 D2
Main Street (Leixlip)	33 A1

STREET NAME	PAGE/GRID REFERENCE
Main Street (Lucan)	34 D1
Main Street (Malahide)	3 B2
Main Street (Maynooth)	17 C3
Main Street (Newcastle)	42 D4
Main Street (Raheny)	27 A2
Main Street (Rathcoole)	52 F2
Main Street (Rathfarnham)	46 F4
Main Street (Swords)	2 D2
Main Street (Tallaght)	55 A1
Maitland Street	67 B2
Malachi Place	72 E2
Malachi Road	70 E3
Malahide	3 B2
Malahide Demesne	3 A3
Malahide Road	13 C4
Malahide Road (Artane)	26 E2
Malahide Road (Balgriffin)	14 D3
Malahide Road (Coolock)	26 F1
Malahide Road (Marino)	26 D4
Malahide Road (Swords)	2 E2
Malahide Roundabout (Swords)	2 D2
Malborough Court	70 D2
Malborough Court	60 E2 [8]
Mallin Avenue	74 D2
Malone Gardens	76 F2
Malpas Court	75 A2
Malpas Place (off Malpas Street)	75 A2
Malpas Street (off New Street)	75 A2
Malpas Terrace	75 A2
Mander's Terrace	75 C4
Mangerton Road	36 F4
Mannix Road	25 A4
Manor Avenue	46 E3
Manor Close	57 A2
Manor Court	17 C3
Manor Crescent	21 B1
Manor Drive	14 D4
Manor Green	57 A2
Manor Grove	46 D2
Manor Hall Apts. (Mount Brown)	74 D1
Manor Heath	57 A1
Manor Mews (off Norseman Place)	70 E3
Manor Park (Ballinteer)	57 A2
Manor Park (Palmerston)	35 C2
Manor Place (Clonsilla)	21 A1
Manor Place (Stoneybatter)	70 E3
Manor Rise	57 A2
Manor Road	35 C2
Manor Square	21 A1
Manor Street	70 E3
Manor Villas	46 F1 [4]
Manorfields	21 B1
Mantua Park	2 D1
Maolbuille Road	25 A2
Mapas Avenue	60 E2
Mapas Road	60 E2
Maple Avenue (Carpenterstown)	22 E3
*Maple Avenue (off Blackthorn Drive)	58 D2
Maple Close	22 E3
Maple Drive (Carpenterstown)	22 E3
Maple Drive (Dunboyne)	7 B2
Maple Drive (Harold's Cross)	46 F2 [6]
Maple Glen	22 E3
Maple Green	22 E3
Maple Grove (Bray)	67 B2
Maple Grove (Carpenterstown)	22 E3
Maple Grove (Rathcoole)	52 F2
Maple House	76 D3
Maple Lawn	22 E3
Maple Lodge	23 A4
Maple Manor	59 C3
Maple Road	47 C2
Maples Road	58 D2
Maplewood Avenue	54 E1
Maplewood Close	54 E1
Maplewood Court	54 E1
Maplewood Drive	54 E1
Maplewood Green	54 E1
Maplewood Lawn	54 E1
Maplewood Park	54 E1
Maplewood Road	54 E1
Maplewood Way	54 E1
Maretimo Gardens East	49 A3

STREET NAME	PAGE/GRID REFERENCE
Maretimo Gardens West	49 A3 [4]
Maretimo Place	49 A3 [17]
Maretimo Road	49 A3 [2]
Maretimo Terrace	49 A3 [16]
Maretimo Villas	49 A3 [18]
Marewood Crescent	24 F1
Marewood Drive	11 C4
Marewood Drive	24 F1
Marewood Grove	24 F1
Margaret Place	76 F2
Marguerite Road	25 A4
Marian Court	14 F4
Marian Crescent	46 E4
Marian Drive	46 E4
Marian Grove	46 E4
Marian Park (Baldoyle)	27 C1
Marian Park (Blackrock)	59 A1
Marian Park (Templeogue)	46 E4
Marian Road	46 E4
Marianella	47 A2
Mariavilla	17 C2
Marie Villas	67 C2 [55]
Marigold Avenue	13 C4
Marigold Court	13 C4
Marigold Crescent	13 C4
Marigold Drive	13 C4
Marigold Grove	13 C4
Marigold Park	13 C4
Marina House Apts	49 C4 [32]
Marina Village	3 B2
Marine Avenue	60 E1
Marine Court (Dalkey)	60 E1
Marine Court (Dún Laoghaire)	50 D4 [17]
Marine Cove	28 D1 [4]
Marine Drive	39 A4
Marine Parade	60 E1
Marine Road	50 D4
Marine Terrace (Bray)	68 D2 [17]
Marine Terrace (Dún Laoghaire)	50 D4 [9]
Marine View	48 F3
Marine Villas	30 D1 [7]
Mariners Court	27 C2 [1]
Mariners Cove	30 E2
Mariner's Port	72 E3
Marino	25 C4
Marino Avenue	26 D4
Marino Avenue East	60 E4
Marino Avenue West	60 E4
Marino Court	25 C4 [13]
Marino Crescent	25 C4
Marino Green	25 C4
Marino Mart	25 C4 [9]
Marino Park	25 C4
Marino Park Avenue	25 C4
Marino Villas	26 D3 [3]
Marion Villas	74 E2
Mark Street	72 D4
Market House	67 C2
Market Square	70 F3
Market Square	67 C2 [49]
Market Square Apts.	71 A3
Market Street South	74 E1
Mark's Alley West	74 F1
Mark's Lane	72 D4
Marlay View	57 B2
Marlborough Court	71 C3
Marlborough Lane	47 B1 [25]
Marlborough Mews	70 D2
Marlborough Park	60 D1 [9]
Marlborough Place	71 C3
Marlborough Road (Donnybrook)	47 B1
Marlborough Road (Glenageary)	60 E1
Marlborough Road (Nth Circular Rd)	70 D2
Marlborough Street	71 C3
Marlborough Terrace	68 D2 [16]
Marley Avenue	57 A1
Marley Close	57 A1
Marley Court North	57 A1
Marley Court South	57 A1
Marley Drive	57 A1
Marley Grove	57 A1
Marley Lawn	57 A1
Marley Rise	57 A1
Marley Villas	57 A1 [1]

STREET NAME	PAGE/GRID REFERENCE
Marley Walk	57 A1
Marlfield	59 C3
Marlfield Close	54 F3
Marlfield Court	54 F3
Marlfield Crescent	54 F3
Marlfield Green	54 F3
Marlfield Grove	54 F3
Marlfield Lawn	54 F3
Marlfield Mall	54 F3
Marlfield Place	54 F3
Marmion Court Flats	70 F3
Marne Villas	70 F2
Marrowbone Lane	74 E2
Marrowbone Lane Close (off Marrowbone Lane)	74 E1
Marrowbone Lane Flats	74 E1
Marshal Court Apts.	74 E1
Marshal Lane (Marshalsea Lane)	74 E1
Marshalsea Court	70 E4
Marshalsea Lane	70 E4
Marsham Court	58 E1
Mart Lane	59 B3
Martello Avenue	50 D4 [14]
Martello Court	4 D4
Martello Mews	48 E1
Martello Terrace (Booterstown)	48 F3 [1]
Martello Terrace (Bray)	67 C1 [2]
Martello Terrace (Dun Laoghaire)	50 E4 [4]
Martello Terrace (Sutton)	29 B3 [2]
Martello View	39 B4 [3]
Martello Wood	39 B4 [6]
Martin Grove	24 D4
Martin Savage Park	23 C3
Martin Street	75 A3
Martin White Chalets	39 A4 [4]
Martin's Row	36 E2
*Martin's Terrace (off Hanover Street East)	72 D4
Mary Street	71 A3
Mary Street Little	71 A4
Maryfield Avenue	26 E2 [1]
Maryfield Crescent	26 E2
Maryfield Drive	26 D2
Maryland	64 E2 [5]
Mary's Abbey	71 A4
Mary's Lane	71 A4
Maryville Road	26 F3
Mask Avenue	26 E2
Mask Crescent	26 E2
Mask Drive	26 E2
Mask Green	26 E2
Mask Road	26 E2
Mather Road North	48 E3
Mather Road South	48 D3
Matt Talbot Court	71 C2
Maunsell Place	71 A2
Maxwell Court	47 A1 [18]
Maxwell Lane	47 A2
Maxwell Road	47 A1
Maxwell Street	74 E2
May Lane	70 F4
May Park	26 D3
*May Street (off Fitzroy Ave)	25 B4
Mayberry Park	45 A4
Mayberry Road	44 F4
Mayeston Boulevard	11 B3
Mayeston Close	11 B3
Mayeston Court	11 B4
Mayeston Crescent	11 B4
Mayeston Downs	11 C4
Mayeston Drive	11 B3
Mayeston Lawn	11 B3
Mayeston Rise	11 B4
Mayeston Square	11 B4
Mayeston Walk	11 C4
Mayfair	3 C2
Mayfield	47 A2
Mayfield Park	35 B4
Mayfield Road (Kilmainham)	73 C2
Mayfield Road (Terenure)	46 F2
Mayfield Terrace (Ballinteer)	57 C2
Mayfield Terrace (Bray)	67 C3 [17]
Mayne Bridge	14 F3
Maynetown	14 F3
Maynooth	18 D2

STREET NAME	PAGE/GRID REFERENCE
Maynooth Park	18 D4
Maynooth Road (Celbridge)	31 C1
Maynooth Road (Dunboyne)	7 A3
Mayola Court	47 B4
Mayor Square	72 E3
Mayor Street Lower	72 D3
Mayor Street Upper	72 F3
Mayville Terrace	60 F1 [11]
Maywood Avenue	27 B2
Maywood Close	27 B2
Maywood Crescent	27 B3
Maywood Drive	27 B2
Maywood Grove	27 B2
Maywood Lawn	27 B3
Maywood Park	27 B2
Maywood Road	27 B2
McAuley Avenue	26 F2
McAuley Drive	26 F2
McAuley Park	26 F2
McAuley Road	26 F2
McCabe Villas	48 E1
McCarthy Terrace	74 D2
McCreadies Lane	3 A3
McDowell Avenue	74 D1
McGrane Court	57 C1 [5]
McKee Avenue	24 E1
McKee Park	69 C1
McKee Road	24 E1
McKelvey Avenue	11 A4
McKelvey Road	11 A4
McMahon Street	75 A3
McMorrough Road	46 F2 [14]
Meade's Terrace	76 D1
Meadow Avenue	57 B1 [1]
Meadow Close (Dundrum)	57 A1
Meadow Close (Newtown Park Ave)	59 A1
Meadow Copse	21 C1
Meadow Court	60 D4 [2]
Meadow Dale	21 C1 [1]
Meadow Downs	21 C1
Meadow Drive	21 C1
Meadow Green	21 C1
Meadow Grove	57 B1
Meadow Mount	57 A1
Meadow Park	57 A1
Meadow Park Avenue	47 A4
Meadow Vale	59 B2
Meadow View (Dunboyne)	7 B2
Meadow View (Nutgrove Avenue)	57 A1
Meadow Villas	57 A1 [2]
Meadow Way	21 C1
Meadowbank	46 F3
Meadowbrook	17 C4
Meadowbrook Avenue (Maynooth)	17 C4
Meadowbrook Avenue (Sutton)	28 D1
Meadowbrook Close	17 C4
Meadowbrook Court	17 C4
Meadowbrook Crescent	17 C4
Meadowbrook Drive	17 C4
Meadowbrook Lawn	28 D1
Meadowbrook Lawns	17 C4
Meadowbrook Park	28 D1
Meadowbrook Road	17 C4
Meadowfield	58 E4
Meadowlands	59 C1
Meadowlands Avenue	59 C1
Meadowlands Court	59 C1 [17]
Meadowlands Mews	59 C1 [18]
Meadowview Grove	33 C2
Meakstown Cottages	11 B3
Meath Market	74 F1
Meath Place (Bray)	67 C2
Meath Place (Meath Street)	74 F1
Meath Road	68 D2
Meath Square	74 F1
Meath Street	74 F1
*Meath Terrace (on Meath Place)	74 F1
*Meathville Terrace (on Long Lane)	75 A2
Meenan Square	48 D3 [5]
Meetinghouse Lane	71 A4
Méile an Rí Crescent	34 F3
Méile an Rí Drive	34 F3
Méile an Rí Green	34 F3
Méile an Rí Park	34 F3
Méile an Rí Road	34 F3
Méile an Rí View	34 F3
Mellifont Avenue	50 D4
Mellowes Avenue	24 D1
Mellowes Court	24 D2 [3]
Mellowes Crescent	24 D2 [4]
Mellowes Park	24 D1
Mellowes Road	24 D1
Mellows Bridge	70 F4
Melrose Avenue (Clondalkin)	43 C1
Melrose Avenue (Fairview)	25 C4
Melrose Court	25 C4 [16]
Melrose Crescent	43 C1
Melrose Green	43 C1
Melrose Grove	43 C1
Melrose Lawn	34 F4
Melrose Park (Clondalkin)	43 C1
Melrose Park (Swords) (Swords)	2 E3
Melrose Park The Avenue	2 E3
Melrose Park The Close	2 E3
Melrose Park The Crescent	2 E3
Melrose Park The Drive	2 E3
Melrose Park The Green	2 E3
Melrose Park The Grove	2 E3
Melrose Park The Heights	2 E3
Melrose Park The Lawn	2 E3
Melrose Park The Park	2 E3
Melrose Park The Rise	2 E3
Melrose Park The Villa	2 E3
Melrose Park The Walk	2 E3
Melrose Road	34 F4
Melville Close	11 B4
Melville Court	11 B4
Melville Cove	11 B4
Melville Crescent	11 B4
Melville Drive	11 B4
Melville Green	11 B4
Melville Grove	11 B4
Melville Lawn	11 B4
Melville Park	11 B4
Melville Rise	11 B4
Melville Square	11 B4
Melville Terrace	11 B4
Melville View	11 B4
Melville Way	11 B4
Melvin Road	46 F2
Memorial Court	69 B4
Memorial Road (Custom House Quay)	71 C3
Memorial Road (Inchicore Road)	73 A1
Mercer House	75 B2
Mercer Street Lower	75 B1
Mercer Street Upper	75 B2
Merchamp	26 F4
Merchants Arch (off Temple Bar)	71 B4
Merchant's Court	70 F4
Merchant's Hall (Merchants Quay)	70 F4
Merchant's House	70 F4
Merchant's Quay	70 F4
Merchant's Road	39 A1
Merchant's Square	72 F3
Meretimo Villas	68 D3 [2]
Merlyn Drive	48 D1
Merlyn Park	48 D1
Merlyn Road	48 D1
Merrion	48 E1
Merrion Close	76 D1
Merrion Court	48 E1 [1]
Merrion Crescent	48 E2 [3]
Merrion Gates	48 E1 [2]
Merrion Grove	48 E3
Merrion Hall	48 E4
Merrion Park	48 E3
Merrion Place	75 C2
Merrion Road	39 A4
Merrion Row	75 C2
Merrion Square East	76 D2
Merrion Square North	76 D1
Merrion Square South	76 D1
Merrion Square West	76 D1
Merrion Strand	48 E1
Merrion Street Lower	76 D1
Merrion Street Upper	75 C2
Merrion View Avenue	48 D1 [1]
Merrion Village	48 E1
Merry Bush	39 A4 [34]
Merrycourt	8 E2
Merton Avenue	74 F3
Merton Drive	47 B1
Merton Park	74 F3
Merton Road	47 B2
Merville Avenue (Fairview)	25 C4
Merville Avenue (Stillorgan)	58 F1
Merville Road	58 F1
Mespil Estate	76 D3
Mespil Lodge	76 D3
Mespil Road	76 D3
Metropolitan Apts.	73 A1
Michael Collins Park	35 A4
Michael Collins Park	44 D1
Middle Third	26 E3
Middle Third Terrace	26 E3
Milesian Avenue	2 E2
Milesian Court	2 E2
Milesian Grove	2 E2
Milesian Lawn	2 E2
Milestown	6 F4
Milestown	19 C1
Milford	3 A2
Military Road (Killiney)	60 E4
Military Road (Kilmainham)	73 C1
Military Road (Phoenix Park)	36 F2
Military Road (Rathmines)	75 B4
Mill Bank	34 D1 [15]
Mill Bridge (Swords)	2 D2
Mill Brook Apts.	35 C1
Mill Court Avenue	43 C1
Mill Court Drive	43 C1
Mill Field (Enniskerry)	66 E3
Mill House	62 F3
Mill Lane (Ashtown)	23 B3 [1]
Mill Lane (Leixlip)	33 A1
Mill Lane (Loughlinstown)	64 E2
Mill Lane (Newmarket)	74 F2
Mill Lane (Palmerstown)	35 C1
Mill Park	44 D1
Mill Road (Blanchardstown)	22 F2
Mill Road (Saggart)	53 A2
Mill Street (Dun Laoghaire)	50 D4 [19]
Mill Street (The Coombe)	74 F2
Millar's Hall	74 F2
Millar's Hall	74 F1
Millbank	14 F2
Millbourne Avenue	25 A4
Millbrook Avenue	27 A1
Millbrook Court	73 C1
Millbrook Drive	27 A1
Millbrook Grove	27 A1
Millbrook Lawns	55 A1
Millbrook Road	27 A1
Millbrook Terrace	73 B1
Millbrook Village	47 C1 [17]
Millennium Bridge	71 B4
Millers Wood	67 B3
Millfarm	7 C2
Millfield (Portmarnock)	14 F2
Millgate Drive	45 C3
Millmount Avenue	25 A4
Millmount Grove	47 B3
Millmount Place	25 B4
*Millmount Terrace (Drumcondra)	25 B4
Millmount Villas	25 A4 [1]
Millrace Avenue	53 A2
Millrace Court	53 A2
Millrace Crescent	53 A2
Millrace Green	53 A2
Millrace Park	53 A2
Millrace Road	23 B3
Millrace Walk	53 A2
Millrose Estate	36 E4 [2]
Millstead	22 F2
Millstream	14 F2
Millstream Road	33 C2
Milltown (Clonskeagh)	47 C2
Milltown (Peamount)	42 F2
Milltown Bridge Road	47 C2
*Milltown Collonade (on Milltown Road)	47 B2
Milltown Drive	47 A3
Milltown Grove (Churchtown)	47 A3
Milltown Grove (Clonskeagh)	47 B2 [6]
Milltown Hill	47 B2 [7]
Milltown Park	47 B1
Milltown Path	47 B2
Milltown Road	47 B2
*Milltown Terrace (Dundrum)	47 B3 [4]
Millview	44 E1 [7]
Millview Close	3 A3
Millview Cottages	73 A2
Millview Court	3 A2
Millview Lawns	3 A3
Millview Road	3 A3
Millwood Court	27 A1
Millwood Park	27 A1
Millwood Villas	27 A1
Milton Hall	1 C2
Milton Terrace	2 D2
Milton Terrace	67 C2 [13]
Milward Terrace	68 D2 [13]
Mine Hill Lane	63 B3
Minnow Brook	46 F2
*Minstrel Court (Charles Sheil's Houses)	58 F2
Misery Hill	72 E4
Moat Lane	1 A2
Moatfield Avenue	26 F1
Moatfield Park	26 F1
Moatfield Road	26 F1
Moatview Avenue	13 B4
Moatview Court	13 B4
Moatview Drive	13 B4
Moatview Gardens	13 B4
Moatview Terrace	13 B4 [5]
Mobhi Court	25 A3 [16]
Mobhi Road	25 A3
Moeran Road	45 C1
Moira Road (off Oxmanstown Road)	70 D3
Moland House	71 C3
Moland Place	71 C3
Molesworth Close	1 A2
Molesworth Place	75 C1
Molesworth Street	75 C1
Mollison Avenue	14 D4
Molyneux Yard	74 F1
Monalea Grove	55 C1
Monalea Park	55 C1
Monalea Wood	55 C1
Monaloe Avenue	59 C3
Monaloe Court	59 B3 [6]
Monaloe Crescent	59 B3 [4]
Monaloe Drive	59 C3
Monaloe Park	59 C3
Monaloe Park Road	59 C3
Monaloe Way	59 C3
Monasterboice Road	46 D1
Monastery	66 E3
Monastery Crescent	44 E1
Monastery Drive	44 E1
Monastery Gate	44 F1
Monastery Gate Avenue	44 F1
Monastery Gate Close	44 F1
Monastery Gate Copse	44 F1
Monastery Gate Green	44 F1
Monastery Gate Lawn	44 F1
Monastery Gate Villas	44 F1
Monastery Grove	66 E2
Monastery Heath	44 E1
Monastery Heath Avenue	44 E1
Monastery Heath Court	44 E1
Monastery Heath Green	44 E1
Monastery Heath Square	44 E1
Monastery Heights	44 E1 [1]
Monastery Park	44 E1
Monastery Rise	44 E1
Monastery Road	44 E1
Monastery Walk	44 E1
Monck Place	70 F1
Monks Hill	66 E2
Monks Meadow	4 D4
Monksfield	44 F1
Monksfield Court	44 F1

STREET NAME	PAGE/GRID REFERENCE		STREET NAME	PAGE/GRID REFERENCE		STREET NAME	PAGE/GRID REFERENCE		STREET NAME	PAGE/GRID REFERENCE	
Monksfield Downs	44	F1	Mount Andrew Avenue	34	F2	Mount Symon Avenue	21	C2	Moy Glas Green	34	E3
Monksfield Grove	44	F1	Mount Andrew Close	34	F1	Mount Symon Close	21	C2	Moy Glas Grove	34	E3
Monksfield Heights	44	F1	Mount Andrew Court	34	F1	Mount Symon Crescent	21	B2	Moy Glas Lawn	34	E3
Monksfield Lawn	44	F1	Mount Andrew Crescent	34	F1	Mount Symon Dale	21	B2	Moy Glas Park	34	E3
Monksfield Meadows	44	F1	Mount Andrew Dale	34	F2	Mount Symon Drive	21	C2	Moy Glas Road	34	E3
Monksfield Walk	44	F1	Mount Andrew Grove	34	F1	Mount Symon Estate	21	B2	Moy Glas Vale	34	E3
Monkstown	49	B4	Mount Andrew Place	34	F1	Mount Symon Green	21	B2	Moy Glas View	34	E3
Monkstown Avenue	59	B1	Mount Andrew Rise	34	F1	Mount Symon Lawn	21	C2	Moy Glas Way	34	E3
Monkstown Crescent	49	C4	Mount Anthony Estate	47	A1 [22]	Mount Symon Park	21	C2	Moy Glas Wood	34	E3
Monkstown Farm	59	C1	Mount Anville Lawn	48	D4	Mount Symon Rise	21	B2	Moyclare Avenue	28	D1
Monkstown Gate	49	C4 [29]	Mount Anville Park	48	D4	Mount Talbot	44	F1	Moyclare Close	28	D1
Monkstown Grove	59	C1	Mount Anville Road	48	D4	Mount Tallant Avenue	46	F2	Moyclare Drive	28	D1
Monkstown Road	49	B4	Mount Anville Wood	48	D4	Mount Temple Road	70	E3	Moyclare Gardens	28	D1 [6]
Monkstown Square	59	B1 [12]	Mount Argus Avenue	46	F1	Mount Venus Road	56	D4	Moyclare Park	28	D1
Monkstown Valley	49	B4	Mount Argus Close	46	F1	Mount View Road	22	D2	Moyclare Road	28	D1
Montague Court	75	B2	Mount Argus Court	46	F1	Mount Wood	59	C1	Moycullen Road	35	C3
Montague Lane	75	B2	Mount Argus Crescent	46	F1	Mountain Park	55	A1	Moygaddy	18	D1
Montague Place	75	B2	Mount Argus Green	46	F1	Mountain View	54	D2	Moyglare	17	A1
Montague Street	75	B2	Mount Argus Grove	46	F1	Mountain View	64	E3	Moyglare Abbey	17	B2
Monte Vella	60	F2 [9]	Mount Argus Park	46	F1	Mountain View Apts.	67	C3 [11]	Moyglare Hall	17	C2
Montebello Terrace	68	D2 [2]	Mount Argus Road	46	F1	Mountain View Avenue	46	F1 [3]	Moyglare Meadows	17	C2
Montpelier Court	70	D3	Mount Argus Square	46	F1 [15]	Mountain View Cottages (Castleknock)	22	D4	Moyglare Road	17	C2
Montpelier Drive	70	D3	Mount Argus Terrace	46	F1	Mountain View Cottages (Ranelagh)	47	B1 [13]	Moyglare Village	17	C2
Montpelier Gardens	70	D3	Mount Argus View	46	F1				Moyle Crescent	44	E1
Montpelier Hill	70	D3	Mount Argus Way	46	F1	Mountain View Court	71	C2	Moyle Road	24	E3
Montpelier Manor	49	B4 [2]	Mount Auburn	60	E3 [2]	Mountain View Court (Harold's Cross)	46	F1 [16]	Moyne	14	F3
Montpelier Parade	49	B4	Mount Bellew Crescent	34	F2				Moyne Court	47	B1 [22]
Montpelier Park	70	D3	Mount Bellew Green	34	F2	Mountain View Court (off Summerhill Place)	71	C2	Moyne Park	14	F3
Montpelier Place	49	B4 [1]	Mount Bellew Rise	34	E2				Moyne Road (Balgriffin)	14	E3
Montpelier Square	70	D4	Mount Bellew Way	34	E2	Mountain View Drive	57	A1	Moyne Road (Ranelagh)	47	B1
Montpelier View	54	D2	Mount Brown	73	C1	Mountain View Park	47	A4	Moynihan Court	55	B1 [6]
Montpelier Walk	54	D2 [2]	Mount Carmel Avenue	47	C4	Mountain View Road (Ballybrack)	60	E4 [5]	Moyville	56	E2
Montrose Avenue	26	D2	Mount Carmel Park	55	C1				Moyville Lawns	56	E1
Montrose Close	26	D2	Mount Carmel Road	47	C4	Mountain View Road (Ranelagh)	47	B1	Muckross Avenue	46	D2
Montrose Court	26	D2	Mount Dillon Court	26	E2				Muckross Crescent	46	D2
Montrose Crescent	26	D1	Mount Drinan Avenue	2	E3	Mountain Villa	60	E4 [3]	Muckross Drive	46	D2 [1]
Montrose Drive	26	D1	Mount Drinan Crescent	2	E3	Mountainview Drive	67	C4	Muckross Green	46	D2
Montrose Grove	26	D2	Mount Drinan Grove	2	E3	Mountbrook	48	E3 [2]	Muckross Grove	46	D2
Montrose Park	26	D2	Mount Drinan Lawn	2	E3	Mountdown Avenue	45	C3	Muckross Parade	71	B1
Moore Lane	71	B3	Mount Drinan Park	2	E3	Mountdown Drive	45	C3	Muckross Park	46	D2
Moore Street	71	B3	Mount Drinan Walk	2	E3	Mountdown Park	45	C3	Muirfield Drive	36	F4 [1]
Moorefield	60	E4	Mount Drummond Avenue	74	F4	Mountdown Road	45	C3	Mulally's Lane	52	F2
Moore's Cottages	59	A1 [3]	Mount Drummond Court	74	F4	Mountfield	3	B3	Mulberry Crescent	22	F4
Mooretown	1	B1	Mount Drummond Square	75	A4	Mountgorry Wood Apts.	2	E2	Mulberry Drive	22	E4
Mooretown Avenue	1	C1	Mount Eagle Court	58	E3	Mountjoy Parade	71	C1	Mulberry Park	22	E4
Mooretown Grove	1	C1	Mount Eagle Drive	58	E3	Mountjoy Place	71	C2	Muldowney Court	3	C3
Mooretown Park	1	C1	Mount Eagle Green	58	E3	Mountjoy Square	71	C2	Mulgrave Street	50	D4
Moorfield	35	A4	Mount Eagle Grove	58	E3	Mountjoy Square Apts	71	C2	Mulgrave Terrace	50	D4
Moorfield Avenue	35	A4	Mount Eagle Lawn	58	E3	Mountjoy Square Apts.	71	B2	Mulhuddart	9	A4
Moorfield Close	35	A4 [2]	Mount Eagle Park	58	E3	Mountjoy Square East	71	C2	Mulhuddart Bridge	9	A4
Moorfield Drive	35	A4	Mount Eagle Rise	58	D3	Mountjoy Square North	71	C2	Mulhuddart Wood	9	A4
Moorfield Green	35	A4	Mount Eagle View	58	E3	Mountjoy Square South	71	C2	Mullauns	42	D1
Moorfield Grove	35	A4	Mount Eagle Way	58	E3	Mountjoy Square West	71	B2	Mullen Bridge	18	D3
Moorfield Lawns	35	A4	Mount Eden Road	47	C1	Mountjoy Street	71	A2	Mullinastill Road	64	D2
Moorfield Parade	35	A4	Mount Eustace	9	B2	Mountjoy Street Middle	71	A2	Mullingar Terrace	36	E2 [10]
Moorfield Walk	35	A4	Mount Eustace Avenue	9	B2	Mountpleasant Avenue Lower	75	B4	Mulroy Road	24	E4
Moracrete Cottages	73	C4	Mount Eustace Close	9	A2	Mountpleasant Avenue Upper	75	B4	Mulvey Park	47	C3
Moran's Cottages	47	B1 [12]	Mount Eustace Drive	9	B2	Mountpleasant Parade	75	B4	Munster Street	24	F4
Moreen Avenue	58	D2	Mount Eustace Green	9	B2	Mountpleasant Place	75	C4	Munster Terrace	60	E1 [16]
Moreen Close	58	D2	Mount Eustace Grove	9	A2	Mountpleasant Square	75	B4	Murphy's Lane	63	B4
Moreen Lawn	58	D2 [2]	Mount Eustace Park	9	B2	Mountpleasant Terrace	75	B4	Murphy's Lane	66	E1
Moreen Park	58	D2	Mount Eustace Rise	9	B2	*Mountpleasant Terrace Upper (off Mountpleasant Place)	75	C4	Murphystown Road	58	E3
Moreen Road	58	D2	Mount Eustace Walk	9	B2				Murragh	14	F2
Moreen Walk	58	D2	Mount Gandon	34	D1 [9]	*Mountpleasant Terrace Upper (Mountpleasant Villas)	75	C4	Murray's Cottages	36	F3 [4]
Morehampton Lane	76	E4	Mount Garrett	9	B2				Murtagh Road	70	E3
Morehampton Mews	76	E4	Mount Harold Terrace	46	F1 [1]	Mountpleasant Villas	75	C4	Muskerry Road	36	E3
Morehampton Road	76	E4	Mount Hybla Court	23	A4	Mountpleasant Villas	67	B2 [13]	Mutton Lane	56	E4
Morehampton Square	76	E4	Mount Hybla House	23	A4	Mountsandel	59	B4	Myra Cottages	73	A1
Morehampton Terrace	47	C1	Mount Merrion	48	E4	Mountshannon Road	73	C2	Myra Manor	3	A4
Morgan Place	70	F4	Mount Merrion Avenue	48	F3	Mounttown Cottages	49	C4 [26]	Myrtle Avenue	60	D1 [3]
Morgans Place	23	A3	Mount Norris Villas	68	D2 [19]	Mounttown Park	59	C1 [3]	Myrtle Grove (Bray)	67	B1 [3]
Moritz House	55	B2	Mount Olive Grove	27	B1	Mounttown Road Lower	59	C1	Myrtle Grove (Stillorgan)	58	F1
Morning Star Avenue	70	F3	Mount Olive Park	27	B1	Mounttown Road Lower	59	C1	Myrtle Park	60	D1
Morning Star Road	74	D2	Mount Olive Road	27	B1	Mounttown Road Upper	49	C4	Myrtle Square	14	F4
Mornington Avenue	50	E4 [1]	Mount Prospect Avenue	26	F4	Mourne Road	36	F4	Myrtle Street	71	A2
Mornington Grove	26	E2	Mount Prospect Drive	26	F4	Mourne Road	73	A3			
Mornington Park	26	E2	Mount Prospect Grove	26	F4	Moy Elta Road	72	E2			
Mornington Road	47	B1	Mount Prospect House	27	A4 [4]	Moy Glas Avenue	34	E3			
Morrogh Terrace	25	C3 [2]	Mount Prospect Lawn	26	F4	Moy Glas Chase	34	E3	**N**		
Moss Street	71	C4	Mount Prospect Park	26	F4	Moy Glas Close	34	E3			
Mount Albany	59	A1	Mount Salus Road	60	F2	Moy Glas Court	34	E3	Naas Road (Kingswood)	43	C4
Mount Albion Road	57	B1	Mount Sandford	47	C1 [14]	Moy Glas Dale	34	E3	Naas Road (Rathcoole)	52	F1
Mount Albion Road	57	B1 [3]	Mount St. Annes	47	B2	Moy Glas Dene	34	E3	Naas Road (Saggart)	53	B1
Mount Alton	55	C1	Mount Street Crescent	76	E2	Moy Glas Drive	34	E3	Naas Road (Walkinstown)	45	A1
Mount Alton Court	56	D1	Mount Street Lower	76	D1	Moy Glas Glen	34	E3	Nagle Court	18	D2
Mount Andrew	34	F2	Mount Street Upper	76	D2				Nangor Crescent	44	D1 [5]
									Nangor Place	43	C1 [2]
									Nangor Road (Clondalkin)	44	D1

STREET NAME	PAGE/GRID REFERENCE
Nangor Road (Fox & Geese)	44 F1
Nangor Road (Grange Castle)	43 A2
Nanikin Avenue	27 A3
Nash Street	36 F3
Nashville Park	30 E2
Nashville Road	30 D2
Nassau Street	75 C1
Naul Road (Brackenstown Road)	1 A3
Naul Road (Cloghran)	1 C4
Navan Road	23 A3
Navan Road (Blanchardstown)	22 E1
Navan Road (Cabra)	24 D4
Navan Road (Clonee)	8 E3
Navan Road (Dunboyne)	7 B2
Navan Road (Mulhuddart)	8 F4
Neagh Road	46 E2
Neilstown Avenue	35 A3
Neilstown Cottages	35 A4 [3]
Neilstown Crescent	35 A3
Neilstown Drive	35 A3
Neilstown Gardens	35 A3
Neilstown Park	35 A3
Neilstown Road	35 A3
Neilstown Village Court	35 A3 [1]
Nelson Street	71 A1
Nephin Road	24 D4
Neptune Terrace	60 E1 [17]
Nerano Road	60 Inset
Nerney's Court	71 B2
Nethercross Court	2 D1
Nethercross Court	2 D1
Neville Road	47 A2
Nevinstown Lane	1 C3
New Bancroft Hall	55 A1 [11]
New Bancroft Place	55 A1 [9]
New Bancroft Square	55 A1 [12]
New Bawn Drive	55 A1
New Bawn Park	55 A2
New Bride Street	75 A2
New Bridge	32 F2
New Brighton Terrace	67 C2 [47]
New Cornelscourt	59 B3 [7]
New Grange Road	59 A1
New Grove Estate	14 E4
New Ireland Court	73 C2
New Ireland Road	73 C2
New Lucan Road	35 B1
New Nangor Road	43 C1
New Park Lodge	59 A2 [3]
New Park Road	59 A1
New Rathmore Terrace	67 B2 [23]
New Ravenswell Row	67 B2 [20]
New River Road	23 A2
New Road (Clondalkin)	44 E2
New Road (Howth)	30 E3
New Road (Inchicore)	36 F3
New Road (Swords)	2 D2 [5]
New Row	36 E2 [12]
New Row Place	75 A2
New Row South	74 F2
New Row Square	74 F2
New Street	3 B2
New Street Garden's (off New Street)	75 A2
New Street North (off Church Street)	70 F3
New Street South	75 A2
New Vale	64 E3
New Vale Cottages	64 D3
New Vale Crescent	64 E3
New Wapping Street	72 F3
Newbridge Avenue	39 A3
Newbridge Drive	39 A3
Newbrook Avenue	27 B1
Newbrook Road	27 B1
Newbury Avenue	13 A4
Newbury Drive	13 A4
Newbury Grove	13 A4
Newbury Lawns	13 B4
Newbury Park	13 A4
Newbury Terrace	13 A4 [1]
Newcastle	41 C4
Newcastle Demesne	41 B4
Newcastle Farm	41 B4
Newcastle Lyons	42 D4
Newcastle Manor	42 D4
Newcastle Road (Lucan)	34 D2
Newcastle Road (Rathcoole)	52 E1
Newcomen Avenue	72 D1
Newcomen Bridge	72 D2
Newcomen Court	72 D1
Newcourt (Bray)	68 D4
Newcourt (Swords) (Swords)	2 D1
Newcourt Avenue	68 D3
Newcourt Mews	2 D1
Newcourt Road	68 D3
Newcourt Villas	67 C3 [8]
Newgrange Road	24 F4
Newgrove Avenue	39 B4
Newhall Court	54 D2
Newington Terrace	47 A1 [27]
Newlands Avenue	44 E2
Newlands Court	26 D2 [1]
Newlands Cross	44 E2
Newlands Drive	44 E2
Newlands Manor	44 D3
Newlands Manor Court	44 D3
Newlands Manor Drive	44 D3
Newlands Manor Fairway	44 D3
Newlands Manor Green	44 D3
Newlands Manor Park	44 D3
Newlands Park	44 E2
Newlands Road (Clondalkin)	44 E2
Newlands Road (Ronanstown)	34 F3
Newman Place	18 D3
Newmarket	74 F2
Newmarket Street	74 F2
Newpark	59 A2
Newport Street	74 E1
Newtown (Dunboyne)	7 A3
Newtown (Glencullen)	62 E3
Newtown (Rathfarnham)	56 E3
Newtown (Tinnehinch)	66 E4
Newtown Avenue (Blackrock)	49 A3
Newtown Avenue (Coolock)	26 F1
Newtown Bridge	7 A2
Newtown Close	13 C4
Newtown Cottages (Coolock)	26 F1
Newtown Cottages (St. Margaret's)	11 A1
Newtown Court (Coolock)	13 C4
Newtown Court (Maynooth)	17 B4
Newtown Court (Rathgar)	47 A3 [5]
Newtown Drive	26 F1
Newtown Glendale	20 D4
Newtown Grove	17 C3
Newtown House	47 A3 [12]
Newtown Lower	51 C4
Newtown Park (Blackrock)	59 A1
Newtown Park (Coolock)	26 F1
Newtown Park (Leixlip)	20 D4
Newtown Park (Tallaght)	55 B1
Newtown Park Court	59 A1 [8]
Newtown Road (Celbridge)	32 D4
Newtown Road (Coolock)	13 C4
Newtown Road (Maynooth)	17 B4
Newtown Road (Maynooth)	17 C3
Newtown Upper	52 D4
Newtown Villas (Blackrock)	49 A3 [1]
Newtown Villas (Braemor Road)	47 A3 [4]
Newtown Way	13 C4
Newtownpark Avenue	49 A4
Newtownpark House	59 A1 [11]
Newtownsmith	50 E4
Niall Street	70 D3
Nicholas Avenue	70 F1
Nicholas Street	75 A1
Ninth Lock Road	44 D1
No2 Nth. Road Extension	39 B1
Noel Purcell Park	75 B1
Nore Road	24 E3
Norfolk Road	24 F4
Norseman Court (off Norseman Place)	70 E3
Norseman Place	70 E3
North Avenue	48 E3
North Bull Island	27 B4
North Circular Road (Phibsborough)	71 C1
North Circular Road (Phoenix Park)	70 D2
North Clarence St Flats	72 D2
North Great George's St	71 B2
North Quay Extension	39 A2
North Road (Finglas)	24 D1
North Road (Phoenix Park)	23 B4
North Road (Phoenix Park)	69 B1
North Strand Road	72 E1
North Street	2 D1
North Wall	72 E3
North Wall Quay	72 E4
Northbrook Avenue (Ranelagh)	75 C4
Northbrook Avenue Lower	72 E1
Northbrook Avenue Upper	72 E1
Northbrook Lane	75 C4
Northbrook Road	75 C4
Northbrook Terrace	72 E1
*Northbrook Villas (on Northbrook Road Ranelagh)	75 C4
Northcote Avenue	49 C4
Northcote Place	49 C4 [23]
Northcote Terrace	49 C4 [20]
Northern Close	13 B3
Northern Cross Route	11 B3
Northern Cross Route	23 A2
Northland Drive	24 F3 [2]
Northland Grove	24 F3 [1]
Northumberland Avenue	50 D4
Northumberland Park	50 D4 [11]
Northumberland Place (Dún Laoghaire)	50 D4 [10]
Northumberland Place (Grand Canal St. Upr.)	76 E2
Northumberland Road	76 E2
Northumberland Square	71 C3
Northway Estate	11 A4
Northwood	12 E4
Norton's Avenue	70 F1
Norwood	64 E1
Norwood Park	47 C1 [7]
Nottingham Street	72 E1
Novara Avenue	67 C2
Novara Mews	67 C2 [57]
Novara Park	67 C2 [7]
Novara Terrace	67 C2 [27]
Nugent Road	47 A4
Nunciature Road (Phoenix Park)	23 C4
Nun's Lane	26 E3
Nuns Walk	26 E3
Nurney Lawn	14 D4
Nutgrove Avenue	47 A4
Nutgrove Avenue	47 B4 [14]
Nutgrove Court	47 A4 [2]
Nutgrove Crescent	57 A1
Nutgrove Park (Clonskeagh)	47 C2
Nutgrove Way	57 A1
Nutley Avenue	48 D1
Nutley Lane	48 D2
Nutley Park	48 D2
Nutley Road	48 D1
Nutley Square	48 D2 [1]

O

STREET NAME	PAGE/GRID REFERENCE
O'Neill's Park	18 D3
Oak Apple Green	47 A2
Oak Avenue	12 F4
Oak Close	44 F1
Oak Court	12 F4
Oak Crescent	12 F4
Oak Dene	60 E3
Oak Downs	44 D2
Oak Drive (Fox & Geese)	44 F1
Oak Drive (Santry)	12 F4
Oak Glen Park	67 C4
Oak Glen View	67 C4
Oak Green	12 F4
Oak Grove	12 F4
Oak Hall	3 B3
Oak House	76 D3
Oak House (Swords)	1 Inset
Oak Lawn (Castleknock)	22 F3
Oak Lawn (Santry)	12 F4
Oak Lodge	23 A4
Oak Rise (Clondalkin)	44 D2
Oak Rise (Santry)	12 F4
Oak Road (Donnycarney)	26 D3
Oak Road (Fox & Geese)	44 F1
Oak View	12 E4
Oak Way	44 D2
Oakbury Court	39 A4 [44]
Oakcourt Avenue	35 C2
Oakcourt Close	35 C2
Oakcourt Drive	35 C2
Oakcourt Grove	35 C2
Oakcourt Lawn	35 C2
Oakcourt Park	35 C2
Oakdale Close	55 B3
Oakdale Crescent	55 B3
Oakdale Drive (Firhouse)	55 B3
Oakdale Drive (Sallynoggin)	59 C2
Oakdale Grove	55 B3
Oakdale Park	55 B3
Oakdale Road	55 B3
Oakdown Road	47 A4
Oakfield Place	75 A3
Oaklands Avenue	2 D2
Oaklands Court	39 A4 [38]
Oaklands Crescent	47 A2
Oaklands Drive (Rathgar)	47 A2
Oaklands Drive (Sandymount)	39 A4
Oaklands Park (Sandymount)	39 A4
Oaklands Park (Swords)	2 D2
Oaklands Terrace	46 F2
Oaklawn	19 C4
Oaklawn Close	19 C4
Oaklawn West	19 C4
Oakleigh	31 C4
Oakleigh Court	3 A3 [3]
Oakley Court	47 B1 [10]
Oakley Grove	49 A4
Oakley Park (Blackrock)	49 A4
Oakley Park (Clontarf)	26 F4
Oakley Park (Ranelagh)	47 B1 [23]
Oakley Road	47 B1
Oakley Square	47 B1 [20]
Oakpark Avenue	25 C1
Oakpark Close	25 C1
Oakpark Drive	25 C1
Oakpark Grove	25 C1
Oakton Court	60 E4 [1]
Oakton Drive	60 D4
Oakton Green	60 D4 [3]
Oakton Park	60 D4
Oakton Park	64 D1
Oaktree Avenue	22 E3
Oaktree Drive	22 E3
Oaktree Green	22 E3
Oaktree Grove	22 E3
Oaktree Lawn	22 E3
Oaktree Road	58 F1
Oakview Avenue	21 C1
Oakview Close	21 C1
Oakview Court	21 C1
Oakview Drive	21 C1
Oakview Grove	21 C1 [2]
Oakview Lawn	21 C1
Oakview Park	21 C1
Oakview Rise	21 C1
Oakview Walk	21 C1
Oakview Way	21 C1
Oakwood	49 C4 [7]
Oakwood Apts.	27 B3 [3]
Oakwood Avenue (Glasnevin)	24 E1
Oakwood Avenue (Swords)	1 C2
Oakwood Close	24 E1
Oakwood Grove Estate	35 A4
Oakwood Park	24 E1
Oakwood Road	24 E1
Oatfield Avenue	35 B3
Oatfield Close	35 B3
*Oatfield Crescent (off Oatfield Drive)	35 B2
Oatfield Drive	35 B3
Oatfield Grove	35 B3
Oatfield Lawn	35 B3
Oatfield Park	35 B3
Obelisk Avenue	59 A1 [12]
Obelisk Court (Malahide)	3 C2 [3]
Obelisk Court (Stillorgan)	59 A1
Obelisk Grove	59 A1
Obelisk Lane	18 E4
Obelisk Rise	59 A1
Obelisk Walk	59 A1

STREET NAME	PAGE/GRID REFERENCE
Oblate Drive	36 F3 [14]
O'Brien Road	45 C1
O'Brien's Place North	25 A3 [13]
Observatory Court	75 B4
Observatory Lane	47 A1 [14]
O'Byrne Road	67 C3
O'Byrne Villas	67 C3 [9]
O'Carolan Road	74 F2
O'Casey Avenue	35 C4
O'Connell Avenue	71 A1
O'Connell Bridge	71 B4
O'Connell Gardens	39 A3
O'Connell Street	71 B3
O'Curry Avenue (off O'Curry Road)	74 F2
O'Curry Road	74 F2
O'Daly Road	25 A3
Odd Lamp Road	36 F1
O'Devaney Gardens	70 D3
O'Donnell Gardens	60 D1 [1]
O'Donoghue Street	36 F3
O'Donovan Road	74 F3
O'Donovan Rossa Bridge	71 A4
O'Dwyer Road	45 C1 [4]
Offaly Bridge	18 E1
Offaly Road	24 F4
Offington Avenue	29 B2
Offington Court	29 B2
Offington Drive	29 B2
Offington Lawn	29 B2
Offington Manor Apts	29 B1 [4]
Offington Park	29 B1
Ogham	60 D3
O'Hanlon's Lane	3 B2
O'Hara Avenue	75 A4
O'Hogan Road	36 E3 [1]
O'Hogan Road	36 E3
Oisin Court	39 A4 [35]
Olaf Hall	58 D2 [8]
Olaf House Apts. (Ushers Quay)	70 F4
Olaf Road	70 E3
Olcovar	64 E3
Old Bawn Avenue	55 A2
Old Bawn Bridge	55 A2
Old Bawn Close	55 A2
Old Bawn Court	55 A1 [5]
Old Bawn Drive	55 A2
Old Bawn Park	55 A2
Old Bawn Road	55 A1
Old Bawn Terrace	55 A2
Old Bawn Way	55 A2
Old Belgard Road	44 F4
Old Blessington Road	55 A1
Old Brazil Way	1 A2
Old Bridge Road	46 D4
Old Brighton Terrace	67 C2 [46]
Old Cabra Road	70 D1
Old Camac Bridge	73 B1
Old Carrickbrack Road	30 D4
Old Connaught	67 A1
Old Connaught Avenue	67 B1
Old Connaught Grove	67 B2
Old Connaught View	67 B2
Old Corduff Road	22 E1
Old Cornmill Road	33 C2
Old County Glen	73 C4
Old County Road	73 B4
Old Dublin Road (Stillorgan)	48 E4
Old Dunleary	49 C4
Old Estuary Mill	2 F2
Old Fairgreen	7 B2
Old Fort Road	1 A2
Old Greenfield	17 C3
Old Greenfield	17 C4
Old Hill	20 D4
Old Kilmainham	73 C1
Old Kilmainham Village	74 D1
Old Mill Court	74 F2
Old Mountpleasant	75 C4
Old Naas Road (Bluebell)	36 E4
Old Naas Road (Brownsbarn)	43 C4
Old Naas Road Cottages	36 E4 [1]
Old Navan Road	22 F2
Old Quarry (Dalkey)	60 F2
Old Quarry (Kilshane)	10 D2
Old Quay	29 B2
Old Quay Mews	29 B2
Old Quay Terrace	29 B2
Old Rathmichael	64 D3
Old Rathmore Terrace	67 B2 [22]
Old Ravenswell Row	67 B4 [29]
Old Rectory	34 D1 [11]
Old Rectory Park	47 C4
Old Road	14 E2
Old Street	3 B2
Old Yellow Walls Road	3 A2
Oldbawn	55 A2
Oldbridge	34 E3
Oldbridge Close	34 E3
Oldbridge Court	34 E3
Oldbridge Glen	34 E3
Oldbridge Green	34 E3
Oldbridge Grove	34 E3
Oldbridge Park	34 E3
Oldbridge View	34 E3
Oldbridge Walk	34 E3
Oldbridge Way	34 E3
Oldcarton	18 F1
Oldcastle Avenue	29 B2
Oldcastle Drive	43 B1
Oldcastlepark	43 B1
Oldcastlepark Close	43 B1
Oldcastlepark Green	43 B1
Oldcastlepark Grove	43 B1
Oldcastlepark Lawn	43 B1
Oldcastlepark View	43 B1
Oldchurch Avenue	43 C1
Oldchurch Close	43 C1
Oldchurch Court	43 C1
Oldchurch Crescent	43 C1
Oldchurch Drive	43 C1
Oldchurch Grove	43 C1
Oldchurch Lawn	43 C1
Oldchurch Park	43 C1
Oldchurch Way	43 C1
Oldcourt	67 B3
Oldcourt Avenue (Boghall Road)	67 B3
Oldcourt Avenue (Bohernabreena)	55 B2
Oldcourt Close	55 B2
Oldcourt Cottages	55 B3
Oldcourt Drive	67 B3
Oldcourt Farm	55 B2
Oldcourt Grove	67 B4
Oldcourt Lawn	55 B2 [1]
Oldcourt Lodge	55 B2
Oldcourt Manor	55 B3
Oldcourt Park	67 B3
Oldcourt Road	55 B3
Oldcourt Terrace	67 C3 [15]
Oldcourt View	55 B2
Oldfarm	22 E3
Oldfield Hall	57 C3
Oldtower Crescent	35 A2
Oldtown Avenue	25 A1
Oldtown Cottages	31 C3
Oldtown Mill	31 C3
Oldtown Mill Road	31 C3
Oldtown Park	25 A1 [3]
Oldtown Road	25 A1
O'Leary Road	73 B2
Olivemount Grove	47 C3 [2]
Olivemount Road	47 C3
Olivemount Terrace	47 C3 [6]
Oliver Bond House Flats	70 F4
Oliver Bond Street	70 F4
Oliver Plunkett Avenue (Dun Laoghaire)	59 C1
Oliver Plunkett Avenue (Ringsend)	39 A3
Oliver Plunkett Road	59 C1
Oliver Plunkett Square	59 C1 [1]
Oliver Plunkett Terrace	59 C1 [5]
Oliver Plunkett Villas	59 B1 [3]
Olney Crescent	46 F2
Olney Grove	46 F2 [17]
Omni Park	25 B1
O'Moore Road	36 E3
O'Neachtain Road	25 A3 [14]
O'Neill's Buildings	75 A2
Ongar Chase Estate	21 A1
Ongar Green	21 A1
Ongar Park Estate	21 B1
Ongar Road	21 B2
Ongar Village	21 A1
Ongar-Hartstown Relief Road	21 C2
Ontario Terrace	75 B4
Onward Close	3 C4
Onward Walk	3 C4
Ophaly Court	47 C4
O'Quinns Avenue	74 D1
O'Rahilly House Flats	39 A3 [28]
O'Rahilly Parade	71 B3
Oranmore Road	35 C3
Oratory Mews Court	50 D4 [24]
Orby Avenue	58 E3
Orby Close	58 F3
Orby Court	58 F3
Orby Lawn	58 E3
Orby Park	58 F3
Orby View	58 E3
Orby Village	58 E3
Orby Way	58 E3
Orchard Avenue (Citywest)	53 B1
Orchard Avenue (Clonsilla)	21 C2
Orchard Close	22 D2
Orchard Cottages	59 A1 [1]
Orchard Court	22 E2
Orchard Green	22 D2
Orchard Grove (Blanchardstown)	22 E2
Orchard Grove (Newcastle)	42 D4
Orchard Lane (Blackrock)	59 A1
Orchard Lane (Clondalkin)	44 E1
Orchard Lane (Ranelagh)	75 C4
Orchard Lawns	35 C3
Orchard Lodge	44 E1
Orchard Road (Ballybough)	25 B4
Orchard Road (Raheny)	27 B2
Orchard Road South	47 B2
Orchard Square	47 C3
Orchard Terrace (Bray)	67 C3 [19]
Orchard Terrace (Grangegorman Upper)	70 F2
*Orchard View	70 F2
Orchardstown Avenue	46 E4
Orchardstown Drive	46 E4
Orchardstown Park	46 E4
Orchardstown Villas	56 E1
Orchardton	56 E1 [1]
Ordnance Survey Road	36 E1
O'Reilly Avenue	73 C1
O'Reilly's Cottages	74 F4
Oriel Street Lower	72 E2
Oriel Street Upper	72 D3
Orlagh Avenue	56 D2
Orlagh Close	56 D2
Orlagh Court	56 D2
Orlagh Crescent	56 D2
Orlagh Downs	56 D2
Orlagh Grange	56 D2
Orlagh Green	56 D2
Orlagh Grove	56 D2
Orlagh Lawn	56 D2
Orlagh Lodge	56 D2
Orlagh Meadows	56 D2
Orlagh Park	56 D2
Orlagh Pines	56 D2
Orlagh Rise	56 D2
Orlagh View	56 D2
Orlagh Way	56 D2
Orlagh Wood	56 D2
Ormeau Drive	60 F1 [2]
Ormeau Street	76 F1
Ormond Avenue	1 B1
Ormond Close	1 B1
Ormond Crescent	1 B1
Ormond Drive	1 B1
Ormond Grove	1 B1
Ormond Lawn	1 B1
Ormond Market (off Ormond Quay Upper)	71 A4
Ormond Place	71 A4
Ormond Place (off Ormond Quay Upper)	71 A4
Ormond Quay Lower	71 B4
Ormond Quay Upper	71 A4
Ormond Road	25 B4
Ormond Road South	47 B1
Ormond Square	71 A4
Ormond Street	74 F2
*Ormond Terrace (off Sorrento Road)	60 F2
Ormond View	1 B1
Ormond Way	1 B1
O'Rourke Park	59 C2
Orpen	58 F1
Orpen Close	48 F4
Orpen Dale	48 F4 [2]
Orpen Green	58 F1
Orpen Hill	58 F1
Orpen Rise	58 F1
Orr's Terrace	74 F4
Orwell Bank	47 A3 [7]
Orwell Court	47 A3 [3]
Orwell Gardens	47 A3
Orwell Mews	47 A3 [5]
Orwell Park	46 D4
Orwell Park (Rathgar)	47 A3
Orwell Park (Templeogue)	45 C4
Orwell Park Avenue	46 D3
Orwell Park Close	46 D3
Orwell Park Crescent	46 D3
Orwell Park Dale	45 C4
Orwell Park Drive	46 D3
Orwell Park Glade	45 C3
Orwell Park Glen	46 D3
Orwell Park Green	46 D3
Orwell Park Grove	45 C3
Orwell Park Heights	45 C4
Orwell Park Lawns	45 C3
Orwell Park Rise	45 C4
Orwell Park View	45 C4
Orwell Park Way	46 D3
Orwell Road	47 A2
Orwell Walk	47 A3
Orwell Woods	47 A2
*Osborne Terrace (Northbrook Road)	75 C4
Oscar Square	74 F2
Oscar Traynor Road	26 E1
Oscar Traynor Road (Kilmore)	13 A3
O'Shea's Cottages	59 C3 [4]
Osprey Avenue	45 C3
Osprey Court	64 E3 [3]
Osprey Drive	45 C3
Osprey Lawn	45 C3
Osprey Park	45 C3
Osprey Road	45 C3
Ossory Road	72 E2
Ostman Place	70 E3
O'Sullivan Avenue	72 D1
Oswald Road	39 A3
Otranto Place	60 E1
Otterbrook	46 F4 [16]
Oulart	1 C3
Oulton Road	26 E4
Our Lady's Close (off Our Lady's Road)	74 E2
Our Lady's Road	74 E2
Outer Ring Road	43 B2
Outfarm Lane	22 E3
Outlands	1 B1
Overend Way	57 C1
Ovoca Road	75 A3
Owendoher Haven	56 E1
Owendoher Lodge	56 E1
Owendore Avenue	46 F4
Owendore Crescent	46 F4
Owen's Avenue	73 C1
Owensilla	24 F1
Owenstown Park	48 D3
Oxford Lane	75 C4
Oxford Road	47 B1
Oxford Terrace (on Hawthorn Terrace)	72 E2
Oxmantown Lane	70 F4
Oxmantown Road	70 D2

P

Street Name	Page/Grid Reference
Pace Avenue	8 E4
Pace Crescent	8 E4
Pace Road	8 E4
Pace View	8 E4
Pacelli Avenue	27 C1
Pairc Gleann Trasna	55 A3
Páirc Mhuire	53 A2
Páirc View	53 A2
Pakenham	49 C4 [28]
Pakenham Bridge	21 A2
Pakenham Road	49 C4
Palace Street (off Dame Street)	71 B4
Palmer Park	56 E2
Palmer Park	56 F2
Palmers Avenue	35 B2
Palmers Close	35 B2
Palmers Copse	35 B2
Palmers Court	35 B2
Palmers Crescent	35 B2
Palmers Drive	35 B2
Palmers Glade	35 B2
Palmers Grove	35 B2
Palmers Lawn	35 B2
Palmers Park	35 B2
Palmers Road	35 B2
Palmers Walk	35 B2
Palmerston	35 C1
*Palmerston Close	47 B1 [21]
*Palmerston Close (rere of Palmerston Road)	47 B1
Palmerston Court	47 A1
Palmerston Gardens	47 B2
Palmerston Grove	47 C2 [5]
Palmerston Lane	47 B2
Palmerston Park (Rathgar)	47 B2
Palmerston Place	71 A2
Palmerston Road	47 B1
Palmerston Villas	47 A2
Palmerstown Avenue	35 C2
Palmerstown Close	35 B2
Palmerstown Court	35 C2
Palmerstown Drive	35 C2
Palmerstown Green	35 B2
Palmerstown Heights	35 B2
Palmerstown Lawn	35 B2
Palmerstown Manor	35 B2
Palmerstown Park (Kennelsfort Road)	35 B2
Palmerstown Woods	35 B4
Paradise Place	71 A2
Park Avenue (Brackenstown Road)	1 B2
Park Avenue (Castleknock)	22 F3
Park Avenue (Deans Grange)	59 A1
Park Avenue (Sandymount)	39 B4
Park Avenue (Willbrook)	56 F1
Park Avenue West	70 D3
Park Boulevard	9 B2
Park Close (Sallynoggin)	60 D2
Park Court (Sandymount)	39 A4 [16]
Park Court Apts	23 A3 [4]
Park Crescent (Blackhorse Avenue)	69 A1
Park Crescent (Kimmage)	46 D2
Park Crescent House	24 D4 [6]
Park Drive (Cabinteely)	59 B3
Park Drive (Ranelagh)	47 B1
Park Drive Avenue	22 F3
Park Drive Close	22 F3
Park Drive Court	22 F3
Park Drive Crescent	22 F3
Park Drive Green	22 F3
Park Drive Grove	22 F3
Park Drive Lawn	22 F3
Park Lane (Chapelizod)	36 E2 [1]
Park Lane (Dún Laoghaire)	50 D4 [21]
Park Lane (Sandymount)	39 A4
Park Lawn	27 A4
Park Lodge	22 F3
Park Manor	22 E3
Park Place	69 B4
Park Road (Dun Laoghaire)	50 D4
*Park Road (off Navan Road)	23 C3
Park Road (Sallynoggin)	60 D2
Park Spring's	24 D4 [5]
Park Street	36 F3 [1]
*Park Street (off Hanover St West)	74 F1
Park Terrace (Coombe)	74 F1
Park View (Cabra)	69 C1
Park View (Castleknock)	23 B4
Park View (Clonsilla)	22 D2
Park View (Enniskerry Road)	58 D4
Park View (Mount Prospect Lawns)	26 F4 [1]
Park View (Portmarnock)	15 A1
Park View (Rathgar)	47 A3 [10]
Park View House	9 B2
Park View Lawns	44 D2
Park View Manor	9 B2
Park Villas (Castleknock)	23 A3
Park Villas (Stillorgan)	48 F4 [3]
Park West Avenue	35 C4
Park West Road	35 C4
Park West Road	36 D4
Parker Hill	47 A1 [12]
Parker House	14 F4
Parkgate Street	70 D4
Parkhill Avenue	44 F3
Parkhill Close	45 A3
Parkhill Court	44 F3
Parkhill Drive	44 F3
Parkhill Green	44 F3
Parkhill Heights	45 A3 [1]
Parkhill Lawn	44 F3
Parkhill Rise	44 F3
Parkhill Road	44 F3
Parkhill Way	45 A3
Parkhill West	44 F4
Parklands (Castleknock)	22 F3
Parklands (Maynooth)	18 D3
Parklands (Santry)	12 E4
Parklands Avenue	55 B2
Parklands Close	18 D3
Parklands Court (Maynooth)	18 D3
Parklands Court (Scholarstown Link Road)	55 B2
Parklands Crescent	18 D3
Parklands Drive	55 B2
Parklands Grove	18 D3
Parklands Lawns	18 D3
Parklands Lodge	18 D3
Parklands Rise	18 D3
Parklands Road	55 B2
Parklands Square	18 D3
Parklands View	55 B2
Parklands Way	18 D3
Parkmore	23 A3
Parkmore Drive	46 E2
Parknasilla Avenue	64 D2
Parknasilla Close	64 D2
Parknasilla Lane	64 D2
Parknasilla Rise	64 D2
Parknasillog	65 C2
Parkside View	24 D4 [7]
Parkvale (Dundrum)	57 C1
Parkvale (Sutton)	28 D1
Parkview	23 C3
Parkview (Kilnamanagh)	45 A3 [2]
Parkview (Swords)	1 B2
Parkview Avenue (Harold's Cross)	46 F1
Parkview Court (Blackhorse Avenue)	69 B1
Parkview Court (Harold's Cross)	46 F1 [8]
Parkview Place	39 A3 [14]
Parkview Terrace	67 B2 [16]
Parkwood Avenue	55 A2
Parkwood Grove	55 A2
Parkwood Lawn	55 A2
Parkwood Road	55 A2
Parliament Street	71 A4
Parnell Avenue	74 F4
Parnell Cottages	3 B3
Parnell Court	74 F4
Parnell Drive	9 A4
Parnell Green	9 A4
Parnell Hall	74 E4
Parnell Lane	9 A4
Parnell Place	71 B2
Parnell Road (Bray)	67 C2
Parnell Road (Harold's Cross)	74 E3
Parnell Square East	71 B2
Parnell Square North	71 B2
Parnell Square West	71 B2
Parnell Street (O'Connell Street)	71 B3
Parnell Street (Sallynoggin)	60 D1
Parochial Avenue	15 A4 [2]
Parslickstown Avenue	9 A4
Parslickstown Close	9 A4
Parslickstown Court	9 A4
Parslickstown Drive	9 A4
Parslickstown Gardens	9 A3
Parslickstown Green	9 A4
Parson Court	17 C3
Parson Lodge	17 C3
Parson Street	17 C3
Parson's Court	42 D4
Parsons Hall	17 B3
Partridge Terrace	36 F3 [5]
Pass If You Can	11 A1
Patrician Park	59 C1 [2]
Patrician Villas	48 F4
Patrick Doyle Road	47 B2
Patrick Street (Dun Laoghaire)	50 D4
Patrick Street (Kevin Street Upper.)	75 A1
Patrick's Row	49 A3 [14]
Patrickswell Court	24 D2 [8]
Patrickswell Place	24 D2
Paul Street	70 F1
Pavillion Gate	59 A4
Pea Field	48 F3
Peamount	42 D2
Peamount Road	42 D3
Peamount Road	42 E2
Pear Tree Field	58 F1 [5]
Pearse Avenue	60 D2
Pearse Brothers Park	56 F1
Pearse Close	60 D2 [3]
Pearse Drive	60 D2
Pearse Gardens	59 C2
Pearse Green	60 D2
Pearse Grove	76 E1
Pearse House	72 D4
Pearse Park	60 D2
Pearse Road (Bray)	67 B2 [12]
Pearse Road (Sallynoggin)	60 D2
Pearse Square (Bray)	67 B2
Pearse Square (Pearse Street)	76 E1
Pearse Street (Sallynoggin)	60 D2
Pearse Street (Westland Row)	71 C4
Pearse Villas	60 D2
Pebble Hill	18 D2
Pebble Hill Lodge	18 D2
Peck's Lane	23 A3
Pelletstown Avenue	23 C3
Pemberton	67 A3
Pembroke Cottages (Booterstown)	48 F3 [2]
Pembroke Cottages (Donnybrook)	47 C1 [2]
Pembroke Cottages (Dundrum)	47 C4 [5]
Pembroke Cottages (Ringsend)	39 A2
Pembroke Court	76 F3
Pembroke Gardens	76 E3
Pembroke Lane (Lr Baggot Street)	76 D2
Pembroke Lane (Pembroke Road)	76 E3
Pembroke Park	76 E4
Pembroke Place (Ballsbridge)	76 F4
Pembroke Place (Pembroke St Upr)	75 C3
Pembroke Road	76 E3
Pembroke Row	76 D2
Pembroke Street	39 A3
Pembroke Street Lower	75 C2
Pembroke Street Upper	75 C2
Pembroke Terrace	47 C4 [6]
Penrose Street	76 F1
Percy French Road	45 C1 [3]
Percy Lane	76 E2
Percy Place	76 E2
Peter Place	75 B3
Peter Row	75 A2
Peter Street	75 A2
Peter's Court	71 A1
Peterson's Court	72 D4
Petrie Road	74 F3
Pheasant Run	8 F4
Pheasant Run The Drive	8 F4
Pheasant Run The Green	8 F4
Pheasant Run The Grove	8 F4
Pheasant Run The Park	8 F4
Phelan Avenue	24 D3
Phibblestown Avenue	21 A1
Phibblestown House Apts.	21 B1
Phibsborough	71 A1
Phibsborough Avenue	70 F1
Phibsborough Place	71 A2
Phibsborough Road	71 A1
Philipsburgh Avenue	25 C4
Philipsburgh Terrace	25 C4
Philomena Terrace	39 A3 [41]
*Philomena Terrace (off Oliver Plunket Ave)	39 A3
Phoenix Avenue	23 A3
Phoenix Court (Arbour Hill)	70 D3
Phoenix Court (Castleknock)	23 A3
Phoenix Court (North Circular Road)	70 D2
Phoenix Court Apartments	69 C3
Phoenix Drive	23 A3
Phoenix Gardens	23 A3
Phoenix Manor	70 D2
Phoenix Park	69 A2
Phoenix Park Way	23 B3
Phoenix Place	23 A3
Phoenix Street	36 F3 [2]
Phoenix Street North	70 F4
Phoenix Street West	70 F4
Phoenix Terrace	48 F3
Phoenix View	74 D1
Phrompstown	66 F1
Pickford's Terrace	72 F3
Pig Lane	71 C2
Pigeon House Road (Ringsend)	39 A2
Pigeon House Road (Ringsend)	39 B3
Pike Bridge	18 F3
*Pile's Terrace (Sandwith St Upper)	76 D1
Pilot View	60 F1 [14]
Pim Street	74 E1
Pimlico	74 F1
Pimlico Cottages	74 E1
Pine Avenue	59 A2
Pine Copse Road	57 B1
Pine Court (Deans Grange)	59 A1
Pine Court (Portmarnock)	15 A1
Pine Grove	56 D1 [2]
Pine Grove Park	1 C1
Pine Grove Road	1 C1
Pine Haven	48 F3
Pine Hurst	24 E4
Pine Lawn (Deans Grange)	59 A1
Pine Lawn (Tallaght)	55 A2
Pine Road	39 A3
Pine Valley Avenue	57 B2
Pine Valley Drive	57 B3
Pine Valley Grove	57 B3
Pine Valley Park	57 B3
Pine Valley Way	57 B3
Pinebrook Avenue	26 D2
Pinebrook Close	21 C1
Pinebrook Crescent	26 D2
Pinebrook Downs	21 C1
Pinebrook Drive	26 D2
Pinebrook Glen	21 C1
Pinebrook Grove	26 E2
Pinebrook Heights	21 C1
Pinebrook Lawn	21 C1
Pinebrook Rise	26 D2
Pinebrook Road	26 D2
Pinebrook Vale	21 C1
Pinebrook View	21 C1
Pinebrook Way	21 C1
Pinecroft	62 F1
Pinetree Crescent	44 F4 [1]
Pinetree Grove	44 F3 [1]
Pineview Avenue	55 A2
Pineview Drive	55 A2

STREET NAME	PAGE/GRID REFERENCE
Pineview Grove	55 A2
Pineview Lawn	55 A2
Pineview Park	55 A2
Pineview Rise	55 A2
Pineview Road	55 A2
Pinewood	60 D4
Pinewood Avenue	24 F1
Pinewood Close	67 C4
Pinewood Court	8 F4
Pinewood Crescent	24 F1
Pinewood Drive	24 F1
Pinewood Green	24 F1
Pinewood Grove	25 A1 [1]
Pinewood Park	56 E1
Pinewood Villas	24 F1
Pinewoods	44 D2
Pinnockhill Roundabout	1 C3
Pipe Hill	1 C2
Pleasants Lane	75 B2
Pleasants Place	75 B2
Pleasants Street	75 A2
Pluckstown	51 A2
Plums Road	58 D1
Plunket Hall	2 E2
Plunkett Avenue (Finglas)	24 D1
Plunkett Avenue (Foxrock)	59 A3
Plunkett Crescent	11 A4
Plunkett Drive	24 D1
Plunkett Green	24 D1
Plunkett Grove	24 D1
Plunkett Hall	7 A2
Plunkett Road	24 D1
Poddle Close	46 E1
Poddle Green	46 E1 [6]
Poddle Park	46 E2
Polo Road	69 A2
Poolbeg Quay	39 A3
Poolbeg Street	71 C4
Poole Street	74 F2
Poplar Row	72 E1
Poplar Row Flats	72 E1
Poppintree	11 C4
Poppintree Lane	11 C4
Poppintree Parade	11 C4
Poppintree Park Lane West	11 C4
Poppintree Terrace	11 C4
Port Tunnel (East Wall)	71 C1
Port Tunnel (Santry Entrance)	25 C1
Port View House	39 A2
Porters Avenue	22 D2
Porters Gate	21 B2
Porters Gate Avenue	21 C2
Porters Gate Close	21 B2
Porters Gate Court	21 B2
Porters Gate Drive	21 B2
Porters Gate Green	21 B2
Porters Gate Grove	21 B2
Porters Gate Heights	21 C2
Porters Gate Lawn	21 B2
Porters Gate Rise	21 C2
Porters Gate View	21 B2
Porters Gate Way	21 B2
Porters Road	22 D2
Portersfield Apts.	22 D2
Porterstown	5 A3
Porterstown Road	22 D2
Portland Close	72 D2
Portland Court	71 C1
Portland Court (off Portland Place)	71 C1
*Portland Lock	71 C1
Portland Lock Apts.	71 C1
Portland Place	71 B1
Portland Row	72 D2
Portland Square	71 C1
Portland Street North	71 C1
Portland Street West	74 E1
Portmahon Drive	73 C2
Portmarnock	15 A1
Portmarnock Avenue	4 D4
Portmarnock Crescent	15 A1
Portmarnock Drive	4 D4
Portmarnock Grove	4 D4
Portmarnock Park	4 D4
Portmarnock Rise	15 A1
Portmarnock Walk	4 D4
Portobello Harbour	75 B3
Portobello Harbour Apts	75 A4
Portobello Place	75 B3
Portobello Road	75 A4
Portside Court	72 E1
Pottery Road	59 C2
Pound Hill	17 C1
Pound Lane	17 C3
Pound Park	17 C3
Pound Street	33 A1
Power's Court	76 E2
Power's Square (off John Dillon Street)	75 A1
Prebend Street	70 F3
Premier Square	24 E2
Preston Street	72 D2
*Price's Lane (Aston Quay)	71 B4
Price's Place (Ranelagh)	75 B4
Priestfield Cottages	74 E3
Priestfield Drive	74 E3
Primrose Avenue	71 A2
Primrose Gate	32 E4
Primrose Grove	13 C4
Primrose Hill (Celbridge)	32 D4
Primrose Hill (Dún Laoghaire)	49 C4 [25]
Primrose Lane	34 D1
Primrose Street (off Wellington Street Upper)	71 A2
Prince Arthur Terrace	47 A1 [3]
Prince Edward Terrace Lower	49 A4 [2]
Prince Edward Terrace Upper	49 A4 [3]
Prince of Wales Terrace (Bray)	67 C2 [26]
Prince of Wales Terrace (Sandymount)	39 A4 [7]
Prince's Street North	71 B3
Prince's Street South	72 D4
Princeton	48 D3
Prior Hall	74 D1
Priorswood Road	13 C4
Priory Avenue	48 F4
Priory Chase	31 C4
Priory Close	31 C4
Priory Court (Celbridge)	31 C4
Priory Court (Grange Road)	57 A2 [1]
Priory Crescent	31 C4
Priory Drive (Celbridge)	31 C4
Priory Drive (Stillorgan)	48 F4
Priory East	24 D4
Priory Green	31 C4
Priory Grove (Celbridge)	31 C4
Priory Grove (Stillorgan)	48 F4
Priory Hall	14 E4
Priory Hall (Kimmage)	46 D2
Priory Hall (Stillorgan)	48 F4
Priory Lodge	31 C4
Priory North	24 D3
Priory Road	46 F1
Priory Square	31 C4
Priory View	31 C3
Priory Walk (Celbridge)	31 C4
Priory Walk (Kimmage)	46 D2
Priory Way (Celbridge)	31 C3
Priory Way (Kimmage)	46 D2
Priory West	24 D4
Proby Garden	49 A4
Proby Hall	60 E2
Proby Park	60 E2
Proby Square	49 A4
Proby's Lane	71 B3
Promenade Road	39 A1
Prospect Avenue (Finglas Road)	25 A4
Prospect Avenue (Stocking Lane)	56 E2
Prospect Court	25 A4 [19]
Prospect Court	56 E3
Prospect Drive	56 E2
Prospect Glen	56 E2
Prospect Grove	56 E2
Prospect Heath	56 E2
Prospect Heights	56 E2
Prospect Lane	47 C2 [1]
Prospect Lawn	59 B3
Prospect Lodge	55 C1 [6]
Prospect Meadows	56 E2
Prospect Road	25 A4
Prospect Square	25 A4 [5]
Prospect Terrace (Kilmainham)	73 B1
Prospect Terrace (Sandymount)	39 B3 [1]
Prospect View	56 E2
Prospect Way	25 A4
Protestant Row	75 B2
Proud's Lane	75 B2
Provost Row	70 E3
Prussia Street	70 E2
Pucks Castle Lane	63 C3
Purcell Lane (off Main Street Bray)	67 C2 [60]
Purley Park	3 C4
Purser Gardens	47 A1 [10]
Putland Road	67 C3
Putland Villas	67 C3 [14]
Pyro Villas	74 E2

Q

STREET NAME	PAGE/GRID REFERENCE
Quarry Cottages	26 E3 [3]
Quarry Drive	45 C2
Quarry Road (Cabra)	24 E4
Quarry Road (Ferndale Road)	64 D4
Quarryfield Court	44 E2
Quarryvale Park	35 A2
Quartiere Bloom	71 B4
Queen's Park	49 B4
Queen's Road	50 D4
Queen's Street	70 F4
Quinn's Lane	75 C2
Quinn's Road	64 E3
Quinsborough	51 A4
Quinsborough Road	67 C2

R

STREET NAME	PAGE/GRID REFERENCE
Radcliff Hall	39 B4 [9]
Radcliffe	29 A1 [3]
Radharc na hAbhann	55 A2
Radlett Grove	4 D4
Rafter's Avenue	73 A4
Rafter's Lane	73 A4
Rafter's Road	73 A4
Raglan Hall Apts.	76 E4
Raglan House	39 A4 [42]
Raglan Lane	76 E4
Raglan Road	76 E4
Raheen Avenue	54 E1
Raheen Close	54 E1
Raheen Court	54 E1
Raheen Crescent	54 E1
Raheen Drive (Ballyfermot)	36 D3
Raheen Drive (Tallaght)	54 E1
Raheen Green	54 E1
Raheen Park (Ballyfermot)	36 D3
Raheen Park (Bray)	68 D3
Raheen Park (Tallaght)	54 E1
Raheen Road	54 E1
Raheny	27 A2
Raheny Park	27 A3
Raheny Road	27 A1
Railpark	18 E3
Railway Avenue (Baldoyle)	28 D1
Railway Avenue (Inchicore)	36 F3
Railway Avenue (Malahide)	3 B2
Railway Close	14 F4
Railway Cottages	39 A4 [8]
Railway Court	3 B2 [3]
Railway Mews	14 F4
Railway Road	14 F4
Railway Road	60 F2 [2]
Railway Street	71 C2
Railway Terrace (off Macken St)	76 E1
Rainsford Avenue	74 E1
Rainsford Lane	60 E4 [6]
Rainsford Street	74 E1
Ralahine	60 D4
Raleigh Square	46 D1
Ralph Square	33 A1 [1]
Ramillies Road	36 E3
Ramleh Close	47 C2
Ramleh Park	47 C2
Ramor Park	22 E2
Ranelagh	75 C4
Ranelagh Avenue	75 C4
Ranelagh Road	75 C4
Raphoe Road	46 D1
Rath Geal	43 C1
Rathbeale Court	1 C1 [2]
Rathbeale Crescent	1 C1
Rathbeale Rise	1 C2
Rathbeale Road	1 C1
Rathborne Avenue	23 C3
Rathborne Close	23 C3
Rathborne Drive	23 C3
Rathborne Place	23 C3
Rathborne Way	23 C3
Rathbourne Court	23 C3 [1]
Rathclaren	67 B3 [2]
Rathcoole Interchange (N7 J4)	52 F1
Rathcoole Park	52 F2
Rathcreedan	52 D1
Rathdown Avenue	46 F3
*Rathdown Court (off Templeogue Road)	46 F2 [10]
Rathdown Crescent	46 F3
Rathdown Drive	46 E3
Rathdown Grove	58 D2 [9]
Rathdown Park	46 F3
Rathdown Road	70 F2
Rathdown Square	70 E2
Rathdown Terrace	58 D2 [5]
Rathdown Villas	46 F3
Rathdrum Road	74 D4
Rathfarnham	46 F3
Rathfarnham Mill	46 F4 [12]
Rathfarnham Park	46 F3
Rathfarnham Road	46 F3
Rathfarnham Wood	46 F4
Rathgar	47 A2
Rathgar Avenue	46 F2
Rathgar Court	47 A1 [28]
Rathgar Park	46 F2 [16]
Rathgar Park	47 A2 [7]
Rathgar Place	47 A1
Rathgar Road	47 A1
Rathgar Villas	46 F2 [11]
Rathingle Road	1 B3
Rathland Drive	46 E2 [4]
Rathland Road	46 E2
Rathlawns	52 E2
Rathlin Road	25 A3
Rathlyon Grove	55 C2
Rathlyon Park	55 C2
Rathmichael	63 C3
Rathmichael Dales	64 D3
Rathmichael Haven	64 D3
Rathmichael Hill	63 C2
Rathmichael Lane	63 C2
Rathmichael Manor	64 D2
Rathmichael Park	64 E2
Rathmichael Road	63 C2
Rathmichael Woods	64 E2
Rathmines	47 A1
Rathmines Avenue	47 A1
Rathmines Avenue Court	47 A1 [25]
Rathmines Close	47 A1
Rathmines Park	47 A1 [1]
Rathmines Road Lower	47 A1
Rathmines Road Upper	47 A1
Rathmintan Close	54 D2
Rathmintan Court	54 D2
Rathmintan Crescent	54 D2
Rathmintan Drive	54 D2
Rathmore	14 F2
Rathmore Avenue	9 B2
Rathmore Avenue	58 D1
Rathmore Crescent	9 B2
Rathmore Drive	9 B2
Rathmore Grove	9 B2
Rathmore Park	27 A2
Rathmore Villas	46 F2
Rathsallagh Avenue	64 E2
Rathsallagh Drive	64 E2
Rathsallagh Grove	64 E2
Rathsallagh Park	64 E2
Rathvale Avenue	26 F1
Rathvale Drive	26 F1
Rathvale Grove	26 F1
Rathvale Park	26 F1
Rathvilly Drive	24 D2
Rathvilly Park	24 D2
Ratoath Avenue	24 D2

STREET NAME	PAGE/GRID REFERENCE
Ratoath Drive	23 C1
Ratoath Estate	24 D3
Ratoath Road (Cabra)	24 E4
Ratoath Road (Finglas)	23 C2
Ratoath Road (Hollystown)	9 B1
Ratra Park	23 C4
Ratra Road	23 C4
Ravens Court	24 D2 [5]
Ravens Rock Road	58 E2
*Ravensdale Drive (off Ravensdale Park)	46 E2
Ravensdale Park	46 E2
Ravensdale Road	72 F2
Ravenswell Road	67 C2
Ravenswood	3 A3 [2]
Ravenwood Avenue	21 B1
Ravenwood Crescent	21 B1
Ravenwood Drive	21 B1
Ravenwood Estate	21 B1
Ravenwood Green	21 B1
Ravenwood Lawn	21 B1
Ravenwood Rise	21 B1
Ravenwood Road	21 B1
Ravenwood View	21 B1
Raverty Villas	67 B1 [1]
Rawson Court	76 E2
Raymond Street	74 F3
Rectory Slopes	67 B3
Rectory Way	67 A3
Red Brick Terrace	59 A1 [2]
Red Cow Cottages	35 C1 [4]
Red Cow Interchange	44 F1
Red Cow Lane	70 F3
Redberry	34 D3
Redesdale Crescent	48 D4
Redesdale Road	48 D4
Redfern Avenue	3 C4
Redgap	52 E3
Redmond's Court	27 B1 [3]
Redmond's Hill	75 B2
Redwood	9 B1
Redwood Avenue	45 A4
Redwood Close	45 A4
Redwood Court (Churchtown)	47 A3
Redwood Court (Tallaght)	44 F4
Redwood Drive	44 F4
Redwood Grove	48 F3
Redwood Heights	45 A4
Redwood Lawn	44 F4
Redwood Park	45 A4
Redwood Rise	45 A4
Redwood View	45 A4
Redwood Walk	44 F4
Reginald Square	74 F1
Reginald Street	74 F1
Rehoboth Avenue	74 E3
Rehoboth Place	74 D3
Reilly's Avenue	74 D3
Renoir Apts.	39 A4 [50]
Reuben Avenue	74 D2
Reuben Street	74 D2
Reuben Walk	74 D2
*Rhodaville (off Mountpleasant Ave)	75 B4
Riachville	25 C2 [10]
Rialto Buildings	74 D2
Rialto Cottages	73 C2
Rialto Drive	73 C3
Rialto Park(off Rialto Street)	74 D2
Rialto Street	74 D2
Ribh Avenue	26 F2
Ribh Road	26 F2
Richelieu Park	48 E1
Richmond	59 A1
Richmond Avenue (Fairview)	25 B4
Richmond Avenue (Monkstown)	49 C4
Richmond Avenue South	47 B2
Richmond Cottages (Summerhill)	72 D1
Richmond Cottages North	72 D1
Richmond Court (Marino)	25 C4
Richmond Court (Milltown)	47 B2
Richmond Crescent	72 D1
Richmond Estate	25 C4
Richmond Green	49 C4 [12]
Richmond Grove	49 C4

STREET NAME	PAGE/GRID REFERENCE
Richmond Hall	25 B4 [13]
Richmond Hill (Monkstown)	49 C4
Richmond Hill (Rathmines)	75 B4
Richmond House	25 B4 [12]
Richmond Lane	71 C1
Richmond Lodge	25 B4
*Richmond Manor	75 B4
Richmond Mews	75 B4
Richmond Parade	72 D1
Richmond Park (Herbert Road)	67 A4
Richmond Park (Monkstown)	49 B4
Richmond Place (Rathmines)	75 B4
Richmond Place South (Sth Richmond St)	75 B3
Richmond Road	25 B4
Richmond Row	75 B3
Richmond Street North	72 D1
Richmond Street South	75 B3
Richmond Terrace	68 D2 [12]
Richmond Villas	75 B3
Richview	47 C2
Richview Park	47 B2
Richview Villas	47 C2 [11]
Riddlesford	67 C4
Ridge Hall	64 E1
Ridge Hill	64 E1
Ridgewood Avenue	1 B3
Ridgewood Close	1 B3
Ridgewood Court	1 B3
Ridgewood Green	1 B3
Ridgewood Grove	1 B3
Ridgewood Park	1 B3
Ridgewood Place	1 B3
Ridgewood Square	1 B3
Rinawade Avenue	32 E1
Rinawade Close	32 E1
Rinawade Crescent	32 E1
Rinawade Downs	32 E1
Rinawade Glade	32 E1
Rinawade Green	32 E1
Rinawade Grove	32 E1
Rinawade Lawns	32 E1
Rinawade Park	32 F1
Rinawade Rise	32 E1
Rinawade Vale	32 E1
Rinawade View	32 E1
Ring Street	36 F3 [12]
Ring Terrace	36 F3
Ringsend	39 A3
Ringsend Park	39 A2
Ringsend Road	76 F1
Rinn na Mara	27 A4 [3]
Ripley Court	67 B3
Ripley Hills	67 B3
River Close	64 E1 [23]
River Court	7 B3
*River Court Apts.	73 A1
River Drive	24 D3
River Forest	20 D4
River Forest View (Leixlip)	19 C3
River Forest View (Leixlip)	20 D3
River Gardens	25 A3 [15]
River Lane (Bray)	67 B2
River Lane (Loughlinstown)	64 E2 [1]
River Lane Grove	64 E2 [13]
River Lawns	31 C4
River Mall	2 D2
River Road (Ashtown)	23 C3
River Road (Blanchardstown)	22 F2
River Road Cottages	23 A2
River Valley Avenue	1 C2
River Valley Close	1 B2
River Valley Court	1 B2
River Valley Drive	1 C2
River Valley Grove	1 C3
River Valley Heights	1 C2
River Valley Lawn	1 C2
River Valley Park	1 C2
River Valley Rise	1 C3
River Valley Road	1 C2
River Valley View	1 B2
River Valley Way	1 B2
River View	31 C4
Riverbank (Braemor Road)	47 A3
Riverbank (Dundrum)	57 C1 [10]
Riverbank Hall	24 F3

STREET NAME	PAGE/GRID REFERENCE
Riverdale	20 D4
Riverpark Apts.	69 C4
Riverpark View	9 A4 [3]
Riverrun Apts.	74 D1
Riversdale (Dundrum)	57 C1 [11]
*Riversdale (Herbert Hill)	57 C1
Riversdale (Palmerston)	35 C1
Riversdale Avenue (Clondalkin)	44 E1
Riversdale Avenue (Palmerston)	35 C1
Riversdale Avenue (Terenure)	46 F3
Riversdale Court	35 C1
Riversdale Crescent	44 E1
Riversdale Drive	44 E1
Riversdale Green	35 B4
Riversdale Grove (Kimmage)	46 E2 [1]
Riversdale Grove (Palmerston)	35 B1
Riversdale Park (Clondalkin)	44 E1
Riversdale Park (Palmerston)	35 C1
Riversdale Road	44 E1
Riversdale View	46 F4 [26]
Riverside (Clondalkin)	44 E1 [6]
Riverside (Kimmage)	46 E2 [9]
Riverside (Mulhuddart)	9 A4 [4]
Riverside Avenue	13 A4
Riverside Cottages	46 E4
Riverside Crescent	13 A4
Riverside Drive (Coolock)	13 B4
Riverside Drive (Palmerston)	35 C1
Riverside Drive (Rathfarnham)	47 A3
Riverside Grove	13 A4
Riverside Park	13 A4
Riverside Road	13 A4
Riverside Walk	47 C1 [21]
Riverston Abbey	24 D4
Riverstown Gardens	24 D3 [5]
Rivervale	23 C3
Rivervale Apts.	67 B2 [27]
*Riverview (Grand Canal Docks)	76 E1
Riverview (Oldbawn)	55 A2
Riverview (Palmerston)	35 C1
Riverview Apts.	32 D4
Riverview Court	36 E2 [11]
Riverwood Chase	22 D3
Riverwood Close	22 D3
Riverwood Copse	22 D3
Riverwood Court	22 D3
Riverwood Crescent	22 D3
Riverwood Dale	22 D3
Riverwood Dene	22 D3
Riverwood Drive	22 D3
Riverwood Gardens	22 D3
Riverwood Glebe	22 D3
Riverwood Glen	22 D3
Riverwood Green	22 D3
Riverwood Grove	22 D3
Riverwood Hall	22 D3
Riverwood Heath	22 D3
Riverwood Lawn	22 D3
Riverwood Park	22 D3
Riverwood Place	22 D3
Riverwood Road	22 D3
Riverwood Terrace	22 D3
Riverwood Vale	22 D3
Riverwood View	22 D3
Riverwood Way	22 D3
Robert Emmett Close	70 E4
Robert Place	25 B4 [7]
Robert Street	74 E1
Robert Street (Jones's Road)	25 B4 [6]
Robin Villas	35 C1
Robinhood Park	45 B1
Robinhood Road	45 A1
Robswall	3 C3
Robswall Path	4 D3
Robswall Walk	4 D3
Rochestown Avenue	59 C2
Rochestown House	59 C2 [9]
Rochestown House Apts.	59 C2 [6]
Rochestown Park	60 D2
Rochfort Avenue	34 F2
Rochfort Close	34 F2
Rochfort Crescent	34 F3
Rochfort Downs	34 F2
Rochfort Green	34 F2
Rochfort Park	34 F2
Rochfort Way	34 F3

STREET NAME	PAGE/GRID REFERENCE
Rock Bridge	32 D4
Rock Hall	49 A3
Rock Hill	49 A3
*Rock Lane (Baggot St Lower)	76 D2
Rock Lodge	60 E3
Rock Road	49 A3
Rockbrae Hall	57 C3
Rockbrook	56 E4
Rockfield (Dundrum)	57 C1
Rockfield (Lucan)	34 D3
Rockfield (Maynooth)	18 D4
Rockfield Avenue (Kimmage)	46 D2
Rockfield Avenue (Maynooth)	18 D4
Rockfield Close	22 D3
Rockfield Drive (Clondalkin)	44 D2
Rockfield Drive (Coolmine)	22 D3
Rockfield Drive (Kimmage)	46 D2
Rockfield Gardens	18 D3
Rockfield Green	18 D3
Rockfield Lodge	18 D4
Rockfield Manor	18 D4
Rockfield Park (Coolmine)	22 D2
Rockfield Park (Maynooth)	18 D4
Rockfield Rise	18 D3
Rockfield Square	18 D3
Rockfield Walk	18 D3
Rockford Manor	59 B1
Rockford Park	59 B1
Rockford Terrace	49 B4 [14]
Rockfort Avenue	60 F2
Rockingham Avenue	19 C4
Rockingham Green	19 C4
Rockingham Grove	19 C4
Rockingham Park	19 C4
Rockingham Terrace	2 D2
Rocklands	60 F1 [6]
Rockmeadon Court	46 D1 [5]
Rockstown	30 E2
Rockview	57 C3
Rockville	62 F2
Rockville Crescent	49 B4
Rockville Drive	49 B4
Rockville Drive	63 A1
Rockville Estate	49 A4 [9]
Rockville Park	49 B4
Rockville Road	49 A4
Rockwell Cove Apts.	49 A3 [9]
Rockwood	34 D3
Rocwood	58 F2
Roe Lane	70 E4
Roebuck Avenue	48 E3
Roebuck Castle	48 D3
Roebuck Crescent	47 C3 [10]
Roebuck Downs	47 C3
Roebuck Drive	46 D2
Roebuck Hill	48 D3
Roebuck Lawn	47 C3 [9]
Roebuck Park	47 C4
Roebuck Road	48 D3
Roger Casement Park	67 B2
Roger's Lane	75 C2
Roland Court	47 A1 [20]
Rollins Court	60 D1 [12]
Rollins Villas	60 D1
Ronanstown	35 A4
Roncalli Road	27 C1
Rookwood View	56 E2
Roosevelt Cottages	24 D4 [1]
Rooske Road	7 B3
Ropewalk Place	39 A3 [30]
Rory O'Connor Park	59 B1
Rory O'More Bridge	70 E4
Ros Mór View	56 D2
Rosary Gardens East	50 D4 [2]
Rosary Gardens West	49 C4 [1]
Rosary Road	74 D2
Rosary Terrace (Ringsend)	39 A3
*Rosary Terrace (off Library Road)	50 D4
Rosbeg Court	27 C2
Rosberry	34 E3
Rosberry Avenue	34 E3
Rosberry Court	34 E3
Rosberry Lane	34 E3
Rosberry Park	34 E3
Rosberry Place	34 E3

STREET NAME	PAGE/GRID REFERENCE
Rose Park	59 C1
Rose Vale Court	22 D1 [6]
Roseacre	58 E3
Rosebank	55 A2
Rosebank Court	35 B4 [2]
Rosebank Hall	35 A4 [5]
Rosebank Place	35 A4 [4]
Rosebank View	35 B4 [1]
Rosedale (Clonsilla)	21 B1
Rosedale (Dunboyne)	7 B2
Rosedale Close	21 B1
Rosedale Crescent	21 B1
*Rosedale Terrace	74 F3
Rosedale Terrace (Lower Clanbrassil St)	74 F3
Roseglen Avenue	27 B2
Roseglen Manor	27 B2 [3]
Roseglen Road	27 B2
Rosehaven	22 E3 [1]
Rosehill	59 A1 [5]
Roselawn	34 E1
Roselawn Avenue	22 E2
Roselawn Close	22 F2
Roselawn Court	22 F2
Roselawn Crescent	22 E2
Roselawn Drive (Blanchardstown)	22 E2
Roselawn Drive (Oldcourt)	67 C3
Roselawn Glade	22 E2
Roselawn Grove	22 E2
Roselawn Park	67 C3 [2]
Roselawn Road	22 E2
Roselawn Road	22 F2
Roselawn View	22 E2
Roselawn Walk	22 E2
Roselawn Way	22 F2
Rosemount	25 C3 [10]
Rosemount (Churchtown)	47 C4
Rosemount (Donnycarney)	26 D3
Rosemount Avenue	26 E2
Rosemount Court (Booterstown)	48 F3
Rosemount Court (Dundrum)	47 C4
Rosemount Court (Inchicore Rd)	73 A1
Rosemount Crescent (Roebuck Road)	47 C3
Rosemount Glade	47 C4
Rosemount Hall	47 C4
Rosemount Park	47 C4
Rosemount Park Drive	10 D4
Rosemount Park Road	10 D4
Rosemount Road	70 F1
Rosemount Terrace (Arbour Hill)	70 E3
Rosemount Terrace (Booterstown)	48 E3
Rosemount Terrace (Dundrum)	47 B4 [11]
Rosevale Court	26 F3
Rosevale Mansions	26 F3
Roseville Court	67 B1 [7]
Roseville Terrace	47 C4 [4]
Rosewood Grove	34 F3
Rosmeen Gardens	50 D4
Rosmeen Park	60 D1
Ross Cottages	3 B2 [8]
Ross Road	75 A1
Ross Street	70 D2
Ross View	35 C1
Rossaveal Court	36 D2 [1]
Rossberry Terrace	34 E4
Rossecourt Avenue	34 F3
Rossecourt Green	34 F3
Rossecourt Grove	34 F3
Rossecourt Heights	34 F3
Rossecourt Lane	34 F3
Rossecourt Rise	34 F3
Rossecourt Square	34 F3
Rossecourt Terrace	34 F3
Rossecourt Way	34 F3
Rossfield Avenue	54 D1
Rossfield Close	54 D1 [4]
Rossfield Court	54 D1 [3]
Rossfield Crescent	54 D1
Rossfield Drive	54 D1
Rossfield Gardens	54 D1
Rossfield Green	54 D1
Rossfield Grove	54 D1

STREET NAME	PAGE/GRID REFERENCE
Rossfield Park	54 D1
Rossfield Way	54 D1
Rosslyn	67 C2 [37]
Rosslyn Court	67 C2
Rosslyn Grove	67 C2 [4]
Rossmeen Park (Off Sumerhill Road)	50 E4
Rossmore Avenue (Ballyfermot)	36 D3
Rossmore Avenue (Templeogue)	45 C4
Rossmore Close	46 D4
Rossmore Crescent	46 D4
Rossmore Drive (Ballyfermot)	36 D2
Rossmore Drive (Templeogue)	45 C4
Rossmore Grove	45 C4
Rossmore Lawns	46 D4
Rossmore Park	46 D4
Rossmore Road (Ballyfermot)	36 D2
Rossmore Road (Templeogue)	46 D4
Rostrevor Court	76 E1
Rostrevor Road	47 A3
Rostrevor Terrace (Lr Grand Canal St)	76 E1
Rostrevor Terrace (Orwell Road)	47 A2
Rothe Abbey	73 B2
Rowan Avenue	58 D2
Rowan Close	32 D3
Rowan Grove	67 B2
Rowan Hall	47 C1 [15]
Rowan Hamilton Court	24 E4 [3]
Rowan House	76 D3
Rowan Park	49 B4
Rowan Park Avenue	49 B4
Rowanbyrn	49 B4
Rowanbyrn	59 B1
Rowans Road	58 D2
Rowlagh Avenue	35 A3
Rowlagh Crescent	35 A3
Rowlagh Gardens	35 A3
Rowlagh Green	35 A3
Rowlagh Park	35 A3
Rowserstown Lane	73 B1
Royal Canal Avenue	23 C3
Royal Canal Bank	25 A4
Royal Canal Bank	71 A1
Royal Canal Terrace	70 F2
Royal Hibernian Way	75 C1
Royal Marine Terrace	67 C2 [12]
Royal Oak	12 F4
Royal Terrace East	60 D1
Royal Terrace Lane	60 D1 [10]
Royal Terrace North	60 D1 [2]
Royal Terrace West	60 D1
Royse Road	25 A4
Royston	46 D2
Royston Village	46 D2
Royston Village	46 D2
Ruby Hall	59 C2
Rugby Road	47 B1
Rugby Villas	47 B1 [6]
Rushbrook	22 E2
Rushbrook Avenue	45 C3
Rushbrook Court	45 C4
Rushbrook Crescent	45 C3
Rushbrook Drive	45 C3
Rushbrook Grove	45 C3
Rushbrook Park	45 C3
Rushbrook Road	45 C3
Rushbrook View	45 C3
Rushbrook Way	45 C4
Rusheeney	21 B1
Rusheeney Avenue	21 B1
Rusheeney Close	21 B1
Rusheeney Court	21 B1
Rusheeney Crescent	8 F4
Rusheeney Green	21 C1
Rusheeney Grove	21 B1
Rusheeney Manor	21 B1
Rusheeney Park	21 B1
Rusheeney View	21 C1
Rusheeney Way	21 B1
Rus-in-Urbe Terrace	60 D1 [19]
Russell Avenue (Fortunestown Way)	54 D1
Russell Avenue (Jones's Road)	71 C1
Russell Avenue East	72 E2

STREET NAME	PAGE/GRID REFERENCE
Russell Close	54 D2
Russell Court	54 D2
*Russell Court Apts. (Little Britain Street)	71 A3
Russell Crescent	54 D1
Russell Downs	54 D1
Russell Drive	54 D2
Russell Green	54 D2
Russell Grove	54 D2
Russell House	2 E2
Russell Lane	54 D1
Russell Lawns	54 D2
Russell Meadows	54 D1
Russell Place	54 D1
Russell Rise	54 D1
Russell Street	71 C1
Russell View	54 D2
Russell Walk	54 D1
Russell's Mews	2 E3
Russell's Place	2 E3
Russell's Terrace	2 E4
Rutland Avenue (Clogher Road)	46 E1
Rutland Avenue (Crumlin Road)	74 D4
Rutland Cottages	71 C2
Rutland Court	71 C2
Rutland Grove	46 F1
Rutland Place North	71 C2
Rutland Place West	71 B2
Rutland Street Lower	71 C2
Rutledge Terrace	74 E3
Ryan's Cottages (Harold's Cross)	46 F1 [7]
Ryder's Row	71 A3
Rye Bridge	33 A1
Rye River Avenue	20 D4
Rye River Close	20 D4
Rye River Court	20 D4
Rye River Crescent	20 D4
Rye River Gardens	20 D4
Rye River Grove	20 D4
Rye River Mall	20 D4
Rye River Park	20 D4
Ryecroft	67 C3
Ryemont Abbey	20 D4
Ryevale Lawns	20 D4
Rynville Manor	67 B4

S

STREET NAME	PAGE/GRID REFERENCE
Sackville Court Apts.	71 B2
Sackville Gardens	72 D1
Sackville Place	71 B3
Saddlers Avenue	9 A4
Saddlers Close	9 A4
Saddlers Court	75 B4
Saddlers Crescent	9 A4
Saddlers Drive	9 A4
Saddlers Glade	9 A4
Saddlers Grove	9 A4
Saddlers Lawn	9 A4
Sadleir Hall	7 A2
Saggart	53 B2
Saggart Abbey	53 C2
Saggart Lakes	53 B1
Saint Canice's Court	23 C1
Saint Canice's Square	24 E2
Saint Pappin's Street	12 D4
Saintdoolaghs	14 D3
Saintsbury Avenue	60 E4
Salamanca	48 D4
Salem Court	47 A1 [17]
Salestown	6 D4
Sallowood View	12 E4
Sallowood Walk	12 E4
Sally Park	55 C1
Sally Park Close	55 C1
Sallyglen Road	60 D2
Sallymount Avenue	47 B1
Sallymount Gardens	47 B1 [1]
Sallymount Terrace	47 B1 [14]
Sallynoggin	60 D2
Sallynoggin Park	59 C2
Sallynoggin Road	59 C2
Salmon Pool Apts	69 A4
Salthill	49 C4
*Salthill Place (off Crofton Road)	50 E4
Saltzburg	48 D4

STREET NAME	PAGE/GRID REFERENCE
Sampson's Lane	71 B3
Sanderling Apts.	48 E3
Sandford Avenue (Donnybrook)	47 C1
Sandford Avenue (Donore Avenue)	74 E3
Sandford Close	47 B1
Sandford Gardens (Donnybrook)	47 C1 [10]
Sandford Gardens (off Donore Avenue)	74 F3
Sandford Gardens (Sandford Avenue)	74 F3
Sandford Lodge	47 B1
Sandford Park (off O'Donovan Road)	74 F3
Sandford Park (Sandford Avenue)	74 F3
Sandford Road	47 B1
Sandford Row	47 B1
Sandford Terrace	47 B1
Sandford Wood	1 C1
Sandon Cove	26 E4
Sandwith Street Lower	72 D4
Sandwith Street Upper	76 D1
Sandycove Avenue East	60 E1
Sandycove Avenue North	50 E4
Sandycove Avenue West	60 E1
Sandycove Lane East	60 E1
Sandycove Point	50 E4
Sandycove Road	60 E1
Sandyford	58 D2
Sandyford Downs	58 D3
Sandyford Hall	58 E3
Sandyford Hall Avenue	58 E3
Sandyford Hall Close	58 E4
Sandyford Hall Court	58 E3
Sandyford Hall Crescent	58 E3
Sandyford Hall Drive	58 E4
Sandyford Hall Green	58 E3
Sandyford Hall Grove	58 E4
Sandyford Hall Lawn	58 E3
Sandyford Hall Park	58 E3
Sandyford Hall Place	58 E3
Sandyford Hall Rise	58 E3
Sandyford Hall View	58 E4
Sandyford Hall Walk	58 E4
Sandyford Park	58 D3
Sandyford Road	57 C1
Sandyford View	57 C3
Sandyford Village	58 D3
Sandyhill Avenue	24 F1
Sandyhill Court	11 C4
Sandyhill Gardens	24 F1
Sandyhill Terrace	11 C4
Sandyhill Way	11 C4
Sandymount	39 A4
Sandymount Avenue	39 A4
Sandymount Castle	39 A4 [5]
Sandymount Castle Drive	39 A4 [3]
Sandymount Castle Park	39 B4 [2]
Sandymount Castle Road	39 A4 [2]
Sandymount Court	39 A3 [26]
Sandymount Green	39 A4 [1]
Sandymount Road	39 A3
Sans Souci Park	48 F3
Sans Souci wood	67 C3
Santa Sabina Manor	29 B2
Santry	25 B1
Santry Avenue	12 E4
Santry Close	12 F4
Santry Court	12 F4
Santry Cross	12 D4
Santry Cross (Ballymun)	12 D4
Santry Villas	12 D4
Sarah Bridge	69 B4
Sarah Curran Avenue	56 F1
Sarah Curran Road	56 F1 [1]
Sarah Place	69 B4
Sarney	6 E2
Sarsfield Court (Inchicore)	36 F3
Sarsfield Court (Lucan)	34 D1 [4]
Sarsfield Park	34 D1
Sarsfield Quay	70 E4
Sarsfield Road	36 F3
Sarsfield Street (Phibsborough)	71 A1
Sarsfield Street (Sallynoggin)	60 D1
Sarsfield Terrace	34 D1 [1]

STREET NAME	PAGE/GRID REFERENCE	STREET NAME	PAGE/GRID REFERENCE	STREET NAME	PAGE/GRID REFERENCE	STREET NAME	PAGE/GRID REFERENCE
Sarto Lawn	27 C1	Seafort Cottages	39 A4 [18]	Seven Oaks (Whitehall)	25 B3	Sheelin Walk	64 E1 [14]
Sarto Park	27 C1	Seafort Gardens	39 A3 [10]	Seventh Lock Cottages	36 D4	Sheephill Avenue	9 C4
Sarto Rise	27 C1	Seafort Parade	48 F3	Seventh Lock Place	36 D4	Sheephill Green	9 C4
Sarto Road	27 C2	Seafort Terrace	39 A4 [19]	Seville Place	72 D2	Sheephill Park	9 C4
Saul Road	46 E1	Seafort Villas	39 A4 [20]	Seville Terrace	72 D2	Sheepmoor Avenue	22 D1
Saval Grove	60 E2	Seagrange Avenue	14 F4	Seymour Road	67 C2	Sheepmoor Close	22 D1
Saval Park Crescent	60 E2	Seagrange Drive	27 C1	Shackelton	8 F4	Sheepmoor Crescent	22 D1
Saval Park Gardens	60 E2	Seagrange Road	27 C1	Shakelton	8 F4	Sheepmoor Gardens	22 D1
Saval Park Road	60 E2	Seagrave	14 F2	Shaldon Grange	62 F2	Sheepmoor Green	22 D1
Scariff House	22 F1	Seagrave Close	11 B4	Shalimar Apts.	44 F3 [3]	Sheepmoor Grove	22 D1
Scholarstown Park	56 D2	Seagrave Court	11 B4	Shamrock Cottages	72 D2	Sheepmoor Lawn	22 D1
Scholarstown Road	56 D2	Seagrave Drive	11 B4	Shamrock Hill Mews	47 C1 [23]	Sheepmoor Way	22 D1
School Avenue	26 E2	Seagrave Terrace	11 B4	Shamrock Place	72 D2	Shelbourne Avenue	76 F3
School Street	74 E1	Seagrave Way	11 B4	Shamrock Street	71 A2	Shelbourne Lane	76NS F3
Schoolhouse Court	25 B1	Seamount	3 C3	Shamrock Terrace	72 D2	Shelbourne Park Mews	76 F1
Schoolhouse Lane (Kildare Street)	75 C1	Seamount	48 E3	Shamrock Villas	46 F1	Shelbourne Place	76 F2
Schoolhouse Lane (Santry)	25 B1	Seamount Drive	3 C3	Shanagarry	47 B2 [9]	Shelbourne Road	76 F2
Schoolhouse Lane West (off High Street)	75 A1	Seamount Grove	3 C3	Shanard Avenue	25 A1	Shelbourne Village	76 F1
Schoolhouse Mews	25 B1 [2]	Seamount Heights	3 C3	Shanard Road	25 A1	Shelerin Road	21 C2
Schools Road	67 B4	Seamount Park	3 C3	Shanboley Road	25 C1	Shellys Banks Road	39 B3
Scotstone Bridge	2 D1	Seamount Road	3 C3	Shancastle Avenue	35 A2	Shelmalier Road	72 F2
Scott Park	67 C3	Seamount View	2 E2	Shancastle Close	35 A2	Shelmartin Avenue	25 C4
Scribblestown	23 C3	Seamus Ennis Road	24 E1	Shancastle Crescent	35 A2	Shelmartin Terrace	25 C4 [2]
Scribblestown Avenue	23 C3	Sean Heuston Bridge	70 D4	Shancastle Drive	35 A2	Shelton Drive	46 D2
Scribblestown Close	23 C3	Sean MacDermott Street Lower	71 C2	Shancastle Lawns	35 A2	Shelton Gardens	46 D2
Scribblestown Grove	23 C3	Sean MacDermott Street Upper	71 C2	Shancastle Park	35 A2	Shelton Grove	46 D2
Scribblestown Park	24 D3	Sean Moore Road	39 A3	Shandon Crescent	24 F4	Shelton Park	46 D2
Scribblestown Place	23 C3	Sean O'Casey Avenue	71 C2	Shandon Drive	24 F4	Sherborne	47 A2
Scribblestown Road	23 B3	Sean O'Casey Bridge	72 D4	Shandon Gardens	24 F4	Sheridan Court	71 B2
Scribblestown Road	24 D3	Sean Tracey House	72 D2	Shandon Green	24 F4 [8]	Sheridan Place	71 B2
Sea Road	3 A2	Seapark (Dollymount)	26 F4	Shandon Mill	24 F4 [9]	Sheriff Street Lower	72 D3
Seabank Court (Dalkey)	60 E1 [21]	Seapark (Malahide)	3 C3	Shandon Park (Monkstown)	49 B4	Sheriff Street Upper	72 F3
Seabank Court (Malahide)	3 C2 [1]	Seapark Drive	26 F4	Shandon Park (Phibsborough)	24 F4	Sherkin Court	25 B3
Seabrook Manor	14 E2	Seapark Hill	3 C3	Shandon Road	24 F4	Sherkin Gardens	25 B3
Seabury	48 E1	Seapark Road	26 F4	Shangan Avenue	25 B1	Sherrard Avenue	71 B1
Seabury Avenue	2 F2	Seapoint Avenue (Baldoyle)	15 A4 [1]	Shangan Court	25 A1	*Sherrard Court (off Portland Place)	71 B1
Seabury Close	2 F2	Seapoint Avenue (Blackrock)	49 B3	Shangan Crescent	25 A1		
Seabury Court	2 F2	Seapoint Court (Baldoyle)	15 A4 [7]	Shangan Drive	25 B1	Sherrard Street Lower	71 C1
Seabury Crescent	2 F2	Seapoint Court (Bray)	67 C1	Shangan Gardens	25 B1	Sherrard Street Upper	71 B1
Seabury Dale	2 F2	Seapoint Road	67 C2	Shangan Green	25 B1	Sherrards Court	71 B1
Seabury Downs	2 F2	Seapoint Terrace (Blackrock)	49 B3 [4]	Shangan Hall Apts.	25 A1 [4]	Shielmartin Drive	29 B3
Seabury Drive	3 A2	Seapoint Terrace (Bray)	67 C2 [24]	Shangan Park	25 B1	Shielmartin Park	29 B3 [1]
Seabury Gardens	2 F2	Seapoint Terrace (Ringsend)	39 A3 [4]	Shangan Road	25 A1	Shielmartin Road	29 B3
Seabury Glen	2 F2	Seapoint Villas	67 C2 [20]	Shanganagh Cliffs	64 E2	Shinkeen Bridge	32 E2
Seabury Green	2 F2	Seascout Den	40 D1	Shanganagh Grove	64 E3	Ship Street Great	75 A1
Seabury Grove	2 F2	Seatown Park	2 D1	Shanganagh Road	64 E1	Ship Street Little	75 A1
Seabury Heights	2 F2	Seatown Park The Avenue	2 D1	Shanganagh Terrace	60 E4	Shrewsbury	39 A4
Seabury Lane	2 F2	Seatown Park The Court	2 D1	Shanganagh Vale	60 D4	Shrewsbury Hall	64 E3
Seabury Lawns	2 F2	Seatown Park The Crescent	2 D1	Shanganagh Wood	64 E2 [8]	Shrewsbury House	59 C4
Seabury Meadows	2 F2	Seatown Park The Drive	2 D1	Shanglas Road	25 C1	Shrewsbury Lawn	59 C4
Seabury Orchard	2 F2	Seatown Park The Green	2 D1	Shanid Road	46 F2	Shrewsbury Lodge	59 C3
Seabury Parade	2 F2	Seatown Park The Grove	2 D1	Shankill	64 E3	Shrewsbury Park	48 D1
Seabury Park	2 F2	Seatown Road	2 D1	Shankill View	67 C2 [38]	Shrewsbury Road (Ailesbury Road)	48 D1
Seabury Place	2 F2	Seatown Roundabout (Swords)	2 D1	Shanliss Avenue	25 B1		
Seabury Road	2 F2	Seatown Terrace	2 D2	Shanliss Drive	25 B1	Shrewsbury Road (Shankill)	64 E3
Seabury Vale	2 F2	Seatown Villas	2 D1	Shanliss Gardens	25 A1 [2]	Shrewsbury Woods	59 C4
Seabury View	2 F2	Seatown Walk	2 D2	Shanliss Grove	25 B1	Sibthorpe Lane	76 D4
Seabury Walk	2 F2	Seatown West	2 D1	Shanliss Park	25 B1	Sidbury Court	68 D2 [5]
Seabury Wood	2 F2	Seaview Avenue East	72 F2	Shanliss Road	25 A1	Sidmonton Avenue	67 C2
Seacliff Avenue	27 C1	Seaview Avenue North	26 D4	Shanliss Walk	25 B1	Sidmonton Court	68 D3 [5]
Seacliff Drive	27 C1	Seaview Cottages	63 C4	Shanliss Way	25 B1	Sidmonton Gardens	67 C2 [36]
Seacliff Road	27 C1	Seaview Lawn	64 E2	Shannon Terrace	73 C1	Sidmonton Gardens	67 C2
Seacourt	26 F4	Seaview Park	64 E2	Shanowen Avenue	25 A1	Sidmonton Park	68 D2
Seacrest	67 C3	Seaview Terrace (Donnybrook)	48 D1	Shanowen Crescent	25 B1	Sidmonton Place	67 C2 [6]
Seafield (Shankill)	64 F2	Seaview Terrace (Dun Laoghaire)	49 C4 [15]	Shanowen Drive	25 B1	Sidmonton Road	67 C2
Seafield (Sutton)	28 D1 [2]			Shanowen Grove	25 A1	Sidmonton Square	67 C2 [1]
Seafield Avenue (Clontarf)	26 F4	Seaview Terrace (Howth)	30 D2 [2]	Shanowen Hall	25 B2	Sigurd Road	70 E3
Seafield Avenue (Monkstown)	49 B4	Seaview Wood	64 E2	Shanowen Park	25 A1	Silchester Court	60 D1
Seafield Close	48 E3	Second Avenue (Seville Place)	72 E3	Shanowen Road	25 B1	Silchester Crescent	60 D1
Seafield Court (Loughlinstown)	64 E1	Second Avenue (Tallaght)	44 F4	Shanowen Square	25 B1	Silchester Park	60 D1
Seafield Court (Malahide)	3 B2	Sefton	59 C2	Shanowen Square	25 B2	Silchester Road	60 D1
Seafield Crescent	48 E3	Sefton Green	59 C2	Shanrath Road	25 B1	Silchester Wood	60 D1 [16]
*Seafield Downs (off Kincora Road Clontarf)	26 F4	Sefton Hall	59 A2 [12]	Shantalla Avenue	25 C1	Silken Vale	17 C3
		*Selskar Terrace (Old Mountpleasant)	75 C4	Shantalla Drive	25 C2	Silleachain Lane	20 D4
Seafield Drive	48 E2			Shantalla Park	25 C2	Silloge Avenue	25 A1
Seafield Grove	27 A4 [1]	Serpentine Avenue	39 A4	Shantalla Road	25 C1	Silloge Crescent	25 A1
Seafield Park	48 E2 [1]	Serpentine Park	39 A4	Shanvarna Road	25 B1	Silloge Gardens	25 A1
Seafield Road (Ballybrack)	64 E1	Serpentine Road	39 A4	Sharavogue	60 E2	Silloge Road	25 A1
Seafield Road (Booterstown)	48 E2	Serpentine Terrace	39 A4	Shaw Court Apts.	75 B3	Silver Birches (Dunboyne)	7 B2
Seafield Road (Killiney)	60 E4	Seskin View Avenue	55 A2	Shaw Street	71 C4	Silver Birches (Dundrum)	47 C4
Seafield Road East	26 F4	Seskin View Drive	55 A2	Shaw's Lane	76 F2	Silver Birches Close	7 B2
Seafield Road West	26 F4	Seskin View Park	55 A2	Shea's Court	70 E2	Silver Birches Crescent	7 B2
Seafield Terrace	60 F2 [15]	Seskin View Road	55 A2	Sheelin Avenue	64 E1	Silver Pines	58 F2 [3]
Seafort Avenue	39 A4	Setanta Place	75 C1	Sheelin Drive	64 E1	Silverberry	34 D3
		Seven Houses	60 D1 [13]	Sheelin Grove	64 E1 [7]	Silverdale	34 D3
		Seven Oaks (Inchicore)	36 F3	Sheelin Hill	64 E1 [13]	Silverpine	67 B3

STREET NAME	PAGE/GRID REFERENCE
Silverwood	34 D3
Silverwood Drive	46 E4
Silverwood Road	46 E4
Simmon's Place (off Thompson's Cottages)	71 C2
Simmonscourt Avenue	48 D1 [2]
Simmonscourt Castle	48 D1
Simmonscourt Road	39 A4
Simmonscourt Square	48 D1 [5]
Simmonscourt Terrace	47 C1 [18]
Simmonscourt View	48 D1 [3]
Simmonstown	41 A1
Simmonstown Manor	32 D4
Simmonstown Park	32 D4
Simons Ridge	57 C3
Simpsons Lane	39 A3 [32]
Sion Hill Avenue	46 F1
Sion Hill Court	25 C3 [5]
Sion Hill Road	25 C3
Sion Road	60 D2
Sionhill	48 F3
Sir Ivor Mall	58 F2 [7]
Sir John Rogerson's Quay	72 E4
Sitric Place (off Sitric Road)	70 E3
Sitric Road	70 E3
Skeagh	41 A3
Skelligs Court	22 F1
Skelly's Lane	26 D2
Skreen Road	24 D4
Slade	53 A3
Slade Castle Avenue	53 A2
Slade Castle Close	53 A2
Slade Castle Heights	53 A2
Slade Castle View	53 A2
Slade Road	53 A2
Slade Row	70 D3
Slademore Avenue	26 F1
Slademore Close	26 F1
Slademore Court	13 C4
Slademore Drive	26 F1
Slane Road	73 C4
Slaney Close	24 E3
Slaney Road	24 E3
Slate Cabin Lane	57 C3
Slemish Road	69 B1
Slí an Chanáil	19 C4
Slieve Rua Drive	58 D1
Slievebloom Park	45 C1
Slievebloom Road	45 C1
Slievemore Road	73 A4
Slievenamon Road	73 B3
Sloan Terrace	68 D2 [8]
*Sloan Terrace (on Meath Road)	67 C2
Sloperton	49 C4
Smithfield	70 F4
Smithfield Gate Apts.	70 F3
Smithfield Market Square Apts. (Smithfield)	70 F4
Smithfield Terrace (Smithfield)	70 F4
Smith's Cottages (Donnybrook)	47 B1 [18]
Smith's Lane	46 F1 [13]
Smith's Villas	49 C4 [3]
Smyth Gardens	49 C4 [34]
Snowdrop Walk	13 C4
Snugborough	14 E3
Snugborough Road	22 F1
Snugborough Road (Extention)	22 D2
Somerset Street	76 F1
Somerton	59 C2
Somerton Mews	59 C2
Somerton Road	22 E4
Somerville Avenue	45 C1
Somerville Court	46 D1 [8]
Somerville Drive	46 D1
Somerville Park	45 C1 [7]
Sommerville	47 C4
Sonesta	3 A2
Sophie Baret Residence	48 D4 [2]
Sorbonne	48 D4
Sorrel Dale	22 D2
Sorrel Drive	21 C2
Sorrel Heath	21 C2
Sorrel Park	21 C2
Sorrell Hall	57 C3
Sorrento Close	60 F2 [25]
Sorrento Court	60 F2 [29]
Sorrento Drive	60 F2 [12]
Sorrento Heights	60 F2 [30]
Sorrento Lawn	60 F2 [13]
Sorrento Mews	60 F2 [28]
*Sorrento Park (on Sorrento Rd)	60 F2
Sorrento Road	60 F2
Sorrento Terrace	60 Inset
South Avenue	48 E4
South Bank	2 D1
South Bank (Swords)	1 C1
South Bank Road	39 B3
South Circular Road (Dolphin's Barn)	74 D3
South Circular Road (Islandbridge)	69 B4
South Circular Road (Kilmainham)	73 C2
South Circular Road (Portobello)	74 E3
South City Market (on South Great Georges Street)	75 B1
South Dock Place	76 F1
South Dock Road	76 F1
South Dock Street	76 F1
South Esplanade	68 D2
South Great George's Street	75 B1
South Hill (Howth)	29 C3
South Hill (Milltown)	47 B2
South Hill Avenue	48 F3
South Hill Park	48 E3
South Lotts Road	76 F1
South Park (Cornelscourt)	59 B3
South Park Drive	59 B2
South Richmond View	75 B3
South Winds	60 F1 [4]
South Wood Park	48 F3
Southdene	49 B4 [18]
Southern Cross Avenue	73 A2
Southern Cross Route	57 B3
Southmede	57 C1
Southview Terrace	74 D1
Spa Road (Inchicore)	36 F3
Spa Road (Phoenix Park)	69 B2
Spafield Terrace	39 A4 [13]
Spawell Cottages	45 C4 [1]
Spawell Roundabout	46 D4
Spencer Dock	72 E3
Spencer Dock (North Wall)	72 E3
Spencer Dock (Guild Street)	72 E3
Spencer Place (off Spencer Street N)	72 E1
Spencer Row	71 C3
Spencer Street North	72 E1
Spencer Street South	75 A3
Spencer Terrace (off Cork Street)	74 E2
Spencer Villas	60 E1
Spences Terrace	74 E2
Sperrin Road	73 A4
Spiddal Park	35 C3
Spiddal Road	35 C3
Spire View	24 D4
Spire View	70 F1
Spire View Lane	47 A1
Spitalfields	74 F1
Spring Garden Lane	71 C4
Spring Garden Street	72 D1
Springbank Cottages	53 A2
Springdale Court Apts.	26 F2
Springdale Road	26 F2
Springfield (Cabra)	69 B1
Springfield (Tallaght)	54 D1
Springfield Avenue	46 E4
Springfield Close	31 C4
Springfield Crescent	46 E4
Springfield Drive	46 E4
Springfield Lane	63 A1
Springfield Park (Deans Grange)	59 A2
Springfield Park (Templeogue)	46 E4
Springfield Road	46 E3
Springhill Avenue	59 A1
Springhill Cottages	59 B1 [5]
Springhill Park (Dalkey)	60 E2
Springhill Park (Deans Grange)	59 B1
Springlawn	22 E2
Springlawn Close	22 E2
Springlawn Court	22 E2
Springlawn Drive	22 E2
Springlawn Heights	22 E2
Springlawn Park	22 E2
Springlawn Road	22 E2
Springmount Apts.	24 D2
Springvale	56 E2
Springvale Hall	57 C3
Spruce Avenue	58 D2
St Agatha Court (off William St N)	72 D2
St Agnes Park	46 D1
St Agnes Road	46 D1
*St Agnes Terrace (on St Agnes Rd)	46 D1
St Agnes Terrace (Rathfarnham)	46 F3 [2]
St Aidan's Drive	48 D4
St Aidan's Halting Site	54 D1
St Aidan's Park	25 C4 [6]
St Aidan's Park Avenue	25 C4
St Aidan's Park Road	25 C4
St Aidan's Terrace	67 C2 [23]
St Alban's Park	48 E1
St Alban's Road	74 F3
St Alphonsus Avenue	25 A4 [11]
St Alphonsus Rd	25 A4
St Andrew Street	75 B1
St Andrews	34 F2
St Andrews Drive	34 F2
St Andrews Fairway	34 F2
St Andrews Green	34 F2
St Andrew's Grove	3 B3
St Andrew's Lane (off Exchequer Street)	75 B1
St Andrews Park	1 C1
St Andrews Wood	34 F2
St Anne's Court	27 A3 [2]
St Anne's (Kimmage)	46 E2
St Anne's (Ranelagh)	75 C4
St Anne's Avenue	27 A3
St Anne's Drive	27 A3
St Anne's Park	64 E3
St Anne's Road North	25 A4
St Anne's Road South	74 E3
St Anne's Square (Blackrock)	49 A3 [7]
St Anne's Square (Portmarnock)	14 F2 [6]
St Anne's Terrace (Raheny)	27 A3
St Anne's Terrace (Ranelagh)	75 C4
St Anne's Terrace (Rathcoole)	52 E2
St Ann's Square Lower	14 F2 [5]
St Anthony's Avenue	44 E2
St Anthony's Crescent	45 C2
St Anthony's Place (off Temple Street North)	71 B2
St Anthony's Road	74 D2
St Aongus Court	45 B4
St Aongus Crescent	45 B4
St Aongus Green	45 B4
St Aongus Grove	45 B4
St Aongus Lawn	45 B4
St Aongus Park	45 B4
St Aongus Road	45 B4
St Assam's Avenue	27 A2
St Assam's Drive	27 A2
St Assam's Park	27 A2
St Assam's Road East	27 B2
St Assam's Road West	27 A2
St Attracta Road	24 F4
St Aubyn's Court	64 E1 [5]
St Audoen's Terrace (off High Street)	75 A1
St Augustine Street	70 F4
St Augustine's Park	59 A1
St Barnabas Gardens	72 E2
St Begnet's Villas	60 E1
St Benedicts Gardens	71 B1
St Brendan's Avenue	26 E2
St Brendan's Cottages	39 A3 [6]
St Brendan's Crescent	45 B2
St Brendan's Drive	26 E2
St Brendan's Park	26 F2
St Brendan's Road	25 A4 [12]
St Brendan's Terrace (Coolock)	26 E1
St Brendan's Terrace (Dun Laoghaire)	49 C4 [19]
St Brendan's Terrace (Rockbrook)	56 E4
St Bricin's Park	70 D3
St Bridget's Avenue (North Strand)	72 E1
St Bridget's Drive	45 B2
St Bridget's Flats	47 C2 [8]
St Brigid's Green	26 E2
St Brigid's Grove	26 E2
St Brigid's Avenue	14 F2 [4]
St Brigid's Church Road	58 F1
St Brigid's Cottages (Blanchardstown)	22 F2
St Brigid's Cottages (Clondalkin)	44 F2
St Brigid's Cottages (North Strand)	72 E1
St Brigid's Court	26 E3 [2]
St Brigid's Crescent	26 E2
St Brigid's Drive (Clondalkin)	44 E2
St Brigid's Drive (Killester)	26 E3 [1]
St Brigid's Lawn	26 E2
St Brigid's Park (Blanchardstown)	22 F2
St Brigid's Park (Clondalkin)	44 E2 [1]
St Brigid's Park (Cornelscourt)	59 B3
St Brigid's Road (Artane)	26 E2
St Brigid's Road (Clondalkin)	44 E2
St Brigid's Road Lower	25 A4
St Brigid's Road Upper	25 A4
St Brigid's Terrace	67 C2 [33]
St Broc's Cottages	47 C1 [1]
St Canice's Park	24 F2
St Canice's Road	25 A2
St Catherine's Avenue	74 E3
St Catherines Grove	43 C1 [3]
St Catherine's Lane West	74 F1
St Catherine's Park	60 E1
St Catherine's Road	60 E1
St Catherine's Terrace	29 A1 [2]
St Catherine's View	20 D4
St Clair's Lawn	67 B3
St Clair's Terrace	67 B3 [3]
St Clare's Avenue	74 F4
St Clement's Road	25 A4 [13]
St Colmcille's Way	55 C2
St Columbanus Avenue	47 B3
St Columbanus Place	47 B3 [1]
St Columbanus Road	47 B3
St Columbas Heights	1 C2
St Columbas Rise	1 C2
St Columba's Road	45 B2
St Columba's Road Lower	25 A4
St Columba's Road Upper	25 A4
St Columcille's Crescent	2 D2
St Columcille's Drive	2 D2
St Columcille's Terrace	67 C2 [18]
St Columcills Park	2 D2
St Conleth's Road	45 C2
St Cronan's Avenue	1 B1
St Cronan's Close	1 C2
St Cronan's Cottages	1 C2
St Cronan's Court	1 B1
St Cronan's Grove	1 C1
St Cronan's Lawn	1 B1
St Cronan's Road	67 C2
St Cronan's View	1 B2
St Cronan's Way	1 C2
St David's	26 D2
St David's Court	26 E4 [5]
St David's Park	26 D2
St David's Terrace (Blackhorse Avenue)	70 D2
St David's Terrace (Glasnevin)	25 A3 [3]
St Davids Wood	26 D2
St Declan's Road	25 C4
St Declan's Terrace	25 C4 [5]
St Domhnach's Well Street	28 D1 [3]
St Dominic's Avenue	55 A1
St Dominic's Court	55 A1 [4]
St Dominic's Road	55 A1
St Dominic's Terrace	55 A1
St Donagh's Crescent	27 B1

STREET NAME	PAGE/GRID REFERENCE
St Donagh's Park	27 B1
St Donagh's Road	27 B1
St Eithne Road	24 F4
St Elizabeth's Court	70 E1
St Enda's Drive	56 F1
St Enda's Park	56 F1
St Enda's Road	46 F2
St Finbarr's Court	24 E4 [2]
St Finbarr's Close	45 B3
St Finbarr's Road	24 E4
St Finian's Grove	34 D2
St Finian's Avenue	34 D2
St Finian's Close	34 D2
St Finian's Crescent	34 D2
St Fintan Road	24 F4
St Fintan Terrace	24 F4
St Fintan's Crescent	29 B3
St Fintan's Grove	29 B3
St Fintan's Park (Dean's Grange)	59 B1
St Fintan's Park (Sutton)	29 B2
St Fintan's Road	29 B3
St Fintan's Terrace	35 C1 [5]
St Fintan's Villas	59 B1
St Francis Square	75 A1
St Gabriel's	59 C3
St Gabriel's Court	27 A4 [2]
St Gabriel's Road	26 F4
St Gall Gardens North	47 B3 [2]
St Gall Gardens South	47 B3 [3]
St Gatien Road	56 F1 [2]
St George's Avenue (Clonliffe Road)	25 B4
St George's Avenue (Killiney)	60 E3
St George's Villas (Inchicore)	36 F3 [18]
St Gerard's Road	45 C2
St Helena's Court	24 E2 [3]
St Helena's Drive	24 E2
St Helena's Road	24 E2
St Helen's	60 E1 [22]
St Helen's Road	48 E2
St Helen's Terrace	73 A2
St Helen's Villas	48 F2 [1]
St Helen's Wood	48 E3
St Helier's Copse	48 F4 [1]
St Ignatius Avenue	71 B1
St Ignatius Road	25 A4
St Ita's Road	25 A3 [6]
St Ives	3 B2
St James Avenue (Clonliffe Road)	72 D1
*St James Place (Sandymount Road)	39 A3
St James Terrace (Sandymount)	39 A3 [23]
St James's Avenue (James's Street)	74 D1
St James's Place (Inchicore)	36 F3 [17]
St James's Road	45 B2
St James's Terrace (Dolphin's Barn)	74 D3
*St James's Walk	74 D2
St Jarlath Road	24 F4
*St John Street	74 F2
St John's Court (Donnycarney)	26 D3
St John's	48 E1
St John's Avenue (Clondalkin)	44 D2
St John's Avenue (The Coombe)	74 F2
St John's Close	44 D2
St John's Cottages	73 C1
St John's Court (Beaumont)	26 D1
St John's Court (Clondalkin)	44 D2
St John's Crescent	44 D2
St John's Drive	44 D2
St John's Gate	44 D2
St John's Green	44 D2
St John's Grove	44 D2
*St John's Lane(off Strand Road)	48 E1
St John's Lawn	44 D2
St John's Park (Dun Laoghaire)	49 C4
St John's Park East	44 D2
St Johns Park West	44 D2
St John's Road	44 D2
St John's Road East	48 E1
St John's Road West (Clondalkin)	44 D2
St John's Road West (Islandbridge)	69 C4
St John's Terrace (Mount Brown)	73 C1
St John's Wood (Clondalkin)	44 D2
St John's Wood (Clontarf)	26 E4 [2]
St John's Wood West	44 D2
St Joseph Street (off Leo Street)	71 B1
St Joseph's	23 C2
St Joseph's Avenue (Ballybough)	25 B4 [2]
St Joseph's Avenue (Drumcondra)	25 A4
St Joseph's Cottages	23 C4 [3]
St Joseph's Court	70 E2
St Joseph's Grove	47 C4 [9]
St Joseph's Mansions	72 D2
St Joseph's Parade	71 A1
St Joseph's Place (Dorset Street Lower)	71 B2
St Joseph's Place (Prussia Street)	70 E2
St Joseph's Road (Aughrim Street)	70 E2
St Joseph's Road (Walkinstown)	45 C2
St Joseph's Square	39 C1 [2]
St Joseph's Terrace (Fairview)	25 C4 [4]
St Joseph's Terrace (North Circular Road)	71 C1
St Joseph's Terrace (off Dolphin's Barn)	74 D3
*St Joseph's Terrace (off Pembroke Street)	39 A3
*St Joseph's Terrace (on Tivoli Road)	50 D4
St Joseph's Villas (Summerhill)	72 D1
St Judes Apts.	31 C3 [3]
St Kevin's Avenue (off Blackpitts)	74 F2
St Kevin's Cottages	75 A3
St Kevin's Court	47 A2
St Kevin's Gardens	47 A2
St Kevin's Parade	75 A3
St Kevin's Park (Rathgar)	47 A2
St Kevin's Park (Stillorgan)	58 D1
St Kevin's Road	75 A4
St Kevin's Square	67 C2
St Kevin's Terrace (Bray)	67 C2 [14]
*St Kevin's Terrace (New Bride Street)	75 A2
St Kevin's Villas	60 D1
St Killian's Avenue	45 B2
St Killians Crescent	67 B4
St Killian's Park	44 E1 [1]
St Laurence Grove	36 E2 [4]
St Laurence Park	48 F4
St Laurence Place (Western Way)	71 A2
St Laurence Place East (Lr Sheriff Street)	72 E3
St Laurence Road	36 E2
St Laurence Terrace (Chapelizod)	36 E2 [9]
St Laurence's Terrace (Bray)	67 C2 [17]
St Lawrence Building Apts.	30 D1 [16]
St Lawrence Glen	36 E3 [3]
St Lawrence O'Toole Avenue	14 F2 [1]
St Lawrence Quay	30 D1 [8]
St Lawrence Road (Clontarf)	26 D4
St Lawrence Road (Howth)	30 D1
St Lawrence's Court	26 D4
St Lawrence's Terrace (Howth)	30 D2 [1]
St Loman's Road	34 F2
St Luke's Avenue	74 F2
St Luke's Court	26 D1 [3]
St Luke's Crescent	47 B2 [3]
St Luke's Gate	74 F2
St Maelruans Park	55 A1 [1]
St Maignenn's Terrace	73 C1
St Malachy's Drive	45 C2
St Malachy's Road	25 A3 [7]
St Margaret's Close	60 E1 [30]
St Margaret's (Booterstown)	48 F3
St Margaret's (North Road)	11 B1
St Margaret's Avenue (Kilbarrack)	27 C2
St Margaret's Avenue (Malahide)	3 B3
St Margaret's Avenue (off Pimlico)	74 F1
*St Margaret's Avenue North (Richmond Lane)	71 C1
St Margaret's Court	11 A4 [1]
St Margaret's Halting Site	11 C4
St Margaret's Park	3 B3
St Margaret's Road (Ballymun)	12 D4
St Margaret's Road (Finglas)	11 A4
St Margaret's Road (Malahide)	3 B3
St Margaret's Road (Poppintree)	11 C4
St Margaret's Terrace	74 E2
St Mark's Avenue	35 A2
St Mark's Crescent	35 A3
St Mark's Drive	35 A3
St Mark's Gardens	35 A3
St Mark's Green	35 A3
St Mark's Grove	35 A3
St Marnock's Avenue	14 F2
St Martin's Drive	46 E2
St Martin's Park	46 E1
St Mary's Ave North (Mountjoy Street)	71 A2
St Mary's Avenue (Rathfarnham)	46 F4
St Mary's Avenue West	36 F3
St Mary's Crescent	45 C1
St Mary's Drive	45 C1
St Mary's Lane	76 E2
St Mary's Mansions	71 C2
St Mary's Park (Crumlin)	45 C1
St Mary's Park (Finglas)	23 C2
St Mary's Park (Leixlip)	20 D4
St Mary's Place (Howth)	30 D2 [4]
St Mary's Place North	71 A2
St Mary's Road (Crumlin)	46 D1
St Mary's Road (Howth)	30 D2 [3]
St Mary's Road North (East Wall)	72 E2
St Mary's Road South (Ballsbridge)	76 E3
St Mary's Street	49 C4 [5]
St Mary's Terrace (Arbour Hill)	70 E3
*St Mary's Terrace (Bath Street)	39 A3
St Mary's Terrace (Boghall Road)	67 C4 [6]
St Marys Terrace (Bray)	68 D2 [20]
St Mary's Terrace (Chapelizod)	36 E2 [5]
St Mary's Terrace (Dunboyne)	7 B2 [1]
St Mary's Terrace (Mountjoy Street)	71 A2
St Mary's Terrace (Rathfarnham)	46 F4 [5]
St Mathias Wood	60 D4
St Mel's Avenue	45 B3
St Michael's Close (off High Street)	75 A1
St Michael's Estate	73 A2
St Michael's Hill (off High Street)	75 A1
St Michael's House	47 C4
St Michael's Place	71 A2
St Michael's Road	25 A3 [8]
St Michael's Terrace (Blackpitts)	74 F2
St Michael's Terrace (Dun Laoghaire)	49 C4 [18]
St Michan's Place (off Chancery Street)	71 A4
St Michan's Street	71 A4
*St Mobhi Avenue (on St. Mobhi Road)	25 A3
St Mobhi Boithirin	25 A3
St Mobhi Drive	25 A3
St Mobhi Grove	25 A3 [10]
St Mobhi Road	25 A3
St Mochtas Avenue	22 D3
St Mochtas Chase	22 D2
St Mochtas Close	22 D3
St Mochtas Drive	22 D3
St Mochtas Green	22 D3
St Mochtas Grove	22 D3
St Mochtas Lawn	22 D2
St Mochtas Road	22 D3
St Mochtas Vale	22 D3
St Mura's Terrace	72 F2
*St Nathy's House	47 B4 [5]
St Nathy's Villas	47 B4 [17]
St Nessan's Apts	30 E2 [3]
St Nessan's Close	30 D2 [9]
St Nessans Court	30 D2 [12]
St Nessan's Terrace	30 D2 [5]
St Nicholas Place	75 A1
St Oliver's Park	35 B3
St Pappin's Green	24 F2
St Pappin's Road	25 A2
St Patrick's Avenue (Clondalkin)	44 D1 [1]
St Patrick's Avenue (Dalkey)	60 F2 [1]
St Patrick's Avenue (Fairview)	72 E1
St Patrick's Avenue (Portmarnock)	14 F2
St Patrick's Close (Kevin Street Upper)	75 A2
St Patrick's Close (Kill O'The Grange)	59 C1 [9]
St Patrick's Cottages	46 F4
St Patrick's Crescent (Kill O'The Grange)	59 C1
St Patrick's Crescent (Rathcoole)	52 E2
St Patrick's Parade	25 A4
St Patrick's Park (Blanchardstown)	22 E2
St Patricks Park (Celbridge)	31 C3
St Patrick's Park (Celbridge)	32 D3
St Patricks Park (Clondalkin)	44 D1
St Patrick's Park (Dunboyne)	7 B2
St Patricks Park (Stepaside)	58 E4
*St Patrick's Place (off Royal Canal Bank)	25 A4
St Patrick's Road (Clondalkin)	35 A4
St Patrick's Road (Dalkey)	60 F2 [8]
St Patrick's Road (Drumcondra)	25 A4
St Patrick's Road (Walkinstown)	45 C2
St Patrick's Square (Bray)	67 C1 [9]
St Patrick's Square (Dalkey)	60 F2 [4]
St Patrick's Terrace (Inchicore)	36 F3 [9]
St Patrick's Terrace (Kill O' the Grange)	59 C1 [7]
St Patrick's Terrace (Nth Brunswick St)	70 F3
*St Patrick's Terrace (off Fitzroy Avenue)	25 B4
*St Patrick's Terrace (Russell Street)	71 C1
St Patrick's Villas	39 A3 [3]
St Paul's Terrace	60 E1 [5]
St Peter's Avenue	70 F1
St Peter's Close	71 A1
St Peter's Crescent	45 C2
St Peter's Drive	45 C2
St Peter's Park	7 B2
St Peter's Road (Bray)	67 B1
St Peter's Road (Phibsborough)	24 F4
St Peter's Road (Walkinstown)	45 C2
St Peter's Square	71 A1
St Peter's Terrace (Bray)	67 B1 [2]
St Peter's Terrace (Dun Laoghaire)	60 E1 [6]
St Peter's Terrace (Howth)	30 D2
St Peter's Terrace (Walkinstown)	45 C2 [1]
St Philomenas	9 C4
St Philomena's Court	9 C4
St Philomena's Park	9 C3
St Philomena's Road	24 F4 [1]
St Raphaels Avenue	31 C4
St Ronan's Avenue	35 A3
St Ronan's Close	35 A3
St Ronan's Crescent	35 A3
St Ronan's Drive	35 A3
St Ronan's Gardens	35 A3
St Ronan's Green	35 A3
St Ronan's Grove	35 A3
St Ronan's Park	35 A3
St Ronan's Way	35 A3
St Stephen's Green East	75 C2
St Stephen's Green North	75 C2
St Stephen's Green South	75 B2
St Stephen's Green West	75 B2
St Sylvester Villas	3 B3
St Teresa's Gardens	74 E2
St Teresa's Place	25 A4 [9]
St Teresa's Road (Crumlin)	46 D2

STREET NAME	PAGE/GRID REFERENCE
St Teresa's Road (Glasnevin)	25 A4 [8]
St Thomas Mead	48 E3
St Thomas Road (Ardee Street)	74 F2
St Thomas's Road (Mount Merrion)	48 E3
St Ultan's Flats	75 B3
St Vincent Street North	71 A1
St Vincent Street South	75 A3
St Vincent Street West	73 A2
St Vincent's Cottages	23 C4 [2]
St Vincent's Court	25 C3 [7]
St Vincent's Park	49 A4
St Werburghs	2 E2
St Wolston's Abbey	32 D4
St. Agnes Terrace	46 D1 [4]
St. Andrews Court	34 D1 [17]
St. Anns Court	71 B2
St. Anthony Crescent	74 D2
St. Anthony's Place	71 B2
St. Audoen's House Flats	70 F4
St. Berach's Place	27 B1 [6]
St. Catheryn's Court	39 B4 [7]
St. Cronan's Cottages	1 C2
St. Cuthbert's Road	43 B1
St. James Court	39 A4 [49]
St. Jame's Wood	73 B2
St. Jame's Wood (Suir Road)	73 B2
St. James's	26 D4
St. James's Court Apts.	74 E1
St. John's Court	25 B1
St. John's Well Way	73 C1
St. Joseph's Court	70 E2
St. Joseph's Place	70 E2
St. Kevins Church Apts.	75 A3
St. Laurence Court	36 E3
*St. Laurence O'Toole Court	72 D3
*St. Mary's Court (on Church Road)	72 F2
St. Michan's House Flats	71 A4
St. Patrick's Court	74 F3
*St. Samson Court	14 D3
St. Samson Square	14 D3
St. Vincent's Court	26 D3
St. Wolstan's Abbey	32 E2
St. James Place	39 A4 [31]
Stable Lane (Harcourt Street)	75 B2
Stable Lane (Leeson St Lr)	75 C2
Stable Lane (Smithfield)	70 F4
Stackstown	61 B1
Stacummy Bridge	32 F4
Staffordstown	5 C2
Staffordstown Little	5 C1
Stamer Street	75 A3
Stanford Green	45 C1
Stanhope Street	70 F3
Stanley Street	70 F3
Stannaway Avenue	46 D1
Stannaway Court	46 D2 [3]
Stannaway Drive	46 E1
Stannaway Road	46 E1
Stapolin	14 F4
Stapolin Avenue	14 F4
Stapolin House	14 F4
Stapolin Lawns	14 F4
Station Close	35 A4
Station Road (Dunboyne)	7 B3
Station Road (Glenageary)	60 E1
Station Road (Killiney)	60 E4
Station Road (Leixlip)	19 C4
*Station Road (off Clover Hill Road)	35 A4
Station Road (Portmarnock)	14 E2
Station Road (Raheny)	27 A2
Station Road (Shankill)	64 E2 [6]
Station Road (Sutton)	29 A1
Station View Apts.	22 E3 [3]
Station Way	14 D4
Stationcourt	22 D3
Stationcourt Hall	22 D3
Stationcourt Park	22 D3
Stationcourt View	22 D3
Stationcourt Way	22 D3
Steelstown	51 C3
Steelstown Interchange (N7 J5)	51 B3
Steeple Gate	39 A3 [46]

STREET NAME	PAGE/GRID REFERENCE
Steeven's Gate Apts.	74 D1
Steeven's Lane	70 D4
Stella Avenue	25 A3
Stella Gardens	39 A3
Stella Maris Apts.	17 C4
Stepaside	58 E4
Stepaside	62 E1
Stepaside Lane	62 E1
Stepaside Park	58 E4
Stepaside Park	62 E1
Stepaside Village	58 E3
Stephen Street Lower	75 B1
Stephen Street Upper	75 B1
Stephen's Lane	76 D2
Stephen's Place	76 D2
Stephen's Road	73 B2
Sterling Square Apts.	8 D3
Stewart Hall	71 A3
Stillorgan	58 F1
Stillorgan Court	58 E1 [2]
Stillorgan Grove	48 F4
Stillorgan Heath	58 E1 [3]
Stillorgan Heath	58 E1
Stillorgan Park	48 F4
Stillorgan Park	49 A4
Stillorgan Park Avenue	58 F1
Stillorgan Road (Donnybrook)	48 D1
Stillorgan Road (Foxrock)	59 A2
Stillorgan Road (Mount Merrion)	48 E3
Stillorgan Road (Stillorgan)	58 F1
Stillorgan Wood	58 E1
Stirling Park	47 A3 [2]
Stirrup Lane (off Church Street)	70 F3
Stockhole	13 A2
Stockhole Lane	12 F1
Stocking Avenue	56 D2
Stocking Lane	56 D3
Stocking Wood	56 D3
Stocking Wood Copse	56 D3
Stocking Wood Drive	56 D3
Stocking Wood Green	56 D3
Stocking Wood Hall	56 D3
Stocking Wood Manor	56 D3
Stocking Wood Rise	56 D3
Stocking Wood Way	56 D3
Stockton Court	23 A3
Stockton Drive	23 A3
Stockton Green	23 A3
Stockton Grove	23 A3
Stockton Lawn	23 A3
Stockton Park	23 A3
Stokes Place	75 B2
Stone Mason's Green	57 A2
Stone Mews	47 A1 [8]
Stonebridge	21 B2
Stonebridge Avenue	21 B2
Stonebridge Close	64 E3 [2]
Stonebridge Drive	21 B2
Stonebridge Lane	64 D2 [1]
Stonebridge Road (Clonsilla)	21 B2
Stonebridge Road (Shankill)	64 D2
Stonemasons Green	57 A2 [5]
Stonemasons Green	57 A2
Stonemasons Way	57 A2
Stonepark Abbey	46 F4
Stonepark Court	46 F4
Stonepark Orchard	46 F4 [17]
Stoneview Place	50 D4 [13]
Stoney Park	52 F2
Stoney Road (Dundrum)	47 C4
Stoney Road (East Wall)	72 E2
Stoneybatter	70 E3
Stoneylea Terrace	67 C3 [10]
Store Street	71 C3
Stormanstown Road	25 A2
Stradbrook Close	59 B1
Stradbrook Gardens	49 B4 [8]
Stradbrook Grove	49 B4
Stradbrook Hall	49 B4 [20]
Stradbrook Hill	59 B1 [4]
Stradbrook Lawn	49 B4
Stradbrook Park	49 B4
Stradbrook Road	49 B4
Straffan Avenue	17 C4

STREET NAME	PAGE/GRID REFERENCE
Straffan Close	17 C4
Straffan Court	17 C4
Straffan Crescent	17 C4
Straffan Drive	17 C4
Straffan Green	17 C4
Straffan Grove	17 C4
Straffan Lawn	17 C4
Straffan Park	17 C4
Straffan Place	17 C4
Straffan Road	17 C4
Straffan Way	17 C4
Straffan Wood	17 C4
Straleek	41 B1
Stralem Court	21 B1
Stralem Crescent	21 B1
Stralem Grove	21 B1
Stralem Mews	21 B1
Stralem Terrace	21 B1
Strand Court	3 B2 [12]
Strand Lane	48 E1 [3]
Strand Road (Baldoyle)	15 A4
Strand Road (Ballybrack)	64 E1
Strand Road (Bray)	67 C2
Strand Road (Merrion)	48 E1
Strand Road (Portmarnock)	4 D4
Strand Road (Portmarnock)	14 F2
Strand Road (Portmarnock)	15 A1
Strand Road (Sandymount)	39 B4
Strand Road (Sutton)	29 B2
Strand Street (Malahide)	3 B2
Strand Street (Ringsend)	39 A3
Strand Street Great	71 A4
Strand Street Little	71 A4
Strand Terrace	47 B2 [2]
Strandmill Avenue	14 F2
Strandmill Park	15 A2
Strandmill Road	15 A2
Strandville Avenue (North Strand)	72 E1
Strandville Avenue East (Clontarf)	26 D4
Strandville House	26 D4 [4]
Strandville Place	72 E1
Strangford Drive	42 D4
Strangford Gardens	72 E2
Strangford Road	72 E2
Strasbur Terrace	39 A3 [21]
Stratford	47 A3 [21]
Strathmore Road	60 E4
Streamstown Lane	2 F4
Streamville Court	64 E1 [10]
Streamville Road	27 A1
Strong's Court	71 B2
Suffolk Street	75 B1
Sugarloaf Crescent	67 C3
Sugarloaf Terrace	67 C3 [21]
Suir Road	73 B2
Sullivan Street	69 C3
Summer Arch	71 C1
Summer Arch (off Summer Street North)	71 C1
Summer Place	71 C2
*Summer Row (off Summer Street North)	71 C1
Summer Street North	71 C2
Summer Street South	74 E1
Summerfield (Blanchardstown)	22 E2
Summerfield (Ringsend)	39 A3 [33]
Summerfield (Tallaght)	55 A2 [1]
Summerfield Avenue	22 E2
Summerfield Close	22 E2
Summerfield Close	60 F2 [10]
Summerfield Green	22 E2
Summerfield Lawns	22 E2
Summerfield Meadows	22 E2
Summerfield Rise	22 E2
Summerhill	71 C2
Summerhill Court	50 E4 [3]
Summerhill Parade (Dun Laoghaire)	50 D4 [6]
Summerhill Parade (Summerhill)	72 D1
Summerhill Place	71 C2
Summerhill Road (Dún Laoghaire)	50 D4
Summerhill Road (Dunboyne)	7 A2

STREET NAME	PAGE/GRID REFERENCE
Summerseat	8 D4
Summerseat Cottage	8 D4
Summerseat Court	8 D4
Summerville	39 B1
Summerville Park	47 A1
*Summerville Terrace (on Dalkey Ave)	60 F2
Sunbury Court	47 A2
Sunbury Gardens	47 A2
Suncroft Avenue	14 F2 [3]
Suncroft Drive	54 D2
Suncroft Park	54 D2
Sundale Avenue	54 D2
Sundale Close	54 D2
Sundale Crescent	54 D1
Sundale Green	54 D1
Sundale Grove	54 D2
Sundale Heights	54 D1
Sundale Lawn	54 D1
Sundale Meadows	54 D1
Sundale Parade	54 D1
Sundale Park	54 D2
Sundale Road	54 D2
Sundale Villas	54 D1
Sundale Walk	54 D1
Sundrive Park	46 E1
Sundrive Road	46 E1
Sunnybank Apts.	69 B4
Sunnybank Court	47 C4 [1]
Sunnybank Court	67 B1 [8]
Sunnyside	62 F3
Sunville Green	46 D1 [1]
Susan Terrace	74 F2
Susanville Road	25 B4
Sussex Road	76 D3
Sussex Street	50 D4 [16]
Sussex Terrace	76 D3
Sutton	29 A1
Sutton Castle Apts.	29 B3
Sutton Court	28 D1 [1]
Sutton Downs	28 D1
Sutton Grove	28 D1
Sutton Lane	63 A3
Sutton Lawns	28 D1
Sutton Park	28 D1
Sutton Road	67 B2 [9]
Sutton Villas	67 B2 [17]
Swallowbrook	8 F4
Swallowbrook Crescent	8 F4
Swallowbrook Park	8 F4
Swallowbrook View	8 F4
Swan Alley	74 F1
Swan Grove	75 C4
Swan Hall (Belgard Square)	54 F1 [10]
Swan Place	76 D4
Swan Yard (off Harry Street)	75 B1
Swanbrook	67 C4
Swan's Nest Avenue	27 B1
Swan's Nest Court	27 B1 [2]
Swan's Nest Road	27 B1
Swanville Place	47 A1 [4]
Swanward Court	74 E4
Sweeney's Terrace	74 F2
Sweetbriar Lane	58 D1
Sweetman's Avenue	49 A3 [21]
Sweetman's Avenue	49 A3
Sweetmount Avenue	47 B4
Sweetmount Drive	57 B1
Sweetmount House	47 B4 [18]
Sweetmount Park	47 B4
Sweetmount Park	57 B1
Swift Hall	59 B4
Swiftbrook (Tallaght)	54 D1
Swiftbrook Avenue	54 D1
Swiftbrook Close	54 D1
Swiftbrook Drive	54 D1
Swiftbrook Park	54 D1
Swift's Alley	74 F1
Swift's Grove	13 A3
Swift's Row (off Ormond Quay)	71 A4
Swiftwood	53 B1
Swilly Road	24 E4
Swords	2 D1
Swords Manor Avenue	1 B2
Swords Manor Court	1 B1

STREET NAME	PAGE/GRID REFERENCE	STREET NAME	PAGE/GRID REFERENCE	STREET NAME	PAGE/GRID REFERENCE	STREET NAME	PAGE/GRID REFERENCE
Swords Manor Crescent	1 B1	Talbot Memorial Bridge	71 C4	Temple Street West	70 D3	The Beeches (Donaghmede)	27 A1
Swords Manor Drive	1 B1	Talbot Park	2 F3	Temple Terrace	60 F2 [16]	The Beeches (Kilmacud)	58 D1
Swords Manor Grove	1 B2	Talbot Place	71 C3	Temple Villas (Arbour Hill)	70 D3	The Beeches (Monkstown)	49 B4 [21]
Swords Manor View	1 B1	Talbot Road (Killiney)	60 E3 [3]	*Temple Villas	47 B1	The Beeches (Willbrook)	56 F1 [8]
Swords Manor Way	1 B1	Talbot Road (Swords)	2 F3	(on Palmerston Road)		The Belfry (Citywest Road)	53 C2
Swords Road (Collinstown)	12 F2	Talbot Street	71 C3	Templemore Avenue	47 A2	The Belfry (Inchicore)	73 A1
Swords Road (Malahide)	3 A3	Tallaght	55 A1	Templeogue	46 D4	The Belfry (Kilbarrack)	27 B1
Swords Road (Santry)	12 F4	Tallaght Bypass	54 F1	Templeogue Lodge	46 D4	The Belfry Apts.	25 C2 [11]
Swords Road (Santry)	25 B1	Tallaght Bypass	55 A1	Templeogue Road	46 E3	The Birch	57 C1 [12]
Swords Street	70 D3	Tallaght Road	45 C4	Templeogue Wood	46 D4	The Birches	59 A3
Sybil Hill Avenue	26 F3	Tallaght Road	55 B1	Templeroan	56 D1	The Birches Apts.	23 C3 [3]
Sybil Hill Road	26 F3	Tallow Hall (Belgard Square)	54 F1 [7]	Templeroan Avenue	56 D1	The Black Avenue	33 B1
Sycamore Avenue (Cabinteely)	59 B3	Tamarisk Avenue	45 A3	Templeroan Close	56 E1	The Blackthorn	57 C1 [14]
Sycamore Avenue (Castleknock)	22 E3	Tamarisk Close	45 A3	Templeroan Court	56 D1	The Bramblings	26 E3
Sycamore Avenue (Tallaght)	45 A3	Tamarisk Court	45 A3	Templeroan Crescent	56 D1	The Briars	35 C1
Sycamore Close (Cornelscourt)	59 B3	Tamarisk Dale	45 A3	Templeroan Downs	56 E1	The Bridge	64 E3
Sycamore Close (Kilnamanagh)	44 F3	Tamarisk Drive	45 A3	Templeroan Drive	56 D1	The Brokerage Apts.	71 C4
Sycamore Court	59 C2 [3]	Tamarisk Grove	45 A3	Templeroan Green	56 D2	The Burgage	60 F2
Sycamore Crescent (Cabinteely)	59 B3	Tamarisk Heights	45 A3	Templeroan Grove	56 D1	The Castlelands	46 F4 [11]
Sycamore Crescent	48 E4	Tamarisk Lawn	45 A3	Templeroan Lodge	56 D2	The Cedars (Abberley)	64 E1 [21]
(Mount Merrion)		Tamarisk Park	45 A3	Templeroan Meadows	56 E1	The Cedars (Monkstown)	49 B4 [5]
Sycamore Drive (Cabinteely)	59 B3	Tamarisk View	45 A3	Templeroan Mews	56 D1	The Chandler Apts.	23 B3 [2]
Sycamore Drive (Castleknock)	22 E3	Tamarisk Walk	45 A3	Templeroan Park	56 D1	The Charter	12 D4
Sycamore Drive (Dundrum)	57 B1 [4]	Tamarisk Way	45 A3	Templeroan View	56 D1	The Chase	58 F2
Sycamore Drive (Tallaght)	45 A3	Tandys Lane	33 C3	Templeroan Way	56 D1	The Cherries	57 A2 [2]
Sycamore Green (Cabinteely)	59 B3	Tandys Lane	34 D3	Templeview Avenue	14 D4	The Claremont Apts.	12 D4
Sycamore Grove (Cabinteely)	59 B4	Taney Avenue	47 C4	Templeview Close	14 D4	The Cloisters (Grace Park Road)	25 B3 [5]
Sycamore Grove (Foxrock)	59 A2 [7]	Taney Court	47 C4	Templeview Copse	14 D4	The Cloisters	46 F2
Sycamore House	76 D3	Taney Crescent	47 C4	Templeview Court	14 D4	(Mount Tallant Avenue)	
Sycamore House (Shankill)	64 E2 [11]	Taney Drive	47 C4	Templeview Crescent	14 D4	The Close (Ballinteer)	57 C2
Sycamore House (Sutton)	28 D1	Taney Grove	47 C4	Templeview Downs	14 D4	The Close (Ballyboden)	56 E2
Sycamore House (Swords)	1 Inset	Taney Lawn	47 C4	Templeview Drive	14 D4	The Close (Beaumont)	25 C1
Sycamore Lawn (Cabinteely)	59 B3	Taney Manor	47 C4	Templeview Green	14 D4	The Close (Celbridge)	31 C3
Sycamore Lawn (Castleknock)	22 E3	Taney Park	47 C4	Templeview Grove	14 D4	The Close (Dunboyne Castle)	7 A3
Sycamore Park (Castleknock)	22 E3	Taney Rise	47 C4	Templeview Lawn	14 D4	The Close (Grange Manor)	34 D3
Sycamore Park (Finglas)	24 E1	Taney Road	47 C4	Templeview Park	14 D4	The Close (Lutterell Hall)	7 B2
Sycamore Park (Tallaght)	45 A3	Tangier Lane	75 B1	Templeview Place	14 D4	The Close (Manorfields)	21 B1
Sycamore Road (Dundrum)	57 B1	(off Grafton Street)		Templeview Rise	14 D4	The Close (Mount Merrion)	48 E3
Sycamore Road (Finglas)	24 E1	Tara Crescent	55 B2 [3]	Templeview Row	14 D4	The Close (Oldtown Mill)	31 C3 [2]
Sycamore Road (Fox & Geese)	45 A1	Tara Hill Crescent	46 F4	Templeview Square	14 D4	The Close (Plunkett Hall)	7 A2
Sycamore Road	48 E4	Tara Hill Grove	46 F4 [2]	Templeview Vale	14 D4 [1]	The Close (Tallaght)	44 F3
(Mount Merrion)		Tara Hill Road	46 F4	Templeview View	14 D4	The Close (Tallaght)	55 A2 [2]
Sycamore Street	71 B4	Tara Lawn	27 A1	Templeview Walk	14 D4	The Close (Temple Manor)	31 C4
Sycamore View	22 E3	Tara Street	71 C4	Templeview Way	14 D4	The Close (Templeogue)	46 D3
Sycamore Walk	59 B4	Tassagard Greens	53 B2	Templeville Avenue	46 D3	The Coachworks	75 A3
Sydenham	50 D4 [23]	Tassagart Drive	53 A2	Templeville Drive	46 D3	The Coombe	74 F1
Sydenham Court	39 A4 [53]	Tay Lane	52 E2	Templeville Park	46 E3 [1]	The Coppice (Palmerstown)	35 C1
Sydenham Mews	68 D3	Taylors Court	56 E1	Templeville Road	46 D3	The Coppins (Celbridge)	32 D3
*Sydenham Place	47 C4	Taylor's Hill	57 A3	Tenterfields	74 E2	The Coppins (Foxrock)	59 A3
(on Kilmacud Rd Upr)		Taylor's Lane (Ballyboden)	56 E1	Terenure	46 F2	The Copse	33 B2 [1]
Sydenham Road (Ballsbridge)	39 A4 [4]	Taylor's Lane (Pimlico)	74 F1	Terenure Park	46 F2	The Copse (Ballinteer)	57 B2 [3]
Sydenham Road (Dundrum)	47 C4	Temple Bar	71 B4	Terenure Place	46 F2 [3]	The Copse (Drumcondra)	25 B3
Sydenham Villas (Bray)	68 D3 [6]	Temple Buildings	71 A2	Terenure Road East	46 F2	The Court (Ballinteer)	57 B2
Sydenham Villas (Dundrum)	57 C1	Temple Cottages	71 A2	Terenure Road North	46 F2	The Court (Ballybrack)	60 E4
Sydney Avenue	49 A3	Temple Court (Arbour Hill)	70 D3	Terenure Road West	46 E2	The Court (Carrickmines)	59 B4
Sydney Parade Avenue	48 E1	Temple Court (Blackrock)	49 A3 [25]	Terminal Road North	39 C2	The Court (Celbridge)	31 C3
Sydney Terrace	49 A3	Temple Court (Off Hogan Place)	76 E1	Terminal Road South	39 C2	The Court (Clontarf)	26 D4
Sylvan Avenue	45 A3	Temple Court Apts.	12 E4	Termon Court	11 C4 [1]	The Court (Donnybrook)	47 C2
Sylvan Close	44 F3	Temple Crescent	49 B4	Terrace Place (off Bella St)	71 C2	The Court (Dunboyne Castle)	7 B3
Sylvan Drive	44 F3	Temple Gardens (Milltown)	47 B2	Tetrarch Grove	7 C1	The Court (Glenamuck Road)	63 A1
Symphony House	75 C3	Temple Gardens (Santry)	12 E4	Texas Lane	3 A2	The Court (Larch Hill)	12 F4
Synge House	47 A3	Temple Grove	32 D3	The Alders	49 B4 [6]	The Court (Lutterell Hall)	7 B2
Synge Lane	75 A3	Temple Hill	49 B4	The Anchora Apts.	3 B2 [10]	The Court (Mulhuddart)	9 A4
Synge Place	75 B3	*Temple Hill	46 E2	The Anchorage	4 D3	The Court (Oldtown Mill)	31 C3
Synge Street	75 B3	(on Terenure Road West)		The Anchorage	49 C4 [33]	The Court (Plunkett Hall)	7 A2
Synge Way	35 C4	Temple Lane North	71 B2	The Appian Way	76 D4	The Court (Raheny)	27 B3 [2]
Synnott Place	71 B1	Temple Lane South	71 B4	The Arches	17 C3	The Court (Sadleir Hall)	7 A2
Synnott Row	71 B1	Temple Manor (Celbridge)	31 C4	The Avenue (Ballinteer)	57 C2	The Court (Shankill)	64 E3
Synnott Row	71 B1	Temple Manor (Dunboyne)	7 B2	The Avenue (Ballyboden)	56 E2	The Court (Sutton)	29 A1
Synnott Terrace	49 C4 [16]	Temple Manor (Greenhills)	45 C3	The Avenue (Carrickmines)	63 A1	The Court (Tallaght)	44 F3
Synod Hall	75 A1	Temple Manor Avenue	45 C3	The Avenue (Celbridge)	32 D3	The Court (Tallaght)	44 F3
		Temple Manor Close	45 C3	The Avenue (Dunboyne Castle)	7 B3	The Court (Temple Manor)	31 C4
T		Temple Manor Court	45 C3	The Avenue (Grange Manor)	34 D3	The Court (Templeogue)	46 D3
		Temple Manor Drive	45 C3	The Avenue (Louisa Valley)	19 C4	The Court (Whitehall)	25 C2
Taaffe's Place	72 E1	Temple Manor Grove	45 C3	The Avenue (Lutterell Hall)	7 B2	The Courthouse	52 F2
Tailors Court	75 A1	Temple Manor Way	45 C3	The Avenue (Manorfields)	21 B1	The Courtyard	71 B2
Tailor's Hall	75 A1	Temple Park	47 B2	The Avenue (Mulhuddart)	9 A4	The Courtyard	76 D1
Talbot	2 F3	Temple Park Apts.	12 E4	The Avenue (Plunkett Hall)	7 A2	The Courtyard (Bray)	67 B2
Talbot Avenue	2 F3	Temple Park Avenue	49 B4	The Avenue	32 D4	The Courtyard (Celbridge)	31 C4
Talbot Court (Blanchardstown)	22 F2	Temple Place	71 B2	(St Wolston's Abbey)		The Courtyard (Clonsilla)	22 D3
Talbot Court (Malahide)	3 A2	Temple Place	75 C4	The Avenue (Tallaght)	44 F3	The Courtyard (Leopardstown)	58 E2
Talbot Downs	22 F2	Temple Road (Blackrock)	49 A3	The Avenue (Templeogue)	46 D3	The Courtyard (Rathfarnham)	46 F4
Talbot Hall (Swords) (Swords)	1 Inset	Temple Road (Rathgar)	47 B2	The Bawn	3 B3	The Courtyard (Templelogue)	46 E3
Talbot Lane (Killiney)	60 E3 [4]	Temple Square	47 B2 [5]	The Bawn Grove	3 B3	The Coutryard (Foxrock)	59 A2 [10]
Talbot Lane (Talbot Street)	71 C3	Temple Street North	71 B2	The Beeches (Abberley)	64 E1 [22]	The Cove	3 A2
Talbot Lodge	48 F4						

STREET NAME	PAGE/GRID REFERENCE
The Covert	35 C1 [1]
The Crescent (Abbeyfarm)	31 C4
The Crescent (Ballinteer)	57 B2 [1]
The Crescent (Ballyboden)	56 E2
The Crescent (Carrickmines)	63 A1
The Crescent (Castleknock)	22 F3 [1]
The Crescent (Donnybrook)	47 C1 [4]
The Crescent (Dunboyne Castle)	7 B3
The Crescent (Grange Manor)	34 D3
The Crescent (Larch Hill)	12 F4
The Crescent (Lucan)	33 C2
The Crescent (Lutterell Hall)	7 A2
The Crescent (Malahide)	4 D3
The Crescent (Mulhuddart)	9 A4
The Crescent (off Beaumont Rd)	25 C2 [8]
The Crescent (Oldtown Mill)	31 C3
The Crescent (Plunkett Hall)	7 A2
The Crescent (Ranelagh)	47 B1
The Crescent (St Wolston's Abbey)	32 D4
The Crescent (Sutton)	29 A1
The Crescent (Swords) (Swords)	2 D2 [4]
The Crescent (Tallaght)	44 E4
The Crescent (Tallaght)	44 F3
The Crescent (Tallaght)	55 A1
The Crescent (Temple Manor)	31 C4
The Crescent (Whitehall)	25 B3
The Croft	32 D2
The Dale	7 B2
The Dale (Ballinteer)	57 B2 [4]
The Dale (Belgard)	44 F4
The Dale (Bray)	67 B2
The Dale (Carrickmines)	63 A1
The Dale (Celbridge)	31 C3
The Dale (Kilnamanagh)	44 F3
The Dale (Manorfields)	21 B1
The Deanery	31 C3 [1]
The Dell	57 A2
The Dingle	35 B2
The Distillery Building Apts.	25 B4 [17]
The Downs (Dunboyne Castle)	7 A3
The Downs (St Wolston's Abbey)	32 D4
The Drive (Abbeyfarm)	31 C4
The Drive (Ballinteer)	57 B2
The Drive (Ballyboden)	56 E1
The Drive (Dunboyne Castle)	7 B3
The Drive (Grange Manor)	34 D3
The Drive (Kilnamanagh)	44 F3
The Drive (Lutterell Hall)	7 B2
The Drive (Manorfields)	21 B1
The Drive (Mulhuddart)	9 A4
The Drive (Oldtown Mill)	31 C3
The Drive (Sadlier Hall)	7 A2
The Drive (Tallaght)	55 A1
The Drive (Temple Manor)	31 C4
The Drive (Woodbrook Glen)	67 C1
The Drive Apts.	56 E1
The Dunes	15 A1
The Elm (Rockfield)	57 C1
The Elms	64 E4
The Elms (Celbridge)	32 D2
The Elms (Dunboyne)	7 B2
The Elms (Elm Park)	48 E2
The Elms (Loughlinstown)	64 E1 [4]
The Elms Apts.	23 C3 [2]
The Fairways (Portmarnock)	14 E2
The Fairways (Woodbrook Glen)	67 C1
The Fairways Apts.	8 D3
The Falls	46 F3 [5]
The Forum	58 E2
The Fosters	48 E3
The Gables (Dundrum)	57 B1
The Gables (Foxrock)	59 A3 [5]
The Gables (Grange View Road)	43 B1
The Gables (Nutgrove)	57 A1
The Gables (Rathgar)	47 A2
The Gallan	60 D3
The Gallops	58 E3
The Gardens	63 A1
The Garth (Cookstown)	44 E4
The Garth (Kingswood Heights)	44 F3
The Gasworks	76 F1
The Gate	44 D1

STREET NAME	PAGE/GRID REFERENCE
The Gate Lodge	30 E3
The Glade (Ballinteer)	57 B2
The Glade (Kingswood Heights)	44 F3
The Glade (Oldtown Mill)	31 C3
The Glade (Palmerstown)	35 B2
The Glade (St Wolston's Abbey)	32 D4
The Glebe	34 E2
The Glen	58 D3
The Glen (Ballinteer)	57 B2
The Glen (Ballyboden)	56 E1
The Glen (Glenageary Road)	60 D1 [14]
The Glen (Louisa Valley)	19 C4
The Glen (Raheny)	27 B3
The Glens	63 A1
The Golf Links	3 C3
The Goulding Apts.	12 D4
The Grainhouse	74 E2
*The Granary	74 E1
The Grange (Deans Grange)	59 B1
The Grange (Malahide)	3 B4
The Grange (Terenure)	46 F2
The Green (Ballinteer)	57 B2
The Green (Ballyboden)	56 E1
The Green (Beaumont)	25 C1
The Green (Carrickmines)	63 A1
The Green (Celbridge)	31 C3
The Green (Dunboyne Castle)	7 B3
The Green (Larch Hill)	12 F4
The Green (Lutterell Hall)	7 B2
The Green (Malahide)	3 B2
The Green (Manorfields)	21 B1
The Green (Moyglare Abbey)	17 B2
The Green (Mulhuddart)	9 A4
The Green (Oldtown Mill)	31 C3
The Green (Tallaght)	44 F3
The Green (Templeogue)	46 D3
The Green (Woodbrook Glen)	67 C1
The Green Road	60 Inset
The Greenlands	46 F4
The Grove (Abbeyfarm)	31 C4
The Grove (Ballinteer)	57 B2
The Grove (Dunboyne Castle)	7 A3
The Grove (Dundrum)	57 A1
The Grove (Grange Manor)	34 D3
The Grove (Louisa Valley)	19 C4
The Grove (Lutterell Hall)	7 B2
The Grove (Plunkett Hall)	7 A2
The Grove (Raheny)	27 B3 [1]
The Grove (Sadlier Hall)	7 A2
The Grove (St Wolston's Abbey)	32 D4
The Grove (Tallaght)	44 E4
The Grove (Tallaght)	44 F3
The Grove (Tallaght)	55 A1
The Grove (Whitehall)	25 B3
The Grove (Woodbrook Glen)	67 C1
The Haggard (Howth)	30 D2 [6]
The Hall	46 F2
The Hampton	12 D4
The Haven (Glasnevin)	25 A3 [17]
The Haven (Malahide)	3 B2
The Hawthorns (Abberley)	64 E1 [20]
The Heath (Tallaght)	44 F4
The Heath (Templeogue)	46 D3
The Heath (The Heath)	57 B2
The Hedgerows	59 A3
The Heights (Ballinteer)	57 B2
The Heights (Dunboyne Castle)	7 B3
The Hill	58 D3
The Hill (Ballinteer)	57 C2
The Hill (Malahide)	3 B3
The Hill (Monkstown)	49 C4
The Hill (Mulhuddart)	9 A4
The Hill (Stillorgan)	58 F1
The Hole in the Wall Rd	14 E4
The Hollows	34 D2 [3]
The Holly (Rockfield)	57 C1
The Island	36 E2
The Killigeen	52 D4
The Kilmore Apts	12 D4
The Kilns	14 F2
The Lakelands	46 F4 [8]
The Larches (Abberley)	64 E1 [16]
The Laurels	47 B4
The Laurels (Bluebell)	36 E4 [3]
The Laurels (Dollymount)	26 F4

STREET NAME	PAGE/GRID REFERENCE
The Laurels (Rathfarnham)	46 F4 [13]
The Laurels (Tallaght)	55 A1 [10]
The Laurels (Terenure)	46 F2
The Lawn (Ballinteer)	57 B2
The Lawn (Ballyboden)	56 E2
The Lawn (Finglas)	24 E2
The Lawn (Kinsaley)	2 E3
The Lawn (Moyglare Abbey)	17 B2
The Lawn (Oldtown Mill)	31 C3
The Lawn (Plunkett Hall)	7 A2
The Lawn (Tallaght)	44 E4
The Lawn(Woodbrook Glen)	67 C1
The Lawns (Abbeyfarm)	31 C4
The Lawns (Temple Manor)	31 C4
The Lime (Rockfield)	57 C1
The Linden	57 C1 [13]
The Links	14 F2
The Little Grove	32 D4
The Lodge (Balgriffen)	14 E3
The Lodge (Clontarf)	26 D4
The Lodge (Glenageary)	60 D1
The Lodge Apts.	23 C3 [6]
The Maieston	12 D4
The Mall (Baldoyle)	15 A4 [4]
The Mall (Leixlip)	33 A1
The Mall (Lucan)	34 D1
The Mall (Malahide)	3 B2
The Malt House	74 E2
The Maltings	67 C2
The Maltings Apts.	70 E4
The Manor (Kimmage)	46 D2 [7]
The Manor (Templeogue)	46 D4
The Maples (Bird Avenue)	47 C3
The Maples (Monkstown)	49 B4 [4]
The Mayne	8 E2
The Meadow	57 B2
The Meadows (Dunboyne)	7 B2
The Meadows (Killester)	26 F3
The Meadows (Newtownpark Ave)	59 A1
The Meadows (Oldtown Mill)	31 C3
The Meadows East	44 F4
The Meadows West	44 E4
The Mews	71 B2
The Mews (Clontarf)	26 E4
The Mews (Dollymount)	27 A4 [5]
The Mews (Killester)	26 E3
The Mews (Rathmines)	47 A1 [19]
The Mews (Templeogue)	46 E3
The Mews Apts.	23 C3 [5]
The Mill	74 E2
The Mill Pond Apts.	44 D1 [4]
The Mills	22 F2
The Moorings	75 B4
The Moorings	39 A3 [38]
The Moorings (Chapelizod)	36 E2
The Moorings (Malahide)	3 C3
The Moorings Apts.	76 E3
The New Road	23 B1
The Northumberlands	76 E2
The Nurseries (Ballybrack)	60 E4 [4]
The Nurseries (Mulhuddart)	9 B4
The Nurseries (Oldcourt)	67 B3
The Nurseries (Swords)	1 C3
The Oaks (Rockfield)	57 C1
The Oaks (Abberley)	64 E1 [17]
The Oaks (Ballinteer)	57 B2
The Oaks (Belgard)	44 E4
The Oaks (Celbridge)	32 D3
The Oaks (Churchtown)	47 B4
The Oaks (Dollymount)	27 A4
The Oaks (Hollystown)	9 C1
The Oaks (Loughlinstown)	64 D1 [1]
The Oaks (Swords)	1 B3
*The Observatory (Windmill Lane)	72 D4
The Old Forge	34 D3
The Old Presbytery	39 A3 [34]
The Orchard	14 D4
The Orchard	49 B3 [5]
The Orchard (Carpenterstown)	22 D3 [1]
The Orchard (Deans Grange)	59 A1
The Orchard (Killester)	26 E3
The Orchard (Kimmage)	46 E2
The Orchard (Lucan)	34 D1 [14]

STREET NAME	PAGE/GRID REFERENCE
The Orchard (Oldtown Mill)	31 C3
The Orchard (Palmerston)	35 B1
The Orchard Apts.	35 B3
The Oval	35 C2
The Paddock (Ashtown)	23 C4
The Paddock (Moyglare Abbey)	17 B2
The Paddock (Oldtown Mill)	31 C2
The Paddock's (Clontarf)	26 E4 [6]
The Paddocks (Dalkey)	60 F1 [3]
The Paddocks (Dunboyne)	7 B2
The Paddocks (Kilmainham)	73 B2
The Paddocks (Swords)	2 D2
The Palms	48 D3
The Park	58 D3
The Park (Abbeyfarm)	31 C4
The Park (Beaumont)	25 C1
The Park (Celbridge)	31 C3
The Park (Dunboyne Castle)	7 B3
The Park (Grange Manor)	34 D3
The Park (Larch Hill)	12 F4
The Park (Louisa Valley)	19 C4
The Park (Oldtown Mill)	31 C3
The Park (Plunkett Hall)	7 A2
The Park (Tallaght)	44 F3
The Park (Tallaght)	55 A2
The Park (Templeogue)	46 D3
The Park Apts.	75 B4
The Park Lands	46 F4 [7]
The Pines (Ballinteer)	57 B2 [1]
The Pines (Castleknock)	23 A3
The Pines (Killester)	26 E3
The Pines (Kilmacud)	58 D1 [3]
The Pines (Oldcourt)	67 B3
The Place (Carrickmines)	63 A1
The Place (Dunboyne Castle)	7 B3
The Plantation	76 D2
The Plaza Apts.	9 B2
The Poplars	49 B4 [7]
The Priory (Cabra)	24 D4
The Priory (Grange Road)	56 F1
The Priory (Malahide)	3 B2 [4]
The Quarry	4 D2 [4]
The Ramparts	63 C1
The Rectory	27 A2
The Rectory	58 D4
The Rise (Ballinteer)	57 B2
The Rise (Ballyboden)	56 E2
The Rise (Carrickmines)	63 A1
The Rise (Dalkey)	60 E2
The Rise (Glasnevin)	25 A2
The Rise (Malahide)	3 B3
The Rise (Manorfields)	21 B1
The Rise (Mount Merrion)	48 E4
The Rise (Newcastle)	42 D4
The Rise (Tallaght)	44 E4
The Rise (Tallaght)	44 F3
The Road (Manorfields)	21 B1
The Rookery	56 D2
The Rose	9 B2
The Rowan (Rockfield)	57 C1
The Rowans (Abberley)	64 E1 [18]
The Sand Holes	22 F4 [1]
The Scalp	63 A4
The Slopes	49 C4
The Spinnaker	4 D3
The Spruce	9 B2
The Square (Greenogue Ind Est)	42 E4
The Square (Irishtown)	39 A3 [5]
The Square (Larch Hill)	12 F4
The Square (Lucan)	34 D1 [5]
The Square (Tallaght)	54 F1
The Stables	48 E3 [1]
The Stables Apts.	23 C3 [4]
The Steeple (Moyglare Abbey)	17 B2
The Steeples	36 E3
The Stiles Road	26 E4
The Summit (Howth)	30 E3
The Sweepstakes	39 A4 [22]
The Sycamore (Rockfield)	57 C1
The Sycamores	64 E1 [3]
The Tallow Apts.	23 C3 [7]
The Terrace	63 A1
The Thatch Road	25 C2
The Thicket	59 A3
The Tower (Smithfield)	70 F4

STREET NAME	PAGE/GRID REFERENCE
The Turnpike	12 D4
The Vale	35 C1
The View (Ballinteer)	57 B2
The View (Carrickmines)	63 A1 [1]
The View (Celbridge)	31 C3
The View (Dunboyne Castle)	7 A3
The View (Larch Hill)	12 F4
The View (Manorfields)	21 B1
The View (Oldtown Mill)	31 C3
The View (St Wolston's Abbey)	32 D4
The View (Tallaght)	44 F3
The View (Tallaght)	55 B1
The Village (Clonsilla)	21 C3
The Village (Drumcondra)	25 B3 [2]
The Village (Raheny)	27 B3
The Village Centre	34 D1 [12]
The Village Court	34 D1 [13]
The Village Gate	60 F2
The Walk (Ballinteer)	57 B2
The Walk (Carrickmines)	63 A1
The Walk (Dunboyne Castle)	7 B3
The Walk (Louisa Valley)	19 C4
The Walk (Manorfields)	21 B1
The Walk (Oldtown Mill)	31 C3
The Walk (Tallaght)	55 A1
The Walk (Templeogue)	46 D3
The Walled Gardens	32 D2
The Walled Orchard	33 B1
The Warren	2 F3
The Water Rill	2 E2
The Waxworks Apts.	23 C3 [8]
The Way (Dunboyne Castle)	7 B3
The Weir	36 E2
The Wicklow Way	61 C4
The Willow	9 B2
The Willow (Rockfield)	57 C1
The Willows	39 A4 [45]
The Willows (Abberley)	64 E1 [19]
The Willows (Celbridge)	32 D3
The Willows (Glasnevin)	24 F3
The Willows (Monkstown)	49 B4 [3]
The Willows (Orwell Road)	47 A3 [1]
The Wood	58 D3
The Wood	64 E3
The Wood (Carrickmines)	63 A1
The Wood (Tallaght)	55 A2
The Woodlands (Celbridge)	32 D3
The Woodlands (Rathfarnham)	46 F4 [9]
The Woods	25 C3 [9]
Theresa House	46 F4 [20]
Third Avenue (Seville Place)	72 E3
Third Avenue (Tallaght)	44 F4
Thirlestane Terrace	74 F1
Thomas Court	74 E1
Thomas Davis Court	27 C1 [4]
Thomas Davis Street (West)	36 F3
Thomas Davis Street South	74 F1
Thomas Lane	71 B3
Thomas Moore Court	27 C1 [3]
Thomas Moore Road	45 C1
Thomas Street	74 E1
Thomas Street West	74 E1
Thomastown Crescent	60 D2 [2]
Thomastown Road	60 D3
Thomond	64 E2 [9]
Thomond Road	36 E3
Thompson's Cottages	71 C2
Thor Place	70 D3
Thormanby Grove	30 D2 [10]
Thormanby Lawns	30 D2
Thormanby Lodge	30 E2
Thormanby Road	30 E2
Thormanby Woods	30 E2
Thorn Wood	48 E3
Thornberry Apts.	8 F4
Thorncastle Court Apts.	39 A2 [3]
Thorncastle Street	39 A2
Thorncliff	47 B2 [8]
Thorncliffe Park	47 B3
Thorndale Avenue	26 D2
Thorndale Court	25 C2 [4]
Thorndale Crescent	26 D2
Thorndale Drive	26 D3
Thorndale Grove	26 D3
Thorndale Lawns	26 D2
Thorndale Park	26 D2
Thornfield Square	44 E1
Thornhill Gardens	31 C2
Thornhill Heights	31 C2
Thornhill Lane	27 A4
Thornhill Meadows	31 C2
Thornhill Road (Bray)	67 A4
Thornhill Road (Kilmacud)	48 E4
Thornhill View	67 B1 [5]
Thornleigh Avenue	1 Inset
Thornleigh Close	1 Inset
Thornleigh Court	1 Inset
Thornleigh Green	1 Inset
Thornleigh Grove	1 Inset
Thornleigh Lane	1 Inset
Thornleigh Park	1 Inset
Thornleigh Place	1 Inset
Thornleigh Road	1 Inset
Thornleigh Row	1 Inset
Thornville Avenue	27 B1
Thornville Drive	27 B2
Thornville Park	27 C1
Thornville Road	27 B1
Thornville Terrace	27 B2 [1]
Three Rock Close	45 B3 [1]
Three Rock Grove	57 B3
Three Rock Road	58 E2
Thundercut Alley	70 F3
Tibradden Close	45 B2 [1]
Tibradden Drive	45 B2
Tibradden Grove	45 B3
Tibradden Lane	56 F4
Tibradden Road	56 F3
Ticknick	63 B2
Ticknock Avenue	57 C3
Ticknock Dale	57 C3
Ticknock Drive	57 C3
Ticknock Grove	57 C3
Ticknock Hill	57 C3
Ticknock Park	57 C3
Ticknock Road	57 B4
Ticknock Way	57 C3
Tiknock	61 B1
Tiknock Bridge	61 B1
Timard	17 A1
Timber Mills Apts.	26 E2
Tinkers Hill	21 A4
Tinkler's Path	36 E1
Tinnehinch	66 E4
Tinnehinch Bridge	66 E4
Tivoli Avenue	46 F1
Tivoli Close	59 C1
Tivoli Road	49 C4
Tivoli Terrace East	50 D4
Tivoli Terrace North	49 C4
Tivoli Terrace South	49 C4
Tobernea Terrace	49 B3 [2]
Tolka Cottages	24 F3
Tolka Estate	24 F2
Tolka Estate Road	24 F3
Tolka Quay	39 A2
Tolka Quay Road	39 A2
Tolka Road	25 B4
Tolka Vale	24 E3
Tolka Valley Road	24 D3
Tolka Valley View	24 D2
Tolka View	22 F2 [2]
Tom Clarke House	25 B4 [1]
Tom Kelly Road	75 B3
Tonduff Close	45 B3
Tonguefield Road	46 E1 [1]
Tonlegee Avenue	26 F1
Tonlegee Drive	26 F1
Tonlegee Road	27 A1
Tootenhill	52 D2
Tootenhill (Rathcoole)	52 E2
Tor an Rí Close	34 F3
Tor an Rí Court	34 F3
Tor an Rí Lane	34 F3
Tor an Rí Parade	34 F3
Tor an Rí Terrace	34 F3
Tor an Rí Walk	34 F3
Torca Road	60 F2
Torca View	60 F2 [33]
Torcaill	3 C4
Torlogh Gardens	25 C4 [8]
Torlogh Parade	25 C3 [1]
Torquay Road	58 F2
Torquay Wood	58 F2
Tory Square	22 F1
Tourmakeady Road	25 B2 [1]
Tourville Lodge	46 F3 [6]
Tower Avenue	46 F2
Tower Road	36 D1
Tower Road (Castleknock)	22 F4
Tower Road (Clondalkin)	44 D1
Tower Terrace (off Kilmainham Lane)	73 B1
Tower View Cottages	24 F4 [2]
Townsend Street	71 C4
Townyard House Apts.	3 B2 [9]
Townyard Lane	3 B2
Traders Wharf	49 C3
Traders Wharf Apts. (Ushers Quay)	70 F4
Trafalgar Lane	49 B4
Trafalgar Terrace (Blackrock)	49 B3
Trafalgar Terrace (Bray)	67 C2 [31]
Tramway Court (Sutton)	29 A1
Tramway Court (Tallaght)	55 A1 [8]
Tranquility Grove	26 D1
Traverslea Close	60 D1
Traverslea Woods	60 D1
Traynor Place (O'Reilly Ave)	73 C1
Treepark Avenue	45 A3
Treepark Close	45 A3
Treepark Drive	45 A3
Treepark Road	45 A3
Trees Avenue	48 E4
Trees Road Lower	48 E4
Trees Road Upper	48 E4
Treesdale	48 F4
Tresilian	59 A3
Trideat Apts.	39 A4 [33]
Trim Road	26 D1
Trimelston Apts.	47 C3
Trimleston Avenue	48 E2
Trimleston Drive	48 E2
Trimleston Gardens	48 E2
Trimleston Park	48 E2
Trimleston Road	48 E2
Trinity Hall (Rathgar)	47 A2
Trinity Square	72 D4
Trinity Street	71 B4
Trinity Terrace	72 D1
Tristan House Apts.	36 E2 [15]
Tritonville Avenue	39 A3 [8]
Tritonville Close	39 A3 [22]
Tritonville Court	39 A4
Tritonville Crescent	39 A3 [9]
Tritonville Mews	39 A3 [45]
Tritonville Road	39 A3
Trosyrafon Terrace	68 D2 [1]
Tuansgate Apts.	54 F1 [1]
Tubber Lane Road	33 B2
Tubbermore Avenue	60 F2
Tubbermore Road	60 F2
Tuckett's Lane	30 D2
Tudor Court	2 F2
Tudor Lawns	58 F2
Tudor Road	47 B1
Tulip Court	13 C4
Tullyhall	34 D4
Tullyhall Avenue	34 D4
Tullyhall Close	34 D4
Tullyhall Court	34 D4
Tullyhall Crescent	34 E4
Tullyhall Drive	34 E4
Tullyhall Green	34 D4
Tullyhall Park	34 D4
Tullyhall Rise	34 E4
Tullyhall Way	34 D4
Tullyvale	63 C1
Turnapin Cottages	12 F3
Turnapin Green	12 F3
Turnapin Grove	12 F3
Turnapin Lane	12 F3
Turnberry	28 D1
Turnberry Square	28 D1
Turnpike Road	45 A2
Turnstone Apts.	48 E3
Turret Road	35 C2
Turrets Flats	47 A1 [9]
Turvey Avenue	73 B1
Tuscany Downs	27 A2
Tuscany Park	28 D1
Twin Cottages	49 A4 [5]
Tymon Close	55 A2
Tymon Crescent	54 F2
Tymon Farm	45 C4
Tymon Grove	55 A2
Tymon Heights	55 B2
Tymon Lane	45 B4
Tymon Lawn	55 A2
Tymon Lodge Apts.	45 B3
Tymon North	45 B4
Tymon North Avenue	45 B4
Tymon North Court	45 B4 [1]
Tymon North Gardens	45 B4
Tymon North Green	45 B4
Tymon North Grove	45 B4
Tymon North Lawn	45 B4
Tymon North Park	45 B4
Tymon North Place	45 B4 [2]
Tymon North Road	45 B4
Tymonville Avenue	45 B4
Tymonville Court	45 A4
Tymonville Crescent	45 A4
Tymonville Drive	45 A3
Tymonville Grove	45 B3
Tymonville Lawn	45 B4
Tymonville Park	45 B4
Tymonville Road	45 A4
Tynan Hall	44 F3
Tynan Hall Avenue	44 F3
Tynan Hall Grove	44 F3
Tynan Hall Park	44 F3
Tyrconnell Park	36 F3
Tyrconnell Road	36 F3
Tyrconnell Street	36 F3 [6]
Tyrconnell Villas	36 F3 [7]
Tyrellstown Boulevard	9 B2
Tyrellstown Way	9 B2
Tyrone House	71 C3
Tyrone Place	73 A2
Tyrrell Place	71 C1
*Tyrrel's Lane (off Fitzwilliam St Ringsend)	39 A3

U

STREET NAME	PAGE/GRID REFERENCE
UCD Village Belgrove	48 D3
Ullardmor	60 F2 [27]
Ulster Street	24 F4
Ulster Terrace (North Strand)	72 D1
Ulster Terrace (Stillorgan Grove)	58 F1 [4]
Ulverton Close	60 F1 [5]
Ulverton Court	60 F1 [13]
Ulverton Road	60 F1
*Ulysses House Apts. (Little Britain Street)	71 A3
University Village Apartments	17 C2
Upper Cliff Road	30 E2 [2]
Upper Dargle Road	67 A2
Upper Garville Avenue	47 A2
Upper Glen Road	36 E1
Upper Kilmacud Road Extension	58 E1
Uppercross	34 F1
Uppercross Court	55 A1 [7]
Uppercross Road	73 C2
Urney Grove	60 E2 [7]
Usher Lane	1 A2
Usher Street	70 F4
Ushers Court Apts.	70 F4
Usher's Island	70 E4
Usher's Quay	70 F4

V

STREET NAME	PAGE/GRID REFERENCE
Vale Terrace (on lower Dargle Road)	67 B2 [7]
Vale View	67 B2 [21]
Vale View Avenue	59 B3
Vale View Close	59 B3

STREET NAME	PAGE/GRID REFERENCE
Vale View Grove	59 B3
Vale View Lawn	59 B3
Valentia House	71 B1
Valentia Parade	71 B1
Valentia Road	25 B3
Valeview Crescent	24 D2 [6]
Valeview Drive	24 D2
Valeview Gardens	24 D2 [2]
Valley Drive	63 C1
Valley Park Avenue	24 D2 [1]
Valley Park Drive	23 C2
Valley Park Road	23 C2
Valley View	1 B1
Vanessa Close	31 C3
Vanessa Lawns	31 C3
Vauxhall Avenue	74 D2
Vavasour Square	76 F2
Venetian Hall	26 E3
Ventry Drive	24 D4
Ventry Park	24 E4
Ventry Road	24 E4
Verbena Avenue (Foxrock)	59 A3
Verbena Avenue (Kilbarrack)	27 C1
Verbena Grove	27 C1
Verbena Lawn	27 C1
Verbena Park	27 C1
Verdemont	22 D2
Vergemount	47 C1 [12]
Vergemount Hall	47 C1 [9]
Vergemount Park	47 C1 [6]
Verney House	62 F3
Vernon Avenue	26 F4
Vernon Court (Clontarf)	39 C1 [3]
Vernon Court (Vernon Avenue)	26 F4
Vernon Drive	26 F3
Vernon Gardens	26 F4
Vernon Grove (Clontarf)	26 F4
Vernon Grove (Rathgar)	47 A2
Vernon Heath	26 F4
Vernon Park	26 F4
Vernon Rise	26 F3
Vernon Street	75 A2
Vernon Wood	39 C1 [4]
Veronica Terrace	39 A3 [40]
*Veronica Terrace	39 A3
(off Oliver Plunket Ave)	
Verschoyle Avenue	53 C2
Verschoyle Close	53 C2
Verschoyle Court	76 D2
Verschoyle Crescent	53 C2
Verschoyle Drive	53 C2
Verschoyle Glen	53 C2
Verschoyle Green	53 C2
Verschoyle Heights	53 C2
Verschoyle Mews	76 D2
Verschoyle Park	53 C2
Verschoyle Place	76 E2
(off Lr Mount St)	
Verschoyle Rise	53 C2
Verschoyle Vale	53 C2
Verville Court	26 E4
Vesey Mews	49 C4
Vesey Park	34 D2
Vesey Place	49 C4
Vesey Terrace	34 D1 [2]
*Vevay Arcade (on Vevay Road)	67 C3
Vevay Crescent	67 C2 [58]
Vevay Road	67 C3
Vevay Villas	67 C3 [18]
Vicar Street	74 F1
Vicars Court	8 F4
Vico Road	60 F3
*Vico Terrace (0ff Vico Road)	60 F3
Victoria Avenue (Bray)	68 D2
Victoria Avenue (Donnybrook)	47 C1
Victoria Cottages	39 A3 [44]
*Victoria Cottages	39 A3
(off Irishtown Rd)	
Victoria Lane	25 B4 [9]
*Victoria Lane	47 A2
(off South Zion Road)	
Victoria Quay	70 E4
Victoria Road	46 F2
Victoria Road (Clontarf)	26 E4
Victoria Road (Dalkey)	60 F2

STREET NAME	PAGE/GRID REFERENCE
Victoria Road (Killiney)	60 E3
Victoria Street	75 A3
Victoria Terrace	39 B1
Victoria Terrace (Dalkey)	60 F2 [11]
Victoria Terrace	50 D4 [8]
(Dun Laoghaire)	
Victoria Terrace (Dundrum)	47 C4
Victoria Village (Rathgar)	46 F2 [7]
Victoria Village (Rathgar)	47 A2
Victoria Villas (Clontarf)	26 D4
Victoria Villas (Rathgar)	46 F2 [5]
Viking Place	70 E3
Viking Road	70 E3
*Villa Bank (Royal Canal Bank)	71 A1
Villa Blanchard	22 F2
Villa Building Apts.	30 D1 [15]
Villa Nova	48 F4
Villa Park Avenue	24 D4
Villa Park Drive	24 D4
Villa Park Gardens	24 D4
Villa Park Road	24 D4
Village Court Apts.	46 F4 [6]
*Village Gate Arcade	67 C2
(on Main Street Bray)	
Village Green (Rathfarnham)	46 F3 [4]
Village Green (Tallagh)	55 A1
Village Heights	9 A4
Village Square (Tallagh)	55 A1
Village Weir	34 D1 [7]
Villarea Park	60 E1
Villiers Road	47 A2
Vintage Court	74 E2
Violet Hill Drive	24 F3
Violet Hill Park	24 F3
Violet Hill Road	24 F3
Virginia Drive	24 D2
Virginia Hall (Belgard Square)	54 F1 [8]
Virginia Heights	54 F1
Virginia Park	24 D2
Viscount Avenue	12 F4

W

STREET NAME	PAGE/GRID REFERENCE
Wadelai Green	25 A2
Wadelai Road	25 A2
Wade's Avenue	27 A3
Wainsfort Avenue	46 D3
Wainsfort Crescent	46 D3
Wainsfort Drive	46 D2
Wainsfort Gardens	46 D3
Wainsfort Grove	46 E3
Wainsfort Manor	46 D3
Wainsfort Manor Crescent	46 D3
Wainsfort Manor Drive	46 D3
Wainsfort Manor Green	46 D3
Wainsfort Manor Grove	46 D3
Wainsfort Park	46 E3
Wainsfort Road	46 D3
Waldemar Terrace	47 B4 [12]
Walker's Cottages	75 B4
Walker's Court	75 B4
Walkinstown	45 B1
Walkinstown Avenue	45 B1
Walkinstown Close	45 B1
Walkinstown Crescent	45 B1
Walkinstown Cross	45 C2
Walkinstown Drive	45 B1
Walkinstown Green	45 B1
Walkinstown Parade	45 B1
Walkinstown Park	45 B1
Walkinstown Road	45 C1
Wallace Road	45 C1 [2]
Walnut Avenue (Clondalkin)	44 F3
Walnut Avenue (Whitehall)	25 B3
Walnut Close	44 F3
Walnut Court	25 B2
Walnut Drive	44 F3
Walnut Lawn	25 B3
Walnut Park	25 B3
Walnut Rise	25 B3
Walnut View	56 E2 [5]
Walsh Road	25 A3
Waltersland Road	58 F1
Waltham Terrace	48 F4
Walton Hall (Swords)	1 Inset

STREET NAME	PAGE/GRID REFERENCE
Walworth Road	75 A3
Warburton Terrace	68 D2 [7]
Ward's Hill	74 F2
Warner's Lane	75 C3
Warren Avenue	22 E3
Warren Close	22 E3
Warren Court	28 D1 [5]
Warren Crescent	22 E4
Warren Green (Carpenterstown)	22 E3
Warren Green (Sutton)	28 D1
Warren Manor	2 F3
Warren Park	22 E3
Warren Street	75 A3
Warrenhouse Road	28 D1
Warrenmount	74 F2
Warrenmount Place	74 F2
Warrenpoint	26 E4 [1]
Warrenstown	9 B4
Warrenstown Close	9 B4
Warrenstown Court	9 B4
Warrenstown Drive	9 B4
Warrenstown Garth	9 B4
Warrenstown Green	9 B4
Warrenstown Grove	9 B4
Warrenstown Lawn	9 B4
Warrenstown Park	9 B4
Warrenstown Place	9 B4
Warrenstown Rise	9 B4
Warrenstown Row	9 B4
Warrenstown Vale	9 B4
Warrenstown View	9 B4
Warrenstown Walk	9 B4
Warrenstown Way	9 B4
Warrington Lane	76 E2
Warrington Place	76 E2
Warwick Terrace	76 D4
Wasdale Grove	46 F2
Wasdale House	46 F3 [8]
Wasdale Park	46 F3
Washington Lane	46 E4
Washington Park	46 E4
Washington Street	74 F3
Waterfall Avenue	25 B4
Waterfall Road	26 F3
Watergate Estate	55 A1
Waterloo Avenue	72 E1
Waterloo Lane	76 D4
Waterloo Mews	76 E3
Waterloo Road	76 D4
Watermeadow Drive	54 F2
Watermeadow Park	55 A2
Watermill	27 B3
Watermill Avenue	27 A3
Watermill Close	55 A2
Watermill Drive	27 A3
Watermill Grove	55 A2
Watermill Lawn (Raheny)	27 A3 [1]
Watermill Lawn (Tallaght)	55 A2
Watermill Park	27 A3
Watermill Road	27 A3
Watermint Court	24 D3 [3]
Waterside Apts.	76 F1
Waterside Avenue	2 E2
Waterside Close	2 E2
Waterside Court	2 E2
Waterside Crescent	3 C4
(Portmarnock)	
Waterside Crescent (Swords)	2 E2
Waterside Drive	2 E2
Waterside Green	2 E3
Waterside Grove	2 E2
Waterside King's Hall	2 E2
Waterside Lawn	2 E2
Waterside Park	2 E2
Waterside Place	2 E3
Waterside Rise	2 E2
Waterside Road	2 E2
Waterside Walk	2 E2
Waterside Way	2 E2
Waterstown	35 C1
Waterstown Avenue	35 C1
Waterville Road	22 F1
Waterville Row	22 F1
Waterville Terrace	22 F1
Watery Lane	2 D1

STREET NAME	PAGE/GRID REFERENCE
Watery Lane (Clondalkin)	44 E1
Watery Lane (Swords)	1 C1
Watkins Buildings	74 F2
Watling Street	70 E4
Watson Avenue	60 D4
Watson Drive	60 D4
Watson Park	60 D4
Watson Road	60 D3
Watson's Estate	60 D3
Waverley Avenue	25 C4
Waverley Terrace (Bray)	67 C2 [28]
Waverley Terrace	46 F1 [12]
(Harolds Cross Road)	
Waynestown	5 C1
Wayside Cottages	62 F2
Weaver Lane	71 A1
Weaver's Close	74 F2
Weaver's Row (Clonsilla)	21 C2
Weavers Row (The Coombe)	74 E2
Weaver's Square	74 F2
Weaver's Street	74 F2
Weaver's Walk	21 C2
Webster's Cottages	49 A4 [8]
Wedgewood Estate	58 D2
Weirview	34 D1
Weirview Drive	58 F1
Weldon's Lane	15 A4
Well Road	2 D2 [2]
Wellesley Place	71 C1
Wellington Cottages	45 C3 [2]
Wellington Court (Bray)	67 C2 [56]
Wellington Court	46 D2 [5]
(Whitehall Road West)	
*Wellington Gardens	47 B1
(off Oakley Road)	
Wellington House	76 E4
Wellington Lane (Tallaght Road)	45 C3
Wellington Lane	76 E4
(Wellington Road)	
Wellington Lodge	39 A4 [52]
Wellington Park	46 D3
Wellington Place (Leeson Street)	76 E4
Wellington Place North	71 A2
Wellington Quay	71 B4
Wellington Road (Ballsbridge)	76 E4
Wellington Road (Phoenix Park)	69 B4
Wellington Road (Templeogue)	46 D3 [1]
Wellington Street	50 D4 [1]
(Dun Laoghaire)	
Wellington Street Lower	71 A2
Wellington Street Upper	71 A2
Wellmount Avenue	24 D2
Wellmount Court	24 D2
Wellmount Crescent	24 D2
Wellmount Drive	24 D2
Wellmount Green	24 D2
Wellmount Parade	24 D2
Wellmount Park	24 D2
Wellmount Road	24 D2
Wellpark Avenue	25 B3
Wellview Avenue	9 A3
Wellview Crescent	9 A3
Wellview Green	9 A3
Wellview Grove	9 A3
Wellview Park	9 A3
Wendell Avenue	4 D2
Wentworth Apartments	76 E1
Werburgh Street	75 A1
Wesbury	58 E1
Wesley Heights	57 C2
Wesley House	76 D4
Wesley Lawns	57 C2
Wesley Place	74 F3
Wesley Road	47 A2
West Park Drive	24 F2
West Pier (Dun Laoghaire)	49 C3
West Pier (Howth)	30 D1
West Road	72 E2
West Terrace	36 F3
Westbourne Avenue	43 C1
Westbourne Close	43 C1
Westbourne Court	46 F3
Westbourne Drive	43 C1
Westbourne Grove	43 C1
Westbourne Lodge	56 D1

STREET NAME	PAGE/GRID REFERENCE
Westbourne Rise	43 C1
Westbourne Road	46 F3
Westbourne Terrace	67 C2 [52]
Westbourne View	43 C1
Westbrook	46 D2
Westbrook Lawns	53 C2
Westbrook Park	33 C2
Westbrook Road	47 B3
Westbury	34 D3
Westbury Avenue	34 D3
Westbury Close	34 D3
Westbury Drive	34 D2
Westbury Grove	33 C3 [1]
Westbury Park	34 D3
Westcourt	74 D1
Westend Gate	22 F3
Westend Village	22 E2
Western Parkway	35 B2
Western Parkway Motorway	22 E4
Western Road	74 E3
Western Way	71 A2
Westerton Rise	57 C1 [1]
Westfield Park	68 D3
Westfield Road	46 F1
Westfield Terrace	49 A3 [10]
Westhampton Place	46 F2 [2]
Westhaven	8 F4
Westland Row	76 D1
Westmanstown	42 D3
Westminster Court	59 A3 [6]
Westminster Lawns	58 F2
Westminster Park	59 A2
Westminster Road	59 A3
Westmoreland Park	47 B1 [4]
Westmoreland Street	71 B4
Weston Avenue	47 B4
Weston Avenue (Leixlip)	33 B1
Weston Close (Churchtown)	47 B4
Weston Close (Leixlip)	33 B1
Weston Court	33 B2
Weston Crescent	33 B1
Weston Drive	33 B1
Weston Green	33 B1
Weston Grove	47 B4
Weston Heights	33 B2
Weston Lane (Leixlip)	33 B1
Weston Lawn	33 B1
Weston Meadow	33 B2
Weston Park (Churchtown)	47 B4
Weston Park (Leixlip)	33 B1
Weston Road	47 B4
Weston Terrace	47 B4 [9]
Weston Way	33 B2
Westpark (Coolock)	26 F2
Westpark (Rathcoole)	52 F2
Westpark (Tallaght)	55 A1
Westview Terrace	67 C2 [29]
Westway Close	9 C4
Westway Grove	9 C4
Westway Lawns	22 F1
Westway Park	9 C4
Westway Rise	9 C4
Westway View	9 C4
Westwood Avenue	23 C2
Westwood Road	23 C2
Wexford Street	75 B2
Wharton Terrace	74 F4
Whately Hall	8 F4
Whately Hall	8 F4
Whately Place	58 E1
Wheatfield	67 C3
Wheatfield Grove	4 D4
Wheatfield Road (Palmerstown)	35 C2
Wheatfield Road (Portmarnock)	4 D4
Wheatfields Avenue	35 B3
Wheatfields Close	35 B3
Wheatfields Court	35 B3
Wheatfields Crescent	35 B3
Wheatfields Drive	35 B3
Wheatfields Grove	35 B3
Wheatfields Park	35 B3
Wheaton Court	36 F3 [20]
Whelan House Flats	39 A3 [29]
Whelan's Terrace	49 A3 [19]
Whitaker Hall	71 A2
Whitchurch Drive	56 F2
Whitchurch Road	56 F2
White Gables	64 D2
White Hall (Ballymount Road)	44 F3
White Oak	47 C3
White Oaks	67 B4
Whiteacre Close	25 B1
Whiteacre Court	25 B1
Whiteacre Crescent	25 B1
Whiteacre Place	25 B1
Whitebank Road	39 B3
Whitebarn Road	47 A4
Whitebeam Avenue	47 C2
Whitebeam Road	47 C2
Whitebeams Road	58 D2
Whitebrook Park	54 E1
Whitechapel Avenue	22 D2
Whitechapel Court	22 D2
Whitechapel Crescent	22 D2
Whitechapel Green	22 D2
Whitechapel Grove	22 D2
Whitechapel Lawn	22 D2
Whitechapel Park	22 D2
Whitechapel Road	22 D2
Whitechurch Abbey	56 F1 [4]
Whitechurch Avenue	56 F2
Whitechurch Close	56 F2
Whitechurch Court	56 F2
Whitechurch Crescent	56 F2
Whitechurch Drive	56 F2
Whitechurch Green	56 F2
Whitechurch Grove	56 F2
Whitechurch Hill	56 F2
Whitechurch Lawn	56 F2
Whitechurch Park	56 F2
Whitechurch Pines	56 F1
Whitechurch Place	56 F2
Whitechurch Road	46 F4
Whitechurch Road	56 F2
Whitechurch Stream	56 F1
Whitechurch View	56 F2
Whitechurch Walk	56 F2
Whitechurch Way	56 F2
Whitecliff	56 F1
Whitefriar Garden Flats (off Whitefriar Street)	75 A1
Whitefriar Place	75 B1
Whitefriar Street	75 A1
Whitehall	25 B2
Whitehall Close	46 D3
Whitehall Gardens	46 D2
Whitehall Mews	59 A2
Whitehall Park	46 D3
Whitehall Road (Churchtown)	47 A4
Whitehall Road (Kimmage)	46 D2
Whitehall Road West	46 D2
Whitehall Square	45 C2
Whites Gate (Phoenix Park)	23 A4
White's Lane North	71 A2
White's Road	23 A4
White's Villas	60 F1 [10]
Whitestown	22 D1
Whitestown Avenue	22 D1
Whitestown Crescent	22 D1
Whitestown Drive (Blanchardstown)	22 D1
Whitestown Drive (Tallaght)	54 E2
Whitestown Gardens	22 D1
Whitestown Green	22 D1
Whitestown Grove	22 D1
Whitestown Park	22 D1
Whitestown Road	54 F2
Whitestown Walk	22 D1
Whitestown Way	54 F2
Whitethorn	35 B3
Whitethorn Avenue	26 D2
Whitethorn Close	26 D2
Whitethorn Crescent (Artane)	26 D2
Whitethorn Crescent (Coldcut Road)	35 B3
Whitethorn Drive	35 B3
Whitethorn Gardens	35 B3
Whitethorn Grove (Artane)	26 D2
Whitethorn Grove (Celbridge)	32 D3
Whitethorn Park (Artane)	26 D2
Whitethorn Park (Coldcut Road)	35 B3
Whitethorn Rise	26 D2
Whitethorn Road (Artane)	26 D2
Whitethorn Road (Milltown)	47 C2
Whitethorn Walk (Foxrock)	59 A2 [8]
Whitethorn Walk (Kill O'The Grange)	59 C2 [2]
Whitethorn Way	35 B3
Whitton Road	46 F2
Whitworth Avenue	71 C1
*Whitworth Parade (off Saint Patrick's Road)	25 A4
Whitworth Place	25 A4 [16]
Whitworth Road	25 A4
Whitworth Terrace (off Russell Ave)	71 C1
Wicklow Lane (off Wicklow Street)	75 B1
Wicklow Street	75 B1
Wicklow Way	65 A4
Wigan Road	25 A4
Wikeford Hall (Swords)	1 Inset
Wilderwood Grove	45 C4
Wilfield	39 A4 [15]
Wilfield Park	39 A4
Wilfield Road	39 A4
Wilford Court	67 B1
Wilfrid Road	46 F1
Wilfrid Terrace	46 F1 [5]
Willans Avenue	21 A1
Willans Drive	21 A1
Willans Green	21 A1
Willans Rise	21 A1
Willans Row	21 A1
Willans Way	21 A1
Willbrook	46 F4
Willbrook Downs	56 F1
Willbrook Estate	56 F1
Willbrook Grove	46 F4
Willbrook House	75 C4
Willbrook Lawn	46 F4
Willbrook Park	46 F4
Willbrook Road	46 F4
Willbrook Street	46 F4
William Beckett House	76 D2
William Dargan Bridge	47 B4
William Pallister House	46 F4 [22]
William Street North	72 D1
William Street South	75 B1
William's Lane	71 B3
William's Park	47 A1
Williams Place Lower (Buckingham Street Upper)	71 C1
William's Place South	75 A2
William's Place Upper	71 B1
William's Place Upper (off Portland Place)	71 B1
Willie Bermingham Place	73 C1
Willie Nolan Road	15 A4
Willington Avenue	45 C3
Willington Court	45 C3
Willington Crescent	45 C3
Willington Drive	45 C3
Willington Green	45 C3
Willington Grove	45 C3
Willington Lawn	45 C3 [1]
Willington Park	45 C3
Willow Avenue	32 E4
Willow Avenue (Clondalkin)	44 D2
Willow Avenue (Loughlinstown)	64 D1
Willow Bank	49 C6
Willow Bank Drive	56 E1
Willow Bank Park	56 E1
Willow Brook	32 E4
Willow Court (Clondalkin)	44 D2
Willow Court (Loughlinstown)	64 D1
Willow Cove	32 E4
Willow Crescent	32 E4
Willow Crescent	64 D1
Willow Drive	32 E4
Willow Drive	44 D2
Willow Gate	57 B1
Willow Green	32 E4
Willow Grove (Clondalkin)	44 D2
Willow Grove (Cornelscourt)	59 B3
Willow Grove (Kill O'The Grange)	59 C1 [13]
Willow House	76 D3
Willow Lawn	32 E4
Willow Lodge	23 A4
Willow Mews	48 E1
Willow Park (Dunboyne)	7 B2
Willow Park (Foxrock)	59 A2 [6]
Willow Park (Loughlinstown)	64 D1
Willow Park Avenue	24 F1
Willow Park Close	24 F1
Willow Park Crescent	24 F1
Willow Park Drive	25 A1
Willow Park Grove	24 F1
Willow Park Lawn	24 F1
Willow Park Road	24 F1
Willow Place (Booterstown)	48 F3
Willow Place (Loughlinstown)	64 D1
Willow Rise	32 E4
Willow Road (Dundrum)	57 B1
Willow Road (Fox & Geese)	45 A1
Willow Terrace	48 F2
Willow Vale	60 D4
Willow View	32 E4
Willow Wood Close	21 C2
Willow Wood Downs	21 C2 [1]
Willow Wood Green	21 C2
Willow Wood Grove	21 C2
Willow Wood Lawn	21 C2
Willow Wood Park	21 C1
Willow Wood Rise	21 C1
Willow Wood View	21 C2
Willow Wood Walk	21 C1
Willowbank	57 C1
Willowbrook Grove	31 C3
Willowbrook Lawns	31 C3
Willowbrook Lodge	31 C3
Willowbrook Park	31 C3
Willowfield	39 B4
Willowfield Avenue	47 C4
Willowfield Park	47 C4
Willowmount	48 F3 [3]
Willows Court	21 C2
Willows Drive	21 C2
Willows Green	21 C2
Willows Road	21 C2
Willsbrook Avenue	34 E2
Willsbrook Crescent	34 F1
Willsbrook Drive	34 E2
Willsbrook Gardens	34 E1
Willsbrook Green	34 E2
Willsbrook Grove	34 E1
Willsbrook Park	34 E1
Willsbrook Place	34 E1
Willsbrook Road	34 E2
Willsbrook View	34 E2
Willsbrook Way	34 E1
Wilmont Avenue	60 E1 [1]
Wilson Crescent	48 D4
Wilson Road	48 E4
Wilson Terrace	74 F1
Wilson's Place	76 D1
Wilton Court	76 D3
Wilton Place	76 D3
Wilton Terrace	76 D3
Windele Road	25 A3 [12]
Windermere	21 B2
Windermere	39 B4 [8]
Windgate Rise	30 D3
Windgate Road	30 D3
Windmill Avenue(Crumlin)	46 D1
Windmill Avenue(Swords)	1 C2
Windmill Crescent (Swords)	1 A2
Windmill Crescent (Crumlin)	46 D1 [2]
Windmill Lands	1 C2
Windmill Lane	72 D4
Windmill Lane Apts.	72 D4
Windmill Park	22 D3 [2]
Windmill Park	46 D1
Windmill Rise	1 C2
Windmill Road	46 D1
Windmill Terrace	22 D3 [3]
Windmillhill	51 C3
Windrush	64 E2 [7]
Windsor Avenue	25 C4

STREET NAME	PAGE/GRID REFERENCE	STREET NAME	PAGE/GRID REFERENCE	STREET NAME	PAGE/GRID REFERENCE	STREET NAME	PAGE/GRID REFERENCE
Windsor Court	59 B1 [1]	Woodfarm Cottages	35 C1 [6]	Woodlawn Rise	12 F4	Woodview Heights (Dunboyne)	7 B3
Windsor Drive	59 B1	Woodfarm Drive	35 C2	Woodlawn Terrace	47 B4 [2]	Woodview Heights (Lucan)	33 C2
Windsor Mews	3 B2 [5]	Woodfield	56 D2	Woodlawn View	12 F4	Woodview House	48 F3
Windsor Park	59 B1	Woodfield Cottages	36 F3 [8]	Woodlawn Villas	59 C1 [16]	Woodview Park	27 A1
Windsor Place	75 C2	Woodfield Place	36 F3 [15]	Woodlawn Walk	12 F4	(Ardara Avenue)	
Windsor Road	47 B1	Woodford	58 E2	Woodlawn Way	12 F4	Woodview Park (Castleknock)	23 A3
Windsor Terrace	50 D4	Woodford Avenue	44 F1	Woodleigh	47 A2 [2]	Woodville Avenue	34 E1
(Dun Laoghaire)		Woodford Close	44 F1	Woodley Court	58 D1 [4]	Woodville Close	34 E1
Windsor Terrace (Malahide)	3 B3	Woodford Court	46 F1 [10]	Woodley Park	58 D1	Woodville Court	26 E1
Windsor Terrace (Ranelagh)	75 A4	(Harold's Cross)		Woodley Road	60 D3	Woodville Green	34 E1
Windsor Villas	25 C4 [3]	Woodford Court (Monksfield)	44 F1	Woodpark	25 A3 [20]	Woodville Grove	34 E1
Windy Arbour	47 C3	Woodford Crescent	44 E1	Woodpark (Ballinteer)	57 B2	Woodville House	26 D1 [4]
Winetavern Street	71 A4	Woodford Downs	44 F1	Woodpark (Blanchardstown)	22 F2	Woodville Lawn	34 E1
Wingfield	62 E1	Woodford Drive	44 E1	Woods End	22 F2	Woodville Road	25 A4 [7]
Winston Ville	26 D4 [12]	Woodford Garth	44 E1	Woodscape	34 D3	Woodville Walk	34 E1
Winter Garden Apts	72 E4	Woodford Green	44 F1	Woodside (Clontarf)	26 F4	Wormwood Gate	70 F4
Winton Avenue	47 A2	Woodford Grove	44 F1	Woodside (Howth)	30 D2	(off Bridge Street Lower)	
Winton Grove	46 F2 [19]	Woodford Heights	44 F1	Woodside (Leixlip)	19 C4	Wyattville	64 D1
Winton Road	76 D4	Woodford Hill	44 F1	Woodside (Rathfarnham)	47 A3	Wyattville Close	64 D1
Wogansfield	33 A1	Woodford Lawn	44 F1	Woodside Drive	47 A3	Wyattville Hill	64 D1
Wolfe Tone Avenue	50 D4 [4]	Woodford Meadows	44 E1	Woodside Grove	47 A3	Wyattville Park	64 D1
Wolfe Tone Close	71 A3	Woodford Parade	44 E1	Woodside Hall	57 C3	Wyattville Road	64 D1
Wolfe Tone Quay	70 D4	Woodford Park	44 F1	Woodside Road	57 C3	Wyckham Grove	57 C1
Wolfe Tone Square East	67 C3	Woodford Park Road	44 E1	Woodstock Court	47 B1 [2]	Wyckham Park Road	57 B1
Wolfe Tone Square Middle	67 C3	Woodford Rise	44 F1	Woodstock Gardens	47 B1 [24]	Wyckham Place	57 C1
Wolfe Tone Square North	67 C3	Woodford Road	44 E1	Woodstock Park	56 D1	Wyckham Way	57 C1
Wolfe Tone Square South	67 C3	Woodford Terrace	44 F1	Woodstown	55 C2	Wynberg Park	49 B4
Wolfe Tone Square West	67 C3	Woodford View	44 F1	Woodstown Abbey	55 C2	Wyndham Park	67 C2
Wolfe Tone Street	71 A3	Woodford Villas	44 E1	Woodstown Abbey	56 D2	Wynnefield Park	47 A1 [21]
Wolseley Street	74 F3	Woodford Walk	44 F1	Woodstown Avenue	55 C2	Wynnefield Road	47 A1
Wolstan Haven Avenue	31 C3	Woodford Way	44 F1	Woodstown Close	55 C2	Wynnsward Drive	47 C2
Wolstan Haven Road	31 C3	Woodhaven	47 C2 [10]	Woodstown Court	55 C2 [2]	Wynnsward Park	47 C2
Wolverton Glen	60 E2	Woodhazel Close	25 A1	Woodstown Crescent	55 C2	Wyteleaf Grove	14 D4
Wood Avens	35 A3	Woodhazel Terrace	25 A1	Woodstown Dale	55 C2	Wyvern Estate	60 E3
Wood Dale Close	55 B2	Woodlands (Blakestown Road)	22 D1 [2]	Woodstown Drive	55 C2		
Wood Dale Crescent	55 B2	Woodlands (Malahide)	14 F1	Woodstown Gardens	55 C2		
Wood Dale Drive	55 B2	Woodlands (Maynooth)	17 B3	Woodstown Green	55 C2		
Wood Dale Green	55 B2	Woodlands (Rathgar)	47 A2 [1]	Woodstown Heath	55 C2	**X**	
Wood Dale Green	55 C2	Woodlands Avenue	59 C3	Woodstown Height	55 C2		
Wood Dale Grove	55 C2	(Cornelscourt)		Woodstown Hill	55 C2	Xavier Avenue	72 E1
Wood Dale Oak	55 C2 [1]	Woodlands Avenue (Stillorgan)	48 E4	Woodstown House	46 F4 [21]		
Wood Dale View	55 C2	Woodlands Court	15 A1	Woodstown Lane	56 D2	**Y**	
Wood Lane	70 E4	Woodlands Drive	59 C3	Woodstown Lawn	55 C2		
Wood Quay	71 A4	(Johnstown Road)		Woodstown Meadow	55 C2	Yale	48 D3
Wood Street	75 A1	Woodlands Drive (Stillorgan)	48 E4	Woodstown Parade	55 C2	Yankee Terrace	49 A4
Woodbank Avenue	23 C2	Woodlands Park	59 C3	Woodstown Park	55 C2	Yarnhall Street	71 A3
Woodbank Drive	23 C2	(Johnstown Road)		Woodstown Place	55 C2	Yeates Hall	59 B4
Woodberry (Carpenterstown)	22 E3	Woodlands Park	48 F4	Woodstown Rise	55 C2	Yeates Way	35 C4
Woodberry (Lucan)	34 D3	(Mount Merrion)		Woodstown Road	55 C2	Yeats Court	39 A4 [54]
Woodbine Avenue	48 E2	Woodlands Road	59 C3	Woodstown Vale	55 C2	Yellow Meadows Ave	44 F1
Woodbine Close	27 A1	Woodlawn	12 F4	Woodstown Walk	55 C2	Yellow Meadows Drive	44 E1
Woodbine Drive	27 A1	Woodlawn Avenue	12 F4	Woodstown Way	55 C3	Yellow Meadows Estate	44 F1
Woodbine House	48 E2 [4]	Woodlawn Close	12 F4	Woodthorpe	58 E1 [5]	Yellow Meadows Grove	44 E1
Woodbine Park (Booterstown)	48 E2	Woodlawn Court	12 F4	Woodtown Way	56 D3	Yellow Meadows Lawn	44 E1
Woodbine Park (Raheny)	27 A1	Woodlawn Crescent	47 B4	Woodvale Avenue	21 C1	Yellow Meadows Park	44 E1
Woodbine Road (Booterstown)	48 E2	(Churchtown)		Woodvale Crescent	21 C1	Yellow Meadows Vale	44 E1
Woodbine Road (Raheny)	27 A1	Woodlawn Crescent	12 F4	Woodvale Drive	21 C1	Yellow Road	25 C2
Woodbine Terrace (Dundrum)	47 C4 [2]	(Coolock Lane)		Woodvale Garth	21 C1	Yellow Walls	3 A2
Woodbrook Court	22 D3	Woodlawn Drive	12 F4	Woodvale Green	21 C1	Yellow Walls Road	3 A2
Woodbrook Crescent	22 D3	Woodlawn Green	12 F4	Woodvale Grove	21 C1	Yellownook Avenue	59 C3
Woodbrook Downs	64 E4	Woodlawn Grove (Churchtown)	47 B4 [7]	Woodvale Park	21 C1	Yewlands Terrace	46 F2
Woodbrook Glen	67 C1	Woodlawn Grove	12 F4	Woodvale Way	21 C1	York Avenue	47 A1
Woodbrook Hall	22 D3	(Coolock Lane)		Woodview	64 E2 [12]	York Road (Dun Laoghaire)	49 C4
Woodbrook Lawn	67 C3	Woodlawn Park (Churchtown)	47 B4	Woodview (Celbridge)	32 D2	York Road (Rathmines)	47 A1
Woodbrook Park	22 D3	Woodlawn Park (Coolock Lane)	12 F4	Woodview (Lucan)	33 C2	York Road (Ringsend)	39 A2
(Carpenterstown)		Woodlawn Park	59 C1 [4]	Woodview Close	27 A1	York Street	75 B2
Woodbrook Park (Templelogue)	46 D4	(Dun Laoghaire)		Woodview Cottages	46 F3 [1]		
Woodbrook Square	22 D3	Woodlawn Park (Tallaght)	55 C2	Woodview Court (Dunboyne)	7 B3	**Z**	
*Woodchester House	75 A1	Woodlawn Park Avenue	55 B1	Woodview Court (Stillorgan)	58 F1 [1]		
Woodcliff Heights	30 E2	Woodlawn Park Drive	55 B1	Woodview Court Apts.	33 C2	York Terrace	49 C4 [4]
Woodfarm Avenue	35 C2	(Firhouse)		Woodview Drive	67 C3 [4]	Zardoz Court	76 F4
		Woodlawn Park Grove	55 C2	Woodview Grove	22 E2	Zion Road	47 A2
						Zoo Road	69 B3
						Zuma Terrace	74 F4
						(on Mount Drummond Ave)	

LIST OF STREETS NOT NAMED ON MAP BUT SHOWN AS SMALL NUMBERS

PAGE/ GRID REF — STREET NAME

1 A2
1 Grove Court (Brackenstown Road)

1 C1
1 Elmwood Court
2 Rathbeale Court

2 D2
1 St Columcille's Crescent
2 Well Road
3 Colmcille Court
4 The Crescent (Swords)
5 New Road (Swords)

2 F3
1 Blizzard Apts.

3 A2
1 Hillcrest (Malahide)

3 A3
1 Castle Oaks
2 Ravenswood
3 Oakleigh Court

3 B2
1 Fair Haven
2 Haven View
3 Railway Court
4 The Priory (Malahide)
5 Windsor Mews
6 Fisherman's Green
7 Broadmeadow Mews
8 Ross Cottages
9 Townyard House Apts.
10 The Anchora Apts.
11 James's Terrace Upper
12 Strand Court

3 B3
1 Castle Court Apts.

3 C2
1 Seabank Court (Malahide)
2 Clearwater Apts.
3 Obelisk Court (Malahide)

4 D4
1 Alder Court
2 The Quarry

7 B2
1 St Mary's Terrace (Dunboyne)
2 Avondale Square

7 B3
1 Congress Park
2 Hamilton Court (Dunboyne)

9 A4
1 Ashmount
2 Ashfield Park (Huntstown Way)
3 Riverpark View
4 Riverside (Mulhuddart)

11 A4
1 St Margaret's Court

11 C4
1 Termon Court

12 E4
1 Domville Court

13 A4
1 Newbury Terrace

13 B4
1 Greenlawns
2 Clonshaugh Rise
3 Ferrycarrig Green
4 Clonshaugh Court
5 Moatview Terrace
6 Glin Close
7 Glin Court

14 D4
1 Templeview Vale
2 Elmfield Close
3 Clonmellon Grove
4 Beechbrook Grove

14 F2
1 St Lawrence O'Toole Avenue
2 Church Avenue (Portmarnock)
3 Suncroft Avenue
4 St Brigid's Avenue
5 St Ann's Square Lower
6 St Anne's Square (Portmarnock)
7 Hazel Court

15 A4
1 Seapoint Avenue (Baldoyle)
2 Parochial Avenue
3 Back Lane (Baldoyle)
4 The Mall (Baldoyle)
5 Breffni Gardens

6 Brookstone Lane
7 Seapoint Court (Baldoyle)
8 College Street (Baldoyle)
9 Admiral Court

17 C3
1 Kelly's Lane (Maynooth)
2 Fagan's Lane
3 Coates Lane
4 Geraldine Court
5 Court House Square
6 Leinster Cottages
7 Charter House

18 D3
1 Leinster Lodge Apts.
2 Leinster Court

20 D4
1 Cypress Springs

21 C1
1 Meadow Dale
2 Oakview Grove

21 C2
1 Willow Wood Downs
2 Cedar Grove

22 D1
1 Briarwood Park
2 Woodlands (Blakestown Road)
3 Briarwood Road
4 Ashcroft Grove
5 Ashcroft Court
6 Rose Vale Court
7 Blake's Court

22 D2
1 Coolmine Mews
2 Kirkfield

22 D3
1 The Orchard (Carpenterstown)
2 Windmill Park
3 Windmill Terrace

22 E3
1 Rosehaven
2 Luttrell Park Heath
3 Station View Apts.

22 F2
1 Herbert Crescent
2 Tolka View
3 Catherine's Well

22 F3
1 The Crescent (Castleknock)
2 Castleknock Court
3 Ashleigh Court

22 F4
1 The Sand Holes

23 A3
1 Beech Park Crescent
2 Hadleigh Green
3 Beechpark Close
4 Park Court Apts
5 Castleknock Manor

23 B3
1 Mill Lane (Ashtown)
2 The Chandler Apts.

23 B4
1 Castleknock Gate

23 C2
1 Eastwood

23 C3
1 Rathbourne Court
2 The Elms Apts.
3 The Birches Apts.
4 The Stables Apts.
5 The Mews Apts.
6 The Lodge Apts.
7 The Tallow Apts.
8 The Waxworks Apts.

23 C4
1 Baggot Terrace
2 St Vincent's Cottages
3 St Joseph's Cottages
4 Ashtown Lodge

24 D1
1 Cardiffsbridge Grove
2 Casement Close (off Barry Road)

24 D2
1 Valley Park Avenue
2 Valeview Gardens
3 Mellowes Court
4 Mellowes Crescent
5 Ravens Court
6 Valeview Crescent
7 Church View (Finglas)
8 Patrickswell Court

24 D3
1 Clearwater Court
2 Cassian Court
3 Watermint Court
4 Compass Court Apts.
5 Riverstown Gardens

24 D4
1 Roosevelt Cottages
2 Convent View Cottages (Cabra)
3 Convent View Crescent
4 Lyndon Gate
5 Park Spring's
6 Park Crescent House
7 Parkside View
8 Doreen House Apts.

24 E1
1 Georges Road
2 Gofton Hall
3 Heath Square

24 E2
1 Ballygall Place
2 Glenhill Villas
3 St Helena's Court
5 Johnstown Gardens
6 Collins Row
7 Glebe View (Finglas)

24 E4
1 Kilkieran Court
2 St Finbarr's Court
3 Rowan Hamilton Court
4 Dunmanus Court

24 F2
1 Drapier Green
2 Glasnamana Place
3 Johnstown House

24 F3
1 Northland Grove
2 Northland Drive
3 Glasnevin Oaks
4 Bellevue Cottages
5 Cremore Villas
6 Addison Hall
7 Botanic Hall
8 Addison Avenue

24 F4
1 St Philomena's Road
2 Tower View Cottages
3 Delvin Road
4 Bengal Terrace
5 Fertullagh Road
6 Connaught Parade
7 Clareville Court
8 Shandon Green
9 Shandon Mill

25 A1
1 Pinewood Grove
2 Shanliss Gardens
3 Oldtown Park
4 Shangan Hall Apts.

25 A3
1 Claremont Avenue
2 Church Avenue (Glasnevin)
3 St David's Terrace (Glasnevin)
4 Barron Place
5 Comyn Place
6 St Ita's Road
7 St Malachy's Road
8 St Michael's Road
9 Addison Place
10 St Mobhi Grove
11 Clonmore Court
12 Windele Road
13 O'Brien's Place North
14 O'Neachtain Road
15 River Gardens
16 Mobhi Court
17 The Haven (Glasnevin)
18 Glenavon Court
19 Hillcrest Court
20 Woodpark
21 James Joyce Court

25 A4
1 Millmount Villas
2 De Courcy Square
3 Enniskerry Road (Phibsborough)

4 Devery's Lane
5 Prospect Square
6 Glendalough Road
7 Woodville Road
8 St Teresa's Road (Glasnevin)
9 St Teresa's Place
10 Botanic Villas
11 St Alphonsus Avenue
12 St Brendan's Road
13 St Clement's Road
14 Botanic Park
15 Lindsay Grove
16 Whitworth Place
17 Botanic Square
18 Botanic Mews
19 Prospect Court

25 B1
1 Ailesbury
2 Schoolhouse Mews

25 B2
1 Tourmakeady Road

25 B3
1 Clonturk Avenue
2 The Village (Drumcondra)
3 Clare Park Villas
4 Beaucourt
5 The Cloisters (Grace Park Road)
6 Clonturk Court
7 All Hallows Lane

25 B4
1 Tom Clarke House
2 St Joseph's Avenue (Ballybough)
3 Clonturk Gardens
4 Kingston Lodge
5 Holycross Avenue
6 Robert Street (Jones's Road)
7 Robert Place
8 College Manor
9 Victoria Lane
10 Edgewood (Richmond Road)
11 College Mews
12 Richmond House
13 Richmond Hall
14 Brook House
15 Distillery Loft Apts.
16 Clonliffe Square
17 The Distillery Building Apts.

25 C1
1 Ivy Court
2 Beaumont Court
3 Beaumont Wood

25 C2
1 Chestnut Court
2 Dromnanane Road
3 Dromnanane Park
4 Thorndale Court
5 Laragh Flats
6 Collindale
7 Beaumont Hall
8 The Crescent (off Beaumont Rd)
9 Grace Park Lawns
10 Riachville
11 The Belfry Apts.

25 C3
1 Torlogh Parade
2 Morrogh Terrace
3 Calderwood Grove
4 Croydon Terrace
5 Sion Hill Court
6 Collins Court (Collins Avenue)
7 St Vincent's Court
8 Collins Close
9 The Woods
10 Rosemount

25 C4
1 Annadale Avenue
2 Shelmartin Terrace
3 Windsor Villas

PAGE/GRID REF	STREET NAME
	4 St Joseph's Terrace (Fairview)
	5 St Declan's Terrace
	6 St Aidan's Park
	7 Fairview Green
	8 Torlogh Gardens
	9 Marino Mart
	10 Fairview Passage
	11 Fairview Terrace
	12 Caragh Court
	13 Marino Court
	14 Fairview Court
	15 Bushfield Square
	16 Melrose Court
	17 Elton Court (Marino)
	18 Belmount Court
26 D1	1 Kilbarron Court
	2 Cromcastle Close
	3 St Luke's Court
	4 Woodville House
	5 Kilmore Court
	6 Cromcastle Court
26 D2	1 Newlands Court
26 D3	1 Cherrymount Crescent
	2 Cherrymount Grove
	3 Marino Villa
26 D4	1 Brighton Avenue (Clontarf)
	2 Hollybrook Court Drive
	3 Hollybrook Court
	4 Strandville House
	5 Haddon Park
	6 Crescent House
	7 Kilronan Court
	8 Glenbrian Hall
	11 Hollybrook Mews
	12 Winston Ville
26 E1	1 Lismeen Grove
	2 Brookville Crescent
	3 Coolock Village Close
26 E2	1 Maryfield Avenue
	2 Artane Cottages Lower
	3 Artane Cottages Upper
	4 Brookwood Abbey
26 E3	1 St Brigid's Drive (Killester)
	2 St Brigid's Court
	3 Quarry Cottages
	4 Killester Court
	5 Killester Park
26 E4	1 Warrenpoint
	2 St John's Wood (Clontarf)
	3 Lambourne Village
	4 Knights Bridge
	5 St David's Court
	6 The Paddock's (Clontarf)
26 F1	1 Elton Court (Coolock)
	2 Ayrefield Park
26 F2	1 Gorsefield Court
26 F4	1 Park View (Mount Prospect Lawns)
	2 Hunter's Row
27 A1	1 Elton Walk
	2 Glentworth Park
	3 Invermore Grove
	4 Curracloe Drive
	5 Laracor Gardens
	6 Gables
27 A3	1 Watermill Lawn (Raheny)
	2 St Anne's Court
27 A4	1 Seafield Grove
	2 St Gabriel's Court
	3 Rinn na Mara
	4 Mount Prospect House
	5 The Mews (Dollymount)
	6 Doyles Lane
27 B1	1 Howth Junction Cottages
	2 Swan's Nest Court
	3 Redmond's Court
	4 Briarsfield Walk
	5 Briarfield Villas

PAGE/GRID REF	STREET NAME
	6 St. Berach's Place
27 B2	1 Thornville Terrace
	2 Greendale Court
	3 Roseglen Manor
27 B3	1 The Grove (Raheny)
	2 The Court (Raheny)
	3 Oakwood Apts.
27 C1	1 Bayside Crescent
	2 Emily Lawless Court
	3 Thomas Moore Court
	4 Thomas Davis Court
	5 James Joyce Court
27 C2	1 Mariners Court
	2 Del Val Court
28 D1	1 Sutton Court
	2 Seafield (Sutton)
	3 St Domhnach's Well Street
	4 Marine Cove
	5 Warren Court
	6 Moyclare Gardens
29 A1	1 James McCormack Gardens
	2 St Catherine's Terrace
	3 Radcliffe
29 B1	1 Corrbridge Terrace (off Claremont Road)
	2 Avalon Apts.
	3 Corr Castle Apts
	4 Offington Manor Apts
29 B3	1 Shielmartin Park
	2 Martello Terrace (Sutton)
30 D1	1 Dunbo Terrace
	2 Evora Terrace
	3 Findlater Building Apts.
	4 Dunbo Hill
	5 Howth Terrace
	6 Harbour View (Howth)
	7 Marine Villas
	8 St Lawrence Quay
	9 Island View Apts.
	10 Howth House Apts
	11 Abbey Terrace
	12 Evora Crescent
	13 Cuan na Mara
	14 Howth Peninsula Apts.
	15 Villa Building Apts.
	16 St Lawrence Building Apts.
30 D2	1 St Lawrence's Terrace (Howth)
	2 Seaview Terrace (Howth)
	3 St Mary's Road (Howth)
	4 St Mary's Place (Howth)
	5 St Nessan's Terrace
	6 The Haggard (Howth)
	7 Hillside Terrace
	8 Dungriffan Villas
	9 St Nessan's Close
	10 Thormanby Grove
	12 St Nessans Court
	13 Crosstrees Court
	15 Forge Court
	16 Campbell Court
30 E2	1 Cannon Rock View
	2 Upper Cliff Road
	3 St Nessan's Apts
31 C2	1 Crodaun Court
31 C3	1 The Deanery
	2 The Close (Oldtown Mill)
	3 St Judes Apts.
33 A1	1 Ralph Square
	2 Liffey View Apts.
33 B2	1 The Copse
33 C3	1 Westbury Grove
34 D1	1 Sarsfield Terrace
	2 Vesey Terrace
	3 Hanbury Lane (Lucan)
	4 Sarsfield Court (Lucan)
	5 The Square (Lucan)
	6 Dispensary Lane (Lucan)
	7 Village Weir

PAGE/GRID REF	STREET NAME
	8 Brookvale
	9 Mount Gandon
	10 Gandon Mews
	11 Old Rectory
	12 The Village Centre
	13 The Village Court
	14 The Orchard (Lucan)
	15 Mill Bank
	16 Gandon Court
	17 St. Andrews Court
34 D2	1 Arthur Griffith Court
	2 Adams Town Court
	3 The Hollows
34 E1	1 Edmondsbury Court
34 F1	1 Latouka Apts.
34 F2	1 Liffey Hall
	2 Foxford Court
34 F3	1 Foxborough Hall
	2 Foxborough Crescent
35 A3	1 Neilstown Village Court
	2 Liscarne Dale
	3 Collinstown Crescent
35 A4	1 Ballymanagin Lane
	2 Moorfield Close
	3 Neilstown Cottages
	4 Rosebank Place
	5 Rosebank Hall
35 B4	1 Rosebank View
	2 Rosebank Court
35 C1	1 The Covert
	2 Glenside Villas
	3 Clarkeville Terrace
	4 Red Cow Cottages
	5 St Fintan's Terrace
	6 Woodfarm Cottages
35 C2	1 Culmore Park
	2 Glenaulin Green
35 C4	1 Cherry Orchard Way
36 D2	1 Rossaveal Court
36 D3	1 Le Fanu Drive
36 E2	1 Park Lane (Chapelizod)
	2 Maidens Row
	3 Hibernian Terrace
	4 St Laurence Grove
	5 St Mary's Terrace (Chapelizod)
	6 Isolde Gardens
	7 Liffey Terrace
	8 Clayton Terrace
	9 St Laurence Terrace (Chapelizod)
	10 Mullingar Terrace
	11 Riverview Court
	12 New Row
	13 Isolde House Apts.
	14 Distillery House Apts.
	15 Tristan House Apts.
36 E3	1 O'Hogan Road
	2 Lynch's Lane
	3 St Lawrence Glen
	4 Convent Lawns
36 E4	1 Old Naas Road Cottages
	2 Millrose Estate
	3 The Laurels (Bluebell)
	4 Hollybrooke
36 F3	1 Park Street
	2 Phoenix Street
	3 Inchicore Terrace North
	4 Murray's Cottages
	5 Partridge Terrace
	6 Tyrconnell Street
	7 Tyrconnell Villas
	8 Woodfield Cottages
	9 St Patrick's Terrace (Inchicore)
	10 Abercorn Terrace
	11 Granite Terrace
	12 Ring Street
	13 Inchicore Square
	14 Oblate Drive

PAGE/GRID REF	STREET NAME
	15 Woodfield Place
	16 Hampton Court (Tyrconnell Road)
	17 St James's Place (Inchicore)
	18 St George's Villas (Inchicore)
	19 Abercorn Square
	20 Wheaton Court
36 F4	1 Muirfield Drive
	2 Bernard Curtis House
	3 La Touche Court (Bluebell)
	4 Grove Court (Bluebell)
	5 Landsdowne Valley Park
39 A2	1 Fishermans Wharf
	2 Alexandra Quay
	3 Thorncastle Court Apts.
39 A3	1 Cambridge Street
	2 Fitzwilliam Street (Ringsend)
	3 St Patrick's Villas
	4 Seapoint Terrace (Ringsend)
	5 The Square (Irishtown)
	6 St Brendan's Cottages
	7 Cambridge Avenue
	8 Tritonville Avenue
	9 Tritonville Crescent
	10 Seafort Gardens
	11 Leukos Road
	12 Clonlara Road (Ringsend)
	13 Kyle-Clare Road
	14 Parkview Place
	15 Canon Mooney Gardens
	16 Caroline Row
	17 Havelock Terrace
	18 Dodder Terrace
	19 Ennis Grove
	20 Londonbridge Drive
	21 Strasburg Terrace
	22 Tritonville Close
	23 St James Terrace (Sandymount)
	24 Cambridge Court
	25 Lansdowne Hall
	26 Sandymount Court
	28 O'Rahilly House Flats
	29 Whelan House Flats
	30 Ropewalk Place
	31 Kennedy Court
	32 Simpsons Lane
	33 Summerfield (Ringsend)
	34 The Old Presbytery
	35 Caroline Row
	36 Fitzwilliam Quay
	37 Fitzwilliam Point
	38 The Moorings
	39 Magdalen Terrace
	40 Veronica Terrace
	41 Philomena Terrace
	42 Celestine Avenue
	43 George Reynolds Flats
	44 Victoria Cottages
	45 Tritonville Mews
	46 Steeple Gate
	47 Fairfield Court
	48 Baggot Rath House
	49 Fairview Avenue (Ringsend)
39 A4	1 Sandymount Green
	2 Sandymount Castle Road
	3 Sandymount Castle Drive
	4 Sydenham Road (Ballsbridge)
	5 Sandymount Castle
	6 Churchill Terrace
	7 Prince of Wales Terrace (Sandymount)
	8 Railway Cottages
	9 Martin White Chalets
	10 Gilford Court
	11 Homelee

PAGE/GRID REF	STREET NAME
	12 Lynton Court
	13 Spafield Terrace
	14 Adair
	15 Wilfield
	16 Park Court (Sandymount)
	17 Dromard Terrace
	18 Seafort Cottages
	19 Seafort Terrace
	20 Seafort Villas
	21 Claremont Court (Sandymount)
	22 The Sweepstakes
	23 Ballsbridge Park
	24 Lansdowne Square
	25 Ballsbridge Gardens
	26 Ballsbridge Avenue
	27 Ballsbridge Wood
	28 Lansdowne Woods
	29 Cannon Mews
	30 Cannon Place
	31 St.James Place
	32 Glenesk Court
	33 Trideat Apts.
	34 Merry Bush
	35 Oisin Court
	36 Claremont Court
	37 Argyle House Apts.
	38 Oaklands Court
	39 Ballsbridge Court
	40 Anglesea House
	41 Elbin House
	42 Raglan House
	43 Clyde House
	44 Oakbury Court
	45 The Willows
	46 Gilford Pines
	47 Hollyrood Apts
	48 Herbert Court
	49 St. James Court
	50 Renoir Apts.
	51 El Greco Apts.
	52 Wellington Lodge
	53 Sydenham Court
	54 Yeats Court
	55 Avondale Mews
39 B1	1 Alverno
	2 Haddon Court
39 B3	1 Prospect Terrace (Sandymount)
39 B4	1 Gilford Terrace
	2 Sandymount Castle Park
	3 Martello View
	4 Bethany House
	5 Hempenstal Terrace
	6 Martello Wood
	7 St. Catheryn's Court
	8 Windermere
	9 Radcliff Hall
39 C1	1 Churchgate Avenue
	2 St Joseph's Square
	3 Vernon Court (Clontarf)
	4 Vernon Wood
43 C1	1 Bawnogue Cottages
	2 Nangor Place
	3 St Catherines Grove
44 D1	1 St Patrick's Avenue (Clondalkin)
	2 Leinster Terrace
	3 Beech Row (Nangor Road)
	4 The Mill Pond Apts.
	5 Nangor Crescent
	6 Cherrywood Villas
44 D2	1 Church View (Clondalkin)
	2 Green Isle Court
44 E1	1 St Killian's Park
	2 Monastery Heights
	3 Bettysford
	4 Castle Crescent
	5 Friar's Walk
	6 Riverside (Clondalkin)
	7 Millview

PAGE/GRID REF	STREET NAME
44 E2	1 St Brigid's Park (Clondalkin)
44 F1	1 Knockmitten Close
	2 Knockmitten Lane North
44 F3	1 Pinetree Grove
	2 Belgard Close
	3 Shalimar Apts.
44 F4	1 Pinetree Crescent
45 A3	1 Parkhill Heights
	2 Parkview (Kilnamanagh)
45 B2	1 Tibradden Close
	2 Ballymount Cottages
45 B3	1 Three Rock Close
45 B4	1 Tymon North Court
	2 Tymon North Place
45 C1	1 Field Avenue
	2 Wallace Road
	3 Percy French Road
	4 O'Dwyer Road
	5 Esposito Road
	6 Landsdowne Valley
	7 Somerville Park
	8 Harty Court
45 C2	1 St Peter's Terrace (Walkinstown)
45 C3	1 Willington Lawn
	2 Wellington Cottages
45 C4	1 Spawell Cottages
46 D1	1 Sunville Green
	2 Windmill Crescent (Crumlin)
	3 Father Kit Court
	4 St. Agnes Terrace
	5 Rockmeadon Court
	6 Brug Chroimlinn
	7 Looceville Court
	8 Somerville Court
46 D2	1 Muckross Drive
	2 Lorcan O'Toole Court
	3 Stannaway Court
	4 Beechfield Mews
	5 Wellington Court (Whitehall Road West)
	7 The Manor (Kimmage)
46 D3	1 Wellington Road (Templeogue)
46 D4	1 Hillcrest (Templeogue)
	2 Hillcrest Manor
46 E1	1 Tonguefield Road
	2 Cloyne Road
	3 Faughart Road
	4 Clonmacnoise Grove
	5 Bedford Court
	6 Poddle Green
	7 Larrisa Court
46 E2	1 Riversdale Grove (Kimmage)
	2 Hazel Park
	3 Kimmage Court
	4 Rathland Drive
	5 Brookfield Green
	6 Brookfield Court (Kimmage)
	7 Hazelbrook Apts.
	8 Clonard Court
	9 Riverside (Kimmage)
	10 Baroma
	11 Clonallen
	12 Cranford Court (Kimmage)
46 E3	1 Templeville Park
	2 Fortfield Court
46 E4	1 Butterfield Meadow
	2 Brookmount Court
46 F1	1 Mount Harold Terrace
	2 Le Bas Terrace
	3 Mountain View Avenue
	4 Manor Villas
	5 Wilfrid Terrace
	6 Fitzpatrick's Cottages

PAGE/GRID REF	STREET NAME
	7 Ryan's Cottages (Harold's Cross)
	8 Parkview Court (Harold's Cross)
	9 Gandon Close
	10 Woodford Court (Harold's Cross)
	11 Kenilworth Manor
	12 Waverley Terrace (Harolds Cross Road)
	13 Smith's Lane
	14 Kengar Mews
	15 Mount Argus Square
	16 Mountain View Court (Harold's Cross)
	17 Casimir Court
	18 Kerrygold House
	19 Kennilworth Lodge
46 F2	1 Ashdale Park
	2 Westhampton Place
	3 Terenure Place
	4 Eagle Hill Avenue
	5 Victoria Villas (Rathgar)
	6 Maple Drive (Harold's Cross)
	7 Victoria Village (Rathgar)
	8 Frankfort Court
	9 Frankfort Flats
	10 Rathdown Court (off Templeogue Road)
	11 Rathgar Villas
	12 Greenlea Place
	13 Brighton Green
	14 McMorrough Road
	15 Earls Court (Terenure)
	16 Rathgar Park
	17 Olney Grove
	18 Eaton Hall
	19 Winton Grove
	20 Beechlawn Manor
	21 Beechlawn Mews
	22 Eaton Court (Terenure)
	23 Carlisle Court
	24 Fairfield House
	25 Beaumont House
	27 Loughmorne House
46 F3	1 Woodview Cottages
	2 St Agnes Terrace (Rathfarnham)
	3 Dodder Park Drive
	4 Village Green (Rathfarnham)
	5 The Falls
	6 Tourville Lodge
	7 Le Brett Terrace
	8 Wasdale House
	9 Crannagh Castle
	10 Crannagh Court
46 F4	1 Willbrook Grove
	2 Tara Hill Grove
	3 Beaufort Villas
	4 Glenann
	5 St Mary's Terrace (Rathfarnham)
	6 Village Court Apts.
	7 The Park Lands
	8 The Lakelands
	9 The Woodlands (Rathfarnham)
	10 Beaufort Court
	11 The Castlelands
	12 Rathfarnham Mill
	13 The Laurels (Rathfarnham)
	14 Loftus Square
	15 Blackburn Square
	16 Otterbrook
	17 Stonepark Orchard
	18 Castle Court (Rathfarnham)
	19 A.W. Pugin House
	20 Theresa House
	21 Woodstown House

PAGE/GRID REF	STREET NAME
	22 William Pallister House
	23 Frances Ball House
	24 De Bret House
	25 Hogan House
	26 Riversdale View
47 A1	1 Rathmines Park
	2 Leinster Square
	3 Prince Arthur Terrace
	4 Swanville Place
	5 Castlewood Terrace
	6 Castlewood Place
	7 Grosvenor Park
	8 Stone Mews
	9 Turrets Flats
	10 Purser Gardens
	11 Esker Villas
	12 Parker Hill
	13 Alma Terrace
	14 Observatory Lane
	15 Belgrave Place (Rathmines)
	16 Cambridge Villas
	17 Salem Court
	18 Maxwell Court
	19 The Mews (Rathmines)
	20 Roland Court
	21 Wynnefield Park
	22 Mount Anthony Estate
	23 Louis Lane
	24 Castlewood Close
	25 Rathmines Avenue Court
	26 Cosy Lodge
	27 Newington Terrace
	28 Rathgar Court
47 A2	1 Woodlands (Rathgar)
	2 Woodleigh
	3 Highfield Court
	4 Cowper Mews
	5 Garville Place
	6 Garville Drive
	7 Rathgar Park
	8 Orwell Mews
	9 Stratford
	10 Garville Court
47 A3	1 The Willows (Orwell Road)
	2 Stirling Park
	3 Orwell Court
	4 Newtown Villas (Braemor Road)
	5 Newtown Court (Rathgar)
	7 Orwell Bank
	8 Crannagh Way
	9 Landore
	10 Park View (Rathgar)
	11 Ard Na Gréine
	12 Newtown House
	13 Dodder Vale
47 A4	1 Castle Court (Rathfarnham)
	2 Nutgrove Court
47 B1	1 Sallymount Gardens
	2 Woodstock Court
	3 Collier's Avenue
	4 Westmoreland Park
	5 Field's Terrace
	6 Rugby Villas
	7 Beechwood Park (Rathmines)
	8 Bushfield Avenue
	9 Charleston Court Flats
	10 Oakley Court
	11 Cullenswood Road
	12 Moran's Cottages
	13 Mountain View Cottages (Ranelagh)
	14 Sallymount Terrace
	15 Chelmsford Lane
	16 Belgrave Villas (Rathmines)
	17 Bushfield Place
	18 Smith's Cottages (Donnybrook)

PAGE/ GRID REF		STREET NAME

		19 Beechdale Mews
		20 Oakley Square
		21 Palmerston Close
		22 Moyne Court
		23 Oakley Park (Ranelagh)
		24 Woodstock Gardens
		25 Marlborough Lane
		26 Castlewood Court
47	B2	1 Dartry Cottages
		2 Strand Terrace
		3 St Luke's Crescent
		4 Balnagowan
		5 Temple Square
		6 Milltown Grove (Clonskeagh)
		7 Milltown Hill
		8 Thorncliff
		9 Shanagarry
		10 Dodder Bank
47	B3	1 St Columbanus Place
		2 St Gall Gardens North
		3 St Gall Gardens South
		4 Milltown Terrace (Dundrum)
47	B4	1 Glenbower Park
		2 Woodlawn Terrace
		3 Beaumont Close
		4 Briarly Court
		5 St Nathy's House
		6 Ardtona Avenue
		7 Woodlawn Grove (Churchtown)
		8 Henley Court
		9 Weston Terrace
		10 Frankfort
		11 Rosemount Terrace (Dundrum)
		12 Waldemar Terrace
		13 Airfield Drive
		14 Nutgrove Avenue
		16 Annadale
		17 St Nathy's Villas
		18 Sweetmount House
		19 Camberley Oaks
		20 Camberley Elms
47	C1	1 St Broc's Cottages
		2 Pembroke Cottages (Donnybrook)
		3 Belmont Park (Donnybrook)
		4 The Crescent (Donnybrook)
		5 Harmony Avenue
		6 Vergemount Park
		7 Norwood Park
		8 Brookvale Road (Donnybrook)
		9 Vergemount Hall
		10 Sandford Gardens (Donnybrook)
		11 Auburn Road (Donnybrook)
		12 Vergemount
		13 Eglinton Square
		14 Mount Sandford
		15 Rowan Hall
		16 Cedar Hall
		17 Millbrook Village
		18 Simmonscourt Terrace
		19 Brookfield (Donnybrook)
		20 Harmony Court
		21 Riverside Walk
		22 Eglinton Wood
		23 Shamrock Hill Mews
		24 Donnybrook Castle
		25 Argyle Square
47	C2	1 Prospect Lane
		2 Beech Hill Villas
		3 Beech Hill Crescent
		4 Beech Hill Terrace
		5 Palmerston Grove
		6 Clonskeagh Drive
		7 Clonskeagh Square

		8 St Bridget's Flats
		9 Crannagh
		10 Woodhaven
		11 Richview Villas
		12 Byrne's Terrace
47	C3	1 Annaville Grove
		2 Olivemount Grove
		3 Friarsland Avenue
		4 Harlech Villas
		5 Gledswood Drive
		6 Olivemount Terrace
		7 Glenard Hall
		8 Belfield Close
		9 Roebuck Lawn
		10 Roebuck Crescent
47	C4	1 Sunnybank Court
		2 Woodbine Terrace (Dundrum)
		3 Alexandra Villas
		4 Roseville Terrace
		5 Pembroke Cottages (Dundrum)
		6 Pembroke Terrace
		7 Claremont Terrace
		8 Glenville Terrace
		9 St Joseph's Grove
48	D1	1 Merrion View Avenue
		2 Simmonscourt Avenue
		3 Simmonscourt View
		4 Ailesbury Close
		5 Simmonscourt Square
48	D2	1 Nutley Square
		2 Donnybrook Close
		3 Donnybrook Green
		4 Greenfield Manor
48	D3	1 Hopkins Square
		2 Finglas Square
		3 Hayden Square
		4 Hyde Square (Fosters Avenue)
		5 Meenan Square
48	D4	1 Edenwood (Goatstown)
		2 Sophie Baret Residence
48	E1	1 Merrion Court
		2 Merrion Gates
		3 Strand Lane
48	E2	1 Seafield Park
		2 Bellevue Court
		3 Merrion Crescent
		4 Woodbine House
48	E3	1 The Stables
		2 Mountbrook
48	E4	1 Greygates
		2 Beaufield Mews
		3 Ashurst (Mount Merrion)
48	F2	1 St Helen's Villas
48	F3	1 Martello Terrace (Booterstown)
		2 Pembroke Cottages (Booterstown)
		3 Willowmount
		4 Cherbury Mews
48	F4	1 St Helier's Copse
		2 Orpen Dale
		3 Park Villas (Stillorgan)
		4 Cedar Square (Stillorgan)
		5 Grove House Gardens
49	A3	1 Newtown Villas (Blackrock)
		2 Maretimo Road
		3 Ben Inagh Park
		4 Maretimo Gardens West
		5 Craigmore Gardens
		6 George's Place (Blackrock)
		7 St Anne's Square (Blackrock)
		8 Bath Place
		9 Rockwell Cove Apts.
		10 Westfield Terrace
		11 Idrone Mews

		12 Brusna Cottages
		13 Collins Court (Blackrock)
		14 Patrick's Row
		15 Eagle Hill
		16 Maretimo Terrace
		17 Maretimo Place
		18 Maretimo Villas
		19 Whelan's Terrace
		20 Carbury Place
		21 Sweetman's Avenue
		22 Lisalea
		23 Frascati Court
		24 Frascati Hall
		25 Temple Court (Blackrock)
49	A4	1 Avondale Park (Blackrock)
		2 Prince Edward Terrace Lower
		3 Prince Edward Terrace Upper
		4 Lindenvale
		5 Twin Cottages
		6 Fieldview Cottages
		7 Cullen's Cottages
		8 Webster's Cottages
		9 Rockville Estate
		10 Avoca Hall
		11 Brookfield Grove
		12 Brookfield Court (Blackrock)
49	B3	1 Ardenza Terrace
		2 Tobernea Terrace
		3 Ardenza Park
		4 Seapoint Terrace (Blackrock)
		5 The Orchard
49	B4	1 Montpelier Place
		2 Montpelier Manor
		3 The Willows (Monkstown)
		4 The Maples (Monkstown)
		5 The Cedars (Monkstown)
		6 The Alders
		7 The Poplars
		8 Stradbrook Gardens
		9 Brighton Terrace (Monkstown)
		10 Belgrave Place (Monkstown)
		11 Belgrave Terrace (Monkstown)
		12 Brooklawn Avenue
		13 Brooklawn Wood
		14 Rockford Terrace
		15 Beaupark Downs
		16 Drayton Close
		17 Heathfield
		18 Southdene
		19 Arundel
		20 Stradbrook Hall
		21 The Beeches (Monkstown)
		22 Brighton Lane
		23 Knocknagow
49	C4	1 Rosary Gardens West
		2 Barrett Street
		3 Smith's Villas
		4 York Terrace
		5 St Mary's Street
		7 Oakwood
		8 Harbour Terrace
		9 Grosvenor Terrace (Dun Laoghaire)
		10 Clifton Lane
		11 Clifton Avenue
		12 Richmond Green
		13 Clifton Terrace
		14 Alma Place
		15 Seaview Terrace (Dun Laoghaire)
		16 Synnott Terrace
		17 Bentley Villas
		18 St Michael's Terrace (Dun Laoghaire)
		19 St Brendan's Terrace (Dun Laoghaire)

		20 Northcote Terrace
		21 Knapton Court
		22 Knapton Lawn
		23 Northcote Place
		24 Cambridge Terrace (Dun Laoghaire)
		25 Primrose Hill (Dún Laoghaire)
		26 Mounttown Cottages
		27 Knapton Terrace
		28 Pakenham
		29 Monkstown Gate
		30 Alma Park
		31 Clearwater Cove
		32 Marina House Apts
		33 The Anchorage
		34 Smyth Gardens
50	D4	1 Wellington Street (Dun Laoghaire)
		2 Rosary Gardens East
		3 Desmond Avenue
		4 Wolfe Tone Avenue
		5 Charlemont Avenue
		6 Summerhill Parade (Dun Laoghaire)
		7 Haddington Terrace
		8 Victoria Terrace (Dun Laoghaire)
		9 Marine Terrace (Dún Laoghaire)
		10 Northumberland Place (Dún Laoghaire)
		11 Northumberland Park
		12 Dungar Terrace
		13 Stoneview Place
		14 Martello Avenue
		15 Crosthwaite Terrace
		16 Sussex Street
		17 Marine Court (Dún Laoghaire)
		18 Charlemont Terrace
		19 Mill Street (Dun Laoghaire)
		20 Anglesea Lane
		21 Park Lane (Dún Laoghaire)
		23 Sydenham
		24 Oratory Mews Court
		25 Crofton Terrace
		26 Connaught Place
		27 Albert Terrace (Dún Laoghaire)
		28 Crofton Mansions
50	E4	1 Mornington Avenue
		2 Martello Terrace (Dun Laoghaire)
		3 Summerhill Court
52	F2	1 Eaton House
54	D1	1 Brookfield Court (Tallaght)
		2 Jobstown Village Square
		3 Rossfield Court
		4 Rossfield Close
		5 Glenshane Dale
		6 Glenshane Place
54	D2	1 Elm House Apartments
		2 Montpelier Walk
54	F1	1 Tuansgate Apts.
		2 Abberley Square Apts.
		3 Aengus Hall (Belgard Square)
		4 Alen Hall (Belgard Square)
		5 Horan Hall (Belgard Square)
		6 Losset Hall (Belgard Square)
		7 Tallow Hall (Belgard Square)
		8 Virginia Hall (Belgard Square)

PAGE/GRID REF — STREET NAME

9 Loftus Hall (Belgard Square)
10 Swan Hall (Belgard Square)

55 A1
1 St Maelruans Park
2 High Street (Tallaght)
3 Avonbeg Court
4 St Dominic's Court
5 Old Bawn Court
6 College View (Tallaght)
7 Uppercross Court
8 Tramway Court (Tallaght)
9 New Bancroft Place
10 The Laurels (Tallaght)
11 New Bancroft Hall
12 New Bancroft Square
13 Courthouse Square Apts.

55 A2
1 Summerfield (Tallaght)
2 The Close (Tallaght)
3 Allenton Crescent

55 B1
1 Bolbrook Drive
3 Bolbrook Avenue
4 Bolbrook Close
5 Avonmore Avenue
6 Moynihan Court

55 B2
1 Oldcourt Lawn
2 Killininny Court Apts
3 Tara Crescent

55 B3
1 Ely Crescent
2 Ely Grove
3 Ely Green
4 Ferncourt Drive
5 Ferncourt Crescent
6 Beechdale Close

55 C1
1 Brookmount Lawns
2 Knocklyon Mews
3 Homeville Court
4 Homeville
5 Balrothery Cottages
6 Prospect Lodge
7 Castle Side

55 C2
1 Wood Dale Oak
2 Woodstown Court
3 Knocklyon Gate Apts

56 D1
1 Coolamber Court
2 Pine Grove
3 Ballyroan Court

56 E1
1 Orchardton

56 E2
1 Beechview
2 Cypress Avenue
3 Larch Drive
4 Beech Walk
5 Walnut View

56 F1
1 Sarah Curran Road
2 St Gatien Road
3 Fonthill Abbey
4 Whitechurch Abbey
5 Edenbrook Court
6 Forthill Court
8 The Beeches (Willbrook)

57 A1
1 Marley Villas
2 Meadow Villas
3 Barton Court

57 A2
1 Priory Court (Grange Road)
2 The Cherries
3 Elm Way (Grange Wood)
5 Stonemasons Green

57 B1
1 Meadow Avenue
2 Hawthorn Drive
3 Mount Albion Road
4 Sycamore Drive (Dundrum)
5 Hillview Glade
6 Hillview Court

57 B2
1 The Crescent (Ballinteer)
2 Ballinteer Court
3 The Copse (Ballinteer)
4 The Dale (Ballinteer)

57 C1
1 Westerton Rise
2 Ashgrove Terrace
3 Eagle Terrace (Dundrum)
4 Castle Court (Dundrum)
5 McGrane Court
6 Ballyolaf Manor
7 Castleview (Dundrum)
8 Ashgrove Court
9 Dundrum Gate Apts
10 Riverbank (Dundrum)
11 Riversdale (Dundrum)
12 The Birch
13 The Linden
14 The Blackthorn

57 C2
1 Clonlea Wood
2 College Park Court
3 College Park Drive

58 D1
1 Drummartin Crescent
2 Carrick Lawn
3 The Pines (Kilmacud)
4 Woodley Court

58 D2
1 Balally Terrace
2 Moreen Lawn
3 Blackthorn Grove
4 Blackthorn Court
5 Rathdown Terrace
6 Blackthorn Green
7 Blackthorn Close (Sandyford)
8 Olaf Hall
9 Rathdown Grove

58 D3
1 Churchlands

58 E1
1 Dale Close
2 Stillorgan Court
3 Stillorgan Heath
4 Convent Court
5 Woodthorpe

58 E3
1 Glencairn Garth

58 F1
1 Woodview Court (Stillorgan)
2 Ard Lorcain Villas
3 Grange Cottages
4 Ulster Terrace (Stillorgan Grove)
5 Pear Tree Field
6 Dunstaffnage Hall Apts

58 F2
1 Leopardstown Court
2 Leopardstown Lawn
3 Silver Pines
4 Ellesmere
5 Ballymoss Parade
6 Arkle Square
7 Sir Ivor Mall
8 Fey Yerra

58 F4
1 Ballyogan Park

59 A1
1 Orchard Cottages
2 Red Brick Terrace
3 Moore's Cottages
4 Hawthorn Manor
5 Rosehill
6 Ardagh Close
7 Newtown Park Court
8 Galloping Green
9 Avila Apts
10 Newtownpark House
11 Obelisk Avenue

59 A2
1 Knocksinna Grove
2 Knocksinna Court
3 New Park Lodge
4 Foxrock Mount
5 Chestnut Park
6 Willow Park (Foxrock)
7 Sycamore Grove (Foxrock)
8 Whitethorn Walk (Foxrock)
9 Birch Dale (Foxrock)
10 The Courtyard (Foxrock)
11 Kelston Hall
12 Sefton Hall

59 A3
1 Brighton Cottages
2 Kilteragh Pines

3 Avalon
4 Brighton Lodge
5 The Gables (Foxrock)
6 Westminster Court

59 B1
1 Windsor Court
2 Grange Grove
3 Oliver Plunkett Villas
4 Stradbrook Hill
5 Springhill Cottages
6 Grange Terrace
7 Abbey Court (Monkstown)
9 Faber Grove
10 Deans Court
11 Devon Close
12 Monkstown Square

59 B3
1 Kerrymount Close
4 Monaloe Crescent
5 Clonkeen Lawn
6 Monaloe Court
7 New Cornelscourt

59 C1
1 Oliver Plunkett Square
2 Patrician Park
3 Mounttown Park
4 Woodlawn Park (Dun Laoghaire)
5 Oliver Plunkett Terrace
6 Fitzgerald Park
7 St Patrick's Terrace (Kill O' the Grange)
8 Dunedin Drive
9 St Patrick's Close (Kill O'The Grange)
10 Highthorn Woods
11 Aspen Park (Kill O'The Grange)
12 Birch Dale (Kill O'The Grange)
13 Willow Grove (Kill O'The Grange)
14 Carriglea Court (Kill O'The Grange)
16 Woodlawn Villas
17 Meadowlands Court
18 Meadowlands Mews

59 C2
1 Hillview Cottages
2 Whitethorn Walk (Kill O'The Grange)
3 Sycamore Court
4 Hazel Lawn (Kill O'The Grange)
5 Eaglewood Apts
6 Rochestown House Apts.
7 Eaglewood House
8 Eaglewood Mews
9 Rochestown House

59 C3
1 Little Meadow
2 Cabinteely Court
3 Cabinteely Park
4 O'Shea's Cottages
5 Little Orchard

59 C4
1 Kilbogget Villas
2 Church Villas

60 D1
1 O'Donnell Gardens
2 Royal Terrace North
3 Myrtle Avenue
4 Emmet Street (Sallynoggin)
5 Eden Villas
6 Laurel Hill
7 Granite Hall
8 Magenta Place
9 Marlborough Park
10 Royal Terrace Lane
11 Beechwood Grove
12 Rollins Court
13 Seven Houses
14 The Glen (Glenageary Road)
15 Glengara Close
16 Silchester Wood
17 Carlisle Terrace (Dún Laoghaire)

18 Durham Place
19 Rus-in-Urbe Terrace

60 D2
1 Honey Park
2 Thomastown Crescent
3 Pearse Close

60 D3
1 Auburn Road (Cabinteely)
2 Granville Crescent

60 D4
1 Annabeg
2 Meadow Court
3 Oakton Green

60 E1
1 Wilmont Avenue
2 Congress Gardens
3 Albert Park
4 Claremont Villas
5 St Paul's Terrace
6 St Peter's Terrace (Dun Laoghaire)
7 Findlater Street (Dun Laoghaire)
8 Devitt Villas
9 Dixon Villas
10 Glen Terrace
11 Glasthule Buildings
12 Hastings Terrace
13 Brighton Terrace (Dun Laoghaire)
14 Lawson Terrace
15 Killiney Terrace
16 Munster Terrace
17 Neptune Terrace
18 Cliff Terrace
19 Beaufort
20 Ballygihen Villas
21 Seabank Court (Dalkey)
22 St Helen's
23 Chester Square
24 Dundela Haven
25 Arkendale Woods
26 Arkendale Court
27 Adelaide Villas (Dun Laoghaire)
28 Adelaide Terrace (Dun Laoghaire)
29 Atmospheric Road
30 St Margaret's Close
31 Avondale Court (Dalkey)

60 E2
1 Barnhill Lawn
2 Killiney Towers
3 Barnhill Park
4 Kilcolman Court
5 Edwin Court
6 Fairlawns
7 Urney Grove
8 Malborough Court
9 Castlepark Court

60 E3
1 Hill Cottages
2 Mount Auburn
3 Talbot Road (Killiney)
4 Talbot Lane (Killiney)

60 E4
1 Oakton Court
2 Dale View Park
3 Mountain Villa
4 The Nurseries (Ballybrack)
5 Mountain View Road (Ballybrack)
6 Rainsford Lane
7 Firgrove

60 F1
1 Carysfort Drive
2 Ormeau Drive
3 The Paddocks (Dalkey)
4 South Winds
5 Ulverton Close
6 Rocklands
7 Bayswater Terrace
8 Bullock Steps
9 Liscanor
10 White's Villas
11 Mayville Terrace
12 Castlelands Grove
13 Ulverton Court
14 Pilot View
15 Bailey View

PAGE/GRID REF	STREET NAME
	16 Castlelands
	17 Churchill Mews
	18 Bartra Rock Apts.
60 F2	1 St Patrick's Avenue (Dalkey)
	2 Railway Road
	3 Anastasia Lane
	4 St Patrick's Square (Dalkey)
	5 Cats Ladder
	6 Dalkey Grove
	7 Barnhill Grove
	8 St Patrick's Road (Dalkey)
	9 Monte Vella
	10 Summerfield Close
	11 Victoria Terrace (Dalkey)
	12 Sorrento Drive
	13 Sorrento Lawn
	14 Coliemore Villas
	15 Seafield Terrace
	16 Temple Terrace
	17 Grosvenor Terrace (Dalkey)
	18 Charlotte Terrace
	19 Heany Avenue
	20 Desmond Cottages
	21 Ardbrugh Villas
	22 Burmah Close
	23 Dalkey Court
	24 Kilbegnet Close
	25 Sorrento Close
	26 Craiglands
	27 Ullardmor
	28 Sorrento Mews
	29 Sorrento Court
	30 Sorrento Heights
	31 Ardbrugh Close
	32 Castle Cove (Dalkey)
	33 Torca View
63 A1	1 The View (Carrickmines)
64 D1	1 The Oaks (Loughlinstown)
	2 Cherry Court (Loughlinstown)
	3 Cois Coillte
64 D2	1 Stonebridge Lane
64 E1	1 Killiney Court
	2 Killiney Oaks
	3 The Sycamores
	4 The Elms (Loughlinstown)
	5 St Aubyn's Court
	6 Ennel Court
	7 Sheelin Grove
	8 Glencarr Court
	9 Domville Grove
	10 Streamville Court
	12 Bayview Glade
	13 Sheelin Hill
	14 Sheelin Walk
	16 The Larches (Abberley)
	17 The Oaks (Abberley)

PAGE/GRID REF	STREET NAME
	18 The Rowans (Abberley)
	19 The Willows (Abberley)
	20 The Hawthorns (Abberley)
	21 The Cedars (Abberley)
	22 The Beeches (Abberley)
	23 River Close
64 E2	1 River Lane (Loughlinstown)
	2 Clonasleigh
	3 Beechfield Haven
	4 Athgoe Drive
	5 Maryland
	6 Station Road (Shankill)
	7 Windrush
	8 Shanganagh Wood
	9 Thomond
	10 Beechwood House
	11 Sycamore House (Shankill)
	12 Woodview
	13 River Lane Grove
	14 Corbawn Glade
64 E3	1 Guilford Terrace
	2 Stonebridge Close
	3 Osprey Court
	4 Cluain na Greine Court
64 E4	1 Kiltuck Park
67 B1	1 Raverty Villas
	2 St Peter's Terrace (Bray)
	3 Myrtle Grove (Bray)
	4 Arbutus Grove
	5 Thornhill View
	6 Fernbrook
	7 Roseville Court
	8 Sunnybank Court
67 B2	1 Auburn Villas (Bray)
	2 Glenburgh Terrace
	3 Dargle Court
	4 Ashley Heights
	5 Dargle Crescent
	6 Copper Beech Grove
	7 Vale Terrace (on lower Dargle Road)
	9 Sutton Road
	10 Dargan Street
	11 Fairgreen Road
	12 Pearse Road (Bray)
	13 Mountpleasant Villas
	15 Diamond Terrace
	16 Parkview Terrace
	17 Sutton Villas
	18 Esmonde Terrace
	19 Old Ravenswell Row
	20 New Ravenswell Row
	21 Vale View
	22 Old Rathmore Terrace
	23 New Rathmore Terrace
	25 Gertrude Terrace
	26 Herbert View
	27 Rivervale Apts.
	29 Bruce's Terrace

PAGE/GRID REF	STREET NAME
67 B3	1 Ballynoe Court
	2 Rathclaren
	3 St Clair's Terrace
	4 Killarney Court
	5 Kilgrastor Court
	6 Glenbrook
	8 Brickfield Lane
67 B4	1 Ballywaltrim Cottages
	2 Ballymorris
67 C1	1 St Patrick's Square (Bray)
	2 Martello Terrace (Bray)
67 C2	1 Sidmonton Square
	3 Eglington Road
	4 Rosslyn Grove
	5 James Connolly Square
	6 Sidmonton Place
	7 Novara Park
	8 St Cronan's Road
	9 Cill Manntan Park
	10 Kilmantain Place
	11 Father Colohan Terrace
	12 Royal Marine Terrace
	13 Milton Terrace
	14 St Kevin's Terrace (Bray)
	15 Darley Cottages
	16 Brabazon Cottages
	17 St Laurence's Terrace (Bray)
	18 St Columcille's Terrace
	20 Seapoint Villas
	21 Dunbur Terrace
	22 Elmgrove Terrace
	23 St Aidan's Terrace
	24 Seapoint Terrace (Bray)
	25 Goldsmith Terrace
	26 Prince of Wales Terrace (Bray)
	27 Novara Terrace
	28 Waverley Terrace (Bray)
	29 Westview Terrace
	30 Augustine Villas
	31 Trafalgar Terrace (Bray)
	32 Fairgreen Terrace
	33 St Brigid's Terrace
	34 Loretto Avenue
	35 Loretto Terrace
	36 Sidmonton Gardens
	37 Rosslyn
	38 Shankill View
	39 Florence Terrace (Bray)
	40 Florence Villas (Bray)
	41 Carlton Terrace
	42 Carlton Villas (Clontarf)
	43 Alexander Terrace (Bray)
	44 Belton Terrace
	45 Church Terrace (Bray)
	46 Old Brighton Terrace
	47 New Brighton Terrace
	48 Killarney Villas
	49 Market Square

PAGE/GRID REF	STREET NAME
	50 Fairgreen Court
	51 Bayview (Bray)
	52 Westbourne Terrace
	53 King Edward Court
	54 Loretto Villas
	55 Marie Villas
	56 Wellington Court (Bray)
	57 Novara Mews
	58 Vevay Crescent
	59 Bull Lane (Off Main Street)
	60 Purcell Lane (off Main Street Bray)
67 C3	1 Cherry Tree Drive
	2 Roselawn Park
	4 Woodview Drive
	5 Kennedy Park
	7 Newcourt Villas
	9 O'Byrne Villas
	10 Stoneylea Terrace
	11 Mountain View Apts.
	14 Putland Villas
	15 Oldcourt Terrace
	16 Lauderdale Terrace
	17 Mayfield Terrace (Bray)
	18 Vevay Villas
	19 Orchard Terrace (Bray)
	20 Bray Head Terrace
	21 Sugarloaf Terrace
67 C4	3 Bentley Avenue
	6 St Mary's Terrace (Boghall Road)
68 D2	1 Trosyrafon Terrace
	2 Montebello Terrace
	3 Esplanade Terrace
	4 Brennans Terrace
	5 Sidbury Court
	6 Dargan Court
	7 Warburton Terrace
	8 Sloan Terrace
	9 Belgrave Villas (Bray)
	10 Belgrave Terrace (Bray)
	11 Claremount Terrace
	12 Richmond Terrace
	13 Milward Terrace
	14 Brennans Parade
	15 Claddagh Terrace
	16 Marlborough Terrace
	17 Marine Terrace (Bray)
	18 Jones Terrace
	19 Mount Norris Villas
	20 St Marys Terrace (Bray)
	21 Fitzwilliam Terrace
	23 Convent View (Bray)
68 D3	1 Eaton Court (Bray)
	2 Meretimo Villas
	3 Grosvenor Avenue
	4 Brookfield Avenue (Bray)
	5 Sidmonton Court
	6 Sydenham Villas (Bray)